*The Encyclopædia of*
ASSOCIATION FOOTBALL

*Other Encyclopaedias published by Robert Hale & Company*

BY PAT BESFORD
Swimming

BY WEBSTER EVANS
Golf

BY A. N. GAULTON
Rugby League Football

BY MAURICE GOLESWORTHY
Cricket
Boxing

BY KEN HAWKES AND GERARD LINDLEY
Bowls

BY J. R. JONES
Rugby Football
*(Second edition edited by Maurice Golesworthy)*

BY ANTHONY PRITCHARD AND KEITH DAVEY
Motor Racing

BY CHARLES STRATTON
Show Jumping

BY ANNE SUNNUCKS
Chess

BY MELVYN WATMAN
Athletics

*The Encyclopædia of*

# Association Football

COMPILED BY

Maurice Golesworthy

FOREWORD BY
Sir Stanley Rous, C.B.E.

*Eleventh Edition*

ROBERT HALE · LONDON

First edition November 1956
Second edition January 1957
Third edition February 1958
Reprinted June 1958
Fourth edition November 1959
Fifth edition October 1961
Sixth edition *(completely re-written and reset)* 1963
Seventh edition October 1965
Eighth edition November 1967
Ninth edition November 1969
Tenth edition November 1970
Eleventh edition *(completely revised and reset)* November 1973


ISBN  0  7091  4047  9


Robert Hale & Company
63 Old Brompton Road,
London, S.W.7


Photoset and Printed
by Redwood Press Limited
Trowbridge, Wiltshire

# *Foreword*

by

## SIR STANLEY ROUS, C.B.E.
President of F.I.F.A.

For more than a century, Association Football has been played and has prospered in an organised regulated manner. It was formed and moulded in the first place by the British and they have had a distinctive part to play in its history and evolution. The credit for the development of what has now become a truly international sport is due to many men—to the brilliant players who, over the years, have excited the emotions of the public and drawn them to the artistry of the game; to the referees who have married justice and discipline and common sense on the field of play; to the teachers who have enlightened the young at home and spread the word abroad; to the legislators who have kept football basically a simple game and brought to it a spirit of service without thought of personal reward.

Thus the game, organised in many stirring competitions like the F.A. Cup and the Football League, has a history bristling with facts and achievements, of individuals and clubs and countries which, over such a long time, assumes massive proportions. The first obvious merit of *The Encyclopædia of Association Football* is that it collects this great mass into one compact volume, invaluable for settling quickly and accurately the manifold arguments and discussions which a great game continually throws up!

But as President of F.I.F.A., I am particularly happy to note that since the book was first published in 1956, a great deal more space has been given to records and information concerning the game abroad. One often feels that the days of exploration are long gone, that there is little new to be learned about the world, that football among many other things is established finally in all corners of the earth.

Yet the fact is that there has never been a more exciting time in football as an international game. In recent years, dozens of new countries have been formed, in Africa and Asia. All have clamoured for membership of F.I.F.A. and a place in the international football sun formerly so firmly held by the "older" nations of Europe and South America. All these new countries need help. They need financial help. They need coaching assistance. They have to be helped organise their game in every possible sense. And they have to be helped play the game in the very best spirit and to take their place in the international brotherhood of football nations above and beyond and apart from any political considerations. This is the present great challenge to F.I.F.A. and it is a responsibility which excites me very much as I travel around the world and see these new nations find their football feet, as it were.

The spread of international television has brought the great occasions of Europe and South America home to our own public. The ever-increasing interest in the World Cup, and the great European competitions, have added a new dimension to spectating. The spread of fast jet travel has allowed journalists to range ever further to record these things, and the "Encyclopædia" has kept pace with all this in recognising that Santos and Benfica and Milan are no longer remote from Manchester and Birmingham.

I find this volume very useful as a quick, reliable reference book, and I suggest that it should be on every football-lover's library shelf. I commend it to you with pleasure.

# Introduction

In years gone by I often felt the need for a standard reference book of Soccer records for although one's shelves might be crammed with football books it was difficult to find the answer to a particular query at a particular time. Various interesting facts and records had become buried within the pages of so many previous publications amidst a mass of information.

To the best of my knowledge there had never been a book on Association Football which contained all the facts and records of the game arranged for easy reference in alphabetical order.

My experience as a sports writer, newspaper librarian and respondent of readers' questions for national sports magazines convinced me that the lack of such a reference book was a serious omission, and so, in 1956, I compiled the first edition of *The Encyclopædia of Association Football* with the hope that this would fill that gap on the sportsman's bookshelf.

The grand reception given to this publication surpassed even my expectations and its success has been a great source of satisfaction to me as well as an encouragement to maintain and improve the standard of each edition.

In recent years there appears to have been more widespread interest in soccer records and statistics and many of the facts and figures set out in this publication have been re-produced elsewhere among an ever increasing number of similar books. The knowledge that so many professional writers are also using this Encyclopædia as a work of reference has kept the need for accuracy uppermost in my mind as I have no wish to be the means by which errors are perpetuated. This latest edition has, therefore, not been completed without many long hours of checking and rechecking records which had already been examined many times before. In this connection I am especially indebted to my collection of that remarkable weekly sporting paper *The Athletic News* which has enabled me to check contemporary reports. Experience has shown that it is surprising what one finds when one gets right back to the source.

The years since the appearance of the first edition of this Encyclopædia have been particularly busy in the football world with more changes than in the previous 40 or 50 years. Apart from changes on the domestic front the greatest development has been in the outlook of the average football fan. No longer is he (or she) interested only in the progress of the game at home for the increase in the number of international competitions has broadened the soccer horizon until today names like Real Madrid, Santos, Juventus, Benfica, Eusebio, Beckenbauer, and Rivelino, mean as much to British fans as Arsenal, Leeds United, Tottenham Hotspur, Celtic, Rangers, Bobby Moore or Billy Bremner.

I have attempted to keep abreast of these developments by increasing the amount of information about football abroad, although as yet, I am still restricting the number of sections on foreign countries to those that have met the home countries in international matches.

In this completely revised 11th edition I have also decided to include biographies of great players. The choice is difficult as space restricts the number and no doubt those critics who have in the past deplored the omission of biographies will now have scope to criticise the omission of this or that favourite.

With regard to these biographies please note that the totals of appearances and goals given are for League games only with figures in brackets being appearances as substitute.

A word about the record victories and record defeats given under each club heading may save some arguments. Please note that only games in the Football League, Scottish League, F.A. Cup (Proper), Football League Cup, and Scottish F.A. or League Cup have been considered. And for these records 9—3 is, for example, considered a bigger win or defeat than 8—2, 10—2 before 9—0, etc., etc.

The division of the various sections under appropriate headings continues to be something of a problem, but I have done my utmost to overcome this difficulty with liberal cross-references, and just to make sure that no fact is lost you will find there is an index which contains all the players, other personalities and clubs mentioned throughout.

In compiling this book the aim for quick and easy reference has been constantly at the back of my mind and I hope that you will find it both interesting and useful.

MAURICE GOLESWORTHY

## ACKNOWLEDGEMENTS

This book is published with special thanks to The Football Association and The Football League for their valuable assistance and for allowing me to include information from their official histories (*The History of The Football Association* and *The Story of The Football League*).
In addition I would like to thank the officials of all other Associations, Leagues and clubs, both at home and abroad, as well as such friends as Jack Rollin and Morley Farror who provided valuable information. Thanks also to Leslie Parsons for compiling the index.

M.G.

# List of Illustrations

## ABANDONED

On Nov. 26, 1898, a First Division game between Sheffield Wednesday and Aston Villa was abandoned because of bad light after 79½ min. play. Sheffield Wednesday were leading 3—1. The remaining 10½ min. were played on Mar. 13, 1899, during which time Sheffield Wednesday scored a further goal. The final result was officially recorded as 4—1.

Today, according to the rules of the Football League and most other Leagues, a match which is not completed must be replayed IN FULL, or the score at the time of abandonment taken as the final result. The choice—in the case of the Football League—rests entirely with the League Management Committee.

The Football League ordered the result to stand after Barrow v. Gillingham, Division IV game, Oct. 9, 1961, was abandoned 15 min. before time, owing to bad light. The game had started late after Gillingham had missed a train and chartered a plane to fly up. The result at time of abandonment was Barrow 7, Gillingham 0.

In Feb. 1904 a Second Round F.A. Cup tie at Tottenham had to be abandoned at half-time when Aston Villa were leading 1—0 because the crowd invaded the pitch and it was found impossible to clear them off. The F.A. ordered the tie to be re-played at Villa Park but Tottenham won 1—0.

The First Division game between Middlesbrough and Oldham Athletic, on April 3, 1915, was abandoned after 55 min. when Oldham's left-back, W. Cook, refused to leave the field when ordered off by the referee.

Middlesbrough were leading 4—1 and the Football League ordered the result to stand. Cook was suspended for 12 months. Oldham missed the League Championship by two points that season.

The F.A. Cup Semi-final between Sheffield United and Liverpool, at Fallowfield, Manchester, in 1899, was abandoned at half-time because the crowd had encroached on to the pitch. Prior to the interval the game had been interrupted while police forced the crowd back beyond the touchlines.

The Scotland v. Austria International at Hampden Park, May 8, 1963, was abandoned 9 min. before full-time after persistent fouling and two players sent off.

Austria v. Greece, international in Vienna, Nov. 5, 1967, was abandoned after 85 minutes following a series of vicious fouls and an invasion of the pitch by spectators.

The Swiss Cup Final of 1967 was abandoned when Lausanne left the field. The Swiss F.A. subsequently rejected a protest by Lausanne and awarded the match to F.C. Basle.

Tunisia v. Nigeria, Dec. 10, 1961, was abandoned after 65 minutes when the Nigerians left the field. The match was awarded to Tunisia.

## ABERDEEN F.C.

Founded 1903. Joined Scottish League, Division II, 1904, Division I, 1905. Honours: Champions, Division I, 1954-5. Runners-up, 1910-11, 1936-7, 1970-71, 1971-2. Scottish Cup: Winners, 1947, 1970. Finalists, 1937, 1953, 1954, 1959, 1967. Scottish League Cup: Winners, 1946, 1956. Runners-up, 1947. Record attendance: 45,061 v. Hearts, Scottish Cup, 4th Round, Mar. 13, 1954. Address: Pittodrie Stadium, Aberdeen AB2 1QH. (Tel. 0224 21428). Nickname: Dons. Colours: Scarlet shirts, scarlet shorts with two white stripes down seams. Record League goalscorer: B. Yorston, 38 goals, Division I, 1929-30. Record victory: 13—0 v. Peterhead, Feb. 9, 1923. Record defeat: 9—2 v. Dundee, April 17, 1909.

## ADMISSION CHARGES
### FOOTBALL LEAGUE

1919-20: Minimum charge raised from 6d. to 1s.

1942-3: Minimum charge raised from 1s. to 1s. 3d. (1s. 6d. in the League South).

1951-2: Minimum charge raised from 1s. 3d. to 1s. 6d.

Subsequent increases: 1952–3, 1s. 6d.; 1955-6, 2s.; 1960-61, 2s. 6d.; 1965-6, 4s.; 1968-9, 5s.; 1970-71, 6s.; 1972-3, 40p.

## A.F.C. BOURNEMOUTH

Founded 1899 as Boscombe F.C. Became Bournemouth and Boscombe Athletic in 1932 and adopted their present title in 1972. Joined Football League, Division III(S) in 1923. Honours: Runners-up, Division III(S), 1947-8. Runners-up, Division IV, 1970-71. Record attendance: 28,799 v. Manchester United, F.A. Cup, 6th Round, Mar. 2, 1957. Address: Dean Court,

Bournemouth (Tel. 35381). Nickname: Cherries. Colours: Red and black striped shirts, black shorts and stockings. Record League goal-scorer: E. MacDougall, 42 goals, Division IV, 1970-71. Record victory: 11—0 v. Margate, F.A. Cup, 1st Round, Nov. 20, 1971. Record defeat: 8—1 v. Bradford City, Division III, Jan. 24, 1970.

## AGE
### Oldest (Football League)
The oldest player ever to appear in the Football League is N. McBain. At the age of 52 years 4 months, he played in goal for New Brighton v. Hartlepools United, Mar. 15, 1947.

R. Suter is the oldest Englishman ever to appear in the Football League. Born in July, 1878, he last played in goal for Halifax Town v. Darlington, April 24, 1929. He was 50 years 9 months old.

G. Shenton was 36 years old when he made his Football League debut for Port Vale v. Barnsley, Division II, Nov. 17, 1928.

A. Cunningham was 38 years 2 days old when he made his Football League debut for Newcastle United v. Leicester City, Division I, Feb. 2, 1929.

The oldest player ever to appear in a Football League, First Division game—Sir Stanley Matthews, aged 50 years 5 days, when he made his final League appearance for Stoke City v. Fulham, Feb. 6, 1965.

J. Cockroft was 38 years 5 months old when he made his First Division debut —Sheffield United v. Preston North End, Nov. 6, 1948.

### Oldest (F.A. Cup)
W. Meredith is the oldest player ever to appear in the F.A. Cup competition proper. He was 49 years 8 months when he played for Manchester City v. Newcastle United, semi-finals, Mar. 29, 1924.

The oldest player ever to appear in an F.A. Cup Final—W. Hampson, right-back Newcastle United, 1924, aged 41 years 8 months.

### Oldest (Internationals)
The oldest player to make his debut in the International Championship is L. Compton. He was 38 years 2 months when he played centre-half for England v. Wales, Nov. 15, 1950.

The oldest player to appear in the International Championship is W. Meredith. He was nearly 46 when he played for Wales v. England, Mar. 15, 1920.

### Youngest Player (Football League)
The youngest player ever to appear in the

Football League is A. Geldard, for Bradford v. Millwall, Division II, Sept. 16, 1929. He was 15 years 156 days old. C. C. Buchanan is often mentioned as the youngest Football League debutant. He made his League debut for Wolverhampton Wanderers v. West Bromwich Albion, Sept. 26, 1942, at the age of 14. However, this distinction cannot be recognised as it occurred during the war.

Next to Geldard is K. Roberts, 15 years 158 days when making his League debut for Wrexham v. Bradford, Division III(N), Sept. 1, 1951.

The youngest ever to appear in Division I is D. Forster, who kept goal for Sunderland v. Leicester City, Aug. 22, 1964, 15 years 185 days.

R. Parry played in Division I for Bolton Wanderers v. Wolverhampton Wanderers, Oct. 13, 1951, when 15 years 207 days old.

R. Stockhill was 15 years 280 days when making his League debut in Division III(N) for York City, at Wigan, Aug. 31, 1929.

The youngest goal scorer in the Football League is R. Dix, 15 years 180 days, for Bristol Rovers v. Norwich City, Division III(S), Mar. 3, 1928. He had made his League debut 7 days earlier v. Charlton Athletic.

### Youngest Player (F.A. Cup)
A. Jeffrey appeared for Doncaster Rovers v. Aston Villa on his 16th birthday, F.A. Cup, 4th Round, Jan. 29, 1955.

The youngest to appear in the Final —H. Kendall, 17 years 345 days, for Preston North End v. West Ham United, May 2, 1964.

### Youngest Player (Scottish League)
A. Edwards, aged 16 years and 5 days, is the youngest player to appear in First Division of the Scottish League—Dunfermline v. Hibernian, Mar. 19, 1962. Here again there may be argument for goalkeeper, R. Simpson, played for Queen's Park at the age of 14 during the war.

### Youngest (Internationals)
The youngest players ever to appear in the International Championship are:

England—D. Edwards, Manchester United, 18 years 6 months, left-half, v. Scotland, April 2, 1955. A. Brown, Sheffield United, 18 years 10 months, centre-forward, v. Wales, Feb. 29, 1904.

Ireland—W. K. Gibson, Cliftonville, 17 years, v. Wales, Feb. 24, 1894. N. Kernoghan, Belfast Celtic, 17 years 3 months, outside-right, v. Wales, Mar. 11, 1936. J. Nicholson, Manchester United 17 years 8 months, inside-left, v. Scotland, Nov. 9, 1960.

Scotland—D. Law, Huddersfield Town, 18 years 7 months, v. Wales, Oct. 18, 1958.

Wales—J. Charles, Leeds United, 18 years 1 month, centre half-back, v. Ireland, Mar. 8, 1950.

The youngest internationals among foreign countries include: G. Dorval, 15, outside-right for Brazil, v. Argentine, 1957. A. R. Nascimento (Pele), 16 years 9 months, inside-left for Brazil v. Argentine, July 1957. F. Brichant, 16, Belgium v. England (Amateurs), Feb. 24, 1914. A. Bickel (Grasshoppers), 16, Switzerland, 1935.

### Youngest (Inter-League)

N. Kernoghan, Belfast Celtic, was the youngest player ever to play in an inter-League match. He appeared for the Irish League v. The Football League, Sept. 25, 1935, aged 16 years 9 months.

### AIRDRIEONIANS F.C.

Founded 1878. Promoted to Scottish League, Division I, 1903. Honours: Runners-up, Division I, 1922-3, 1923-4, 1924-5, 1925-6. Champions, Division II, 1902-3. (B) 1954-5. Runners-up, 1965-6. Scottish Cup: Winners, 1924. Record attendance: 26,500 v. Hearts, Scottish Cup, 4th Round, Mar. 8, 1952. Address: Broomfield Park, Airdrie (Tel. Airdrie 26-62067). Colours: White, with red V, white shorts. Record goal-scorer in Division I: H. G. Yarnall, 39 goals, 1916-17. Record victory: 11—1 v. Falkirk, Division A, April 28, 1951. Record defeat 11—1 v. Hibernian (H.), Division I, Oct. 24, 1959.

### ALBANIA

The Albanian F.A. was formed in 1930 and a National League first came into being in 1936 but for many years they remained isolated from the international scene. It was not until 1965 that Albania met any of the home countries. Then they were grouped with Ireland in the World Cup Qualifying Competition.

The address of the Albanian F.A. which first joined F.I.F.A. in 1932 is Federation Albanaise de Football, Rruga Kongresi I Permetir Nr. 41, Tirana. Colours: red shirts, black shorts.

May 7, 1965 Ireland 4, Albania 1; Belfast
Nov. 24, 1965 Albania 1, Ireland 1; Tirana

### ALBION ROVERS F.C.

Founded 1881. Joined Scottish League, Division II, 1903. Honours: Champions, Division II, 1932–3. Runners-up, 1913–14,

1937-8, 1947-8. Scottish Cup: Finalists, 1920. Record attendance: 27,381 v. Rangers, Scottish Cup, 2nd Round, Feb. 8, 1936. Address: Cliftonhill Park, Coatbridge (Tel. 20 21865). Colours: Primrose shirts, white sleeves and shorts. Record goal-scorer: J. Renwick, 41 goals, Division II, 1932-3. Record victory: 10—0 v. Brechin City, Division II, 1937-8. Record defeat: 9—1 v. Motherwell, Division I, 1936-7.

### ALDERSHOT F.C.

Founded 1927. Joined Football League, Division III(S), 1932. Best in Division III(S), 10th, 1938-9. Record attendance: 19,138 v. Carlisle United, F.A. Cup, 4th Round (replay), Jan. 28, 1970. Address: Recreation Ground, Aldershot (Tel. 20211). Nickname: Shots or Soldiers. Colours: Red shirts with blue collars, cuffs and numbers, white shorts, stockings red with blue trim. Record League goal-scorer: R. Howfield, 23 goals, Division IV, 1961-2. Record victory: 8—1 v. Gateshead, Division IV, Sept. 13, 1958. Record defeat: 9—0 v. Bristol City, Division III(S), Dec. 28, 1946.

### ALLOA ATHLETIC F.C.

Founded 1878. Joined Scottish League, Division II, 1921. Honours: Champions, Division II, 1921-2. Runners-up, 1938-9. Only one season in First Division (1922-3); not promoted in 1939 owing to outbreak of war. Record attendance: 13,000 v. Dunfermline, Scottish Cup, 3rd Round (replay), Feb. 1939. Address: Recreation Ground, Alloa (Tel. 025-92 2695). Nickname: Wasps. Colours: Gold shirts with black trim, black shorts. Record League goal-scorer: W. Crilley, 49 goals, Division II, 1921-2. Record victory: 9—2 v. Forfar Athletic, Division II, Mar. 18, 1933. Record defeat: 10—0 v. Dundee, Division II, Mar. 8, 1947.

### AMATEUR CUP

See FOOTBALL ASSOCIATION AMATEUR CHALLENGE CUP.

### AMATEUR FOOTBALL ALLIANCE

With the rapid increase in professionalism throughout the country in the early years of this century many of the old amateur clubs felt that they were not getting the same consideration and attention from the Football Association. The situation was aggravated when the F.A. instructed all County Associations to admit professional clubs to membership, and, in 1907, the true amateurs of the "old school" decided that the time had come for them to break away from the F.A. to form an amateur association of their own.

Accordingly, a meeting was called at the Holborn Restaurant at which the following resolution was adopted: "It is essential for the good of the game of Association football as played by amateurs that an Amateur Football Association be formed."

Clubs represented at this meeting included Cambridge University, Clapham Rovers, Corinthians, Old Carthusians, Old Etonians, Old Westminsters and the Swifts.

Many other amateur clubs, big and small, decided to accept the new Association as their governing body in preference to the F.A. The "split" continued until 1914 when representatives of both Associations got together and the amateurs decided once again to recognise the F.A. as being the governing body of the game in England.

The Amateur Football Association, however, still continued with some measure of independence.

Eventually in May, 1934, the title was changed to the AMATEUR FOOTBALL ALLIANCE, and representation was secured on the International Selection Committee of the F.A. and the Amateur Cup Committee.

The amateurs introduced a Senior Cup competition of their own in 1907 with a trophy presented by the Corinthians. This should not be confused with the much older Amateur Cup Competition instituted by the F.A.

Today, as always, the members of the A.F.A. are mainly composed of clubs from London Insurance and Banking offices, Government Departments, Public Schools, Old Boys' clubs, Hospitals, Southern Amateur League clubs and, of course, Oxford and Cambridge Universities, numbering in all some 350 to 400 clubs, competing in something like 40 League and Cup competitions.

## AMATEURS (FOOTBALL LEAGUE)

The greatest number of amateurs to appear in a Football League team since normal football was resumed in 1946 is three—B. Joy, K. O'Flanagan and A. Gudmundsson for Arsenal v. Stoke City, Oct. 19, 1946.

After World War II amateurs in Football League matches became increasingly rare until in 1972 the F.A. decided that as from the start of season 1974-5 amateurs would no longer be recognised as such, and that all footballers, paid or unpaid, would be classed as "Players".

An attempt has been made below to list the principal amateurs who played more than a dozen games in the Football League in peace-time since the competition recommenced in 1919.

J. C. Burns, l.h., 263 appearances, Queen's Park Rangers, Brentford, 1927-36; W. V. Gibbins, c.f. or i.f., 176, West Ham United, Brentford, Bristol Rovers, Southampton, 1923-34; G. H. Armitage, c.h.b., 165, Charlton Athletic, 1923-30; W. I. Bryant, c.h.b., 131, Millwall, 1925-31; J. F. Mitchell, g., 120, Preston North End, Manchester City, 1920-26; Dr. V. E. Milne, c.h.b., 133, Aston Villa, 1924-9 (had previously played as a professional with Aberdeen and Aston Villa); H. L. Coates, i.l., 101, Southampton, 1928-34; B. H. Baker, g., 95, Everton, Chelsea, Oldham Athletic, 1920-29; M. Woosnam, c.h.b., 89, Manchester City, 1919-25; B. Joy, c.h.b., 87, Fulham, Arsenal, 1933-47; M. J. Pinner, g., 89, Aston Villa, Sheffield Wednesday, Queen's Park Rangers, Manchester United, Chelsea, Swansea Town, Leyton Orient, 1959-63; G. Bromilow, c.f., 84, Southport, 1955-59; W. J. Slater, r.h.b., 81, Blackpool, Brentford, Wolverhampton Wanderers, 1949-54; J. R. Roxburgh, f., 80, Leicester City, Aston Villa, Sheffield United, 1920-27; Dr. J. A. Paterson, o.r., 70, Arsenal, 1920-26; A. E. Knight, f.b., 69, Portsmouth, 1919-22; W. H. Fitchford, f., 69, Port Vale, 1919-23; C. T. Mortimore, c.f., 66, Aldershot, 1949-53; J. E. Beswick, h.b., 58, Stoke City, 1921-7; R. Boreham, i.r., 51, Arsenal, 1921-4; M. Edelston, i.r., 51, Brentford, Reading, 1937-47; T. H. Robinson, h.b., 47, Brentford, Northampton Town, 1954-58; H. J. McIlvenny, c.f., 43, Bradford, 1946-50; P. Thompson, c.f., 42, Wrexham, 1955-7; A. H. Gibbons, c.f., 39, Tottenham Hotspur, 1937-9; F. P. Kippax, o.l., 31, Burnley, Liverpool, 1946-9; G. P. Keizer, g., 29, Arsenal, Charlton Athletic, 1930-32; N. Middleboe, h.b., 28, Chelsea, 1919-32; M. Costello, c.f., 28, Aldershot, 1956-7; C. W. Harbidge, h.b., 25, Reading, Charlton Athletic, 1920-22; J. Brennan, h.b., 23, Manchester City, 1919-22; W. Holmes, c.f., 23, Doncaster Rovers, Blackburn Rovers, 1950-53; H. P. Evans, r.h.b., 23, Cardiff City, 1920-22; G. H. Smithies, c.f., 21, Preston North End, Birmingham, 1929-31; A. Roxburgh, f., 19, Leicester City 1920-22; W. W. Parr, o.r., 18, Blackpool, 1935-9; S. C. P. O'Connell, i.l., 16, Chelsea, 1954-6; W. Steffen, l.b., 15, Chelsea, 1946-7; J. Surtees, f., 14, Durham City, 1921-3; Rev. H. Davies, f., 14, Wrexham, 1924-8; Dr. K. O'Flanagan, o.r., 14, Arsenal, 1946-7; J. Nicholls, i.r., 13, Newport County, Cardiff City, 1923-5.

A few of the above players subsequently turned professional, but for the most part, such men have been ignored when compiling this list, and in any case, the number of appearances given are amateur only.

The record for the longest period a player appeared as an amateur before turning professional with the same Football League club is held by R. Hawkes. He played for Luton Town, usually as a left-half, for 10 seasons before signing professional forms at the start of season 1911-12.

H. S. Stapley, an amateur centre-forward, was Glossop's principal goal-scorer in Division II for four seasons 1908-12. This is a Football League record for the greatest number of consecutive seasons that an amateur has headed a club's scoring list. During those four seasons Stapley scored 67 goals in 135 appearances.

The only amateurs to head their side's scoring list in the Football League for any season since World War I are W. V. Gibbins, 18 goals for West Ham United, Division I, 1930-31; C. F. Mortimore, 15 goals for Aldershot, Division III(S), 1949-50; G. Bromilow, 22 goals for Southport, Division III(N), 1955-6, and 8 in 1956-7.

The first amateur club to seek admission to the Football League were the Argonauts. Formed in 1928, they immediately applied for membership of Division III(S). They came third in a poll of six clubs. Only two being elected. The Argonauts tried again in 1929 when again they were third. In the 1930 election —their last attempt—they polled no votes. In the hope that they would gain admission to the League they had provisionally booked Wembley Stadium as their home ground.

## AMATEURS (INTERNATIONALS)

The last amateur to appear in a full international for England was B. Joy who played centre-half v. Belgium, Brussels, May 9, 1936. The same player finally appeared for England v. Scotland, Oct. 14, 1944, but this being a war-time game it is not rated a full international.

England last fielded 11 amateurs in a full international on Mar. 18, 1895, v. Wales, at Queen's Club, London. The result was a draw 1—1.

## APPEARANCES (LEAGUE) Consecutive

The record for the number of consecutive appearances in the Football League is held by H. Bell, Tranmere Rovers' centre-half. From the opening of the 1946-7 season Bell did not miss a match until he was dropped for the visit of Gateshead, Aug. 30, 1955—a total of 401 consecutive Division III(N) appearances. Altogether, Bell's appearances totalled 459 for he also played in 26 F.A. Cup, 22 Liverpool Senior Cup, and 10 Cheshire Bowl games.

In the Argentine goalkeeper J. Saldumnere made 412 consecutive appearances for Racing Mar-del-Plata before he broke a leg. This run was spread over 18 years.

Returning to the Football League the runner-up to Bell is N. J. Trollope who made 368 consecutive appearances for Swindon Town, Apr. 3, 1961 to Aug. 24, 1968 inclusive. 324 Football League, 25 F.A. Cup, and 19 Football League Cup. R. Powell made 284 consecutive League appearances in goal for Chesterfield, 1952-8. Plymouth Argyle full-back, P. Jones, made 279 consecutive League appearances from April, 1947 to Nov. 7, 1953, when he was forced to drop out of the side with an ankle injury.

R. Middleton made 277 consecutive Football League appearances with Chesterfield and Derby County, although if one includes war-time Football League (N) 1945-6 season's appearances then Middleton's run totalled 319, for it began in that season. Then followed 210 consecutive peace-time League games for Chesterfield before he was transferred to Derby County in June 1951. There he added another 67 consecutive appearances before being dropped from their side on Jan. 17, 1953.

J. Whatley made 276 consecutive appearances (246 in Football League) in goal for Bristol Rovers, Aug. 1922- April 1928.

R. McKinlay, Nottingham Forest, centre-half made 265 consecutive Football League appearances from April 1959 to October 1965.

A. Ingham, Queen's Park Rangers, full-back, 249 consecutive appearances, 1956-61.

E. Ditchburn, made 247 consecutive Football League appearances in goal for Tottenham Hotspur from April 1948 until Mar. 1954.

## General

A. McNamara appeared in all four divisions of the Football League inside a period of 12 months. He made his last appearance for Everton (Division I), Oct. 12, 1957, and his debut for Bury (Division III), Sept. 27, 1958. Between these dates he played for Liverpool (Division II) and for Crewe Alexandra (Division IV).

Outside-left, R. Clarke, appeared in three divisions of the Football League in three successive matches. He was playing for Cardiff City in Division III(S) in 1946-7. Near the end of the season he was transferred to Manchester City in time to make one appearance in Division II before his new club was promoted to Division I.

During 1961 goalkeeper, C. Brodie, appeared in Division IV, I and III in three consecutive Football League appearances. He made his last League appearance for

Aldershot in Division IV, Feb. 4, 1961, subsequently transferred to Wolverhampton Wanderers where he made one Division I appearance before the end of the season. His next appearance was with Northampton Town in Division III, Sept. 30, 1961.

R. Straw played in all six divisions of the Football League in the space of eight seasons 1952-60 while with Derby County and Coventry City.

**Most Appearances**

Here is a list of players with 500 or more peacetime Football League and/or Scottish League games to their credit:

| | | | | |
|---|---|---|---|---|
| J. Dickinson | Portsmouth | l.h. | 1946–65 | 764‡ |
| R. Sproson | Port Vale | h.b. | 1950–72 | 757(5)‡ |
| S. Matthews | Stoke City (twice), Blackpool | o.r. | 1932–65 | 701 |
| I. Allchurch | Swansea Town (twice), Newcastle United, Cardiff City | i.f. | 1949–68 | 692(2) |
| W. Meredith | Northwich Victoria, Manchester City (twice), Manchester United | o.r. | 1893–1924 | 682 |
| T. Paine | Southampton | o.l. or o.r. | 1956–73 | 668(4) |
| R. Allen | Port Vale, West Bromwich Albion, Crystal Palace | f. | 1946–65 | 637 |
| R. Collins | Celtic, Everton, Leeds United, Bury, Oldham Athletic | i.f. | 1949–73 | 636(1) |
| J. Charlton | Leeds United | c.h. | 1952–73 | 630‡ |
| J. Shaw | Sheffield United | c.h. | 1948–66 | 629‡ |
| P. Broadbent | Brentford, Wolverhampton Wanderers, Shrewsbury Town, Aston Villa, Stockport County | i.f. | 1950–70 | 628(1) |
| R. Ferrier | Motherwell | o.l. | 1918–37 | 626‡ |
| A. G. Rowley | West Bromwich Albion, Fulham, Leicester City, Shrewsbury Town | c.f. | 1946–65 | 619 |
| D. Blakey | Chesterfield | c.h. | 1948–67 | 613‡ |
| E. Hine | Barnsley (twice), Leicester City, Huddersfield Town, Manchester United | i.r. | 1921–38 | 612 |
| R. McKinlay | Nottingham Forest | c.h. | 1951–70 | 611(3)‡ |
| J. W. Spence | Manchester United, Bradford City, Chesterfield | o.r. | 1919–38 | 611 |
| J. Brownsword | Hull City, Scunthorpe United | l.b. | 1946–65 | 610 |
| R. Charlton | Manchester United | c.f. | 1956–73 | 604(2)‡ |
| R. C. Simpson | Queen's Park, Third Lanark, Newcastle United, Hibernian, Celtic | g. | 1946–70 | 604 |
| J. Scoular | Portsmouth, Newcastle United, Bradford | w.h. | 1946–64 | 602 |
| R. F. Kelly | Burnley, Sunderland, Huddersfield Town, Preston North End, Carlisle United | i.r. | 1913–36 | 601 |
| A. Iremonger | Notts County, Lincoln City | g. | 1905–27 | 600 |
| S. Bloomer | Derby County (twice), Middlesbrough | i.r. | 1892–1914 | 600 |
| J. Atyeo | Portsmouth, Bristol City | c.f. | 1951–66 | 599 |
| J. Haynes | Fulham | i.f. | 1952–70 | 598‡ |
| L. Allchurch | Swansea (twice), Sheffield United, Stockport County | o.r. | 1953–71 | 597(3) |
| H. Bell | Tranmere Rovers | c.h. | 1946–61 | 595‡ |
| S. Milburn | Chesterfield, Leicester City, Rochdale | r.b. | 1946–65 | 591 |
| R. Ashman | Norwich City | l.b. | 1946–64 | 590‡ |
| A. McNair | Celtic | r.b. | 1904–25 | 588‡ |
| E. Lowe | Aston Villa, Fulham, Notts County | l.h. | 1946–65 | 587 |
| W. McGarry | Port Vale, Huddersfield Town, Bournemouth | w.h. | 1946–63 | 586 |
| W. Milne | Swansea Town | l.b. | 1919–37 | 585‡ |
| E. J. Langley | Leeds United, Brighton, Fulham, Queen's Park Rangers | l.b. | 1952–67 | 583(1) |

| | | | | |
|---|---|---|---|---|
| S. Bartram | Charlton Athletic | g. | 1934–56 | 582‡ |
| M. Keen | Queen's Park Rangers, Luton Town, Watford | h.b. | 1959–73 | 581(1)† |
| G. Farm | Hibernian, Blackpool, Queen of the South | g. | 1947–64 | 581 |
| W. Fotheringham | Airdrie, Dundee, Morton, St. Mirren, Queen of the South | g. | 1919–37 | 580 |
| R. Clayton | Blackburn Rovers | r.h. | 1950–69 | 578(2)‡ |
| J. L. Simpson | Lincoln City, Gillingham | g. | 1957–72 | 576 |
| W. Robb | Birmingham, Rangers, Hibernian, Aldershot | g. | 1913–37 | 571 |
| C. C. Holton | Arsenal, Watford (twice), Northampton Town, Crystal Palace, Charlton Athletic, Leyton Orient | c.f. | 1947–68 | 571 |
| J. McIlroy | Burnley, Stoke City, Oldham Athletic | i.f. | 1950–68 | 569(4) |
| J. Melia | Liverpool, Wolverhampton Wanderers, Southampton, Aldershot, Crewe Alexandra | i.f. | 1955–72 | 569(2) |
| W. Cresswell | South Shields, Sunderland, Everton | l.b. | 1919–36 | 569 |
| J. W. Smith | South Shields, Portsmouth, Bournemouth, Clapton Orient | i.f. | 1919–37 | 569 |
| J. Armfield | Blackpool | r.b. | 1955–71 | 568‡ |
| T. Eglington | Everton, Tranmere Rovers | o.l. | 1946–61 | 566 |
| P. Gallagher | Celtic, Falkirk | i.f. | 1911–32 | 565‡ |
| P. Dobing | Blackburn Rovers, Manchester City, Stoke City | c.f. | 1956–73 | 564† |
| R. Evans | Celtic, Chelsea, Newport County, Morton, Third Lanark, Raith Rovers | c.h. | 1947–68 | 564 |
| W. A. Foulkes | Manchester United | c.h. | 1952–70 | 563(4)‡ |
| R. G. Williamson | Middlesbrough | g. | 1902–23 | 563‡ |
| R. Bentley | Newcastle United, Chelsea, Fulham, Queen's Park Rangers | r.b. or c.f. | 1946–63 | 559 |
| J. W. McCue | Stoke City, Oldham Athletic | l.b. | 1946–62 | 558 |
| A. Sherwood | Cardiff City, Newport County | l.b. | 1946–61 | 558 |
| A. Mullery | Fulham (twice), Tottenham Hotspur | r.h.b. | 1958–73 | 557† |
| T. D. Burden | Chester, Leeds United, Bristol City | w.h. or i.f. | 1946–61 | 557 |
| M. Downie | Kilmarnock, Bradford, Lincoln City, Bradford City, Doncaster Rovers | g. | 1946–64 | 557 |
| T. Cairns | Bristol City, Rangers, Bradford City | i.f. | 1911–32 | 556 |
| M. Owen | Swindon Town | c.f. or c.h. | 1946–63 | 554‡ |
| A. Williams | Bristol City, Oldham Athletic, Watford, Newport County, Swansea City | r.h.b. | 1956–72 | 551(4) |
| F. Else | Preston North End, Blackburn Rovers, Barrow | g. | 1953–70 | 550 |
| D. Blanchflower | Barnsley, Aston Villa, Tottenham Hotspur | r.h. | 1949–64 | 553 |
| S. Hardy | Chesterfield, Liverpool, Aston Villa, Nottingham Forest | g. | 1903–25 | 552 |
| A. Hodgkinson | Sheffield United | g. | 1954–72 | 552‡ |
| W. McStay | Ayr United, Celtic, Hearts | f.b. | 1912–30 | 550 |
| D. H. Harris | Newport County, Portsmouth | h.b. | 1954–71 | 551 |
| D. C. Mackay | Hearts, Tottenham Hotspur, Derby County, Swindon Town | w.h. | 1953–72 | 549(1) |
| H. Gallacher | Airdrie, Newcastle United, Chelsea, Derby County, Notts County, Grimsby Town, Gateshead | c.f. | 1921–39 | 541 |

| | | | | |
|---|---|---|---|---|
| J. D. S. Gordon | Portsmouth (twice), Birmingham City | i.f. | 1951–67 | 541 |
| T. Fowler | Northampton Town, Aldershot | o.l. | 1920–36 | 540 |
| F. Large | Halifax Town, Queen's Park Rangers, Northampton Town (three times), Swindon Town, Carlisle United, Oldham Athletic, Leicester City, Fulham, Chesterfield | i.f. or c.f. | 1958–73 | 539(2)† |
| J. Iley | Sheffield United, Tottenham Hotspur, Newcastle United, Peterborough United | w.h. | 1954–72 | 536(9) |
| F. Tunstall | Sheffield United, Halifax Town | o.l. | 1946–63 | 535 |
| N. Trollope | Swindon Town | l.b. | 1960–73 | 534(1)†‡ |
| R. A. Parry | Bolton Wanderers, Blackpool, Bury | i.f. | 1952–72 | 533(8) |
| J. McColl | Celtic, Stoke City, Partick Thistle, Hibernian, Leith Athletic | c.f. | 1913–32 | 532 |
| A. Black | Leicester City | f.b. | 1919–35 | 530‡ |
| B. Harris | Everton, Cardiff City, Newport County | h.b. | 1955–73 | 531(3)† |
| E. F. Brook | Barnsley, Manchester City | o.l. | 1925–39 | 529 |
| R. Flowers | Wolverhampton Wanderers, Northampton Town | l.h. | 1952–69 | 528 |
| J. McNichol | Brighton, Chelsea, Crystal Palace | i.f. | 1949–63 | 528 |
| R. Crompton | Blackburn Rovers | f.b. | 1896–1920 | 528‡ |
| A. Sturgess | Stoke City, Sheffield United, Norwich City | f.b. | 1902–25 | 525 |
| G. Harrison | Leicester Fosse, Everton, Preston North End, Blackpool | o.l. | 1910–32 | 524 |
| L. Weare | Newport County | g. | 1955–70 | 524‡ |
| R. Moore | West Ham United | l.h.b | 1958–73 | 523(1)†‡ |
| W. Smith | Huddersfield Town, Rochdale | o.l. | 1914–35 | 523 |
| J. Rutherford | Newcastle United, Arsenal, Clapton Orient | o.r. | 1901–27 | 522 |
| R. Robinson | Middlesbrough, Barrow | c.h. | 1946–63 | 522 |
| E Hopkinson | Oldham Athletic, Bolton Wanderers | g. | 1951–70 | 522 |
| A. Ingham | Leeds United, Queen's Park Rangers | f.b. | 1947–63 | 522 |
| J. K. McHale | Huddersfield Town, Crewe Alexandra, Chester | o.r. | 1956–72 | 522(3) |
| A. Black | Leicester City | f.b. | 1919–35 | 522 |
| J. Dawson | Burnley | g. | 1906–29 | 522‡ |
| R. S. Marshall | Sunderland, Manchester City | i.f. | 1920–38 | 521 |
| A. Biggs | Bristol Rovers (twice), Preston North End, Walsall, Swansea Town | c.f. | 1953–69 | 520(1) |
| J. Sewell | Notts County, Sheffield Wednesday, Aston Villa, Hull City | i.f. | 1946–61 | 520 |
| Joe Smith | Bolton Wanderers, Stockport County | i.f. | 1908–27 | 520 |
| A. Archibald | Raith Rovers, Glasgow Rangers | o.r. | 1916–34 | 519 |
| L. Massie | Huddersfield Town, Darlington, Halifax Town, Bradford, Workington | c.f. | 1956–71 | 519(1) |
| D. Welbourne | Grimsby Town, Watford | r.b. | 1957–73 | 517(5)† |
| G. Mee | Blackpool, Derby County, Burnley, Mansfield Town, Accrington Stanley, Rochdale | o.l. | 1920–39 | 517 |
| J. McLaren | Bradford City, Leicester City, Watford | g. | 1922–39 | 517 |
| K. Furphy | Darlington, Workington Watford | h.b. | 1953–69 | 516(6) |
| James Oakes | Port Vale, Charlton Athletic | l.b. | 1923–39 | 515 |
| E. Burgin | Sheffield United, Doncaster Rovers, Leeds United, Rochdale | g. | 1949–66 | 514 |

| | | | | |
|---|---|---|---|---|
| J. Greaves | Chelsea, Tottenham Hotspur, West Ham United | i.f. | 1957–71 | 514(2) |
| G. E. Eastham | Newcastle United, Arsenal, Stoke City | i.f. | 1956–73 | 513(10)† |
| G. Stevenson | Motherwell | i.l. | 1923–39 | 513‡ |
| K. Coote | Brentford | f.b. | 1949–64 | 513‡ |
| E. G. Harrison | Halifax Town, Hartlepool, Barrow (twice), Southport | h.b. | 1957–72 | 512(4) |
| A. Davidson | Hull City | r.b. | 1952–68 | 511‡ |
| E. A. Stuart | Wolverhampton Wanderers, Stoke City, Tranmere Rovers, Stockport County | c.h. | 1952–68 | 511 |
| R. Wylie | Notts County, Aston Villa, Birmingham City | h.b. | 1951–70 | 510 |
| G. Banks | Chesterfield, Leicester City, Stoke City | g. | 1958–73 | 510† |
| J. W. Ruffell | West Ham United, Aldershot | o.l. | 1921–39 | 510 |
| E. Wilson | Brighton & Hove Albion | o.l. | 1922–36 | 509‡ |
| J. Newman | Birmingham City, Leicester City, Plymouth Argyle, Exeter City | w.h. | 1951–72 | 509(1) |
| C. Taylor | Walsall (three times), Newcastle United, Crystal Palace | o.l. | 1958–73 | 508(13) |
| A. D. Holden | Bolton Wanderers, Preston North End | o.l. | 1951–65 | 508 |
| B. C. Trautmann | Manchester City | g. | 1949–64 | 508‡ |
| M. Summerbee | Swindon Town, Manchester City | o.r. | 1959–73 | 508(1)† |
| F. Womack | Birmingham, Torquay United | f.b. | 1908–30 | 507 |
| N. Bullock | Bury | c.h. or c.f. | 1920–35 | 506‡ |
| W. P. Gray | Leyton Orient, Chelsea, Burnley, Nottingham Forest, Millwall | i.f. | 1947–65 | 505 |
| C. Jones | Swansea Town, Tottenham Hotspur, Fulham | o.l. or o.r. | 1952–70 | 504(6) |
| J. Wilson | Workington (twice), Nottingham Forest, Wolverhampton Wanderers, Newport County | r.b. | 1955–73 | 504(2) |
| S. Anderson | Sunderland, Newcastle United, Middlesbrough | r.h. | 1952–66 | 504 |
| E. R. Herod | Charlton Athletic, Brentford, Tottenham Hotspur, Chester, Swindon Town, Clapton Orient | f.b. | 1921–37 | 504 |
| A. Jones | Wrexham | f.b. | 1923–36 | 503‡ |
| G. Wall | Barnsley, Manchester United, Oldham Athletic, Hamilton Academicals | o.l. | 1903–23 | 503 |
| W. Pease | Northampton Town, Middlesbrough, Luton Town, | o.r. | 1920–34 | 502 |
| J. Mathieson | Raith Rovers Middlesbrough, Brentford, Queen of the South | g. | 1923–39 | 502 |
| A. Wilson | Sheffield Wednesday | i.r. or c.f. | 1900–19 | 502‡ |
| G. W. Curtis | Coventry City, Aston Villa | c.h. | 1955–72 | 501(3) |
| J. T. Brittleton | Stockport County, Sheffield Wednesday, Stoke City | h.b. | 1902–25 | 501 |
| M. Hooper | Darlington, Sheffield Wednesday | o.r. | 1921–38 | 500 |

Figures in parentheses indicate appearances as substitute.
† Still adding to this total in 1973–74.
‡ This is to emphasise the fact that these appearances were made for a single club. See also the succeeding item.

## Most Appearances for a Single Club

Included in the preceding list and indicated so ‡ are a number of players whose total of appearances was made with a single club. *Those names are not repeated here.* However, that list also includes other players who can claim the distinction of making over 500 appearances for a single club although the figures given include appearances with more than one club. Those players and their totals for the one club are:

| | | | | |
|---|---|---|---|---|
| J. Brownsword | Scunthorpe United | l.b. | 1950–65 | 600 |
| J. Atyeo | Bristol City | c.f. | 1951–66 | 597 |
| J. L. Simpson | Gillingham | g. | 1957–72 | 571 |
| A. Iremonger | Notts County | g. | 1905–26 | 564 |
| T. Fowler | Northampton Town | o.l. | 1946–61 | 521 |
| W. Smith | Huddersfield Town | o.l. | 1914–34 | 520 |
| E. Hopkinson | Bolton Wanderers | g. | 1952–70 | 519 |
| A. Ingham | Queen's Park Rangers | f.b. | 1950–63 | 519 |
| A. Archibald | Rangers | o.r. | 1917–34 | 513 |
| J. W. Ruffell | West Ham United | l.b. | 1921–38 | 508 |
| J. W. McCue | Stoke City | o.l. | 1946–60 | 502 |

The following have made between 450 and 500 League appearances for a single club:

| | | | | |
|---|---|---|---|---|
| J. Hewie | Charlton Athletic | f.b. | 1951–66 | 495 |
| A. Mitchell | Exeter City | w.h. | 1952–66 | 495 |
| R. H. Morton | Luton Town | w.h. | 1948–64 | 494 |
| D. Meiklejohn | Rangers | r.h. | 1919–36 | 492 |
| W. Liddell | Liverpool | c.f. | 1946–61 | 492 |
| S. Burton | Swindon Town | g. | 1946–62 | 490 |
| D. Gray | Rangers | r.h. | 1925–39 | 490 |
| W. A. Wright | Wolverhampton Wanderers | c.h. | 1946–59 | 490 |
| R. Wilcox | Newport County | c.h. | 1946–61 | 489 |
| H. Bamford | Bristol Rovers | r.b. | 1946–58 | 487 |
| F. Womack | Birmingham | f.b. | 1908–28 | 487 |
| G. Merrick | Birmingham City | g. | 1946–60 | 486 |
| G. W. Curtis | Coventry City | c.h. | 1956–70 | 483(3) |
| G. B. Edwards | Bolton Wanderers | h.b. | 1950–65 | 483 |
| A. Finney | Bolton Wanderers | l.b. | 1922–37 | 483 |
| K. Harvey | Exeter City | c.h. | 1952–69 | 483 |
| B. Jackson | York City | c.h. | 1958–70 | 481 |
| J. W. Spence | Manchester United | o.r. | 1919–33 | 481 |
| W. Walker | Aston Villa | i.l. | 1919–34 | 480 |
| P. P. Harris | Portsmouth | o.r. | 1946–60 | 479 |
| W. Bremner | Leeds United | r.h.b. | 1959–73 | 478(1)† |
| R. McGrory | Stoke City | r.b. | 1921–35 | 478 |
| J. Parry | Derby County | c.h. | 1949–66 | 478 |
| S. Bloomer | Derby County | c.f. | 1892–1906, 1910–14 | 475 |
| G. Barrowcliffe | Derby County | r.b. | 1951–66 | 475 |
| E. Lowe | Fulham | l.h. | 1950–63 | 474 |
| R. W. H. Powell | Chesterfield | g. | 1952–66 | 471 |
| S. Black | Plymouth Argyle | o.l. | 1924–38 | 470 |
| J. Callender | Gateshead | r.h. | 1946–58 | 470 |
| J. Pitt | Bristol Rovers | r.h. | 1946–58 | 470 |
| P. Bonetti | Chelsea | g. | 1959–73 | 467† |
| R. Flowers | Wolverhampton Wanderers | w.h. | 1952–67 | 467 |
| E. T. Vizard | Bolton Wanderers | o.l. | 1910–31 | 467 |
| E. Sagar | Everton | g. | 1929–53 | 466 |
| R. Murray | Stockport County | f.b. | 1952–63 | 465 |
| J. H. Brown | Sheffield Wednesday | g. | 1922–37 | 465 |
| J. Burkitt | Nottingham Forest | l.h. | 1946–62 | 464 |
| G. Farm | Blackpool | g. | 1947–60 | 462 |

| | | | | |
|---|---|---|---|---|
| G. Hair | Leeds United | f.b. | 1950–65 | 462 |
| V. Watson | West Ham United | c.f. | 1920–35 | 462 |
| E. Needham | Sheffield United | l.h. | 1892–1913 | 461 |
| J. B. McAlpine | Queen's Park (Glasgow) | i.l. | 1919–34 | 460 |
| J. Rowland | Newport County | w.h. | 1958–69 | 460 |
| D. T. Williams | Rotherham United | w.h. | 1946–62 | 460 |
| G. Bradford | Bristol Rovers | c.f. | 1949–64 | 459 |
| G. Petherbridge | Bristol Rovers | o.r. | 1946–62 | 459 |
| G. E. Jones | Middlesbrough | f.b. | 1959–73 | 457(5) |
| I. Callaghan | Liverpool | o.l. | 1959–73 | 456(2)† |
| A. Oakes | Manchester City | l.h.b. | 1959–73 | 455(2)† |
| J. Pennington | West Bromwich Albion | l.b. | 1903–22 | 455 |
| W. Amos | Bury | o.l. | 1923–35 | 453 |
| P. Broadbent | Wolverhampton Wanderers | i.f. | 1951–65 | 453 |
| A. Finney | Sheffield Wednesday | o.r. | 1950–66 | 453 |
| E. T. Skeels | Stoke City | h.b. | 1959–73 | 453(11)† |
| R. A. Spiers | Reading | h.b. | 1955–70 | 453 |
| N. Lofthouse | Bolton Wanderers | c.f. | 1946–61 | 452 |
| R. Warren | Bristol Rovers | c.h. | 1935–56 | 452 |
| A. Anderson | Southend United | l.b. | 1950–63 | 451 |
| E. F. Brook | Manchester City | o.l. | 1927–39 | 451 |
| B. Turner | Bury | h.b. | 1957–70 | 451(3) |
| W. Edwards | Leeds United | r.h. | 1924–39 | 450 |
| K. Jobling | Grimsby Town | h.b. | 1953–69 | 450 |
| Joe Smith | Bolton Wanderers | i.l. | 1908–27 | 450 |

† Still adding to this total in 1973–74
Figures in brackets indicate appearances as substitute.
Years given are seasons which cover appearances and do not necessarily coincide with player's stay with the club.

## APPEARANCES (INTERNATIONALS)
**Consecutive**

R. D. Blanchflower, Aston Villa and Tottenham Hotspur, holds the record for the highest number of consecutive appearances in the Home International Championship.

Beginning with the game against Wales, at Swansea, March 19, 1952, he played in every one of Ireland's International Championship games to the end of 1962. An un-interrupted run of 33 consecutive games.

Prior to this run Blanchflower had appeared in four International Championship matches while with Barnsley and Aston Villa.

The English record in the International Championship was set up by W. A. Wright, Wolverhampton Wanderers, with a run of 25 games beginning with that against Scotland at Wembley, April 14, 1951, and ending with that against Scotland on the same ground, April 11, 1959.

In all internationals for England Wright set up a world record with a run of 70 consecutive appearances beginning with the game against France, Oct. 3, 1951, and ending with that against U.S.A., May 28, 1959.

**Most**

In the list of players that follows the total of international appearances does not necessarily mean the total number of caps received. It should be remembered that at the present time only one cap is awarded each season for appearances in the International Championship between the home countries.

War-time and Victory Internationals are not included as they do not rank as full internationals. A list of players with most appearances in those games is given under WAR-TIME FOOTBALL.

*England (30 or more appearances)*

| | *I.C. | O. | Total |
|---|---|---|---|
| R. Moore (West Ham United) | 30 | 77m | 107 |
| R. Charlton (Manchester United) | 32 | 74 | 106dh |

| | | | |
|---|---|---|---|
| W. Wright (Wolverhampton Wanderers) | 38 | 67 | 105c |
| T. Finney (Preston North End) | 29 | 47 | 76 |
| G. Banks (Leicester City, Stoke City) | 23 | 50 | 73 |
| A. Ball (Blackpool, Everton, Arsenal) | 17 | 48m | 65 |
| R. Wilson (Huddersfield Town, Everton) | 15 | 48 | 63h |
| M. Peters (West Ham United, Tottenham Hotspur) | 18 | 44m | 62 |
| J. Greaves (Chelsea, Tottenham Hotspur) | 14 | 43 | 57h |
| J. Haynes (Fulham) | 16 | 40 | 56 |
| S. Matthews (Stoke City, Blackpool) | 24 | 30 | 54ab |
| R. Flowers (Wolverhampton Wanderers) | 15 | 34 | 49 |
| G. Hurst (West Ham United) | 14 | 35 | 49 |
| J. Dickinson (Portsmouth) | 17 | 31 | 48 |
| J. Armfield (Blackpool) | 13 | 30 | 43 |
| R. Crompton (Blackburn Rovers) | 34 | 8 | 42 |
| G. Cohen (Fulham) | 11 | 26 | 37 |
| B. Douglas (Blackburn Rovers) | 11 | 25 | 36 |
| R. Clayton (Blackburn Rovers) | 13 | 22 | 35 |
| J. Charlton (Leeds United) | 9 | 26 | 35d |
| A. Mullery (Tottenham Hotspur) | 8 | 27 | 35d |
| R. Hunt (Liverpool) | 7 | 27 | 34 |
| R. W. Byrne (Manchester United) | 12 | 21 | 33 |
| N. Lofthouse (Bolton Wanderers) | 13 | 20 | 33c |
| R. Springett (Sheffield Wednesday) | 10 | 23 | 33 |
| A. Ramsey (Southampton, Tottenham Hotspur) | 10 | 22 | 32 |
| E. Hapgood (Arsenal) | 13 | 17 | 30 |
| F. Lee (Manchester City) | 7 | 20 | 27d |

*Scotland (30 or more appearances)*

| | | | |
|---|---|---|---|
| G. Young (Rangers) | 29 | 24 | 53c |
| D. Law (Huddersfield Town, Manchester City, Turin, Manchester United) | 25 | 24 | 49gh |
| R. Evans (Celtic) | 21 | 27 | 48 |
| J. Greig (Rangers) | 21 | 22 | 43d |
| W. Bremner (Leeds United) | 16 | 25 | 41d |
| E. Caldow (Rangers) | 18 | 22 | 40 |
| L. Reilly (Hibernian) | 20 | 18 | 38 |
| J. Baxter (Rangers, Sunderland) | 17 | 17 | 34gh |
| R. Collins (Celtic, Everton, Leeds United) | 12 | 19 | 31 |
| A. Morton (Queen's Park Rangers) | 30 | 1 | 31 |
| W. Steel (Morton, Derby County, Dundee) | 17 | 13 | 30a |

*Ireland (30 or more appearances)*

| | | | |
|---|---|---|---|
| T. Neill (Arsenal, Hull City) | 30 | 29 | 59 |
| R. D. Blanchflower (Barnsley, Aston Villa, Tottenham Hotspur) | 37 | 19 | 56b |
| W. Bingham (Sunderland, Luton Town, Everton) | 34 | 22 | 56 |
| J. McIlroy (Burnley) | 36 | 19 | 55b |
| P. Jennings (Watford, Tottenham Hotspur) | 25 | 19 | 44d |
| D. Dougan (Portsmouth, Blackburn Rovers, Aston Villa, Leicester City, Wolverhampton Wanderers) | 23 | 20 | 43d |
| A. McMichael (Newcastle United) | 28 | 13 | 41c |
| J. Nicholson (Manchester United, Huddersfield Town) | 24 | 17 | 41 |
| A. Elder (Burnley, Stoke City) | 24 | 16 | 40 |
| D. Clements (Coventry City, Sheffield Wednesday) | 19 | 15 | 34 |
| P. McParland (Aston Villa, Wolverhampton Wanderers) | 20 | 14 | 34 |
| M. Harvey (Sunderland) | 15 | 17 | 32 |
| G. Best (Manchester United) | 16 | 15 | 31d |
| E. Scott (Liverpool, Belfast Celtic) | 31 | — | 31 |
| R. Peacock (Glasgow Celtic, Coleraine) | 18 | 13 | 31b |
| W. Cunningham (St. Mirren, Leicester City, Dunfermline) | 20 | 10 | 30 |
| O. Stanfield (Distillery) | 30 | — | 30 |

*Wales (30 or more appearances)*

| | | | |
|---|---|---|---|
| I. Allchurch (Swansea, Newcastle United, Cardiff City) | 37 | 31e | 68 |
| C. Jones (Swansea, Tottenham Hotspur, Fulham) | 31 | 28ef | 59 |
| W. Meredith (Manchester City, Manchester United) | 48 | — | 48 |
| S. G. Williams (West Bromwich Albion, Southampton) | 23 | 20 | 43 |
| M. England (Blackburn Rovers, Tottenham Hotspur) | 22 | 19fk | 41 |
| A. J. Kelsey (Arsenal) | 23 | 18 | 41b |
| A. Sherwood (Cardiff City, Newport County) | 30 | 11e | 41 |
| W. J. Charles (Swansea Town, Leeds United, Juventus, Cardiff City) | 19 | 20e | 39b |
| W. Hennessey (Birmingham City, Nottingham Forest, Derby County) | 20 | 19fj | 39 |
| R. Rees (Coventry City, West Bromwich Albion, Nottingham Forest, Swansea City) | 17 | 22f | 39 |
| P. Rodrigues (Cardiff City, Leicester City, Sheffield Wednesday) | 21 | 18fk | 39 |
| T. Ford (Swansea Town, Aston Villa, Sunderland, Cardiff City) | 26 | 12e | 38 |
| M. Hopkins (Tottenham Hotspur) | 16 | 18 | 34 |
| W. Davies (Bolton Wanderers, Newcastle United, Manchester City) | 18 | 15j | 33 |
| R. Paul (Swansea Town, Manchester City) | 23 | 10e | 33 |
| R. Burgess (Tottenham Hotspur) | 22 | 10e | 32a |
| F. Keenor (Cardiff City, Crewe Alexandra) | 32 | — | 32 |
| T. R. Vernon (Blackburn Rovers, Everton, Stoke City) | 18 | 14 | 32 |
| M. Charles (Swansea Town, Arsenal, Cardiff City) | 14 | 17 | 31 |
| G. Sprake (Leeds United) | 29 | 12fk | 31 |
| B. G. Hole (Cardiff City, Blackburn Rovers, Aston Villa, Swansea City | 14 | 16 | 30 |
| W. Lewis (Bangor, Crewe Alexandra, Chester) | 30 | — | 30 |
| T. C. Medwin (Swansea Town, Tottenham Hotspur) | 16 | 14 | 30 |

*I.C.—Home International Championship.
O.—Other internationals.
a—also played for G.B. *v.* Rest of Europe, 1947.
b—also played for G.B. *v.* Rest of Europe, 1955.
c—also played for Rest of U.K. *v.* Wales, 1951.
d—also played for Rest of U.K. *v.* Wales, 1969.
e—include Wales *v.* Rest of U.K., 1951.
f—includes Wales *v.* Rest of U.K., 1969.
g—also played for F.I.F.A. *v.* England, 1963.
h—also played for Rest of Europe *v.* Scandinavia, 1964.
j—includes one game *v.* England, World Cup, 1972.
k—includes two games *v.* England, World Cup, 1972.
m—includes England *v.* Scotland centenary game, 1973
Above figures are correct to June 30th, 1973.

In both amateur and full internationals, V. Woodward made a total of 61 appearances for England. He also played in three "Test" matches against South Africa and six games for Great Britain in the Olympic Games.

*Foreign Countries*

International appearance figures for many of the foreign players are difficult to establish because the status of several so-called international games is sometimes doubtful. This is particularly the case among South American countries where "Internationals" are so numerous and where closer examination reveals that a large percentage of these games could not possibly rate the title of full international.

This being the case the compiler regrets that a few of the figures quoted below can only be regarded as approximate, but this still can be treated as a useful guide to the world's leading players. It is based on records available to June, 1973.

Argentine: A. Roma (Boca Juniors) 49.
Austria: G. Hanappi (S.C. Wacker, S.C. Rapid) 96.
Belgium: P. Van Himst (Anderlecht) 72.
Brazil: Pele (Santos) 110.

Bulgaria: I. Kolev (CFKA Sofia) 75.
Chile: L. Sanchez (Universidad de Chile) 104.
Czechoslovakia: L. Novak (Dukla) 75.
Denmark: B. Hansen (Frem) 51.
Eire: A. Kelly (Preston N.E.) 46.
Finland: S. Mynti (VIFK) 61.
France: R. Marché (R.C. Paris) 63.
Germany (East): H. Frenzel (Locomotiv Leipzig) 52.
Germany (West): U. Seeler (Hamburger SV) 72.
Greece: D. Papaioannou (AEK Athens) 44.
Hungary: J. Bozsik (Honved) 100.
Italy: G. Facchetti (Inter-Milan) 68.
Luxembourg: N. Kettel (Slade Dudelange) 67.
Mexico: G. Pena (Oro, Cruz Azul) 85.
Netherlands: P. Van Heel (Feyenoord) 64.
Norway: T. Svennson (Sandefjord) 104.
Poland: W. Lubanski (Gornik Zabrze) 67.
Portugal: M. Coluna (Benfica) 73.
Soviet Union: A. Shesternev (Moscow Army) 90.
Spain: R. Zamora (Espanol, C.F. Barcelona, Real Madrid) 47.
Sweden: O. Bergmark (Orebro, Roma) 94.
Switzerland: S. Minelli (Servette, Grasshoppers) 79.
Turkey: K. Lefter (Fenerbahce) 48.
Uruguay: P. Rocha (Penarol) 75.
Yugoslavia: D. Dzajic (Red Star Belgrade) 68.

## General

S. Davies played for Wales in six different positions: right-half (two), left-half (one), outside-right (two), inside-right (three), centre-forward (six), and inside-left (four). Total 18 appearances.

T. Pearson (Newcastle United), a Scot, played for England v. Scotland in a war-time Red Cross international match at Newcastle, Dec. 1939. Pearson was called in at the last minute to replace E. Brook (Manchester City) who had been injured in an accident.

S. Mortensen made his international debut (war-time) against his own country. It was at Wembley, Sept. 25, 1943. England were playing Wales. Mortensen was reserve for England, but when the injured Wales left-half, I. Powell, was unable to resume after the interval, it was agreed that Mortensen should take his place.

R. G. Milne (Linfield), a Scot, played 27 times for Ireland, 1894-1906.

S. Macrae, born Port Bannantyne, Bute, Scotland, played for England six times 1883-84.

The decision made in 1971 to alter the international qualification rules so as to enable a player to represent the country of his father's birth will inevitably mean that instances like these just mentioned will become quite commonplace. But these early instances are still interesting.

L. Kubala, one of the finest inside-forwards of the post-war era, has appeared in internationals for three different countries. Born in Hungary he was first capped for that country, but subsequently appeared with Czechoslovakia and with Spain.

A. Di Stefano has also played for three countries: his native Argentine, Colombia and Spain.

Another player to appear for three countries is J. Kennaway who was a Glasgow Celtic goalkeeper in the 1930s. Prior to joining Celtic he had played for Canada v. U.S.A. in 1928, U.S.A. v. Canada in 1930, and while with Celtic he made two appearances for Scotland.

Many players have appeared in internationals for two different countries and here we mention only a few of them.

J. Reynolds of Distillery, West Bromwich Albion and Aston Villa, appeared for England and for Ireland in the 1890s. Reynolds was born at Blackburn.

R. E. Evans (Aston Villa and Sheffield United) played for Wales against England, and for England against Wales, in the early 1900s. He also played for both countries against Scotland and Ireland. Evans was born at Chester.

J. H. Edwards (Shropshire Wanderers) played for England v. Scotland, 1874, and for Wales v. Scotland, 1876.

H. Maschio, Argentine inside-forward was capped for his country in the 1950s and subsequently made appearances for Italy. Others include Lojacono, Montuori, Martino and Sivori, and pre-war—Demaria,

Guaita, Monti, and Orsi.

G. Altafini, led the Brazilian attack on a number of occasions when he was with Palmeiras, and, after transferring to A.C. Milan in 1958, he appeared for Italy.

J. Schiaffino, another brilliant inside-forward, appeared in many internationals for his native country, Uruguay, before being transferred from Penarol to A.C. Milan and subsequently playing for Italy.

J. Santamaria was born in Montevideo and while with Penarol F.C. he appeared in many internationals for Uruguay. In 1957 he was transferred to Real Madrid and subsequently made a number of appearances for Spain.

Other Uruguayans to appear for their own country and for Italy are Ghiggia (1950s) and Faccio (1930s).

I. Beck, Yugoslavian centre-forward of the 1930s made 15 appearances for his country before becoming a naturalised Frenchman and playing in five internationals for France.

Another French international who had previously played for the country of his birth was goalkeeper R. Hiden who moved from Wiener A.C. to Racing Club de Paris in the 1930s.

F. Puskas, the brilliant Hungarian inside-forward made 84 appearances for his country before quitting at the time of the revolution in 1956. After that he made four appearances for Spain.

The first player to appear in an England representative side while not attached to an English club was C. Rutter, right-back of Cardiff City. He played for England "B" v. Holland at Amsterdam, Mar. 26, 1952.

The first professional to appear for England while on the books of a club outside the Football League was J. Baker, Hibernian, who was in the England Under 23 side v. Poland, Sept. 24, 1958. He subsequently appeared in five Full Internationals for England while still with Hibernian.

## APPRENTICE PROFESSIONALS
See under REGISTRATION OF PLAYERS

## ARBROATH F.C.
Founded 1878. Joined Scottish League, Division II, 1902. Honours: Runners-up, Division II, 1934-5, 1958-9, 1967-8, 1971-2. Record attendance: 13,510 v. Rangers, Scottish Cup, 3rd Round, Feb. 23, 1952. Address: Gayfield Park, Arbroath. (Tel. 0241-4 2157). Colours: Maroon shirts, white shorts. Record goalscorer: D. Easson, 45 goals, Division II, 1958-9. Record victory: 36—0 v. Bon Accord, Scottish Cup, 1st Round, Sept. 5, 1885. Record defeat: 8—0 v. Kilmarnock, Division II, Jan. 3, 1949.

## ARGENTINE
Football was introduced into the Argentine by Britishers in the 1860s, when they were, for the most part, engaged in the building of the railways in that country.

The Buenos Aires F.C. was formed by these British residents in 1865 and is, therefore, the oldest football club in the Argentine.

Despite the fact that it was the British who sowed the seed it is really the Italians who must take most credit for the development of the game in the Argentine and today it is one of the foremost soccer loving nations in the world. Italians immigrated to the Argentine in large numbers around the time of World War I.

The Argentinian Football Association was founded as early as 1895 when the British influence was still at its strongest and Sir Thomas Lipton kept interest alive when he presented a cup in 1902 to be competed for annually between the Argentine and Uruguay.

However, it was much later, in the decade before World War II that Argentinian football really became world class. In 1928 the Argentine reached the final of the Olympic Games soccer tournament to draw with Uruguay, 1—1, before losing the replay 2—0. In 1930 they were defeated by the same opponents in the final of the World Cup, but from then on the reputation of the Argentinian footballer as a soccer artist quickly built up to one of such renown that by the time the second World War had come to an end these South Americans were in great demand abroad.

Their early elimination from the final tournaments of the World Cup in 1958 and again in 1962 was followed by violent demonstrations against the Argentine F.A., and no-one will ever forget the fantastic scene at Wembley in the 1966 tournament when the Argentine were eliminated with a 1—0 defeat by England. The game was held up for seven minutes while their captain, A. Rattin, refused to leave the field after being ordered off by the referee.

The Argentinians, rather surprisingly, again failed to qualify for the 1970 final tournament after being defeated by less fancied Peru and Bolivia.

The address of the national association is Associación del Futbol Argentino, Viamonte 1366/76, Buenos Aires. Colours: blue and white striped shirts, black shorts, grey stockings.

| May | 9, 1951 | England 2, Argentine 1; Wembley |
|---|---|---|
| May | 13, 1951 | Eire 0, Argentine 1; Dublin |
| May | 17, 1953 | Argentine 0, England 0; Buenos Aires |
| | | (Abandoned after 23 min, pitch waterlogged) |
| June | 11, 1958 | England 1, Argentine 3; Sweden† |
| June | 2, 1962 | England 3, Argentine 1; Chile† |
| June | 6, 1964 | Argentine 1, England 0; Rio de Janeiro |
| July | 23, 1966 | England 1, Argentine 0; Wembley† |

†World Cup

## ARMFIELD, James Christopher (1935-    )

Voted the best right-back in the world following brilliant display in the World Cup competition in Chile in 1962, this stylish defender, who was among the earliest of the modern attacking full-backs, was an England regular from 1958 to 1966, including a run of 37 consecutive games.

Born in Manchester, young Armfield played mostly rugby at school in Blackpool and represented Lancashire, but following National Service he decided to make soccer his career. He made League debut for Blackpool December 27, 1954, and played over 600 games for them before retiring in May 1971. Two months later he was appointed team-manager of Bolton Wanderers.

Blackpool 1954-71, 566 apps. England internationals 43 (15 as captain). Under-23 games 9. Inter-League games 12.

## ARSENAL F.C.

Founded 1886 as Royal Arsenal, Woolwich. Joined Football League, Division II, 1893. Honours: Champions, Division I, 1930-31, 1932-3, 1933-4, 1934-5, 1937-8, 1947-8, 1952-3, 1970-71. Runners-up, 1925-6, 1931-2, 1972-3. Runners-up, Division II, 1903-4. F.A. Cup: Winners, 1930, 1936, 1950, 1971. Finalists, 1927, 1932, 1952, 1972. Arsenal achieved the "double" in winning both the F.A. Cup and League Championship in 1970-71. League Cup, Runners-up, 1968, 1969. Fairs Cup: Winners, 1970. Record attendance: 73,295 v. Sunderland, Division I, Mar. 9, 1935. Address: Arsenal Stadium, Highbury, N.5 (Tel. 01-226 5841). Nickname: Gunners. Colours: Red shirts, white sleeves, white shorts, red stockings. Record League goal-scorer: E. Drake, 42 goals, Division I, 1934-5. Record victory: 12—0 v. Loughborough Town, Division II, Mar. 12, 1900. Record defeat: 8—0 v. Loughborough Town, Division II, Dec. 12, 1896.

## ASTON VILLA F.C.

Founded 1874 by members of the Villa Cross Wesleyan Chapel, Aston. One of the original members of the Football League 1888. Honours: Champions, Division I, 1893-4, 1895-6, 1896-7, 1898-9, 1899-1900, 1909-10. Runners-up, 1888-9, 1902-3, 1907-8, 1910-11, 1912-13, 1913-14, 1930-31, 1932-3. Champions, Division II, 1937-8, 1959-60. Champions Division III, 1971-2. F.A. Cup: Winners 1887, 1895, 1897, 1905, 1913, 1920 and 1957. Seven F.A. Cup victories is a record. Finalists, 1892, 1924. In season 1896-7 Aston Villa achieved the "double" in winning both the F.A. Cup and League Championship. League Cup: Winners, 1961. Finalists, 1963, 1971. Record attendance: 76,588 v. Derby County, F.A. Cup, 6th Round, Mar. 2, 1946. Address: Villa Park, Birmingham B6 6HE (Tel. 021-327 6604). Nickname: Villans. Colours: Claret shirts, light blue collars and sleeves, white shorts and stockings. Record League goal-scorer: T. Waring, 49 goals, Division I, 1930-31. Record victory: 13 0 v. Wednesbury Old Athletic, F.A. Cup, 1st Round, Oct. 30, 1886. Record defeat: 8—1 v. Blackburn Rovers, F.A. Cup, 3rd Round, 1888-9.

## ATHERSMITH, William Charles (1872-1910)

This speedy outside-right was the first player to gain every possible honour in a single season when he helped Aston Villa win the League and Cup "double" in 1896-7 and also represented England against Scotland, Ireland and Wales. Combined with John Devey to form Villa's finest ever right wing in that club's "golden age"—the 1890s, when they won the League five times and the F.A. Cup twice.

Born Bloxwich, Staffs, he was playing for Bloxwich Wanderers at the age of 12. Joined Villa from Unity Gas Works F.C. in February 1891 and was first capped just over a year later.

Aston Villa 1891-1901, 259 apps. Small

Heath 1901-05, 100 apps. (8 goals). England internationals 12. Inter-League games 7. League champions 1893-4, 1895-6, 1896-7, 1898-9, 1899-1900. F.A. Cup, winners 1895, 1897, runners-up 1892.

## ATTENDANCES
### European Cup
The record attendance: 135,826, Celtic v. Leeds United, semi-final (2nd leg), Hampden Park, April 15, 1970.

### F.A. Amateur Cup
An attendance of 100,000 has been recorded at five F.A. Amateur Cup finals at Wembley—in 1951 (Pegasus v. Bishop Auckland), 1952 (Walthamstow Avenue v. Leyton), 1953 (Pegasus v. Harwich and Parkeston), 1954 (Bishop Auckland v. Crook Town), and 1955 (Bishop Auckland v. Hendon).

### F.A. Cup
For attendances at Final ties see complete list under FOOTBALL ASSOCIATION CHALLENGE CUP.

The record for the Cup Final is 126,047, at Wembley, April 28, 1923, when Bolton Wanderers defeated West Ham United 2—0. This is the official figure. However, several thousands more broke into the ground. Various estimates of the actual number have been given. It is generally considered that in all something like 200,000 spectators gained admission.

The smallest attendance at an F.A. Cup tie in the competition proper was a few hundred who were admitted free to the Norwich City v. Bradford City, 3rd Round (second replay), at Lincoln, in 1915. Officially the game was played behind closed doors so as not to interfere with the production of armaments at nearby factories.

### Football League
Aggregate of attendances at all Football League games in each season:

| | |
|---|---|
| 1946-47 | 35,604,606 |
| 1947-48 | 40,259,130 |
| 1948-49 | 41,271,424 |
| 1949-50 | 40,517,865 |
| 1950-51 | 39,584,987 |
| 1951-52 | 39,015,866 |
| 1952-53 | 37,149,966 |
| 1953-54 | 36,174,590 |
| 1954-55 | 34,133,103 |
| 1955-56 | 33,150,809 |
| 1956-57 | 32,744,405 |
| 1957-58 | 33,562,208 |
| 1958-59 | 33,610,985 |
| 1959-60 | 32,538,611 |
| 1960-61 | 28,619,754 |
| 1961-62 | 27,979,902 |
| 1962-63 | 28,885,852 |
| 1963-64 | 28,535,022 |
| 1964-65 | 27,641,168 |
| 1965-66 | 27,206,960 |
| 1966-67 | 28,902,596 |
| 1967-68 | 30,107,298 |
| 1968-69 | 29,382,172 |
| 1969-70 | 29,600,972 |
| 1970-71 | 28,191,146 |
| 1971-72 | 28,700,729 |
| 1972-73 | 25,448,642 |

The record club average for a single season in Football League is 57,758, Manchester United, Division I, 1967-68.

Record attendance for each division at a single game:

Division I: Manchester United v. Arsenal, at Maine Road, Jan. 17, 1948, 83,260.

Division II: Aston Villa v. Coventry City, Oct. 30, 1937, 68,029.

Division III(S): Cardiff City v. Bristol City, at Ninian Park, April 7, 1947, 51,621.

Division III(N): Hull City v. Rotherham United, at Boothferry Park, Dec. 25, 1948, 49,655.

Division III: Aston Villa v. Bournemouth, at Villa Park, Feb. 12, 1972, 48,110.

Division IV: Crystal Palace v. Millwall, Mar. 31, 1961, 37,774.

The smallest attendance recorded at a Football League game is 13. This number paid to see a Division II match between Stockport County and Leicester City at Old Trafford, Manchester, May 7, 1921, when Stockport County's ground was under suspension.

The smallest attendance at a Football League game in the period since World War II—484, Gateshead v. Accrington Stanley, Division III(N), March 1952.

### Football League Cup
Record attendance at a Final tie: 98,189 in 1969. At any other tie: 63,418, Manchester United v. Manchester City, semi-final, Dec. 17, 1969.

### Friendlies
The record attendance at a friendly game between Football League clubs is 44,840, Newcastle United v. Liverpool, Feb. 14, 1948.

The record attendance at a friendly game played in England between a Football League club and any other club was at Stamford Bridge when Chelsea drew 3—3 with Moscow Dynamo in Nov. 1945. The attendance can only be estimated as several thousands broke into the ground after the gates had been closed. It is recorded as 82,000 but was probably nearer 90,000.

The record for a friendly game in Scotland is 104,679, Rangers v. Eintracht

Frankfurt, at Hampden Park, Oct. 17, 1961.

### Internationals

British record: 149,547, Scotland v. England, Hampden Park, Glasgow, April 17, 1937.

World Record: 199,850, Brazil v. Uruguay, World Cup Final, Rio de Janeiro, July 16, 1950. This is a world record for any football match.

### Mid-Week

The British record for a mid-week match is 135,826, European Cup, semi-final (2nd leg), Celtic v. Leeds United, at Hampden Park, April 15, 1970.

The record in England is 100,000 at Wembley Stadium. This was first established at the England v. Argentine international match on May 9, 1951, and has since been equalled on a number of occasions.

The Football League mid-week record is 72,077, Everton v. Manchester United, Division I, Sept. 4, 1957.

The F.A. Cup mid-week record is 80,407, Derby County v. Birmingham City, Maine Road, Manchester, semi-finals (replay), Mar. 28, 1946.

### Provincial

The record for a game in England outside London is 84,569 at Maine Road, Manchester, Mar. 3, 1934, when Manchester City defeated Stoke City 1—0 in the 6th Round of the F.A. Cup.

### Scottish Cup

The record attendance for a Scottish Cup Final is 146,433, Celtic v. Aberdeen, Hampden Park, Glasgow, April 24, 1937.

For any game other than an international or a Cup Final the British attendance record is also a Scottish Cup match: 143,570, Glasgow Rangers v. Hibernian, semi-final tie, Mar. 27, 1948.

### Scottish League

Record attendance: 118,567, Rangers v. Celtic, Ibrox Stadium, Glasgow, Jan. 2, 1939.

### Scottish League Cup

Record attendance: 107,609, Final tie, Hampden Park, Oct. 23, 1965.

## AUSTRALIA

Organised football in Australia dates from the early 1880s and the Anglo-Australian Association was formed as long ago as 1884, but for more than 50 years soccer was a very poor relation to the Rugby League game so popular in New South Wales and Queensland or the Australian Rules game which is the number one sport in South Australia, Victoria, Tasmania and Western Australia.

The recent boom has brought with it headaches for the authorities. In 1960 the A.S.F.A. was banned for three years from F.I.F.A. for poaching players from Austria. Then, in 1961, feeling against the governing body of Australian soccer grew to such proportions that in November of that year a rival organisation, the Australian Federation of Soccer Clubs was formed and claimed recognition as the leading soccer authority. It quickly gained support and became the official governing body.

Whereas soccer in Australia was a strictly amateur game before the last war, most of the leading clubs now employ part-time professionals and the wages offered together with jobs outside the game have attracted many professionals from Britain.

Australia entered for the World Cup for the first time in 1965 but were eliminated with two defeats by North Korea. In 1969 they were eliminated by Israel.

At the present time Australian soccer is still dominated by migrants who cling together in ethnic groups forming their own clubs with names foreign to Australia. The game will not really gain national status and support until they breed more Australian born players.

Address of the governing body —Australian Soccer Federation, Room 413, 155 King Street, Sydney, N.S.W. 2,000. Colours: Dark green shirts with gold trim, white shorts.

Results of Tests and internationals:

| July | 27, 1925 | Australia 0, England 5; Brisbane |
| July | 4, 1925 | Australia 1, England 2; Sydney |
| July | 11, 1925 | Australia 2, England 8; Maitland |
| July | 18, 1925 | Australia 0, England 5; Sydney |
| July | 25, 1925 | Australia 0, England 2; Melbourne |
| July | 10, 1937 | Australia 5, England 4; Sydney |
| July | 17, 1937 | Australia 0, England 4; Brisbane |
| July | 20, 1937 | Australia 4, England 3; Newcastle |
| May | 26, 1951 | Australia 1, England 4; Sydney |
| June | 30, 1951 | Australia 0, England 17; Sydney † |

| July | 7, 1951 | Australia 1, England 4; Brisbane |
| July | 14, 1951 | Australia 1, England 6; Sydney |
| July | 21, 1951 | Australia 0, England 5; Newcastle |
| May | 28, 1967 | Australia 0, Scotland 1; Sydney |
| May | 30, 1967 | Australia 1, Scotland 2; Adelaide |
| June | 3, 1967 | Australia 0, Scotland 2; Melbourne |
| June | 13, 1971 | Australia 0, England 1; Sydney |
| June | 20, 1971 | Australia 0, England 1; Melbourne |

† 17–0 is England's highest score in international matches—a world record win.

## AUSTRIA

For the greater part of the last 40 years Austria has been rated among the leading football nations of the world. But like most countries they have had their ups and downs in the international field. The early 1930s was one of their better periods when the famous "Wunderteam" beat Scotland 5—0, Germany 6—0, and lost by only the odd goal of seven to a powerful England side at Stamford Bridge.

The second half of the 1950s was one of Austria's down-hill periods and this decline prompted them not to enter for the 1962 World Cup, and although they have since recovered they have still not been restored to their former glory, and failed to qualify for the World Cup in 1966 and 1970.

The British introduced soccer to Vienna in the 1880s and helped form one of the first clubs to play the game in that country, the Cricketers, in 1889.

The first English club to visit Austria was Oxford University in 1899, followed by Southampton in 1901.

The Austrians figured in the earliest international match to be played on the continent of Europe, beating Hungary 5—0 in 1902, and A.C. Wiener (formed 1896) was the first club to defeat an English professional side touring abroad when they beat Sunderland 2—1 in Vienna in 1909.

However, little progress was made in the game in Austria until after the formation of their F.A. in 1926. Today, they control over 1,500 clubs with a membership of over 200,000.

The address of the governing body is: Oesterreichischer Fussball-Bund, Postfach 161, Vienna 1061. Colours: White shirts, black shorts.

Results of international matches:

| June | 6, 1908 | Austria 1, England 6; Vienna |
| June | 8, 1908 | Austria 1, England 11; Vienna |
| June | 1, 1909 | Austria 1, England 8; Vienna |
| May | 14, 1930 | Austria 0, England 0; Vienna |
| May | 16, 1931 | Austria 5, Scotland 0; Vienna |
| Dec. | 7, 1932 | England 4, Austria 3; Chelsea |
| Nov. | 29, 1933 | Scotland 2, Austria 2; Glasgow |
| May | 6, 1936 | Austria 2, England 1; Vienna |
| May | 9, 1937 | Austria 1, Scotland 1; Vienna |
| Dec. | 13, 1950 | Scotland 0, Austria 1; Glasgow |
| May | 27, 1951 | Austria 4, Scotland 0; Vienna |
| Nov. | 28, 1951 | England 2, Austria 2; Wembley |
| May | 7, 1952 | Austria 6, Eire 0; Vienna |
| May | 25, 1952 | Austria 2, England 3; Vienna |
| Mar. | 25, 1953 | Eire 4, Austria 0; Dublin |
| May | 9, 1954 | Austria 2, Wales 0; Vienna |
| June | 16, 1954 | Austria 1, Scotland 0; Zurich* |
| May | 19, 1955 | Austria 1, Scotland 4; Vienna |
| Nov. | 23, 1955 | Wales, 1, Austria 2; Wrexham |
| May | 2, 1956 | Scotland 1, Austria 1; Glasgow |
| May | 14, 1958 | Austria 3, Eire 1; Vienna |
| June | 15, 1958 | England 2, Austria 2; Sweden* |
| May | 29, 1960 | Austria 4, Scotland 1; Vienna |
| May | 27, 1961 | Austria 3, England 1; Vienna |
| April | 4, 1962 | England 3, Austria 1; Wembley |
| April | 8, 1962 | Eire 2, Austria 3; Dublin |
| May | 8, 1963 | Scotland 4, Austria 1; Glasgow† |
| Sept. | 25, 1963 | Austria 0, Eire 0; Vienna‡ |

Oct. 13, 1963   Eire 3, Austria 2; Dublin‡
Oct. 20, 1965   England 2, Austria 3; Wembley
May 22, 1966   Austria 1, Eire 0; Vienna
May 27, 1967   Austria 0, England 1; Vienna
Nov. 6, 1968   Scotland 2, Austria 1; Glasgow*
Nov. 10, 1968   Eire 2, Austria 2; Dublin
Nov. 5, 1969   Austria 2, Scotland 0; Vienna*
May 30, 1971   Eire 1, Austria 4; Dublin§
Oct. 10, 1971   Austria 6, Eire 0; Linz§

† Abandoned after 81 minutes   * World Cup
‡ Nations Cup   § European Championship

## AWAY POINTS

The record for each division is:

| | | | | W. | D. | L. | |
|---|---|---|---|---|---|---|---|
| Division I | 33 points | Arsenal | | 14 | 5 | 2 | 1930–31 |
| | 33 ,, | Tottenham Hotspur | | 16 | 1 | 4 | 1960–61 |
| Division II | 31 ,, | Bristol City | | 13 | 5 | 1 | 1905–06 |
| Division III(S) | 32 ,, | Nottingham Forest | | 14 | 4 | 5 | 1950–51 |
| Division III(N) | 37 ,, | Doncaster Rovers | | 18 | 1 | 2 | 1946–47 |
| Division III | 29 ,, | Bury | | 12 | 5 | 6 | 1960–61 |
| | 29 ,, | Portsmouth | | 12 | 5 | 6 | 1961–62 |
| | 29 ,, | Hull City | | 12 | 5 | 6 | 1965–66 |
| Division IV | 32 ,, | Walsall | | 14 | 4 | 5 | 1959–60 |
| Scottish League: | | | | | | | |
| Division I | 37 ,, | Glasgow Rangers | | 16 | 5 | 0 | 1920–21 |

### No points

Throughout the history of the Football League only five clubs have gone through a season without gaining a single away point:

Division II: Northwich Victoria, 1893-4; Crewe Alexandra, 1894-5; Loughborough Town, 1899-1900; Doncaster Rovers, 1904-5. Division III(N): Nelson, 1930-31.

### AWAY WINS

Doncaster Rovers 18 away wins in Division III(N) in season 1946-7 is a Football League record.

Tottenham Hotspur's eight consecutive away wins in 1960-61 is a Football League record. Their total of 16 away wins that season is a First Division record.

Huddersfield Town were not defeated away from home between Nov. 15, 1924 and Nov. 14, 1925. During that time they played 18 Division I games, winning 12 and drawing six.

Merthyr Town had a run of 61 away games in Division III(S) without a win, Sept. 1922- Sept. 1925. A Football League record.

On Jan. 30, 1937, there was not one away win in all the 35 F.A. Cup and Football League matches played.

The most away wins in any division of the Football League on a single day is eight: Division III, Sept. 27, 1958; Division II, Sept. 12, 1959, and Nov. 25, 1967.

### AYR UNITED F.C.

Founded 1910 by amalgamation of Ayr Parkhouse and Ayr F.C. Joined Scottish League, Division II, 1910. Honours: Champions, Division II, 1911-12, 1912-13, 1927-8, 1936-7, 1958-9, 1965-6. Runners-up, 1910-11, 1955-6, 1968-9. Record attendance: 24,617 v. Celtic, Scottish Cup, 2nd Round, Feb. 3, 1934. Address: Somerset Park, Ayr. (Tel. 0292 63435). Nickname: Honest Men. Colours: White shirts with black trim, black shorts. Record League goal-scorer: J. Smith, 66 goals, Division II, 1927-28. Record Victory: 11—2 v. Clackmannan, Scottish Cup, 1st Round, Jan. 17, 1931. Record defeat: 9—0 v. Rangers, Scottish League, Division I. Nov. 16, 1929, and v. Hearts, Division I, Feb. 28, 1931.

## BAILEY, Norman Coles (1857-1923)

An outstanding personality on the playing field as well as in the administrative side of the game, this London solicitor turned over from rugby to soccer with Clapham Rovers, a club that played both codes. Strong and fearless Bailey appeared in London's first-ever floodlit soccer match in November 1878. Known as the "Prince of half-backs" he was the first man to fill the new right-half berth for England and had a run of 10 consecutive appearances against Scotland, a record for an England half-back not beaten until Billy Wright enjoyed a run of 14 such appearances more than 70 years later.

It was Bailey who seconded the proposal for the legalisation of professionalism when this was put to the F.A. He became a vice-president of that body as well as of the Amateur Football Association.

Old Westminsters, Swifts, Clapham Rovers, 1875-86. Corinthians 1885-89. England internationals 19. F.A. Cup, winners 1880, runners-up 1879.

## BALL, Alan James (1945-    )

This dynamic footballer was the youngest member of England's World Cup-winning team of 1966 and became the first player transferred between British clubs for a fee of over £200,000. This deal took place in December 1971. Born Farnworth, nr. Bolton, he was encouraged by his father, a former professional who became manager of Halifax Town and later Preston North End. Ball junior made League debut with Blackpool in 1962 and after exciting so much interest with that club Everton paid £110,000 for his transfer in August 1966, a new British record. His hard running and quick tackling helped Everton through one of the finest spells in their history before his move to Arsenal.

Blackpool 1962-66, 116 apps. (42 goals), Everton 1966-71, 208 apps. (66 goals), Arsenal 1971-73, 58 apps. (13 goals). England internationals 65. Under-23 games 8. Inter-League games 6 League champions 1969-70. F.A. Cup, runners-up 1968, 1972.

## BALL, THE

According to the Laws of Football, the ball must be spherical with an outer casing of leather or other approved materials. The circumference shall not be more than 28 in., nor less than 27 in., while the weight at the start of the game must be not more than 16 oz., nor less than 14 oz.

The law further stipulates that no material shall be used in the manufacture of the ball which might prove dangerous to the players.

As regards the use of coloured balls, these must be available for all games during the months of Nov., Dec., Jan. and Feb.

The ball selected at the start of a match, coloured or otherwise, must be used throughout the game. It can only be changed if defective, and then must be replaced by a ball of the same type and colour.

### Bursting Ball

The first time the ball burst in a Cup Final at Wembley was in 1946 during the Derby County v. Charlton Athletic tie. Oddly enough, the chances of the ball bursting in a Cup Final were discussed in a B.B.C. broadcast shortly before this particular game, and the referee, Mr. E. D. Smith, of Cumberland, remarked that it was a million to one chance.

The ball also burst when Derby County met Charlton Athletic in a Football League match only five days after the Wembley meeting.

The ball also burst thirty minutes after the start of the following year's Cup Final —Charlton Athletic v. Burnley, 1947.

### BANKS, Gordon, O.B.E. (1937-    )

Discovered by Chesterfield while playing for a Sheffield works club Gordon Banks was snapped up by Leicester City after only a season in the Third Division. Possessing great powers of concentration he has since been acknowledged as one of the world's safest goalkeepers, particularly after brilliant displays in England's World Cup-winning side of 1966. Since making England debut against Scotland in 1963 he has created a record among England goalkeepers for his number of caps. Stoke City paid something like £50,000 for his transfer April 1967. An injury to his right eye in a motoring accident in Oct. 1972 seriously affected his playing career.

Chesterfield 1958-59, 23 app., Leicester City 1959-67, 293 app., Stoke City, 1967-73 194 app. England appearances 73. Under-23 games 2. Inter-League games 5. League Championship · medals nil. F.A. Cup medals, runners-up 1961, 1963. Football

League Cup medals, winners 1972. World Cup medal 1966.

## BARNSLEY F.C.
Founded 1887 as Barnsley St. Peter's. Joined Football League, Division II, 1898. Honours: Champions, Division III(N), 1933-4, 1938-9, 1954-5. Runners-up, 1953-4. Runners-up, Division III, 1967-8. Best in Division II, 3rd 1914-15, 1921-2. F.A. Cup: Winners, 1912. Finalists, 1910. Record attendance: 40,255 v. Stoke City, F.A. Cup 5th Round, Feb. 15, 1936. Address: Oakwell Ground, Barnsley. (Tel. 84113). Nickname: Tykes. Colours: Red shirts, white shorts, red stockings. Record League goal-scorer: C. McCormack, 33 goals, Division II, 1950-51. Record victory: 9—0 v. Loughborough Town, Division II, Jan. 28, 1899, and v. Accrington Stanley (at Accrington), Division III(N), Feb. 3, 1934. Record defeat: 9—0 v. Notts County, Division II, Nov. 19, 1927.

## BASSETT, William Isaiah (1869-1937)
When Billy Bassett was at the height of his fame in the 1890s wingers hugged the touch-line, centering the ball from near the corner-flag, and nobody could pin-point a centre better than this player who stood only 5ft. 5½ inches tall but used his great speed to keep out of trouble. Contemporaries reckoned there was no finer player for the big occasion, and it was Bassett's speed and skill that won the Cup for West Bromwich Albion in 1888 when that club had only been in existence nine years. He also laid on the centres for two of Albion's three goals when they won the trophy again in 1892.

A local lad, Bassett served the Albion for over 50 years, becoming a director in 1905 and Chairman from 1908 until his death.

West Bromwich Albion 1886-99, 262 apps. England internationals 16. Inter-League games 4. F.A. Cup, winners 1888, 1892, runners-up 1895.

## BASTIN, Clifford Sydney (1912-    )
When Arsenal were sweeping all before them in the 1930s they had the coolest head and one of the deadliest shots in football at outside-left—Clifford Bastin, a player who made such a rapid rise to fame that he won all the major football honours before his 21st birthday.

Born at Exeter, Bastin was in Exeter City's League side when still only 15, going to Arsenal for £2,000 soon after turning professional. In 1932-3 he created a record that still stands for a First Division winger by hitting 33 goals. He played his first League game for Arsenal at Everton in October 1929 and his last in the League against Derby in September 1946.

Exeter City 1927-9, 17 apps. (7 goals). Arsenal 1929-47, 350 apps. (150 goals). England internationals 21. Inter-League games 4. League champions 1930-31, 1932-3, 1933-4, 1934-5, 1937-8. F.A. Cup, winners 1930, 1936, runners-up 1932.

## BELGIUM
A strange situation existed in Belgium for many years inasmuch as the F.A. were reluctant to recognise professionalism yet most of the leading clubs employed part-time professionals referred to as "Independent Footballers" because they did not sign contracts with their particular clubs.

That state of affairs was brought to an end in 1962 and there has been a subsequent strengthening of the game in this country although there are still comparatively few full-time professionals, the vast majority being part-timers.

Belgium's most successful clubs in recent years have been Anderlecht and Standard Liege. These two have practically monopolised the League championship since the war.

The Belgian F.A. was formed in 1895 and joined F.I.F.A. in 1904. It became the Royal F.A. in 1920, the prefix being granted by King Albert I. Today there are over 2,200 clubs affiliated.

The Belgians have appeared in five World Cup final tournaments, 1930, 1934, 1938, 1954 and 1970, but they were beaten in every game except that against England in Basle in 1954 when they drew 4-4 after extra time, and against El Salvador in Mexico in 1970 when they won 3-0.

The address of the governing body is Union Royale Belge des Sociétés de Football Association, 14 Rue Guimard, Bruxelles 1040. Colours: White shirts with tri-coloured (black-yellow-red) collars and cuffs, white shorts, white stockings with tri-coloured tops.

Results of international matches:

| | | |
|---|---|---|
| May 21, 1921 | Belgium 0, England 2; Brussels |
| Mar. 19, 1923 | England 6, Belgium 1; Highbury |
| Nov. 1, 1923 | Belgium 2, England 2; Antwerp |
| Dec. 8, 1924 | England 4, Belgium 0; West Bromwich |
| May 24, 1926 | Belgium 3, England 5; Antwerp |

| | |
|---|---|
| May 11, 1927 | Belgium 1, England 9; Brussels |
| Feb. 12, 1928 | Belgium 2, Eire 4; Liege |
| May 19, 1928 | Belgium 1, England 3; Antwerp |
| April 30, 1929 | Eire 4, Belgium 0; Dublin |
| May 11, 1929 | Belgium 1, England 5; Brussels |
| May 11, 1930 | Belgium 1, Eire 3; Brussels |
| May 16, 1931 | Belgium 1, England 4; Brussels |
| Feb. 25, 1934* | Eire 4, Belgium 4; Dublin |
| May 9, 1936 | Belgium 3, England 2; Brussels |
| Jan. 19, 1946† | England 2, Belgium 0; Wembley |
| Jan. 23, 1946† | Scotland 2, Belgium 2; Hampden |
| May 18, 1947 | Belgium 2, Scotland 1; Brussels |
| Sept. 21, 1947 | Belgium 2, England 5; Brussels |
| April 28, 1948 | Scotland 2, Belgium 0; Hampden |
| April 24, 1949 | Eire 0, Belgium 2; Dublin |
| May 22, 1949 | Belgium 3, Wales 1; Liege |
| Nov. 23, 1949 | Wales 5, Belgium 1; Cardiff |
| May 10, 1950 | Belgium 5, Eire 1; Brussels |
| May 18, 1950 | Belgium 1, England 4; Brussels |
| May 20, 1951 | Belgium 0, Scotland 5; Brussels |
| Nov. 26, 1952 | England 5, Belgium 0; Wembley |
| June 17, 1954* | England 4, Belgium 4§; Basle |
| Oct. 21, 1964 | England 2, Belgium 2; Wembley |
| Mar. 24, 1964 | Eire 0, Belgium 2; Dublin |
| May 25, 1966 | Belgium 2, Eire 3; Liege |
| Feb. 25, 1970 | Belgium 1, England 3; Brussels |
| Feb. 3, 1971‡ | Belgium 3, Scotland 0; Liege |
| Nov. 10, 1971‡ | Scotland 1, Belgium 0; Glasgow |

* World Cup
† Victory Internationals
‡ European Championship
§ After extra time

England's scorers in the 9—1 victory in 1927 were Dean 3, Brown 2, Rigby 2, Page and Hulme.

## BENEFITS

Only three players have received benefits with three different Football League clubs. Goalkeeper J. McLaren received benefits with Bradford City, Leicester City and Watford between 1922 and 1939. Outside-right T. Urwin received benefits with Middlesbrough, Newcastle United and Sunderland between 1915 and 1935. Full-back S. Milburn had benefits with Chesterfield, Leicester City and Rochdale between 1946 and 1965.

### Regulations

Football League clubs may, with the consent of the Management Committee, permit a Testimonial match to be arranged on behalf of any player who has completed 10 years or more in the service of a club.

## BERWICK RANGERS F.C.

Founded 1881. Elected to Scottish League, Division II, 1955. Highest in Division II, 8th, 1961-62, 1964-65. Record attendance: 13,238 v. Rangers, Scottish Cup, 1st Round, Jan. 28, 1967. Address: Sheilfield Park, Tweedmouth, Berwick-on-Tweed, Northumberland. (Tel. Berwick 02897 7424). Colours: Black and gold striped shirts, black shorts. Record League goalscorer: K. Bowron, 38 goals, Division II, 1963-64. Record victory: 8-2 v. Dundee United, Division II, Feb. 21, 1958. Record defeat: 9-3 v. Ayr United, Scottish Cup, 1st Round, Jan. 19, 1929.

## BEST, George (1946-  )

The greatest individualist of recent years George Best was Britain's "Footballer of the Year" in 1968 and "European Footballer of the Year" in 1969. A brilliant dribbler Best is also a genius at snapping up scoring chances, using his uncanny ball control and superb balance to weave his way through a defence in exciting fashion.

Made Football League debut with Manchester United against Burnley, Dec. 28, 1963, when aged 17 yrs. 7 months, while his debut in a full international for N. Ireland was made in April 1964 when he was still more than a month short of his 18th birthday. Born Belfast, May 22, 1946.

Manchester United 1963-73, League apps. 349 (134 goals). Irish Internationals

31. League Championship, 1964-65, 1966-67. European Cup winners, 1968.

## BETTING

As long ago as 1892 the F.A. introduced a rule which prevented any club official or players from making bets on matches. At the same time it ruled that each club was made responsible for taking measures to prevent betting by spectators at football matches.

That rule, in a modified form, stood until 1957, when, at the annual meeting of the F.A. Council, it was decided to lift the ban which prevented officials and players from betting on authorised football pools. This was indeed a momentous decision when one considers the strong line which the F.A. has taken against football pools in the past.

It is interesting to note that an Act which was passed in 1920 to make ready-money betting illegal was first introduced into Parliament at the request of the F.A. in 1913.

During season 1935-6 the Football League made an effort to stop the football pools by scrapping the fixture lists and embarking upon a system whereby fixtures were arranged only from week to week, and clubs informed of their matches only in time to make necessary arrangements. Even then everyone was sworn to secrecy so that the pools promoters would be prevented from preparing coupons in time for distribution.

The system had to be abandoned after only a few weeks because it was found that the necessary information was still leaking out to the pools promoters. And in any case attendances showed an alarming drop and clubs were irritated by the many inconveniences the new system created.

In May, 1959, the Football League were successful in obtaining a judgment in the Chancery Division to the effect that their fixture lists are copyright. This meant that the pools would only be able to use their fixtures after agreement with the League who would thereby derive some financial benefit from the pools.

The Football League subsequently made agreements with the Pools, the latest guarantees the League nearly £2,000,000 per annum for the use of their fixtures.

In 1965 the F.A. and the Scottish F.A. agreed with the Pool Promoters Association to receive £60,000 and £15,000 respectively for use of their Cup fixtures.

Prior to this there had often been talk of the game in this country obtaining financial benefit from the pools. But the controlling bodies of the game had refused to be associated with the pools in this way.

As recently as 1949 the Football Association reiterated its uncompromising attitude towards betting in a statement to the Royal Commission on Lotteries, Betting and Gaming.

The F.A. said it was confident that betting had "no influence whatsoever upon results of any matches played under its jurisdiction" but was always mindful that if betting were to gain a hold on the game the present position might well be seriously undermined.

Subsequently, however, in Dec. 1960, the F.A. relaxed its betting ban by announcing that in future clubs would be permitted to run their own pools competitions to raise money and in 1963 they went as far as to approve a scheme for establishing their own Football Pool but this was shelved.

J. Pennington, the captain of West Bromwich Albion, was once involved in a case of attempted bribery. He was offered a sum of £55 (to be shared among his team mates) if they either lost or drew their game with Everton on Nov. 29, 1913. Pennington persuaded the briber to put his offer in writing, and then reported the facts to his club. The police were informed and were present after the game when the man was arrested as he handed over the money, for, as it happened, the match was drawn. The man was sentenced to five months' imprisonment.

There were rumours of bribery and corruption in football in 1960 but although evidence was placed in the hands of the Director of Public Prosecutions this was apparently inconclusive for no further action was taken.

However, in 1963, a national Sunday newspaper published fresh evidence of this kind and following their disclosures the police carried out an extensive investigation. The result was that 10 players and former players, including internationals, received jail sentences and were subsequently suspended from football.

See also under SUSPENSION.

## BIRMINGHAM CITY F.C.

Founded 1875 by members of Trinity Church, Bordesley, as Small Heath Alliance. In 1888 they changed their name to Small Heath F.C. Ltd. and were the first football club to become a limited liability company. The name Birmingham was adopted in 1905, and "City" was added to this in 1945. They were among the original members of the Football League, Division II, 1892. Honours: Champions, Division II, 1892-3, 1920-21, 1947-8, 1954-5. Runners-up, 1893-4, 1900-1, 1902-3, 1971-2. Best in Division I, 6th, 1955-6. F.L. Cup: Winners, 1963. F.A. Cup: Finalists, 1931, 1956 Fairs Cup: Runners-up, 1960, 1961. Record attendance: 66,844 v. Everton, F.A. Cup, 5th Round, Feb. 11, 1939. Address: St. Andrew's, Birmingham B9 4NH (Tel. 021-772 0101). Nickname: Blues. Colours: Royal blue shirts with single broad white stripe down the front, white shorts, blue stockings. Record League goal-scorer: W. Abbot, 38 goals, Division II, 1898-9. Record victory: 12—0 v. Walsall Town Swifts, Division II, Dec. 17, 1892, and v. Doncaster Rovers, Division II, April 11, 1903. Record defeat: 9—1 v. Sheffield Wednesday, Division I, Dec. 13, 1930.

### BLACKBURN ROVERS F.C.
Founded 1875. One of the original members of the Football League in 1888. Honours: Champions, Division I, 1911-12, 1913-14. Champions, Division II, 1938-9. Runners-up, 1957-8. F.A. Cup: Winners 1884, 1885, 1886, 1890, 1891, 1928. Finalists, 1882, 1960. Record attendance: 61,783 v. Bolton Wanderers, F.A. Cup, 6th Round, Mar. 2, 1929. Address: Ewood Park, Blackburn BB2 4JF (Tel. 55432.) Nickname: Blue and Whites. Colours: Blue and white halves, white shorts, white stockings with blue rings. Record League goal-scorer: E. Harper, 43 goals, Division I, 1925-6. Record victory: 11—0 v. Rossendale United, F.A. Cup, 1884-5. Record defeat: 8—0 v. Arsenal, Division I, Feb. 25, 1933.

### BLACKPOOL F.C.
Founded 1887. Amalgamated with South Shore F.C. 1899. Became members of the Football League, Division II, 1896. Not re-elected, 1899. Regained admission to Division II, 1900. Honours: Champions, Division II, 1929-30. Runners-up, 1936-7, 1969-70. Runners-up Division I, 1955-6. F.A. Cup, winners 1953, finalists 1948, 1951. Record attendance: 39,118 v. Manchester United, Division I, April 19, 1952. Address: Bloomfield Road, Blackpool FY1 6JJ (Tel. 46118). Nickname: Tangerines or Seasiders. Colours: Tangerine shirts with white trim, white shorts, tangerine stockings. Record League goal-scorer: J. Hampson, 45 goals, Division II, 1929-30. Record victory: 8—4 v. Charlton Athletic, Division I, Sept. 27, 1952. Record defeat: 10—1 v. Huddersfield Town, Division I, Dec. 13, 1930, and also v. Small Heath, Division II, Mar. 2, 1901.

### BLANCHFLOWER, Robert Dennis "Danny" (1926- )
Born Belfast, Feb. 10, 1926, he attracted attention of English clubs when playing for Glentoran and the Irish League representative side. Barnsley paid £6,500 for him in April 1949 and less than two years later

Aston Villa more than doubled the amount to secure his services. The fee reached £30,000 when he moved to Tottenham in December 1954.

"Footballer of the Year" in 1958 and again in 1961 he was one of the most commanding right half-backs ever seen in the Football League and a great captain. Led Ireland into the last eight of the 1958 World Cup and skippered Tottenham through their remarkable "double" winning campaign of 1960-61. A fantastic football brain, Blanchflower appeared to stroll through his games with effortless ease.

Glentoran 1945-9. Barnsley 1949-51, 68 apps. (2 goals). Aston Villa 1951-4, 148 apps. (10 goals). Tottenham Hotspur 1954-64, 337 apps. (15 goals). Irish internationals 56. Great Britain v. Rest of Europe 1955. Inter-League games, 1 (Irish League), 1 (Football League). League champions 1960-61. F.A. Cup winners 1961, 1962.

### BLOOMER, Stephen (1874-1938)
This talented inside-forward was an individualist dedicated to the task of scoring goals. Indeed, so much did he devote himself to getting the ball into the net that he was sometimes criticised for not doing enough to help his team (!) and his nonchalant style did not meet with everyone's approval. There was, however, no denying his talent for dribbling and shooting, and in 24 internationals he got 28 goals, a total which still stands as a record for the home International Championship.

Born Cradley Heath he made League debut for Derby County at Stoke, September 3, 1892, and scored twice in a 3—1 win. After playing his last game in 1914 he went to Berlin as a soccer coach and was interned there during World War I.

Derby County 1892-1906, 1910-14, 475 apps. (291 goals). Middlesbrough 1906-10, 125 apps. (61 goals). England internationals 24. Inter-League games 16. F.A. Cup, runners-up 1898, 1899.

### BOLTON WANDERERS F.C.
Founded 1874 as Christ Church F.C. Changed to present title in 1877. Among original members of the Football League in 1888. Honours: Champions, Division II, 1908-9. Runners-up, 1899-1900, 1904-5, 1910-11, 1934-5. Champions, Division III, 1972-3. Best in Division I, 3rd, 1891-2, 1920-21, 1924-5. F.A. Cup, winners, 1923, 1926, 1929, 1958. Finalists, 1894, 1904, 1953. Record attendance: 69,912 v. Manchester City, F.A. Cup, 5th Round, Feb. 18, 1933. Address: Burnden Park, Bolton BL3 2QR (Tel. 21101). Nickname: Trotters. Colours: White shirts, navy blue shorts,

white stockings. Record League goal-scorer: J. ("Joe") Smith, 38 goals, Division I, 1920-21. Record victory: 13—0 v. Sheffield United, F.A. Cup, 2nd Round, Feb. 1, 1890. Record defeat: 7—0 v. Manchester City, Division I, Mar. 21, 1936.

## BOYLE, Thomas W. (1889-1940)

Barnsley had a reputation for toughness in the old days and this local discovery was one of the toughest of them all. A great personality, a superb captain and one of the most capable centre-halves of his generation, being especially good in the air and noted for his long-distance headers to his wings. King-pin of the Burnley side that enjoyed a run of 30 First Division games without a defeat in 1920-21.

Barnsley 1906-11, 156 apps. (16 goals). Burnley 1911-23, 186 apps. (31 goals). Wrexham 1923-24, 7 apps. 1 England international. Inter-League games 3. League Championship 1920-21. F.A. Cup winners 1914, runners-up 1910.

## BOZSIK, Joszef (1925-     )

With Honved (previously Kispest) for more than 30 years, latterly as coach, Bozsik was in that great Hungarian side which enjoyed such a tremendous run of success in the 1950s. A brilliant attacking style right-half he helped Hungary beat England 6—3 at Wembley in 1953 and eventually made a record number of appearances for his country. Born Budapest. A member of the Hungarian House of Representatives.

Kispest 1937-49, Honved 1949-63. Hungarian internationals 100. Hungarian League championship 1950, 1952, 1954, 1955. Olympic Gold medal 1952. World Cup finalists 1954.

## BRADFORD CITY F.C.

Founded 1903. Elected to Football League Division II, 1903. Honours: F.A. Cup, winners, 1911. Champions, Division II, 1907-08. Champions, Division III(N), 1928-29. Best in Division I, 5th, 1910-11. Record attendance: 39,146 v. Burnley, F.A. Cup, 4th Round, Mar. 11, 1911 (the oldest Football League club ground record). Address: Valley Parade, Bradford BD8 7DY (Tel. 26565). Nickname: Paraders or Gents. Colours: All claret. Record League goal-scorer: D. Layne, 34 goals, Division IV, 1961-62. Record victory: 11—1 v. Rotherham United, Division III(N), Aug. 25, 1928. Record defeat: 9—1 v. Colchester United, Division IV, Dec. 30, 1961.

## BRAZIL

The only country to have appeared in all nine World Cup tournaments, and the first to win the trophy outright, the Brazilians are truly masters of soccer.

The game is generally considered to have been introduced into the country by Charles Miller, the Brazilian born son of English parents, who became a soccer enthusiast while being educated in England and took a couple of footballs home with him in 1894.

British sailors also helped spread the soccer gospel and it was only a few weeks after H.M.S. *Amethyst* had met Fluminese F.C. that the first League was formed in Rio in 1906.

The game is controlled by the Confederação Brasileira de Desportos. This organisation, founded in 1914, actually controls 20 other sports as well as soccer, but it is the latter which provides its main source of income.

The Brazilians are football fanatics and the country has a number of the most modern and well appointed stadia, including nine with a capacity of 100,000 or more.

In the international sphere Brazil first reached their peak by winning the World Cup in Sweden in 1958. They repeated the performance four years later in Chile but failed in 1966 when, with too many old players, they were out manoeuvred and outclassed.

Brazil probably put more advance planning into their World Cup campaigns than any other country and the set-back they received in England in 1966 was only temporary. In Mexico in 1970 they came back better than ever to win the trophy for the third time and so make it their own property.

In this tournament they gave some magical displays of exciting, skilful, attacking football, and when they demolished the defensive minded Italians 4—1 in the Final there were many who hoped that the inspiration of these talented Brazilians would serve to revolutionise the duller football played in so many other countries.

The address of the governing body: Confederação Brasileira de Desportos, Rua da Alfandega 70, P.O. Box 1078, Rio de Janeiro. Colours: Yellow shirts with green collar and cuffs, blue shorts, white stockings with green and yellow tops.

| | |
|---|---|
| May 9, 1956 | England 4, Brazil 2; Wembley |
| June 11, 1958 | England 0, Brazil 0; Sweden† |
| June 19, 1958 | Wales 0, Brazil 1; Sweden† |

| May 13, 1959 | Brazil 2, England 0; Rio |
| May 12, 1962 | Brazil 3, Wales 1; Rio |
| May 17, 1962 | Brazil 3, Wales 1; San Paulo |
| June 10, 1962 | Brazil 3, England 1; Chile† |
| May 8, 1963 | England 1, Brazil 1; Wembley |
| May 30, 1964 | Brazil 5, England 1; Rio |
| May 14, 1966 | Brazil 3, Wales 1; Rio |
| May 18, 1966 | Brazil "B" 1, Wales 0; Belo Horizonte§ |
| June 25, 1966 | Scotland 1, Brazil 1; Hampden Park |
| June 12, 1969 | Brazil 2, England 1; Rio |
| June 7, 1970 | Brazil 1, England 0; Guadalajara† |
| July 5, 1972 | Brazil 1, Scotland 0; Rio |
| June 30, 1973 | Scotland 0, Brazil 1; Hampden Park |

§ Accorded full international rating by Wales F.A.
† World Cup

## BRECHIN CITY F.C.
Founded 1906. First elected to Division II in 1929. Dropped out after World War II but returned in 1956. Record attendance: 8,022 v. Dundee, Scottish Cup, 2nd Round, Jan. 25, 1964. Address: Glebe Park, Brechin (Tels. 2181 and 2856). Colours: All red. Record victory: 12—1 v. Thornhill, Scottish Cup. 1st Round, Jan. 23, 1926. Record defeat: 10—1 v. Dunfermline Athletic, Division II, Dec. 14, 1929.

## BREMNER, William J.
There is no more determined and whole-hearted player in the game today than this Scot from Stirling who made his League debut for Leeds United at Stamford Bridge, January 23, 1960, soon after his 17th birthday. An excitable and exciting foot-baller who has captained Leeds United through the finest period in their history, a period during which he has been the main driving force. A former Scottish Schoolboy International he made his debut in a full international against Spain in 1965 and has since captained his country.
Leeds United 1959-73, 478(1) apps. (76 goals). Scottish internationals 41. Scottish Under-23 games 3. League Championship medal, 1968-69. F.A. Cup medals runners-up 1965, 1970, 1973, winners 1972. Fairs Cup medal 1968.

## BRENTFORD F.C.
Founded 1888. Elected to Football League, Division III, on its formation in 1920. Honours: Champions, Division II, 1934-5. Champions, Division III(S), 1932-3. Run-ners-up, 1929-30, 1957-8. Best in Division I, 5th, 1935-6. Champions, Division IV, 1962-3. Record attendance: 39,626 v. Preston North End, F.A. Cup, 6th Round, Mar. 5, 1938. Address: Griffin Park, Brentford TW8 ONT (Tel. 01-560 2021). Nickname: Bees. Colours: Red and white striped shirts, black shorts with two white stripes down seams, black stockings with red and white hooped tops. Record League goal-scorer: J. Holliday, 36 goals, Division III(S), 1932-3. Record victory: 9—0 v. Wrexham, Division III, Oct. 15, 1963. Record defeat: 7—0 v. Swansea Town, Division III(S), Nov. 8, 1924, and v. Walsall, Division III(S), Jan. 19, 1957.

## BRIBERY
See BETTING.

## BRIGHTON AND HOVE ALBION F.C.
Founded 1900 as Brighton and Hove Rangers. A club known as Brighton United had been formed two years earlier but had to disband because of lack of support. Bright-on and Hove Rangers became Brighton and Hove Albion in 1901. Joined Football League, Division III, on its formation in 1920. Honours: Champions, Division III(S), 1957-8, Runners-up Division III(S), 1953-4, 1955-6, Runners-up Division III, 1971-2. Champions Division IV, 1964-5. Address: Goldstone Ground, Hove BN3 7DE (Tel. Hove 739535). Record atten-dance: 36,747 v. Fulham, Division II, Dec. 27, 1958. Nickname: Seasiders or Albion. Colours: Blue and white striped shirts, blue shorts with white piping at edge, blue stock-ings. Record League goal-scorer: H. Val-lance, 30 goals, Division III(S), 1929-30. Record victory: 10—1 v. Wisbech, F.A. Cup, 1st Round, Nov. 13, 1965. Record defeat: 9—0 v. Middlesbrough, Division II, Aug. 23, 1958.

## BRISTOL CITY F.C.
Founded 1894 as Bristol South End. Changed to present title, 1897. Joined Foot-ball League, Division II, 1901. Honours: Runners-up, Division I, 1906-7. Cham-pions, Division II, 1905-6. Champions, Division III(S), 1922-3, 1926-7, 1954-5. Runners-up, 1937-8. Runners-up, Division III, 1964-5 F.A. Cup: Finalists, 1909.

Record attendance: 43,335 v. Preston North End, F.A. Cup, 5th Round, Feb. 16, 1935. Address: Ashton Gate, Bristol BS3 2EJ (Tel. 664093). Nickname: Robins. Colours: Red shirts with two white hoops round collar and cuffs, white shorts, red stockings with two white hoops round tops. Record League goal-scorer: D. Clark, 36 goals, Division III(S), 1946-7. Record victory: 11—0 v. Chichester, F.A. 1st Round, Nov. 5, 1960. Record defeat: 9—0 v. Coventry City, Division III(S), April 28, 1934.

## BRISTOL ROVERS F.C.
Founded 1883 as Black Arabs F.C. Changed to Eastville Rovers 1884. Changed to Bristol Eastville Rovers, 1897, and to Bristol Rovers, 1898. Among the original members of Football League, Division III, 1920. Honours: Champions, Division III(S), 1952-53. Record attendance: 38,472 v. Preston North End, F.A. Cup, 4th Round, Jan. 30, 1960. Address: Bristol Stadium, Bristol BS5 6NN (Tel. 558620). Nickname: Pirates. Colours: Blue and white quartered shirts, white shorts and stockings. Record League goal-scorer: G. Bradford, 33 goals, Division III(S), 1952-53. Record victory: 7—0 v. Swansea Town, Division II, Oct. 2, 1954; v. Brighton and Hove Albion, Division III(S), Nov. 29, 1952 and v. Shrewsbury Town, Division III, Mar. 21, 1964. Record defeat: 12—0 v. Luton Town, Division III(S), April 13, 1936.

## BROADCASTING
See also TELEVISION.
The first football match to be broadcast in England was the Football League, Division I, match between Arsenal and Sheffield United at Highbury, Jan. 22, 1927. A week later the F.A. Cup tie between Corinthians and Newcastle United was the second game to be broadcast. Ever since there has been almost continuous arguments about the advisability of allowing important football matches to be broadcast. At different times, both the F.A. and the Football League have banned broadcasting.

The first Cup Final to be broadcast was Cardiff City v. Arsenal on April 23, 1927. The 1928 Final tie between Blackburn Rovers and Huddersfield Town was also broadcast but in 1929 there was a dispute between the F.A. and the B.B.C. over the broadcasting fee, and the F.A. refused to allow the broadcast to be made. The B.B.C. however, succeeded in providing a running commentary of sorts by setting up a broadcasting point near to the ground and engaging about half a dozen commentators to

leave the stadium at regular intervals to broadcast a description of the play up to the moment of their departure. With one commentator following another at intervals of something like 15 min., the B.B.C. was able to provide a complete non-stop description of the game.

Agreement was reached for the 1930 Final, but, following renewed opposition —particularly from the smaller League clubs who complained bitterly that broadcasts adversely affected attendances at their matches—the Football League decided at its annual meeting of June 1, 1931, that no League matches would be broadcast.

Thereafter, the F.A. imposed a ban on the broadcasting of all games under its jurisdiction with the exception of the Cup Final.

The F.A. subsequently permitted the broadcasting of international matches, but the League did not relent until 1937 when it permitted the B.B.C. to broadcast certain matches on overseas wavelengths.

In 1938 more matches were added to the list of those which might be broadcast, but, in most cases, broadcasting was only allowed during the second half of the game.

More broadcasts were permitted during, and immediately after, the war, but, in June 1951, the Football League dealt a major blow to radio listeners when it re-introduced a complete ban on the broadcasting of any of its games.

It was not long, however, before the League relented to the extent of allowing broadcasts of matches providing that no prior announcement was made as to the match chosen, and only the second half was broadcast. That is how the situation stands now.

## BROOK, Eric Fred (1907-1965)
Manchester City made one of the finest deals in their history when they signed this player together with Fred Tilson from Barnsley in March, 1928. Among the game's most dangerous wingers Eric Brook was a human dynamo with a terrific shot. One of his best displays was against Italy in "The Battle of Highbury" in 1934 when he scored twice in six minutes. Despite such brilliant contemporary outside-lefts as Ellis Rimmer (Sheffield Wednesday) and Cliff Bastin (Arsenal) Eric Brook enjoyed one run of 11 consecutive England games, and, indeed, the selectors solved the problem of having Brook and Bastin at the peak of their form by playing the Arsenal winger inside-left to Brook on a number of occasions.

Barnsley 1926-28, 78 apps. (18 goals), Manchester City 1928-29, 451 apps. (157 goals). England internationals 18. Inter-League games 7. League Champions 1937. F.A. Cup, winners 1934, runners-up 1933.

**BROTHERS**
See FAMILIES (Brothers).

**BUCHAN, Charles Murray (1891-1960)**
This master tactician, who captained Sunderland, Arsenal and England, made only seven appearances for his country. Considering that he was one of the finest inside-rights of all time this is surprising, but the reason is that this long-legged genius was too clever for many of his team mates. Buchan formed a link in the famous Sunderland right-wing triangle of Buchan, Mordue and Cuggy, a combination still revered at Roker Park. Went to Sunderland from Leyton for £1,200 in March 1911. In July 1925, at the age of 33, he was one of the first signings made by the great Herbert Chapman after taking over the Arsenal, and played a leading role in laying the foundations of a new tactical set-up at Highbury. When he retired in 1928 Buchan took up journalism.

Leyton 1910-11, 24 apps. (14 goals) in Southern League. Sunderland 1911-25, 380 apps. (209 goals), Arsenal 1925-28, 102 apps. (49 goals). England internationals 6 (plus 1 Victory game). Inter-League games 9. Football League v. The Army 1. League Championship medals 1912-13. F.A. Cup medals, runners-up 1913, 1927.

**BULGARIA**
Bulgaria first entered the international football field in 1924 but it was not until after World War II that they improved enough to make any real impression in world football. A steady improvement culminated in them reaching the final tournament of the World Cup competition, at their fourth attempt, in Chile, in 1962.

Since then the Bulgarians have qualified for the World Cup Finals in 1966 and 1970, but a 1—1 draw with Morocco in Mexico produced their only point in these two tournaments.

They have been more successful in the Olympics, reaching the Final in 1968 before losing 4—1 to Hungary.

The game was first played in Bulgaria in 1894, the first club was formed in 1909, the governing body in 1923 and a national league competition in 1925.

Football clubs as such were disbanded by the new Communist regime in 1946 and the principal teams are all from sports clubs which run football sections. The leading side in the country, C.S.K.A. is fielded by the Central House of the People's Army,

and was formed in 1947. This club won the League Championship nine times in a row 1954-62.

In 1973 there are about 9,000 teams, all amateurs (the leading players are all provided with jobs outside the game), competing in four zonal and 14 regional groups throughout the country.

Address of the governing body: Bulgarian Football Federation, Stade (V.-Levsky), Sofia. Colours: White shirts, green shorts, red stockings.

June 7, 1962: England 0, Bulgaria 0; Chile†

Dec. 11, 1968: England 1, Bulgaria 1; Wembley.

Oct. 18, 1972: Bulgaria 3, Ireland 0; Sofia†

† World Cup

**BURNLEY F.C.**
Founded in 1881 as Burnley Rovers and dropped the title "Rovers" in 1882. One of the original members of the Football League, 1888. Honours: Champions, Division I, 1920-21, 1959-60. Runners-up, 1919-20, 1961-2, Champions, Division II, 1897-8, 1972-3. Runners-up, 1912-13, 1946-7. F.A. Cup: Winners, 1914. Finalists, 1947, 1962. Record attendance: 54,775 v. Huddersfield Town, F.A. Cup, 3rd Round, Feb. 23, 1924. Address: Turf Moor, Burnley (Tel. 27777). Nickname: Clarets. Colours: Claret with blue collars and cuffs, white shorts, white stockings with claret and blue rings at top. Record League goal-scorer: G. W. Beel, 35 goals, Division I, 1927-8. Record victory: 9—0 v. Darwen, Division I, Jan. 9, 1892; v. Crystal Palace, F.A. Cup, 2nd Round (Replay), 1908-9; v. New Brighton, F.A. Cup, 4th Round, Jan. 26, 1957. Record defeat: 10—0 v. Aston Villa, Division I, Aug. 29, 1925, and v. Sheffield United, Division I, Jan. 19, 1929.

**BURY F.C.**
Founded 1885. Joined Football League, Division II, 1894. Honours: Champions, Division II, 1894-5. Runners-up, 1923-4. Best in Division I, 4th, 1925-6. Champions Division III, 1960-61. Runners-up, 1967-8. F.A. Cup: Winners, 1900, 1903. Record attendance 35,000 v. Bolton Wanderers, F.A. Cup, 3rd Round, Jan. 9, 1960. Address: Gigg Lane, Bury (Tel. 061-764 4881). Nickname: Shakers. Colours: White shirts, dark blue shorts, dark blue stockings with white band. Record league goal-scorer: N. Bullock, 31 goals, Division I, 1925-6 Record victory: 12—1 v. Stockton, F.A. Cup, 1st Round (Replay), Feb. 2, 1897 Record defeat: 10—0 v. Blackburn Rovers, F.A. Cup, 1887-8.

## CAMBRIDGE UNITED F.C.

Founded 1919. Originally known as Abbey United. Adopted present title 1949. Elected to Football League, Division IV 1970. Record attendance: 14,000 v. Chelsea, Friendly, May 1, 1970. Colours: Amber shirts with black trim, black shorts, amber stockings. Address: Abbey Stadium, Newmarket Road, Cambridge (Tel. Teversham 2170). Nickname: Abbots. Record League goalscorer: B. Greenhalgh, 18 goals. Division IV, 1971-2 and 1972-3. Record victory: 6—0 v. Darlington, Division IV, Sept. 18, 1971. Record defeat: 5—0 v. Colchester United, League Cup, 1st Round, Aug. 14, 1970.

## CANADA

While football has been played in Canada since about 1880 when it was introduced by Scottish migrants, it is only in the last two decades that any significant progress has been made in the development of the game in this part of the world.

The large increase in the number of European emigrants to Canada after World War II brought a greater enthusiasm for soccer, the main interest being centred around Toronto and Montreal but with many clubs springing up in all parts of the country.

The greatest and most lasting progress is that which has been made recently in the schools and colleges, progress that has already meant an increase in the number of Canadian born players reaching the highest level in their Amateur International team as well as in their professional club sides.

A National Soccer League has been formed and despite the difficulties created by the great distances involved a national championship has been in existence for more than 60 years.

The first Association to be formed in Canada was the Western Association of Ontario in 1880. Eight years later a Canadian team toured Britain, playing 23 games, including one against Scotland in which the visitors were defeated 4—0, and two against the Swifts (one of the most powerful amateur clubs in the country and including six England internationals). The visitors were beaten 1—0 in the first game but forced a 2—2 draw in the second game which was attended by the Prince of Wales.

A second tour by a Canadian team (although referred to as the Canadians the party actually included nine from the U.S.A.) took place in 1891-92 when "internationals" were played against England, Scotland, Ireland, and Wales (twice). All of these were lost but the tourists won 11 of their 49 matches, including victories over Middlesbrough Ironopolis, Lincoln City, Stoke, Walsall Town Swifts, and Swindon.

This tour must have been a strain on their players for in one hectic spell they played six matches in 10 days, including games as far apart as Belfast and Grimsby.

Since then no fully representative international matches or "Tests" have been played between any of the home Associations and Canada. However, representative F.A. teams toured Canada in 1926 (played and won 18 games), 1931 (played and won 17 games), and 1950 (played 11, won 10, drew one). In the 1950 tour one of the 11 games was played in the United States against the U.S. World Cup XI. A twelfth game was also played, Blues v. Whites, at Winnipeg, in aid of the Winnipeg Flood Disaster, but, in this game, each side was a combination of F.A. and Canadian players.

The F.A. of Canada was formed in May 1912 and has been represented on the Council of the English F.A. since 1929.

Address of the governing body: Canadian Soccer Association, 333 River Road, Ottawa, Ontario K1L 8B9. Colours: All red.

## CAPS, INTERNATIONAL

See under INTERNATIONALS and also APPEARANCES (Internationals).

## CAPTAINS

W. A. Wright (Wolverhampton Wanderers) created a world record by captaining England in 90 internationals 1948-59.

## CARDIFF CITY F.C.

Founded 1899 as Riverside F.C. Turned professional as Cardiff City, 1910. Joined Football League, Division II, 1920. Honours: Runners-up, Division I, 1923-4. Runners-up, Division II, 1920-21, 1951-2, 1959-60. Champions, Division III(S), 1946-7. F.A. Cup: Winners 1927. Finalists 1925. Record attendance: 61,566, Wales v. England, Oct. 14, 1961. Club record, 57,800 v. Arsenal, Division I, Apl. 22, 1953. Colours: Blue shirts, white shorts and stockings. Address: Ninian Park, Cardiff CF1 8SX

(Tel. 28501). Nickname: Bluebirds. Record League goal-scorer: S. Richards, 31 goals, Division III (S), 1946-7. Record victory: 9-2 v. Thames, Division III(S), Feb. 6, 1932. Record defeat: 11-2 v. Sheffield United, Div. I, Jan. 1, 1926.

### CAREY, John J. (1919-    )

Manchester United paid only £200 to take this player from St. James's Gate, Dublin, to Old Trafford in 1936 when he was a 17-year-old inside-forward and he proved to be one of the best bargains the club ever secured, distinguishing himself in almost every department as well as gaining a reputation as one of their finest captains. Carey's versatility was such that he played in six different positions in internationals. Never flustered, he captained the Rest of Europe against Great Britain at Hampden Park in May 1947, and was "Player of the Year" in 1948-49. Following his retirement in 1953 Carey became manager of Blackburn Rovers, restoring them to the First Division. He subsequently managed Everton, Leyton Orient and Nottingham Forest before returning to Blackburn Rovers for a spell as general manager 1969-1971.

Manchester United 1936-53, 306 apps. (17 goals). Eire internationals 29, Irish internationals 7 (plus 2 Victory games). League Champions 1951-52. F.A. Cup winners 1948.

### CARLISLE UNITED F.C.

Founded 1903 by the amalgamation of Carlisle Red Rose and Shaddongate United. Joined Football League, Division III(N), 1928. Honours: Champions, Division III, 1964-5. Runners-up, Division IV, 1963-4. Record attendance: 27,500 v. Birmingham City, F.A. Cup, 3rd Round, Jan. 5, 1957 and v. Middlesbrough, F.A. Cup, 5th Round, Feb. 7, 1970. Address: Brunton Park, Carlisle CA1 1LL (Tel. 26237). Nickname: Cumbrians. Colours: Blue shirts, white shorts and stockings. Record League goal-scorer: J. McConnell, 42 goals, Division III(N), 1928-9. Record Victory: 8—0 v. Hartlepools United, Division III(N), Sept. 1, 1928. Record defeat: 11—1 v. Hull City, Division III(N), Jan. 14, 1939.

### CARTER, Horatio Stratton (1913-    )

A master tactician whose skills were so great that he enjoyed the longest international career of any England inside-right, making initial appearance in April 1934 and not playing his last game until more than 13 years later. Turned down by Leicester City as too frail he made League debut for his local club, Sunderland, in October 1932 and helped them win both the League and Cup.

Teamed up with that other great inside-forward, Peter Doherty, at Derby in 1945, and those who saw this pair's display when that club beat Charlton 4—1 in the 1946 Cup Final have never forgotten it. Rounded off League career as player-manager of Hull City, helping them win promotion to the Second Division in 1949. Born Sunderland.

Sunderland 1932-45, 248 apps. (121 goals). Derby Country 1945-48, 67 apps. (34 goals). Hull City 1948-52, 136 apps. (58 goals). England appearances 14. Inter-League games 5. League Champions 1935-6. F.A. Cup winners 1937, 1946. F.A. of Ireland Cupwinners 1953.

### CASUALTIES

See also DISASTERS, INJURIES.

#### Fatal

R. W. Benson, Arsenal full-back, retired from the field when playing against Reading, Feb. 19, 1916, and died soon afterwards. Benson had not played for nearly 10 months. Death was due to a burst blood vessel.

T. Butler, Port Vale, broke his arm in a Division II game with Clapton Orient on Nov. 5, 1923. Septic poisoning set in and he died six days later.

D. Jones, Welsh international full-back, who played for Bolton Wanderers and Manchester City at the end of the 19th century, cut his knee while in training with the latter club; lock-jaw set in and he died.

S. Raleigh, Gillingham centre-forward, died from concussion sustained in a match with Brighton and Hove Albion, Dec. 1, 1934.

J. Thomson, Glasgow Celtic goalkeeper, died after fracturing his skull in a game with Glasgow Rangers, Sept. 5, 1931.

J. Thorpe, Sunderland goalkeeper, died a few days after a game against Chelsea on Feb. 1, 1936. His death was due to diabetes but a coroner's jury found that the illness had been accelerated by the game.

J. Wilkinson, Dumbarton goalkeeper, died from injuries received in a Scottish League match with Rangers, Nov. 12, 1921.

S. Wynne, Bury full-back, collapsed when taking a free-kick against Sheffield United at Bramall Lane, April 30, 1927, and died in the dressing-room. Death was primarily due to pneumonia.

#### Serious Injuries

D. Dooley, Sheffield Wednesday centre-forward fractured a leg in a game against Preston North End, Feb. 14, 1953. Gangrene set in and his leg was amputated.

L. Ritson, Leyton Orient full-back, frac-

41

tured a leg in a game against Northampton Town, Sept. 11, 1948. He recovered, but in 1950 it was discovered that a bone had become diseased and the limb was amputated.

## CELTIC F.C.

Founded 1887 by a number of the Catholics of the East End of Glasgow with the object of raising funds for the maintenance of the "Dinner Tables" of needy children in the Missions of St. Mary's, Sacred Heart, and St. Michael's. One of the original members of the Scottish League, 1890. Honours: Champions, Scottish League, Division 1, 1892-3, 1893-4, 1895-6, 1897-8, 1904-5, 1905-6, 1906-7, 1907-8, 1908-9, 1909-10, 1913-14, 1914-15, 1915-16, 1916-17, 1918-19, 1921-2, 1925-6, 1935-6, 1937-8, 1953-4, 1965-6, 1966-7, 1967-8, 1968-9, 1969-70, 1970-71, 1971-2, 1972-3. Runners-up, 1891-2, 1894-5, 1899-1900, 1900-1, 1901-2, 1911-12, 1912-13, 1917-18, 1919-20, 1920-2, 1927-8, 1928-9, 1930-31, 1934-5, 1938-9, 1954-5. Scottish Cup: Winners, 1892, 1899, 1900, 1904, 1907, 1908, 1911, 1912, 1914, 1923, 1925, 1927, 1931, 1933, 1937, 1951, 1954, 1965, 1967, 1969, 1971, 1972. Finalists, 1889, 1893, 1894, 1901, 1902, 1909 (cup withheld by Scottish F.A. after a riot), 1926, 1928, 1955, 1956, 1961, 1963, 1966, 1970, 1973. Scottish League Cup: Winners, 1957, 1958, 1966, 1967, 1968, 1969, 1970. Finalists, 1965, 1971, 1972, 1973. European Cup: Winners, 1967. Finalists, 1970. Record attendance: 92,000 v. Rangers, Division 1, Jan. 1, 1938. Address: Parkhead, Glasgow (Tel. 041-554 2710). Colours: Green and white hooped shirts, white shorts. Record League goal-scorer: J. McCrory, 50 goals, Division I, 1935-6. Record victory: 11—0 v. Dundee, Division I, Oct. 26, 1895. Record defeat: 8—0 v. Motherwell, Division I, 1936-7.

## CHARLES, William John (1932-    )

Born Cwmdu, near Swansea, January 19, 1932, this powerfully built player was first capped for Wales soon after his 18th birthday. Developed as a centre-half with Leeds United, but two years after his international debut switched to centre-forward, and it was in this position that he was widely acclaimed as the world's most valuable player. Known as "the Gentle Giant", he created a Leeds United record with 42 League goals in 1953-4 and shot them into the First Division in 1955-6. Juventus paid a British record £65,000 fee (£10,000 going to the player) to obtain his transfer in April 1957 and he immediately won the hearts of the Italian fans. Leeds got him back in August 1962 but he returned to Italy only three months later, joining Roma for £70,000. Home to Wales and Cardiff City in August 1963. Rounded off his playing career as player-manager of Hereford United and Merthyr.

Leeds United 1948-57, 1962, 308 apps. (153 goals). Juventus 1957-62, 155 apps. (93 goals). Roma 1962-63, 10 apps (4 goals). Cardiff City 1963-66, 70 apps. (18 goals). Welsh internationals 39. G.B. v. Rest of Europe 1955. Italian League Championship 1957-8, 1959-60, 1960-61. Italian Cup winners 1959, 1960.

## CHARLTON, Robert, O.B.E. (1937-    )

Born Ashington, October 11th, 1937. Joined Manchester United straight from school in 1953 and made League debut (scoring 2 goals) v. Charlton Athletic in October 1956. Soon became famous for his powerful, accurate shooting, and for his ability to work himself into shooting positions. First capped for England in April 1958 (v. Scotland) and went on to create an international record (since beaten) with a total of 106 appearances, playing in all forward positions except outside-right. One of the stars of England's World Cup-winning team in 1966. Survivor of the Munich air crash in 1958. Created England goalscoring record with 49 goals.

Manchester United 1956-73, 604(2) apps. (198 goals). England internationals 106. Inter-League games 8. League Champions 1964-5, 1966-7. F.A. Cup, winners 1963; runners-up 1957, 1958. European Cup winners 1968. Rest of Europe v. Scandinavia 1964. Rest of U.K. v. Wales 1969.

## CHARLTON ATHLETIC F.C.

Founded 1905. Turned professional, 1920. Elected to Division III(S) 1921. Honours: Champions, Division III(S), 1928-9, 1934-5. Runners-up, Division II, 1935-6. Runners-up, Division I, 1936-7. F.A. Cup: Winners, 1947. Finalists, 1946. Record attendance: 75,031 v. Aston Villa, F.A. Cup, 5th Round, Feb. 12, 1938. Address: The Valley, Floyd Road, Charlton, SE7 8AW (Tel. 01-858 3711). Nickname: Haddicks or Valiants. Colours: Red shirts with white trim, white shorts with red stripe down seam, red stockings. Record League goal-scorer: R. Allen, 32 goals, Division III(S), 1934-5. Record victory: 8—1 v. Middlesbrough, Division I, Sept. 12, 1953. Record defeat: 11—1 v. Aston Villa, Division II, Nov. 14, 1959.

## CHELSEA F.C.

Founded 1905. Elected in the same year to the Football League, Division II after application for membership of the Southern

League had been turned down. Honours: Champions, Division I, 1954-5. Runners-up, Division II, 1906-7, 1911-12, 1929-30, 1962-3. F.A. Cup: Winners, 1970. Finalists, 1915, 1967. F.L. Cup: Winners, 1965. Finalists 1972. European Cup winners cup: Winners 1971. Record attendance: 82,905 v. Arsenal, Division I, Oct. 12, 1935. Address: Stamford Bridge, London, SW6 1HS (Tel. 01-385 5545). Colours: Royal blue shirts and shorts with white stripe down seam, white stockings. Record League goal-scorer: J. Greaves, 41 goals, Division I, 1960-61. Record victory, 9—1 v. Worksop, F.A. Cup, 1st Round, Jan. 11, 1908. Record defeat: 8—1 v. Wolverhampton Wanderers, Division I, Sept. 26, 1953.

## CHESTER F.C.
Founded 1884 with amalgamation of Chester Rovers and Kings School Old Boys. Elected to Football League, Division III(N), 1931. Honours: Runners-up, Division III(N), 1935-6. Record attendance: 20,500 v. Chelsea, F.A. Cup, 3rd Round (replay), Jan. 16, 1952. Address: Sealand Road Stadium, Chester CH1 4LW (Tel. 21048). Colours: Royal blue and white striped shirts, white shorts, royal blue stockings with red and white ringed tops. Record League goal-scorer: R. Yates, 36 goals, Division III(N), 1946-7. Record victory: 12—0 v. York City, Division III(N), Feb. 1, 1936. Record defeat: 11—2 v. Oldham Athletic, Division III(N), Jan. 19, 1952.

## CHESTERFIELD F.C.
Founded 1866. Re-formed 1871. Became a limited company in 1899 and elected to Football League, Division II in the same year. Re-organised as Chesterfield Town in 1904. Left the Football League 1909. In 1918 in another re-shuffle, Chesterfield Corporation took control and the club became the first to play municipal football.

Continued in the Midland League until the Football League formed Division III(N) in 1921. Honours: Champions, Division III(N), 1930-31, 1935-6. Runners-up, 1933-4. Champions, Division IV, 1969-70. Best in Division II, 4th, 1946-7. Record attendance: 30,968 v. Newcastle United, Division II, April 7, 1939. Address: Recreation Ground, Chesterfield (Tel. 2318). Nickname: Blues. Colours: Royal blue shirts, white shorts, royal blue stockings with white tops. Record League goal-scorer: J. Cookson, 44 goals, Division III(N), 1925-6. Record victory: 10—0 v. Glossop North End, Division II, Jan. 17, 1903. Record defeat: 9—1 v. Port Vale, Division II, Sept. 24, 1932.

## CHILE
Rather overshadowed by other South American countries, Uruguay, Brazil and Argentina, Chile has never been reckoned a powerful footballing nation, but they have victories to their credit over several European countries, most of them in home matches.

In Chile the home side has the advantage of being acclimatised to the special conditions of playing football at nearly 2,000 ft. above sea level.

As World Cup hosts in 1962 Chile was automatically seeded to the final tournament, and they won through to the semi-finals and to third place in the competition with victories over Switzerland (3—1), Italy (2—0), Russia (2—1) and Yugoslavia (1—0). However, the best they could do in 1966 was a draw with North Korea, while they failed to qualify for the 1970 finals.

The governing body of football in Chile was established in 1895 and is the second oldest in South America. It now controls about 3,000 clubs.

Address of F.A.: Federación de Football de Chile, Huéfanos 1535, Casilla 3733, Santiago. Colours: Red shirts, blue shorts, white stockings.

Results of international matches:
June 25, 1950   Chile 0, England 2; Brazil†
May 24, 1953   Chile 1, England 2; Santiago
Mar. 30, 1960   Eire 2, Chile 0; Dublin
May 23, 1966   Chile 2, Wales 0; Santiago
June 21, 1972   Eire 1, Chile 2; Recife, Brazil

† World Cup

## CLYDE F.C.
Founded 1877. Joined Scottish League, Division I, 1906-7. Honours: Champions, Scottish League, Division II, 1904-5, 1951-2, 1956-7, 1961-2, 1972-3. Runners-up, 1903-4, 1905-6, 1963-4. Best in Division I, 3rd, 1908-9, 1911-12, 1966-7. Scottish Cup: Winners, 1939, 1955, 1958. Finalists, 1910, 1912, 1949. Record attendance: 52,000 v. Rangers, Division I, Nov. 21, 1908. Address: Shawfield Stadium, Glasgow C.5. (Tel. 041-647 6329). Nickname: Bully Wees.

Colours: White shirts with red trim, black shorts. Record League goal-scorer: W. McPhail, 36 goals, Division II, 1951-2. Record victory: 11—1 v. Cowdenbeath, Division B, Oct. 6, 1951. Record defeat: 11—0 v. Rangers, Scottish Cup, 4th Round, 1880-81.

## CLYDEBANK F.C.
Founded 1965. Joined Scottish League, Division II, 1966-7. Honours: none. Record attendance: 14,900 v. Hibernian, Scottish Cup, 1st Round, Feb. 10, 1965. Address: New Kilbowie Park, Clydebank (Tel. 041-952 2887). Colours: Red shirts with broad white vertical stripe on front, black shorts. Record League goal-scorer: A. Moy, 24 goals, Division II, 1967-8. Record victory: 7-1 v. Queen's Park, Division II, Mar. 10, 1971. and v. Hamilton Academicals, Division II, Nov. 20, 1971. Record defeat: 7—0 v. Falkirk (home), Division II, 1969-70.

## COLCHESTER UNITED F.C.
Became a professional club in 1937. Elected to Football League, Division III(S), 1950. Honours: Runners-up, Division IV, 1961-2. Record attendance: 19,072 v. Reading, F.A. Cup, 1st Round, Nov. 27, 1948. Address: Layer Road, Colchester (Tel. 74042). Nickname: The U's. Colours: All white. Record League goal-scorer: R. R. Hunt, 37 goals, Division IV, 1961-2. Record Victory: 9—1 v. Bradford City (H), Division IV, Dec. 30, 1961. Record defeat: 7—0 v. Leyton Orient, Division III(S), Jan. 5, 1952; 7—0 v. Reading, Division III(S), Sept. 18, 1957.

## COLOMBIA
Colombia first hit the football headlines in April 1950 when they tempted many leading players, mostly Argentinians, but including such British stars as Neil Franklin, George Mountford and Charlie Mitten, to join their principal clubs—Santa Fe and Millionarios. These clubs had broken away from their national association at this time, and therefore, were outside the jurisdiction of F.I.F.A. and had no need to comply with transfer regulations.

The departure of star players caused a sensation at the time but conditions in Colombia were not what had been expected and it was not long before the majority of these players returned home.

Address of the governing body—Federación Colombiana de Fútbol, Avenida Jiménez No. 11-28, Ofic. 202, Apartado Aéreo No. 17.602, Bogota, D.E. Colours: Orange shirts with yellow, blue and red stripe, cream shorts, orange stockings. Result of international: May 20, 1970.

Colombia 0, England 4, Bogota.

## COLOURED PLAYERS
Before World War II probably no more than three coloured players had made Football League appearances. These were:

J. Leslie, inside-forward with Plymouth Argyle, 1921-35.

J. Parris, outside-right or left with Bradford, Luton Town, Northampton Town, Bournemouth and Boscombe Athletic, 1928-39. Parris is the only coloured player to appear in the International Championship. He was capped for Wales against Ireland in Dec. 1931.

D. Tull, forward with Northampton Town (then in the Southern League), Tottenham Hotspur, 1908-14.

Following the vast increase of immigrants to Britain since the war many more coloured players have appeared in Football League matches. These include:

T. Balogun, centre-forward with Queen's Park Rangers, 1956-7.

C. Best, inside-forward with West Ham United 1969-.

T. Best, centre-forward with Chester, Cardiff City, Queen's Park Rangers, 1947-50.

R. Brown, centre-half or centre-forward, Stoke City, Watford, 1947-58.

C. Charles, full-back, West Ham United, 1970-.

J. Charles, half-back, West Ham United, 1962-70.

A. Coker, centre-forward, West Ham United, 1970-.

L. Delapenha, inside or outside-right, Portsmouth, Middlesbrough, Mansfield Town, 1948-61.

P. Foley, outside-right, Workington, Scunthorpe United, 1965-68.

G. Francis, outside-right, Leeds United, York City, 1957-64.

R. Heppolette, half-back, Preston North End, 1967-.

A. Johanneson, outside-left, Leeds United, York City, 1960-72.

J. Miller, outside-left, Ipswich Town, 1968-.

S. Mokone, outside-right, Coventry City, Cardiff City, Barnsley, 1952-62.

E. Onyeali, centre-forward, Tranmere Rovers, 1960-61.

C. Podd, full-back, Bradford City, 1970-.

S. Stacey, full-back, Wrexham, Ipswich Town, Charlton Athletic, Bristol City, Exeter City, 1966-73.

## COLOURS
Club colours appear under each club heading and international team colours under the respective countries.

## COMBI, Giampiero (1902-1956)

When this player first kept goal for Italy (against Austria) in 1924 they were beaten 7—1, but he was recalled the following year and established himself as the finest goalkeeper ever to have played for Italy. Combi was in the side that held England to a 1—1 draw in Rome in 1933 and captained his country's World Cup-winning side the following year. With Juventus throughout his career he enjoyed one run of 102 consecutive League appearances.

Juventus 1919-34. 47 Italian internationals. Italian League champions 1926, 1931, 1932, 1933, 1934. World Cup winners 1934.

## CONTINENTAL TOURS

See under TOURS.

## CORINTHIANS A.F.C.

Although this club is no longer in existence (it was amalgamated with the Casuals in 1939), it remains the most famous amateur club in the history of English football.

It was formed in 1882 by N. L. Jackson, then honorary assistant-secretary of the Football Association. He was distressed by England's poor international record against Scotland and considered it would benefit the England international team if a number of leading players could be given the opportunity of playing together more often in the same club side.

It was an unwritten law of the club that only public school and university men should be admitted as members. There were very few exceptions to this rule.

The Corinthians also made a rule never to enter for competitions, and, with the exception of charity matches (the Sheriff of London Shield), this rule was adhered to until 1922-3 season when the club first entered for the F.A. Cup.

No club did more than the Corinthians in developing the passing game in England during the 1880s. The advantages of this style, as opposed to the individual dribbling game, were soon apparent when the Corinthians defeated Blackburn Rovers, 8—1, at Blackburn, in Dec., 1884, when the Rovers were recognised as the best team in the country and were holders of the F.A. Cup.

Other outstandng victories of the Corinthians against professional opponents included a 5—0 win over Preston North End, then F.A. Cup holders and League Champions, at Richmond, Nov. 8, 1889; 10—3 v. Bury, F.A. Cup holders, 1904; 2—1 v. Aston Villa, League champions, 1900.

If the Corinthians had chosen to enter for the F.A. Cup in those earlier days they might well have won it. But when they entered the competition in 1922-3, through a lack of fixtures, the professional game had reached such a high standard that the amateurs were not able to make much of an impression.

Probably their best game in the F.A. Cup competition was against Newcastle United in the 4th Round in 1926-7. They led the powerful Newcastle team (League Champions in that season) by 1—0 until 15 minutes from the end when the professionals equalised and went on to score two more goals.

The Corinthians had been the first English soccer club to play outside Europe when they made a tour of South Africa in 1897.

More players have been drawn from the Corinthians to play for England in full internationals than from any other club (a total of 83). On two occasions the whole England team was composed of Corinthians (see INTERNATIONALS, Club Records).

During the 1880s and 1890s the Corinthians included such great internationals as N. C. Bailey (with 19 full England international appearances to his credit), E. C. Bambridge (18), R. E. Foster (5), G. O. Smith (20), and W. Arnott (14 for Scotland).

Even in the 1920s when teams for full internationals were drawn almost entirely from the professional ranks a number of Corinthians could not be denied a place in these games. Such men were B. Howard Baker (2 full, 10 amateur caps), A. G. Bower (6 full, 13 amateur), F. H. Ewer (2 full, 14 amateur), A. E. Knight (1 full, 28 amateur), F. N. S. Creek (1 full, 5 amateur), A. G. Doggart (1 full, 4 amateur), B. Joy (1 full, 12 amateur).

As already stated the Corinthians finally amalgamated with the Casuals in 1939 and now the Corinthian-Casuals A.F.C. competes in the Isthmian League.

## CORNER KICK

See also LAWS OF THE GAME.

The corner kick was adopted by the F.A. in 1872 (the Sheffield Rules had included the corner kick since 1868), and in the early days these kicks were usually taken by the wing halves. It was not until the late 1890s that the wing forwards began to take corners.

In 1924 the law was altered so that a goal could be scored direct from a corner kick, following a proposal of the Scottish F.A. This alteration brought some confusion in its first season as some thought that it was permissible for the player taking the corner to dribble the ball in from the flag. The F.A. decided against this and before the next season began the wording of the law was altered to make the position clear.

W. Smith was the first player to score direct from a corner-kick in a Football League game—Huddersfield Town v. Arsenal. Division I, Oct. 11, 1924. The first to do so in a home international was A. Cheyne (Aberdeen) for Scotland v. England, Hampden Park, April 13, 1929.

There is thought to have been only one Football League game without a corner kick. That was a Division I match between Newcastle United and Portsmouth, Dec. 5, 1931. Result 0—0.

## COVENTRY CITY F.C.
Founded 1883 by factory workers and known as Singers F.C. until 1898. Reorganised 1908. Elected to Football League, Division II, 1919. Honours: Champions, Division II, 1966-7. Champions, Division III(S), 1935-6. Runners-up 1933-4. Champions, Division III, 1963-4. Runners-up, Division IV, 1958-9. Record attendance: 51,455 v. Wolverhampton W., Division II, April 29, 1967. Address: Highfield Rd., Coventry (Tel. 57171). Nickname: Sky-blues. Colours: Sky blue shirts with navy blue and white trim, sky blue shorts and stockings. Record League goal-scorer: C. Bourton, 49 goals, Division III(S), 1931-2. Record victory: 9—0 v. Bristol City (H), Division III(S), April 28, 1934. Record defeat: 10—2 v. Norwich City (A), Division III(S), Mar. 15, 1930.

## COWAN, James
Stood only 5ft. 6¼ in. in height but was one of the finest centre-halves of his day, winning no less than five League Championship medals during 13 seasons with Aston Villa. Cowan played in the old attacking style being extremely fast—he won the Powderhall Handicap in 1896. The ban on Anglo-Scots kept him out of the Scottish International team until 1896 but he then figured in his country's team against England in three consecutive seasons. Manager of Queen's Park Rangers 1907-15.

Vale of Leven 1888-89. Aston Villa 1889-1902, 317 apps. Scottish internationals 3. League Championship 1893-94, 1895-96, 1896-97, 1898-99, 1899-1900. F.A. Cup, winners 1895, 1897, runners-up 1892.

## COWDENBEATH F.C.
Founded 1881. Re-organised 1905. Promoted to Scottish League Division I 1924. Honours: Champions, Division II, 1913-14, 1914-15, 1938-9. Runners-up 1921-2, 1923-4, 1969-70. Record attendance: 25,586 v. Rangers, Scottish League Cup, Q.F. (2nd leg, Sept. 21, 1949. Address: Central Park,

Cowdenbeath (Tel. 0383–511205). Colours: Royal blue and white striped shirts, white shorts. Record goal-scorer in Division I: W. Devlin, 40 goals, 1925-6. Record victory: 12—0 v. Johnstone, Scottish cup, 1st Round, Jan. 21, 1928. Record defeat: 11—1 v. Clyde, Division B, Oct. 6, 1951.

## CRESSWELL, Warneford (1894-    )
An unorthodox type of full-back who scorned the full-blooded first-time tackle and perfected the art of jockeying an opponent along the touch-line and using his positional sense to great advantage in a more constructive style. Sunderland paid South Shields what was then a record £5,500 transfer fee when they signed him in 1922. Born South Shields. Manager Port Vale, and Northampton Town in the 1930s.

South Shields 1919-22, 97 apps. Sunderland 1922-27, 182 apps. Everton 1927-36, 289 apps. England internationals 7. Inter-League games 5. League Champions 1927-8, 1931-2. F.A. Cup winners 1933.

## CREWE ALEXANDRA F.C.
Founded 1876. One of the original members of the football League, Division II, 1892. Adopted professionalism 1893. Failed to gain re-election to Division II, 1896. Became member of newly-formed Division III(N), 1921. Best in Division II, 10th, 1892-3. Best in Division III(N), 6th, 1921-2, 1922-3, 1931-2, 1935-6. Record attendance: 20,000 v. Tottenham Hotspur, F.A. Cup, 4th Round, Jan. 30, 1960. Address: Gresty Road, Crewe (Tel. 3014). Nickname: Alex. Colours: All red. Record League goal-scorer: J. T. Harkin, 34 goals. Division IV, 1964-5. Record victory: 8—0 v. Rotherham United (H.), Division III(N), Oct. 1, 1932. Record defeat: 13—2 v. Tottenham Hotspur (A.), F.A. Cup, 4th Round (replay), Feb. 3, 1960.

## CRICKETERS
Here is a list of men who have made international appearances in both cricket and Association football: J. Arnold, former Oxford City, Southampton and Fulham outside-left and Hampshire batsman. Capped at football for England v. Scotland, 1933. Capped at cricket for England v. New Zealand (at Lords), 1931.

D. C. S. Compton, Arsenal outside-left and Middlesex batsman. Played in 11 wartime soccer internationals for England as well as one "Victory" international v. Scotland. He made the first of his 78 Test appearances in 1937 against New Zealand at the Oval.

A. Ducat, Arsenal, Aston Villa and Fulham wing-half and Surrey batsman.

Capped at football for England v. Scotland, Wales and Ireland, 1919, v. Scotland and Wales 1920, and v. Ireland, 1921. Capped at cricket v. Australia (at Leeds), 1921.

R. E. Foster, Oxford University inside-left and Worcestershire batsman. Capped at football for England v. Wales, 1900, v. Scotland, Wales, Ireland and Germany, 1901, and v. Wales, 1902. Foster played in 8 Test matches: 3 v. South Africa, 1907, and 5 v. Australia in the winter of 1903-4.

C. B. Fry, Corinthians right-back and Sussex and Hampshire batsman. Capped at football for England v. Ireland, 1901. Played in 26 Test matches, 18 of them against Australia, 8 against South Africa, 1895-1912.

L. H. Gay, Old Brightonians goalkeeper and Cambridge University wicket-keeper. Capped for England v. Scotland, 1893, and v. Scotland and Wales, 1894. Played in one Test against the Australians at Sydney in 1894-5.

W. Gunn, Notts County outside-left and Nottinghamshire batsman. Capped for England v. Scotland and Wales, 1884. Played in 11 Test matches, all of them against Australia, 1886-99.

H. T. W. Hardinge, Sheffield United inside-forward and Kent batsman. Capped for England v. Scotland, 1910. Capped at cricket v. Australia (at Leeds), 1921.

E. Hendren, outside-right with Manchester City, Coventry City and Brentford. Middlesex batsman. Played for England at football in "Victory" international v. Wales, 1920. Played for England at cricket in 51 Tests.

Hon. A. Lyttelton, Old Etonians forward and Middlesex batsman. Capped for England v. Scotland, 1877. Played in 4 Tests against Australia, 1880-84.

H. Makepeace, Everton wing-half and Lancashire batsman. Capped for England v. Scotland, 1906, 1910 and 1912, v. Wales, 1912. Played in 4 Tests in Australia, 1920-21.

C. A. Milton, Arsenal outside-left and Gloucestershire all-rounder. Capped for England v. Austria in 1951 and appeared in 6 Tests in 1958 and 1959.

J. Sharp, Everton outside-right and Lancashire batsman. Played for England v. Ireland, 1903, v. Scotland, 1905, and in 3 Tests v. Australia, 1909.

W. Watson, Huddersfield Town and Sunderland wing-forward or wing-half, and left-handed batsman for Yorkshire and Leicestershire. Appeared for England in "Victory" international v. Wales, 1946. Capped v. Ireland and Italy, 1950, v. Wales and Yugoslavia, 1951. Played the first of 23 Tests for England in 1951 against South Africa.

## CROMPTON, Robert (1879-1941)
One of England's finest full-backs, renowned for his consistency. Between making his international debut against Germany in 1901 (a game not always recognised as a Full international) and his last appearance—against Scotland in April 1914, he missed only five of 45 England games. His 12 appearances against Scotland is still a record for an England right-back.

An outstanding personality both on and off the field Crompton served Blackburn Rovers as a player, director and manager, but although this club has played in eight F.A. Cup Finals and Crompton played for them for nearly 24 years his trophies never included a Cup medal. He also managed Bournemouth for a brief spell 1935-6.

Blackburn Rovers 1896-1920, 528 apps. England internationals 42. Inter-League games 17. League Champions, 1911-12, 1913-14.

## CROSSBAR
The crossbar over the goalmouth was first introduced into Football Association rules in 1875. Before that a tape was used although the word "bar," was mentioned in other rules as far back as 1863.

The Sheffield Association made bars obligatory some time before 1875. But it was not until the international conference—held in Manchester in 1882—that crossbars became generally compulsory.

See also LAWS OF THE GAME, Law 1, Part 6, and Law 10.

## CRYSTAL PALACE F.C.
Founded 1905. Immediately joined Southern League. One of the original members of the Football League, Third Division, 1920. Honours: Runners-up, Division II, 1968-9. Champions, Division III(S), 1920-21. Runners-up, 1928-9, 1930-31, 1938-9. Runners-up, Division III, 1963-4. Runners-up, Division IV, 1960-61. Record attendance: 49,498 v. Chelsea, Division I, Dec. 27, 1969. Address: Selhurst Park, London, SE25 6PU (Tel. 01-653 2223). Nickname: Glaziers. Colours: White shirts with two inch wide claret and blue stripe down front and back, white shorts, light blue stockings with claret tops. Record League goal-scorer: P. Simpson, 46 goals, Division III(S), 1930-31. Record victory: 9—0 v. Barrow, Division IV, Oct. 10, 1959. Record defeat: 11—4 v. Manchester City, F.A. Cup, 5th Round, Feb. 20, 1926.

## CUP MEDALS
See also FOOTBALL ASSOCIATION CHAL-

LENGE CUP, FOOTBALL ASSOCIATION AMATEUR CHALLENGE CUP, SCOTTISH CUP, TROPHIES.

J. Delaney created a unique record by gaining Scottish, English, N. Ireland and Eire Cup medals—Celtic 1937, Manchester United 1948, Derry City 1954, and Cork Athletic 1956 (runners-up).

J. Welford is often referred to as another player with a similar record, but the fact is that he gained only English and Scottish medals.

Only two players have gained winners' medals in both the F.A. Cup and the F.A. Amateur Cup. T. Morren was Middlesbrough's centre-half when they won the Amateur Cup in 1895 and Sheffield United's centre-half when they won the F.A. Cup in 1899. Morren again appeared in the F.A. Cup Final when Sheffield United were beaten in 1901. And R. Chatt was inside-right for Aston Villa when they won the Cup in 1895. Subsequently reinstated as an amateur, he received a winners' medal in the F.A. Amateur Cup with Stockton in 1899.

Three other players have appeared in both the F.A. Cup final and the F.A. Amateur Cup final:

S. B. Ashworth: Oxford City, Amateur finalists, 1903. Manchester City, F.A. Cup winners, 1904.

Rev. K. R. G. Hunt: Wolverhampton Wanderers, F.A. Cup winners, 1908. Oxford City, Amateur Cup finalists, 1913.

R. Topham: Casuals, Amateur Cup finalists, 1894. Wolverhampton Wanderers, F.A. Cup winners, 1893.

Members of Charlton Athletic's team which was defeated 4—1 by Derby County in the 1946 Cup Final each received two medals from the F.A. Gold was scarce at the time and as losers they were presented with bronze medals. The gold medals came later.

F. Gento gained eight European Cup medals with Real Madrid, including six winners' medals.

The following players have won both F.A. and Scottish F.A. Cup winners' medals:

Brady, A. Celtic 1892, Sheffield Wednesday 1896.
Campbell, H. Renton 1888, Blackburn Rovers 1890.
Campbell, J. Celtic 1892, 1899, 1900; Aston Villa 1897.
Cook, W. Celtic 1931, Everton 1933.
Delaney, J. Celtic 1937, Manchester United 1948.
Groves, W. Hibernian 1887, West Bromwich Albion 1892.
Hall, C. Blackburn Rovers 1891, St.

Bernard's 1895.
McPherson, J. Hearts 1891, Nottingham Forest 1898.
Mackay, D. Hearts, 1956, Tottenham Hotspur 1961, 1962, 1967.
Nibloe, J. Kilmarnock 1929, Sheffield Wednesday 1935.
O'Donnell, H. Celtic 1933, Preston North End 1938.
Scott, A. Rangers 1960, Everton 1966.
Simpson, R. Newcastle United 1952, 1955. Celtic 1967.
Smith, J. R. Kilmarnock 1920, Bolton Wanderers 1923, 1926.
Stevenson, W. Rangers 1960, Liverpool 1965.
Welford, J. Aston Villa, 1895, Celtic 1899.

Welford was the only Englishman to collect both F.A. and Scottish F.A. Cup medals.

Wilson, G. Hearts 1906, Newcastle United 1910.
Young, A. Hearts 1956, Everton 1966.

## CULLIS, Stanley (1915-    )

This constructive centre-half showed tremendous powers of concentration, never taking his eyes off the ball when making a tackle. A first-class general he was also a determined player who always had the will to win, a determination he carried with him into the managerial side of the game.

Spent his entire professional career with Wolverhampton Wanderers, joining them in February 1934 from Ellesmere Port and playing his last game (v. Liverpool at Molyneux) in May 1947. He became manager the following year and steered the club to three Championship and 2 F.A. Cup wins. Surprisingly sacked in September 1964 he subsequently managed Birmingham City from December 1965 to March 1970. Born Ellesmere Port.

Wolverhampton Wanderers 1934-47, 155 apps. England internationals 12 (plus 20 war-time games). Inter-League games 3. F.A. Cup runners-up 1939.

## CYPRUS

The Cypriots are enthusiastic about soccer, but with a population of only a little over half a million it is hardly surprising that they have been unable to make much impression at International level.

They withdrew from the 1958 World Cup and did not win a game in this competition until beating N. Ireland 1—0 in Feb. 1973.

Address: Cyprus F.A., Stasinos Steet 10, Engomi 114, P.O. Box 1471, Nicosia.
Colours: Blue shirts, white shorts, blue and white stockings.

APPEARANCES (LEAGUE). Two players who made more than 700 peacetime Football League appearances: Sir Stanley Matthews (*left*) and Jimmy Dickinson. (*Photos*: Central Press and P.A. Reuter).

ARSENAL F.C. This group (the 1932 team) includes six players who helped the club win the Championship four times in five years: back row (*left to right*) Parker, Jones, Moss, Roberts, John, Black; *front row* H. Chapman (manager), Hulme, Jack, Lambert, James, Bastin, T. Whittaker (trainer). (*Photo*: P.A. Reuter).

(*above left*) CAREY, JOHN. One of Ireland's most versatile players who captained Manchester United to their F.A. Cup victory in 1948. Pictured here with the coveted trophy. (*Photo*: Provincial Press Agency) (*above right*) CARTER, RAICH. There has never been a more talented inside-forward than this player who won F.A. Cup medals with both Sunderland and Derby County. (*Photo*: P.A. Reuter).

(*below left*) CHARLES JOHN. " The Gentle Giant " earned himself as big a reputation in the Italian League as he did at home in the Football League. (*Photo*: Sport & General), (*below right*) CHARLTON, JACKIE. In this action shot we see (left to right) Hunter and Charlton (in their white Leeds United strip) and Peplow of Liverpool. Charlton made more appearances for Leeds than any other player. (*Photo*: Syndication International).

(*above*) CHELSEA F.C. The Pensioners have won the Football League Championship once only, and this is the side that achieved that distinction in 1954-55. Back row, Armstrong, Harris, Robertson, Saunders, Willemse, Greenwood ; front row, Parsons, McNichol, Bentley, Stubbs, Lewis. (*Photo*: Provincial Press Agency) (*below*) DEFENSIVE RECORD. This is the Burnley team that created a Football League record for the longest run without defeat in a single season. Back row (players only), Halley, Boyle, Dawson, Jones, Watson ; front row, Nesbitt, Kelly, Anderson, Lindsay, Mosscrop, Smelt. (*Photo*: A. J. Winder).

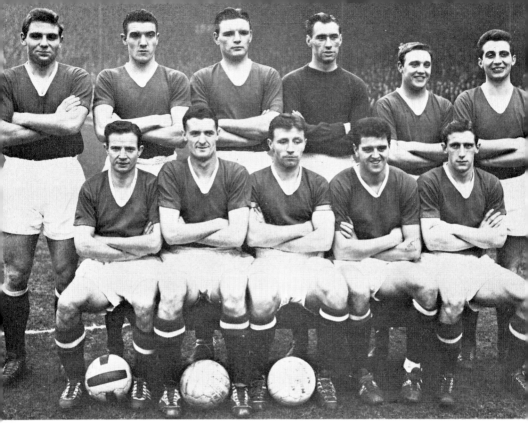

DISASTERS. The pre-Munich air crash Manchester United side of 1957: back row (*left to right*): Edwards, Foulkes, Jones, Wood, Colman, Pegg; front row, Berry, Whelan, Byrne, Taylor, Viollet. (*Photo*: Provincial Press Agency).

DI STEFANO. One of the finest centre-forwards in the game's history seen here in action for Real Madrid against an Egyptian team in 1961. (*Photo: United Press International*)

DOUBLE, THE. (*above*) Preston North End—Old Invincibles—who won both F.A. Cup and League in 1888-89: back row, Mills-Roberts, Graham, Sudell, Holmes, Russell, Tomlinson, Hanbury, Howarth, Drummond; front row, Thomson, Dewhurst, Goodhall, Ross, Gordon. (*Photo: Lancashire Evening Post*) (*below*) Aston Villa, winners of the F.A. Cup and Football League Championship in 1896-97. Back row (players only), Reynolds, Spencer, Evans, Whitehouse, Campbell; middle row, Athersmith, Devey, Wheldon, Cowan (John); on ground, Crabtree, Cowan (James).

DOUBLE. THE. Tottenham Hotspur, 1960–61), the first side to complete the Double this century: back row, Brown, Baker, Henry, Blanchflower, Norman, Mackay ; front row, Jones, White, Smith (R). Allen, Dyson. (Photo: P.A. Reuter)

DOUBLE, THE. Arsenal—who completed the Double in 1970-71. Back row, G. Wright (trainer), McNab, Storey, Simpson, Barnett, Wilson, Roberts, Kennedy, Marinello, D. Howe (coach); front row, George, Radford, Armstrong, Sammels, McLintock, B. Mee (manager), Rice, Kelly, Graham, Nelson. (*Photo*: Kenneth Prater).

EUROPEAN CHAMPION CLUBS CUP. Celtic, 1965-67, the first British club to win the competition. (*Photo*: Central Press Photos).

| Dec. 11, 1968 | Cyprus 0, Scotland 5, Nicosia* |
|---|---|
| May 17, 1969 | Scotland 8, Cyprus 0, Glasgow* |
| Feb. 3, 1971 | Cyprus 0, Ireland 3, Nicosia† |
| April 21, 1971 | Ireland 5, Cyprus 0, Belfast† |
| Feb. 14, 1973 | Cyprus 1, Ireland 0, Nicosia* |
| May 9, 1973 | Ireland 3, Cyprus 0 Fulham* |

\* World Cup
† Nations Cup

## CZECHOSLOVAKIA

Soccer was played in Prague before the formation of the Republic of Czechoslovakia when Bohemia was part of Austria-Hungary. Clubs like SK Slavia and A.C. Sparta were playing the game in the 1880s and 1890s and Slavia, now known as Dynamo, were formed as early as 1882.

The Bohemian F.A. was formed in 1902 and with the visit of British coaches to Prague in the years before World War I the game developed quickly.

In 1920 the Republic of Czechoslovakia came into being and in that same year their international side reached the final of the Olympic Games but disgraced themselves by walking off the field when losing 2—0 to Belgium after one of their number had been sent off by the referee.

The new Czechoslovakian F.A. was formed in 1922 and since then they have always been among the better European footballing nations.

Czechoslovakia reached the final of the World Cup in 1934 when they were beaten 2—1 by Italy after extra time.

They were finalists again in 1962 when a side noted for its strong defence surprised the critics by winning through to meet Brazil. In that final the man who had previously been the star of their defence, goalkeeper V. Schroif, did not maintain his brilliant form and partly because of this they were beaten 3—1.

Czechoslovakia failed to qualify in 1966, and, after reaching Mexico in 1970, their all-amateur side did not collect a single point.

Address of the governing body which now controls about 6,000 clubs is Ceskoslovenský Fotbalový Svaz, Porici 12, Prag 1. Colours: White shirts, white shorts, red, white and blue stockings.

A match against Bohemia is included in these results of international matches:

| June 13, 1908 | Bohemia 0, England 4; Prague |
|---|---|
| May 16, 1934 | Czechoslovakia 2, England 1; Prague |
| May 22, 1937 | Czechoslovakia 1, Scotland 3; Prague |
| Dec. 1, 1937 | England 5, Czechoslovakia 4; Tottenham |
| Dec. 8, 1937 | Scotland 5, Czechoslovakia 0; Ibrox Park |
| May 18, 1938 | Czechoslovakia 2, Eire 2; Prague |
| May 1, 1957 | Wales 1, Czechoslovakia 0; Cardiff* |
| May 26, 1957 | Czechoslovakia 2, Wales 0; Prague* |
| June 8, 1958 | Ireland 1, Czechoslovakia 0; Sweden* |
| June 17, 1958 | Ireland 2, Czechoslovakia 1; Sweden*§ |
| Apr. 5, 1959 | Eire 2, Czechoslovakia 0; Dublin† |
| May 10, 1959 | Czechoslovakia 4, Eire 0; Prague† |
| May 14, 1961 | Czechoslovakia 4, Scotland 0; Bratislava* |
| Sept. 26, 1961 | Scotland 3, Czechoslovakia 2; Hampden* |
| Oct. 8, 1961 | Eire 1, Czechoslovakia 3; Dublin* |
| Oct. 29, 1961 | Czechoslovakia 7, Eire 1; Prague* |
| Nov. 29, 1961 | Scotland 2, Czechoslovakia 4; Brussels* |
| May 29, 1963 | Czechoslovakia 2, England 4; Bratislava |
| Nov. 2, 1966 | England 0, Czechoslovakia 0; Wembley |
| May 21, 1967 | Eire 0, Czechoslovakia 2; Dublin† |
| Nov. 22, 1967 | Czechoslovakia 1, Eire 2; Prague† |
| May 4, 1969 | Eire 1, Czechoslovakia 2; Dublin* |
| Oct. 7, 1969 | Czechoslovakia 3, Eire 0; Prague* |
| June 11, 1970 | England 1, Czechoslovakia 0; Guadalajara* |
| April 21, 1971 | Wales 1, Czechoslovakia 3, Swansea‡ |
| Oct. 27, 1971 | Czechoslovakia 1, Wales 0; Prague‡ |

CZECHOSLOVAKIA

July   2, 1972   Scotland  0,  Czechoslovakia  0;  Porto  Alegre,
                 Brazil
May  27, 1973   Czechoslovakia 1, England 1; Prague

* World Cup      † Nations Cup
‡ European Championship      § After extra time

50

## DARLINGTON F.C.

Founded 1883. Adopted professionalism, 1908. One of the original members of the Football League, Division III(N), 1921. Honours: Champions, Division III(N), 1924-5. Runners-up, 1921-2. Runners-up Division IV, 1965-6. Best in Division II, 15th, 1925-6. Record attendance: 21,864 v. Bolton Wanderers, Football League Cup, 3rd Round, Nov. 14, 1960. Address: Feethams Ground, Darlington (Tel. 65097). Nickname: Quakers. Colours: All white. Record League goal-scorer: D. Brown, 39 goals, Division III(N), 1924-5. Record victory: 9—2 v. Lincoln City, Division III(N), Jan. 7, 1928. Record defeat: 10—0 v. Doncaster Rovers, Division IV, Jan. 25, 1964.

## DEAN, William Ralph (1907—        )

One of the most prolific goal-scorers in the game's history "Dixie" Dean was the finest example of the old style of centre-forward, always in the thick of the fray, spearheading the attack, taking all the bumps but still rising to head the ball into the net or down for his inside-forwards to shoot at goal. In this way Dean netted 379 League goals but he created many more for his colleagues. He scored 12 goals in his first five England games, but the scoring feat which has put his name down to posterity was his 60 First Division goals for Everton when they won the League Championship in 1927-8.

Considering that soon after joining Everton from Tranmere Rovers in March 1925 Dean suffered skull fractures in a motorcycle accident, it is remarkable that this player made such a fine recovery that he headed more goals than any player in First Division football. Born Birkenhead.

Tranmere Rovers 1923-25, 29 apps. (27 goals). Everton 1925-28, 399 apps. (349 goals). Notts County 1938-39, 9 apps. (3 goals). England internationals 16. Inter-League games 6. League Champions 1927-8, 1931-2. F.A. Cup winners 1933. F.A. of Ireland Cup runners-up 1939.

## DEATHS

See CASUALTIES (Fatal); DISASTERS.

## DEBUTS

For youngest and oldest players see AGE. For goal-scoring debuts see GOAL-SCORING (Debuts).

S. Milton had an unhappy Football League debut as goalkeeper for Halifax Town against Stockport County, Jan. 6, 1934. He conceded 13 goals. An unenviable record.

D. Murray conceded 11 goals when making his Football League debut in goal for Crewe Alexandra v. Lincoln City, Division III(N), Sept. 29, 1951.

## DEFEATS

See also under F.A. CHALLENGE CUP (Results), DEFENSIVE RECORDS (Goals) and WITHOUT A WIN.

Manchester United lost their first 12 games of season 1930-31. The club's first victory was against Birmingham (2—0) at Old Trafford, Nov. 1, 1930. This is the worst start to the season any club has ever made in the Football League.

In season 1931-2 Rochdale lost 17 games in succession in Division III(N). On Nov. 7, 1931, they defeated New Brighton, 3—2, then failed to gain another point until drawing 1—1 with the same opponents on Mar. 9, 1932.

Nelson lost every one of their away games in Division III(N) during season 1930-31, the only club to do so in a season of at least 21 away games. After drawing, 1—1, with Halifax Town, Mar. 29, 1930, they played 24 away games without gaining a point.

Only two clubs have ever had 10 or more goals scored against them in more than one Football League game in a single season —Darwen and Rotherham. Darwen suffered three 0—10 defeats in Division II, 1898-9, v. Manchester City, Feb. 18, 1899, v. Walsall, Mar. 3, 1899, v. Loughborough Town, April 1, 1899. All were away matches. Rotherham had two big defeats in Division III(N) during 1928-9: 1—11 v. Bradford City, away, Aug. 25, 1928, 1—10 v. South Shields away, Mar. 16, 1929.

In the Scottish League, Division II, season 1937-8, Brechin City suffered three 10—0 defeats: v. Airdrieonians, v. Albion Rovers, and v. Cowdenbeath.

Other double-figure scores are mentioned under GOAL-SCORING (Teams and General).

## Most Defeats in a Season

*Football League:*

Division I: 30 defeats in 42 games, Leeds United, 1946-7; Blackburn Rovers, 1965-6.

Division II: 31 defeats in 42 games, Tranmere Rovers, 1938-9.

Division III(S): 29 defeats in 42 games, Merthyr Town, 1924-5.

Division III(N): 33 defeats in 40 games, Rochdale, 1931-2.

Division III: 31 defeats in 46 games, Newport County, 1961-2.

Division IV: 31 defeats in 46 games, Bradford, 1968-9, and Barrow 1970-71.

*Scottish League:*

Division I: 31 defeats in 42 games, St. Mirren, 1920-21.

Division II: 30 defeats in 38 games, Lochgelly United, 1923-4. 30 defeats in 36 games, Brechin City, 1962-3.

## DEFENSIVE RECORDS
### Goals

Here are the best defensive records for a single season of at least 42 games in the Football League:

### DIVISION I

| | | Goals | Games |
|---|---|---|---|
| Liverpool | 1968-69 | 24 | 42 |
| | 1970-71 | 24 | 42 |
| Leeds United | 1968-69 | 26 | 42 |

### DIVISION II

| | | | |
|---|---|---|---|
| Manchester United | 1924-25 | 23 | 42 |
| Birmingham City | 1947-48 | 24 | 42 |

### DIVISION III(S)

| | | | |
|---|---|---|---|
| Southampton | 1921-22 | 21 | 42 |
| Plymouth Argyle | 1921-22 | 24 | 42 |

### DIVISION III(N)

| | | | |
|---|---|---|---|
| Port Vale | 1953-54 | 21 | 46 |
| Rochdale | 1923-24 | 26 | 42 |

### DIVISION III

| | | | |
|---|---|---|---|
| Watford | 1968-69 | 34 | 46 |

### DIVISION IV

| | | | |
|---|---|---|---|
| Gillingham | 1963-64 | 30 | 46 |

### SCOTTISH LEAGUE

(a complete season of 30 or more games).

### DIVISION I

| | | | |
|---|---|---|---|
| Celtic | 1913-14 | 14 | 38 |
| | 1916-17 | 17 | 38 |
| Aberdeen | 1970-71 | 18 | 34 |

### DIVISION II

| | | | |
|---|---|---|---|
| Morton | 1966-67 | 20 | 38 |

The worst defensive records for a single season in the Football League are as follows:

### DIVISION I

| | | Goals | Games |
|---|---|---|---|
| Blackpool | 1930-31 | 125 | 42 |
| Ipswich Town | 1963-64 | 121 | 42 |

### DIVISION II

| | | | |
|---|---|---|---|
| Darwen | 1898-99 | 141 | 34 |
| Newport County | 1946-47 | 133 | 42 |

### DIVISION III(S)

| | | | |
|---|---|---|---|
| Merthyr Town | 1929-30 | 135 | 42 |
| Walsall | 1952-53 | 118 | 46 |

### DIVISION III(N)

| | | | |
|---|---|---|---|
| Nelson | 1927-28 | 136 | 42 |
| Rochdale | 1931-32 | 135 | 40 |

### DIVISION III

| | | | |
|---|---|---|---|
| Accrington Stanley | 1959-60 | 123 | 46 |

### DIVISION IV

| | | | |
|---|---|---|---|
| Hartlepools United | 1959-60 | 109 | 46 |

### SCOTTISH LEAGUE
### DIVISION I

| | | | |
|---|---|---|---|
| Leith Athletic | 1931-32 | 137 | 38 |

### DIVISION II

| | | | |
|---|---|---|---|
| Edinburgh City | 1931-32 | 146 | 38 |

Preston North End won the F.A. Cup without conceding a goal in 1888-9. The club's tally for five Cup-ties was 11—0. In the same season they also won the League Championship without losing a game. Their goals tally in the League was 74—15.

Bury also accomplished this Cup feat in 1902-3 when their tally for five ties was 12—0.

The highest number of consecutive F.A. Cup ties without conceding a single goal is 12 by Bradford City in seasons 1910-11 and 1911-12. The run came to an end after three goal-less draws with Barnsley in the 4th Round of 1911-12. In the third replay Bradford City were knocked out 2—3.

Queen's Park (Glasgow) were formed in 1867 and did not have a goal scored against them by a Scottish club until Jan. 16, 1875. Vale of Leven broke the 7-year record.

Since the offside rule was changed in 1925 the record number of games in any one season that a club has prevented their opponents from scoring in Football League games is 30 by Port Vale in Division III(N) in 1953-4.

In Division III(S) in 1925-6, Millwall did not have a goal scored against them in 11 consecutive matches.

Huddersfield Town completed all their Football League matches in Division I, 1924-5, without conceding more than two goals in any one match. Tranmere Rovers did the same in Division III(N), 1937-8.

Cardiff City completed season 1928-9 with the best defensive record in the First Division (59 goals conceded). Nevertheless they were relegated.

**Undefeated**

See also HOME WINS, AWAY WINS.

In the German Regional League I.F.C. Nuremberg were undefeated in 104 games 1918-22.

The record for the longest run without defeat in the Football League is held by Leeds United. After losing 5—1 at Burnley, Oct. 19, 1968, they enjoyed a run of 34 Division I games without a defeat before losing 3—2 at Everton, Aug. 30, 1969.

Liverpool won the championship of Division II, 1893-4, winning 22 of their 28 games, and drawing 6. They followed this by winning their "Test Match" for promotion, then drew their first two games of season 1894-5 in Division I before going down to Aston Villa. A total of 31 games without defeat.

The longest run without defeat in the Football League in a single season was made by Burnley. They were undefeated in 30 matches played between Sept. 4, 1920 (when they lost 0—2, away to Bradford) and Mar. 26, 1921 (when they were beaten 3—0 away to Manchester City). Burnley won the championship that season. Manchester City were runners-up. (Note that Burnley's run applies to League games only. It was interrupted by an F.A. Cup defeat by Hull City.)

In the Scottish League Celtic were undefeated in 63 games from Nov. 13, 1915 to April 21, 1917. Kilmarnock broke this remarkable run, winning 2—0 at Parkhead.

In International matches the longest undefeated run was made by Hungary. After losing 3—5 against Austria, May 14, 1950, they were undefeated in 29 matches before losing 2—3 to Germany in the World Cup Final, July 4, 1954.

The highest number of consecutive F.A. Cup ties played by a single club without defeat is 24 by Blackburn Rovers, set up from Dec. 1883 to Dec. 1886.

In season 1881-2, Blackburn Rovers played 35 matches without defeat before losing 0—1 in the F.A. Cup Final to Old Etonians in Mar., 1882.

Between Mar. 17, 1928 and Mar. 27, 1929, Rangers played 38 consecutive Scottish League, Division I, games without defeat. Hamilton Academicals broke the run, 3—1, at Douglas Park.

Celtic (Glasgow) were undefeated in 33 games after losing in the Scottish Cup Final, April 1966, until beaten by Dundee United, Dec. 12, 1966. In League games only this run extended over 27 from Feb. 1966.

In the Italian League Fiorentina enjoyed a run of 33 games without defeat during season 1955-6.

Liverpool started the 1949-50 season by playing 19 consecutive Division I games without defeat. Of these they won 10. Their first defeat of the season was 2—3 at Huddersfield, Dec. 10, 1949. This is a record start for Division I since World War I.

In Division IV Millwall also played 19 games from the start of a season before suffering their first defeat. This was in 1959-60.

In the Scottish League, Division II, 1963-4, Morton actually *won* their first 23 games before losing 1—3 at East Fife.

Millwall hold the Football League record for the longest home run without defeat. After losing their last home game of 1963-4 they were unbeaten in 59 consecutive League games at The Den before losing 1—2 to Plymouth Argyle, Jan. 14, 1967.

After losing at home 1—3 to Brentford, April 8, 1933, Reading were unbeaten in the Football League on their own ground until Jan. 15, 1936, when they lost 1—2 to Queen's Park Rangers. They had then played 55 consecutive home League games without defeat.

Both Millwall's and Reading's runs were interrupted by Cup defeats at home, and the record home run which included Cup games (both F.A. and Football League Cup) was set up by Gillingham with a total of 52. After losing 2—3 at home to Barrow, April 6, 1963, they were undefeated at Priestfield Stadium until losing 0—1 to Exeter City, April 10, 1965. Gillingham's run included 48 Football League games.

Stockport County had an unbeaten home run of 48 Football League games, plus three F.A. Cup ties, April 2, 1927 to Oct. 5, 1929.

Plymouth Argyle were not beaten at home between Mar. 25, 1921 and Aug. 25, 1923 a total of 47 Football League plus three F.A. Cup games.

In the Spanish League Real Madrid were undefeated at home from Feb. 3, 1957, when they lost 2—3 to Athletico Madrid, until beaten 0—1 by the same club, Mar. 7, 1965. Between these games they won 114 and drew 8 League games on their own ground.

Sunderland were not beaten at home in a Football League game from Sept. 15, 1890 (lost 3—4 to Wolverhampton Wanderers) to Dec. 9, 1893 (lost 2—3 to Blackburn Rovers); 44 home games without defeat, including six draws. There followed another run of 37 undefeated home games, including seven draws, before losing 0—1 to Bury, Sept. 1, 1896. That is a run of 82 home games with only one defeat.

**Fewest Defeats**

The fewest defeats in a season since each division of the Football League contained at least 22 clubs, are listed below:

| DIVISION I | | |
|---|---|---|
| | *Defeats* | *Games* |
| Leeds United | 1968-69 | 2 | 42 |
| Arsenal | 1930-31 | 4 | 42 |

| DIVISION II | | |
|---|---|---|
| Leeds United | 1963-64 | 3 | 42 |
| Tottenham Hotspur | 1919-20 | 4 | 42 |

| DIVISION III(S) | | |
|---|---|---|
| Southampton | 1921-22 | 4 | 42 |
| Plymouth Argyle | 1929-30 | 4 | 42 |

| DIVISION III(N) | | |
|---|---|---|
| Wolverhampton Wanderers | 1923-24 | 3 | 42 |
| Doncaster Rovers | 1946-47 | 3 | 42 |
| Port Vale | 1953-54 | 3 | 46 |

| DIVISION III | | |
|---|---|---|
| Queen's Park Rangers | 1966-67 | 5 | 46 |

| DIVISION IV | | |
|---|---|---|
| York City | 1958-59 | 7 | 46 |
| Millwall | 1964-65 | 7 | 46 |
| Luton Town | 1967-68 | 7 | 46 |
| Swansea City | 1969-70 | 7 | 46 |
| Port Vale | 1969-70 | 7 | 46 |
| Notts County | 1970-71 | 7 | 46 |

*Scottish League*

DIVISION I
(with 18 or more clubs)

| Rangers | 1920-21 | 1 | 42 |
|---|---|---|---|
| | 1928-29 | 1 | 38 |
| | 1967-68 | 1 | 34 |
| Celtic | 1916-17 | 1 | 38 |
| | 1956-57 | 1 | 36 |
| | 1967-68 | 1 | 34 |
| Hearts | 1957-58 | 1 | 34 |

DIVISION II
(with 18 or more clubs)

| Clyde | 1956-57 | 1 | 36 |
|---|---|---|---|
| Morton | 1963-64 | 1 | 36 |
| St. Mirren | 1967-68 | 1 | 36 |

| Raith Rovers | 1937-38 | 2 | 34 |
|---|---|---|---|
| Cowdenbeath | 1938-39 | 2 | 34 |

# DENMARK

It was not until 1971 that the Danes agreed to allow a limited form of professionalism with players given gift vouchers to the value of an amount in the region of £160 per annum. Small indeed, but a significant breakthrough in a country which had been one of the last bastions of the amateur game.

Perhaps even more significant at this time was the introduction of Danish professionals from abroad into their national team, for there is no doubt that their absence had prevented this country from making much of an impression in the international field except, of course, in the amateur Olympic Games where they have been finalists in 1908, 1912 and 1960.

Money talks, and until this break through the Danish national side had failed to develop into a major force because of the regular exodus of their star players to other countries, principally Italy, France, and more recently, Scotland, where they are tempted by professionalism.

Football was begun in Denmark by British residents in about 1876 and the Danish Football Union which now controls something like 1,500 clubs, was formed in 1889.

England suffered their first-ever defeat by a side outside of the United Kingdom when they were beaten 2—1 in Copenhagen in May 1910 in an amateur international, and there was another shock in store for England's full professional side when they met Denmark for the first time in 1948. On that occasion the Danish amateurs held the English professionals to a goalless draw.

Address of the governing body: Dansk Boldspil Union, P.H. Lings-Allé 4, Koben-havn 2100. Colours: Red shirts, white shorts, red stockings.

| Sept. 26, 1948 | Denmark 0, England 0; Copenhagen |
|---|---|
| May 12, 1951 | Scotland 3, Denmark 1; Glasgow |
| May 25, 1952 | Denmark 1, Scotland 2; Copenhagen |
| Oct. 2, 1955 | Denmark 1, England 5; Copenhagen |
| Oct. 3, 1956* | Eire 2, Denmark 1; Dublin |
| Dec. 5, 1956* | England 5, Denmark 2; Wolverhampton |
| May 15, 1957* | Denmark 1, England 4; Copenhagen |
| Oct. 2, 1957* | Denmark 0, Eire 2; Copenhagen |
| Oct. 21, 1964* | Denmark 1, Wales 0; Copenhagen |
| Dec. 1, 1965* | Wales 4, Denmark 2; Wrexham |
| July 3, 1966 | Denmark 0, England 2; Copenhagen |
| Oct. 16, 1968 | Denmark 0, Scotland 1; Copenhagen |
| Dec. 4, 1968* | Eire 1, Denmark 1; Dublin† |
| May 27, 1969* | Denmark 2, Eire 0; Copenhagen |
| Oct. 15, 1969* | Eire 1, Denmark 1; Dublin |
| Nov. 11, 1970‡ | Scotland 1, Denmark 0; Glasgow |

June 9, 1971‡ Denmark 1, Scotland 0; Copenhagen
Oct. 18, 1972* Denmark 1, Scotland 4; Copenhagen
Nov. 15, 1972* Scotland 2, Denmark 0; Glasgow
    * World Cup     † Abandoned
    ‡ European Championship

## DERBY COUNTY F.C.

Founded 1884 as the football section of Derby County Cricket Club. One of the original members of the Football League, 1888. Honours: Champions, Division I, 1971-2. Runners-up, 1895-6, 1929-30, 1935-6. Champions, Division II, 1911-12, 1914-15, 1968-9. Runners-up 1925-6. Champions, Division III(N), 1956-7. Runners-up, Division III(N), 1955-6. F.A. Cup: Winners, 1946. Finalists, 1898, 1899, 1903. Record attendance: 41,826 v. Tottenham Hotspur, Division I, Sept. 20, 1969. Address, Baseball Ground, Derby (Tel. 40105). Nickname: Rams. Colours: White shirts, blue shorts, white stockings. Record League goal-scorers: J. Bowers, Division I, 1930-31, and R. Straw, Division III(N), 1956-7, 37 goals. Record victory: 9—0, v. Wolverhampton Wanderers, Division I, Jan. 10, 1891; v. Sheffield Wednesday, Division I, Jan. 21, 1899. Record defeat: 11—2 v. Everton, F.A. Cup, 1st Round, 1889-90.

## DICKINSON, James William M.B.E. (1925-    )

A player who epitomised all that is best in the game. Made debut with Portsmouth as an amateur in 1943 and after completing service in the Royal Navy turned professional with the club and went on to create an all-time record by making 764 League appearances—his last on his 40th birthday in 1965. He was also an automatic choice for England at left-half for seven seasons and would have made more international appearances but for the fact that his club loyalty was so great that he agreed to switch to centre-half with Portsmouth even though he knew that England would have no place for him in that position.

A gentleman both on and off the field Dickinson was never cautioned by the referee. He played a no frills but so effective and consistent game in the half-back line. Born Alton, Hants.

Portsmouth 1946-65, 764 apprs. England internationals 48. England "B" 3. Inter-League games 11. League Champions 1948-9, 1949-50.

## DISASTERS

The biggest disaster in the history of sport occurred at the National Stadium, Lima, Peru, on Sunday, May 24, 1964. Six minutes before the end of a match between Peru and Argentina, the referee disallowed a goal by the home side and a riot quickly broke out. The police used tear gas, and during the ensuing panic to get out of the stadium 301 people were killed and over 500 injured.

Nearly 80 people were killed and about 200 injured in a stampede at the River Plate Stadium, Buenos Aires, June 23, 1968, following a game between River Plate and Boca Juniors.

The worst disaster in British football history occurred at Ibrox Park, Glasgow, January 2, 1971, when 66 people were killed and over 140 injured in the crush while leaving the ground towards the end of a game between Rangers and Celtic.

On Mar. 9, 1946, 33 people were killed and well over 400 injured at Burden Park, Bolton, before an F.A. Cup-tie between Bolton Wanderers and Stoke City. A section of the crowd was so tightly packed that they got out of hand and were pushed helplessly upon one another as crush-barriers broke. Several thousand pounds were collected for the dependants of those killed and for the injured.

During an International Championship match at Ibrox Park, Glasgow, between Scotland and England on April 5, 1902, part of the West stand collapsed and many people were killed and injured. Officially the casualty list was 25 killed, 24 dangerously injured, 168 seriously injured, 153 injured, and 172 slightly injured. The game, which had been in progress for about 10 minutes, was resumed after a hold-up of half an hour. The result was a draw 1—1 but the match was subsequently declared unofficial and deleted from International records.

Manchester United lost eight of their players when the aircraft bringing the team home from Belgrade crashed at Munich Airport, Feb. 6, 1958. The players who died were R. Byrne, T. Taylor, D. Edwards, G. Bent, E. Colman, M. Jones, D. Pegg, and L. Whelan. The club secretary, coach, trainer and eight sporting journalists were also killed.

On May 14, 1949, the whole of the Torino team, Italian League Champions, including eight internationals, were killed, when the plane returning them from a game in Lisbon crashed at Superga, outside Turin. In addition to the players including all the reserves, the club's manager, trainer and coach were also killed. The total death roll was 28.

Two people were killed and several injured when crush barriers collapsed at Ibrox Park, Glasgow, Sept. 16, 1961, during a game between Rangers and Celtic.

At Hillsborough, Sheffield, on Feb. 4, 1914, during a replayed F.A. Cup-tie between Sheffield Wednesday and Wolverhampton Wanderers a retaining wall collapsed and 75 people were injured. The game was resumed but there was no addition to the score of 1—0 in favour of the Wednesday.

## DI STEFANO LAUTHE, Alfredo (1926- )

The complete footballer, tall and well built with tremendous stamina, this centre-forward was always on the move throughout a game. Born Buenos Aires of Italian descent he joined River Plate in 1942 and was capped seven times by the Argentine before going to Colombia. Came to Europe in 1953 and enjoyed a remarkable career with Real Madrid being renowned both as a strategist and goalscorer. Topped the Spanish League's list of scorers in five of the six seasons 1953-59 and scored a record total of 49 goals in the European Cup, helping his club win that competition five times in a row. European Footballer of the Year in 1957 and 1959.

River Plate 1942-46. Huracan 1946-47, 66 apprcs. (50 goals). River Plate 1947-49, 45 apprcs. (30 goals). Milionarios 1949-53, 292 apprcs. (259 goals). Real Madrid 1953-64, 624 apprcs. (405 goals). International appearances—Argentine 7, Colombia 4, Spain 31. Rest of the World v. England 1963. Spanish League champions 1954, 1955, 1957, 1958, 1961, 1962, 1963, 1964. Argentinian League Champions 1947. European Cup winners 1956, 1957, 1958, 1959, 1960, finalists 1962, 1964. World Club Cup winners·1960.

## DOHERTY, Peter Dermont (1914- )

This red-haired Irishman (born Magerafelt) developed by Glentoran and introduced into the Football League by Blackpool in November 1933 is reckoned by many experts to have been the most complete inside-forward of all time. A natural dribbler, a glutton for work and quick off the mark, no player could read a game better than Peter Doherty who created goals as well as scored them.

When he applied his talent to the managerial side of the game he succeeded in steering Ireland to the last eight of the 1958 world cup.

Blackpool 1933-36, 83 apps. (28 goals). Manchester City 1936-45, 122 apps. (76

goals). Derby County 1945-46, 15 apps. (7 goals). Huddersfield Town 1946-49, 83 apps. (33 goals). Doncaster Rovers 1949-53 106 apps. (55 goals). Irish internationals 16 (plus 2 Victory games). League Champions 1936-7. F.A. Cup winners 1946. Irish Cup winners 1933.

## DONCASTER ROVERS F.C.

Founded 1879. Elected to Football League, Division II, 1901. Failed to gain re-election, 1903. Re-elected 1904. Failed to gain· re-election 1905. Unable to gain re-admission to the League until elected to Division III(N) 1923. Honours: Champions, Division III(N), 1934-5, 1946-7, 1949-50. Runners-up, Division III(N), 1937-8, 1938-9. Champions, Division IV, 1965-6, 1968-9. Best in Division II, 7th 1901-2. Record attendance: 37,149 v. Hull City Division III(N), Oct. 2, 1948. Address: Belle Vue, Doncaster (Tel. 55281). Colours: White shirts with two red hoops and red trim, red shorts, white stockings. Record League goal-scorer: C. Jordan, 42 goals, Division III(N), 1946-7. Record victory: 10—0 v. Darlington, Division IV, January 25, 1964. Record defeat: 12—0 v. Small Heath, Division II, April 11, 1903.

## DOUBLE, THE

Only four clubs have won the Football League Championship and the F.A. Cup in the same season, Preston North End in 1888-9, Aston Villa in 1896-7, Tottenham Hotspur in 1960-61, and Arsenal in 1970-71.

The details of their records are as follows:

### Preston North End

Football League:
Played 22, won 18, drawn 4, lost 0. For 74, against 15. Points 40.
F.A. Cup:

| | |
|---|---|
| Round 1 v. Bootle (a) | 3—0 |
| Round 2 v. Grimsby Town (a) | 2—0 |
| Round 3 v. Birmingham St. George (h) | 2—0 |
| Semi-final v. West Bromwich Albion (at Bramall Lane, Sheffield) | 1—0 |
| Final v. Wolverhampton Wanderers (at The Oval) | 3—0 |

### Aston Villa

Football League:
Played 30, won 21, drawn 5, lost 4. For 73, against 38. Points 47.
F.A. Cup:

| | |
|---|---|
| Round 1 v. Newcastle United (h) | 5—1 |
| Round 2 v. Notts County (h) | 2—1 |
| Round 3 v. Preston North End (after draws 1—1, 0—0, 2nd replay at Sheffield) | 3—2 |

Semi-final v. Liverpool (at Bramall
Lane, Sheffield)               3—0
Final v. Everton (at Crystal Palace)  3—2

Tottenham Hotspur
Football League:
Played 42, won 31, drawn 4, lost 7. For
115, against 55. Points 66.
F.A. Cup:
Round 3 v. Charlton Athletic (h)   3—2
Round 4 v. Crewe Alexandra (h)     5—1
Round 5 v. Aston Villa (a)         2—0
Round 6 v. Sunderland (h) (after
  draw 1—1)                        5—0
Semi-final v. Burnley (at Villa
  Park)                            3—0
Final v. Leicester City (at Wembley)
                                   2—0

Arsenal
Football League:
Played 42, won 29, drawn 7, lost 6. For
71, against 29. Points 65.
F.A. Cup:
Round 3 v. Yeovil (a)              3—0
Round 4 v. Portsmouth (h) (after
  draw 1—1)                        3—2
Round 5 v. Manchester C. (a)       2—1
Round 6 v. Leicester C. (h) (after
  draw 0—0)                        1—0
Semi-final v. Stoke City at Villa Park,
  Birmingham (after draw 2—2 at
  Hillsborough, Sheffield)         2—0
Final v. Liverpool (at Wembley)    2—1

In Scotland two clubs, Celtic and Rangers, have won the Scottish League and
Cup in the same season on several occasions:
  Celtic: 1907, 1908, 1914, 1954, 1967,
  1969, 1971, 1972.
  Rangers: 1928, 1930, 1934, 1935, 1949,
  1950, 1953, 1963, 1964.
In seasons 1948-9 and 1963-4 Rangers
also won the Scottish League Cup. Celtic
achieved this in 1966-7 and 1968-9.

**DRAWS**
The record number of draws by a club in a
single season in the Football League is 22
by Tranmere Rovers, Division III, 1970-71.
In the Scottish League, Division I, the
record is 17, by Falkirk in 1921-2 and 1922-
3.
The record abroad is 22 draws in 52
games by Percira, Colombian League,
1967-8.
Torquay drew 8 consecutive Division III
games Oct 25—Dec. 13, 1969. A Football
League record.
On Saturday, Sept. 18, 1948, there were
nine drawn games in Division I of the Football League, a record for any division of the

League in a single day.
There were 22 drawn games in the Foot-
ball League on Oct. 13, 1962.
The record for drawn games in a single
round of the F.A. Cup is 15 in the 3rd
Round, Jan. 9, 1954.
The following clubs have gone through a
Football League season without a drawn
game: Sunderland, Division I, 1891-2;
Small Heath, Division II, 1893-4; Lincoln
City and Walsall Town Swifts, Division II,
1894-5; Stoke, Division I, 1895-6; Darwen,
Division II, 1896-7.

**DUMBARTON F.C.**
Founded 1872. One of the original members of Scottish League, 1890. Honours:
Scottish League Champions, 1890-91
(shared), 1891-2. Champions, Division II,
1910-11, 1971-2. Runners-up, 1907-8. Scottish Cup, Winners, 1882-3. Finalists, 1880-
81, 1881-2, 1886-7, 1890-91, 1896-7. Record
attendance: 18,000 v. Raith Rovers, Scottish Cup, 7th Round, Mar. 2, 1957.
Address: Boghead Park, Dumbarton (Tel.
3842569). Colours: White shirts with single
gold hoop between two black hoops, white
shorts. Record League goal-scorer: K.
Wood, 38 goals, Division II, 1971-2.
Record victory: 8—0 v. Cowdenbeath,
Division II, Mar. 28, 1964. Record defeat:
8—0 v. Dundee United, Division II, 1935-6,
v. Morton, Division II, 1953-4, v. Third
Lanark, Scottish Cup, 3rd Round, Feb. 22,
1936.

**DUNDEE F.C.**
Founded 1893 by the amalgamation of East
End and Our Boys clubs. Joined Scottish
League, Division I, 1893. Honours: Cham-
pions, Division 1, 1961-2. Runners-up,
1902-3, 1906-7, 1908-9, 1948-9. Champions,
Division B, 1946-7. Scottish Cup: Winners,
1910. Finalists, 1925, 1952, 1964. Scottish
League Cup: Winners, 1952. Finalists 1968.
Record attendance: 43,024 v. Glasgow
Rangers, Scottish Cup, 2nd Round, Feb. 7,
1953. Address: Dens Park, Dundee (Tel.
0382 86104). Colours: White shirts, dark
blue shorts. Record League goal-scorer in
Division I, D. Halliday, 38 goals, 1923-4.
Record victory: 10—0 v. Alloa Athletic
Division II, Mar. 8, 1947, and v. Dunferm-
line Athletic, Division II, Mar. 22, 1947.
Record defeat: 11—0 v. Celtic, Division I,
Oct. 26, 1895.

**DUNDEE UNITED F.C.**
Founded 1910 as Dundee Hibernian.
Changed name to Dundee United in 1923.
Joined Scottish League, Division II, 1910.
Honours: Champions, Division II, 1924-5,
1928-9. Runners-up, 1930-31, 1959-60.

57

Record attendance: 26,500 v. Barcelona, Nov. 16, 1966, and v. Juventus, Mar. 8, 1967. Both Inter-Cities Fairs Cup ties. Address: Tannadice Park, Dundee (Tel. 0382 86289). Colours: Tangerine shirts with black facings, tangerine shorts with black trim. Record League goal-scorer J. Coyle, 41 goals, Division II, 1955-6. Record victory: 14—0 v. Nithsdale Wanderers, Scottish Cup, 1st Round, Jan. 17, 1931. Record defeat: 12—1 v. Motherwell, Division B, 1953-4.

## DUNFERMLINE ATHLETIC F.C.
Founded 1885. Joined Scottish League, Division II, 1921. Honours: Champions, Division II, 1925-6. Runners-up, 1912-13, 1933-4, 1954-5, 1957-8, 1972-3. Best in Division I, 4th, 1961-2. Scottish Cup: Winners, 1961, 1968. Runners-up, 1965. Scottish League Cup: Finalists 1950. Record attendance: 27,816 v Celtic, Division I, April 30, 1968. Address: East End Park, Dunfermline (Tel. 0383 24295). Nickname: Pars. Colours: Black and white stripe shirts, black shorts. Record League goal-scorer: R. Skinner, 53 goals, Division II, 1925-6. Record victory: 11—2 v. Stenhousemuir, Division II, Sept. 27, 1930. Record defeat: 10—0 v Dundee, Division II, Mar. 22, 1947.

## EAST FIFE F.C.
Founded 1903. First promoted to Division I, 1930. Honours: Champions, Division B, 1947-8. Runners-up, Division II, 1929-30, 1970-71. Best in Division I, 3rd, 1951-2, 1952-3. Scottish Cup: Winners, 1938. Finalists, 1927, 1950. Scottish League Cup: Winners, 1948, 1950, 1954. Record attendance: 22,515 v. Raith Rovers, Jan. 2, 1950. Address: Bayview Park, Methil (Tel. 033-32 2323). Colours: Gold shirts with black trim, black shorts. Record League goal-scorer: J. Wood, 42 goals, Division II, 1926-7. Record victory: 13—2 v. Edinburgh City, Division II, Dec. 11, 1937. Record defeat: 9—1 v. Celtic, Division I, Jan. 10, 1931.

## EAST GERMANY
See under GERMANY.

## EAST STIRLING (SHIRE) F.C.
Founded 1881. First joined Scottish League, Division II, 1901. Became East Stirling—Clydebank for season. 1964-5, but reverted to original name on return to Falkirk in 1965. Honours: Champions, Division II, 1931-2, runners-up 1962-3. Record attendance: 10,000 v. St. Mirren, Division II, Nov. 16, 1935. Address: Firs Park, Falkirk (Tel. 0324 23583). Colours: Black and white hooped shirts, black shorts. Record League goal-scorer: M. Morrison, 36 goals, Division II, 1938-9. Record victory: 8—2 v. Brechin City, Division II, Mar. 31, 1962. Record defeat: 10—0 v. Dundee United, Division II, Mar. 25, 1939.

## ECUADOR
With star players emigrating to Uruguay and Brazil this small country has made little impression at International level, but they are as keen on the game as their more illustrious neighbours, having played organised football since about 1912 and been members of F.I.F.A. since 1925.

The controlling body was formed in 1925. Address: Asociación Ecuatoriana de Fútbol, Calle Chimborazo 206, 2° Piso, of 4, Casilla 7447, Guayaquil. Colours: Yellow shirts with blue trim, blue shorts, red stockings.
Result of international matches.
May 25, 1970 Ecuador 0, England 2; Quito June 18, 1972 Ecuador 2, Eire 3; Natal, Brazil.

## EIRE
To avoid confusion between the two Associations which control football in Ireland, i.e., the Football Association of Ireland and the Irish Football Association, the former is generally referred to throughout this encyclopaedia under the Gaelic name, Eire. "Ireland" refers to teams selected by the Irish F.A. (Belfast).

In June 1954, F.I.F.A. decided that the title for international teams representing Eire should be "Republic of Ireland".

In 1973 Northern Ireland is entitled by F.I.F.A. to select players born in Eire for international matches with England, Scotland or Wales, but must restrict itself to its own players for matches with any other countries.

The Football Association of Ireland (Dublin) has taken exception to this arrangement, and have gone so far as to compel its players, before transferring to clubs outside the country, to sign an agreement that they would not play for any country other than Eire. The F.A. of Ireland, were however, forced to abandon this rule.

On the other hand it was not so long ago that the Irish F.A. (Belfast) lifted its ban prohibiting the playing of any matches between clubs of its Association with clubs in membership with the Eire Association.

The first club to be formed in what has since become Eire was Dublin Association in 1883. Their first game was played against Dublin University.

The Football Association of Ireland was formed in June 1921, shortly after many clubs in Southern Ireland broke away from the Irish F.A. (Belfast). The Football League of Ireland came into being two months later.

At first the new Association was not granted recognition by the Associations of England, Scotland and Wales, and the clubs were entirely suspended by the Irish F.A. (Belfast).

The first step towards international recognition was made in August 1923, when the F.A. of Ireland was accepted into membership with F.I.F.A. Next came recognition by the Associations of Great Britain, although this recognition did not extend to the International Championship. The Irish F.A. (Belfast) was still the only authority recognised to represent Ireland, and only its members were allowed to sit on the International Board.

Several clubs from Belfast and Derry were in membership with the F.A. of Ireland (Dublin), but one of the conditions of recognition by the other Associations of Great Britain, was that the membership of these clubs should be cancelled. Another condition was that the title of the new Association should be changed to the F.A. of the Irish Free State.

The Dublin Association tried to reach an agreement with the Irish F.A. (Belfast) whereby the selection and control of international matches concerning Ireland would be dealt with by a committee from the two Associations working on a 50-50 basis. These proposals were not accepted.

Subsequently the Dublin authorities complained to F.I.F.A. and the International Board that the Irish F.A. (Belfast) was still fielding its International XI under the title "Ireland," although it had control in only six of the 32 counties of Ireland. They demanded that the Belfast Association should adopt the title "Northern Ireland". Although this proposal was accepted by F.I.F.A. it was not adopted by the Irish F.A. (Belfast).

In 1989 Eire became the first country outside the United Kingdom to defeat England on English soil. At Goodison Park, Everton, on Sept. 21, 1989, Eire beat England 2—0. For the teams in this game see INTERNATIONALS (England).

Address of governing body: F.A. of Ireland, 80 Merrion Square, Dublin, 2. Colours: Green shirts, white shorts, green and white stockings.

The results of matches with foreign countries are given under each country.

Results of international matches with countries of the United Kingdom:

| Sept. 30, 1946 | Eire 0, England 1; Dublin |
| Sept. 21, 1949 | England 0, Eire 2; Everton |
| May 8, 1957* | England 5, Eire 1; Wembley |
| May 19, 1957* | Eire 1, England 1; Dublin |
| Sept. 28, 1960 | Eire 2, Wales 3; Dublin |
| May 3, 1961* | Scotland 4, Eire 1; Glasgow |
| May 7, 1961* | Eire 0, Scotland 3; Dublin |
| June 9, 1963 | Eire 1, Scotland 0; Dublin |
| May 24, 1964 | Eire 1, England 3; Dublin |
| Sept. 21, 1969 | Eire 1, Scotland 1; Dublin |

* World Cup

## ENGLAND
See INTERNATIONALS (England).

## ENTRANCE CHARGES
See ADMISSION CHARGES.

## EUROPEAN CHAMPION CLUBS CUP
This is one of the most popular football competitions and although only inaugurated in 1955 it was soon firmly established and considered by many to be the forerunner of a European Super League.

Known simply as the European Cup it was prompted by a suggestion of the French football magazine *L'Equipe* and is run under the auspices of the European Union of Football Associations.

Each season the champion club of each of the Associations in the Union are eligible to compete together with the winner of the previous season's competition. Games are played on a home and away basis with the aggregate score of the two games deciding the winner. In the event of a tie being still drawn after extra time in the second game then away goals count double. If still drawn then the winner is decided by a series of penalty kicks. In the final only one game is played.

Here are the results of the finals of this competition together with the attendance at each game and, in brackets, the number of clubs which competed:

| 1955–56 | (16) | Real Madrid 4, Reims 3; Paris, 38,000 |
| 1956–57 | (22) | Real Madrid 2, Fiorentina 0; Madrid, 125,000 |
| 1957–58 | (24) | Real Madrid 3, A.C. Milan 2*; Brussels, 67,000 |
| 1958–59 | (28) | Real Madrid 2, Reims 0; Stuttgart, 80,000 |
| 1959–60 | (27) | Real Madrid 7, Eintracht-Frankfurt 3; Glasgow, 127,621 |
| 1960–61 | (28) | Benfica 3, Barcelona 2; Berne, 30,000 |
| 1961–62 | (29) | Benfica 5, Real Madrid 3; Amsterdam, 65,000 |

| 1962–63 | (30) | A.C. Milan 2, Benfica 1; Wembley, 45,000 |
|---|---|---|
| 1963–64 | (31) | Internazionale 3, Real Madrid 1; Vienna, 74,000 |
| 1964–65 | (31) | Internazionale 1, Benfica 0; Milan, 80,000 |
| 1965–66 | (32) | Real Madrid 2, Partizan 1; Brussels, 38,713 |
| 1966–67 | (33) | Glasgow Celtic 2, Internazionale 1; Lisbon, 65,000 |
| 1967–68 | (31) | Manchester United 4, Benfica 1*; Wembley, 100,000 |
| 1968–69 | (27) | A.C. Milan 4, Ajax Amsterdam 1; Madrid, 50,000 |
| 1969–70 | (33) | Feyenoord 2, Celtic 1*; Milan, 85,000 |
| 1970–71 | (35) | Ajax 2, Panathinaikos 0; Wembley, 83,179 |
| 1971–72 | (35) | Ajax 2, Internazionale 0; Rotterdam, 67,000 |
| 1972–73 | (32) | Ajax 1, Juventus 0; Belgrade, 92,000 |

* After extra time

## EUROPEAN CUP WINNERS CUP

Run on the same lines as the European Cup, the clubs eligible for this competition are the winners (or if unable to compete —the runners-up) of each of the national cups.

In the event of a drawn tie away goals count double, and if still drawn on this basis then the result is decided by a series of penalty kicks.

Results of finals with the number of entrants shown in brackets:

| 1960–61 | (10) | Fiorentina bt. Glasgow Rangers 2–0, 2–1 |
|---|---|---|
| 1961–62 | (23) | Atletico Madrid bt. Fiorentina 3–0† |
| 1962–63 | (25) | Tottenham Hotspur bt. Atletico Madrid 5–1 |
| 1963–64 | (28) | Sporting Lisbon bt. MTK Budapest 1–0*‡ |
| 1964–65 | (30) | West Ham United bt. Munich 1860 2–0 |
| 1965–66 | (31) | Borussia Dortmund bt. Liverpool 2–1* |
| 1966–67 | (32) | Bayern Munich bt. Glasgow Rangers 1–0* |
| 1967–68 | (32) | Milan bt. S.V. Hamburg 3–0 |
| 1968–69 | (27) | Slovan Bratislava bt. Barcelona 3–2 |
| 1969–70 | (33) | Manchester City bt. Gornik Zabrze 2–1 |
| 1970–71 | (33) | Chelsea bt. Real Madrid 2–1† |
| 1971–72 | (34) | Glasgow Rangers bt. Moscow Dynamo 3–2 |
| 1972–73 | (32) | A.C. Milan bt. Leeds United 1–0 |

† After Draw 1–1
* After extra time
‡ After draw 3–3

## EUROPEAN FAIRS CUP

See under UEFA Cup.

## EUROPEAN FOOTBALL CHAMPION-SHIP

Known originally as the Nations Cup this is another competition run under the auspices of the European Union of Football Associations and in this the system of elimination is similar to that of the World Cup.

The qualifying competition for the quarter-finals is split into eight groups with the members of each group playing each other at home and away. The winners of each group then meet on a home and away basis in the quarter-finals, but the semi-finals are on a straight knock-out basis, the games being played on neutral grounds.

The trophy is the Henri Delaunay Cup, named after the secretary of the French Football Federation who originally conceived the idea of an international competition among European nations, but, unfortunately, did not live long enough to see his dream come true.

Results of finals with the number of competing nations shown in brackets:

| 1960 | (17) | Russia 2, Yugoslavia 1; Paris, 17,966 |
|---|---|---|
| 1964 | (29) | Spain 2, Russia 1; Madrid, 120,000 |
| 1968 | (31) | Italy 2, Yugoslavia 0; Rome, 100,000. After draw 1–1 |
| 1972 | (32) | W. Germany 3, Russia 0; Brussels, 43,437 |

## EUROPEAN UNION OF FOOTBALL ASSOCIATIONS
See under UNION OF EUROPEAN FOOTBALL ASSOCIATIONS.

## EUSEBIO da SILVA FERREIRA (1942- )
Reckoned to have one of the strongest shots ever seen in football this negro from Mozambique, Portuguese East Africa, first attracted attention with S.C. Lourenco Marques before Benfica signed him in 1961. An inside-forward with a tremendous turn of speed as well as that powerful right-foot shot he was top scorer with nine goals in the World Cup Final tournament in 1966 and has topped the Portuguese League scoring list seven times. European Footballer of the Year 1961.

S.C. de Lourenco Marques 1957-61. Benfica 1961-. Portuguese internationals 63. Portuguese League champions 1961, 1963, 1964, 1965, 1967, 1968, 1969, 1971, 1972, 1973. Cup winners 1962, 1964, 1969, 1970, 1972. European Cup winners 1962, finalists 1963, 1965. World Club Cup runners-up 1961, 1962.

## EVERTON F.C.
Founded 1878 as St. Domingo Church Sunday School Club. Became Everton, 1879. One of the original members of the Football League, 1888. Moved to Goodison Park, 1892. Honours: Champions, Division I, 1890-91, 1914-15, 1927-8, 1931-2, 1938-9, 1962-3, 1969-70. Runners-up, 1889-90, 1894-5, 1901-2, 1904-5, 1908-9, 1911-12. Champions, Division II, 1930-31. Runners-up, 1953-4. F.A. Cup: Winners, 1906, 1933, 1966. Finalists, 1893, 1897, 1907, 1968. Record attendance: 78,299 v. Liverpool, Division I, Sept. 18, 1948. Address: Goodison Park, Liverpool L4 4EL (Tel. 051-525 5263). Nickname: Toffees. Colours: Royal blue shirts with white neckband, white shorts and stockings. Record League goalscorer: W. Dean, 60 goals, Division I, 1927-8 (Football League record). Record victory 11—2 v. Derby County, F.A. Cup, 1st Round, 1889-90. Record defeat: 10—4 v. Tottenham Hotspur, Division I, Oct. 11, 1958.

## EXETER CITY F.C.
Founded 1904 on amalgamation of St. Sidwell's United and Exeter United. Adopted professionalism and joined the Southern League as Exeter City 1908. One of the original members of the Football League, Division III, 1920. Honours: Runners-up, Division III(S), 1932-3. Record attendance: 20,984 v. Sunderland F.A. Cup, 6th Round (replay), Mar. 4, 1931. Address: St. James's Park, Exeter EX4 6PX (Tel. 54073). Nickname: Grecians. Colours: Red and white striped shirts, red shorts, red stocking with white tops. Record League goal-scorer: F. Whitlow, 34 goals, Division III(S), 1932-3. Record victory: 8—1 v. Coventry City, Division III(S), Dec. 4, 1926; v. Aldershot, Division III(S), May 4, 1935. Record defeat: 9—0 v. Notts County, Division III(S), Oct. 16, 1948, and v. Northampton Town, Division III(S), April 12, 1958.

## FALKIRK F.C.
Founded 1876. Joined Scottish League, Division II, 1902. Division I, 1905. Honours: Runners-up, Division I, 1907-8, 1909-10. Champions, Division II, 1935-6, 1969-70. Runners-up, 1904-5, 1960-61. Scottish Cup: Winners, 1913, 1957. Scottish League Cup: Finalists, 1948. Record attendance: 23,100 v. Celtic, Scottish Cup, 3rd Round, Feb. 21, 1953. Address: Brockville Park, Falkirk (Tel. 0324 24121). Nickname: Bairns. Colours: Navy blue shirts, white shorts. Record League goalscorer: E. Morrison, 43 goals, Division I, 1928-9. Record victory: 10—0 v. Breadalbane, Scottish Cup, 1st Round, Jan. 13, 1923, and also Jan. 23, 1926. Record defeat: 11—1 v. Airdrieonians, Division A, April 28, 1951.

## FAMILIES
### Brothers
There have been many instances of brothers playing with the same League club, far too many to mention here. Included below are cases where brothers appeared together in international matches or in particularly interesting circumstances.

Two pairs of brothers in the same international side is a record set up on April 20, 1955, when L. and I. Allchurch and J. and M. Charles played for Wales against Ireland at Windsor Park, Belfast. They also appeared against Israel at Tel Aviv, Jan. 15, 1958, and against Brazil at Rio de Janeiro, May 12, 1962.

Abegglen. The three brothers, Jean, Max and André ("Trello") Abegglen, all played for Switzerland during the 1930s but never more than two in the same side.

Allchurch. Ivor and Len Allchurch, appeared together in eight internationals for Wales 1955-63.

Bambridge. A. L. and E. C. appeared together for England v. Wales in 1883 and v. Ireland in 1884. Another brother, E. H., had also played for England.

Blanchflower. R. D. ("Danny") Blanchflower, Tottenham Hotspur wing-half, and John Blanchflower, Manchester United

inside-forward, appeared together for Ireland in 10 internationals 1954-8.

Browell. In season 1910-11 Andrew, George and Tom Browell appeared together in Hull City's Division II side.

Carr. In season 1919-20 the brothers William (centre-half), John (outside-right) and George Carr (inside-right) appeared together in the Middlesbrough side in Division I.

Charles. John and Melvyn Charles appeared together for Wales in 15 internationals during the period 1955-62.

Charlton. John and Robert appeared in the same England team on 28 occasions 1965-70.

Corbett. In 1937-8 West Ham United had three brothers on their books who were all recognised as right-half-backs. They were David, James and Robert Corbett.

Cursham. Arthur and Harry of Notts County appeared together for England v. Scotland and Wales in 1882-3.

Doughty. The record number of goals scored in an International Championship match by two brothers is seven by Jack and Roger Doughty of the Druids. That was the number they scored between them in Wales' 11—0 victory over Ireland at Wrexham, 1888.

Evaristo. Mario (outside-left) and Juan (right-half) are two brothers who appeared together for the Argentine in the 1930s.

Forman. The only two brothers to play together for England as professionals before the Charlton brothers were Frank and Frederick Forman of Nottingham Forest. They were in the same England team on three occasions in season 1898-9.

Goodall. John Goodall, Preston North End and Derby County, was capped for England 14 times. His younger brother, Archie, Derby County and Glossop, was capped 10 times, but for Ireland not England. They never opposed each other in these games.

Hargreaves. The brothers Frederick and John of Blackburn Rovers appeared together for England v. Wales, Feb. 26, 1881.

Heron. The only two brothers to appear together both in an international side and an F.A. Cup winning side were Frederick and Hubert Heron of The Wanderers. They played for England v. Scotland, Mar. 4, 1876, and, two weeks later, appeared in their club side which defeated Old Etonians in the Cup Final.

Hollins. Dave Hollins, born Bangor and capped for Wales during the 1960s. Younger brother, John, born Guildford, and capped for England in 1967.

Irvine. William and Robert played together for Ireland v. Wales and Spain in

1963, and v. Wales in 1965.

Jack. Three brothers playing together with each of two Football League clubs is a record. David, Donald and Robert Jack were all with Plymouth Argyle in 1920 and all with Bolton Wanderers in 1923.

Jackson. Twin brothers David and Peter played together with three Football League clubs, Wrexham, Bradford City, and Tranmere Rovers.

Jones. The brothers John (Linfield) and Samuel Jones (Distillery and Blackpool), played alongside each other, as centre-half and left-half respectively, for Ireland v. England, Oct. 14, 1933, and v. Wales, Nov. 4, 1933. Against Wales, their brother-in-law, William Mitchell (Chelsea), completed the half-back line.

Keetley. Four brothers of the Keetley family all played for Doncaster Rovers. Three were with the club at the same time. On Feb. 20, 1926, Joseph, Thomas and Harold Keetley appeared together in the Rovers' forward line v. Wigan Borough in Division III(N). At the end of the season Joseph Keetley left Doncaster Rovers, but another brother, Frank, came to the club from Derby County and he played in the same forward-line as Tom and Harold on more than one occasion during 1926-7.

Koerner. Brothers Albert (outside-left) and Robert (outside-right) appeared together for Austria in several internationals in the 1950s.

Milburn John, James and George Milburn, all brothers and full-backs, were together with Leeds United from Nov. 1935 until the summer of 1937.

Morgan. Twin brothers Ian and Roger each scored for Queen's Park Rangers in the same Football League games a number of times in the 1960s.

Nordhal. The brothers Knut, Bertil and Gunnar won Olympic Gold Medals with the Swedish team in 1948.

O'Donnell. The brothers Frank and Hugh O'Donnell played together with the following clubs: St. Agatha School, Leven, Fifeshire. Denbeath Violet, Wellesley Juniors, Celtic, Preston North End, Blackpool, and Heart of Midlothian.

O'Flanagan. Dr. Kevin and his brother, Michael O'Flanagan played outside-right and centre-forward, respectively, for Eire v. England, Dublin, Sep. 30, 1946.

Perry. Five Perry brothers played for West Bromwich Albion in the 80's and 90's; Charles, Edward, Thomas, Walter and William.

Pyper. Brothers James and John of Cliftonville appeared in same Irish team v. Scotland and Wales, 1897, and v. England, 1900.

Rawson. Brothers Herbert and William of Old Westminsters appeared for England v. Scotland in 1875.

Shaw. David Shaw (Hibernian) and brother Jack Shaw (Rangers), right and left-back respectively, played together for Scotland v. England and v. Switzerland in 1946.

Stephens. On Sept. 21, 1946, Swindon Town defeated Exeter City 2—0 in the Third Division (S). The Stephens twins, Alfred and William, each scored a goal, the first time that twins scored in the same Football League game (see also Morgan).

Topham. The brothers Arthur and Robert of the Corinthians played for England v. Wales in 1894.

Sulon. Gerald and Albert Sulon are twin brothers who have appeared together in the Belgium National team.

Wallbanks. Five Wallbanks brothers were professionals with Football League clubs: John Wallbanks with Barnsley, Chester and Bradford, 1929-35, Frederick with Bradford City, West Ham United and Nottingham Forest, 1932-6, Harold with Fulham, 1946-8, James with Barnsley, Northampton Town, Portsmouth, Millwall and Reading, 1929-47, and Horace with Grimsby Town and Luton Town, 1946-8.

Walter. Fritz and Ottmar Walter are two brothers who have played alongside each other in several international games for Germany, they were inside-left and centre-forward respectively in the German side that won the World Cup in 1954.

Walters. The brothers A. M. and P. M. Walters (Old Carthusians) right and left-back respectively, played together for England in nine international matches in the 1880s.

Two pairs of brothers in the same Football League side is a record:

Charles and Tom Perry, Ezra and Jack Horton for West Bromwich Albion, Division I, 1890-91. Frank and Fred Forman, Arthur and Adrian Capes for Nottingham Forest, Division I, 1896-7. Samuel and John Tonner, Thomas and Owen Williams, for Clapton Orient, Division II, 1921-2 and 1922-3. Peter and John Butler, Antony and Peter Bircumshaw for Notts County, Division III, 1961-2. Cyril and Gilbert Beech or Cliff and Bryn Jones with Ivor and Len Allchurch, Swansea Town, 1953-4. Ray and Pat Brady, Roger and Ian Morgan, Queen's Park Rangers, Division III, 1964-5.

Swansea Town had four pairs of brothers on their books as professionals during 1953-4, for in addition to those mentioned above they also had the brothers Colin and Alan Hole.

**Father and Son**

Two pairs of father and son have won F.A. Cup medals with the same club: Thomas Boyle and Harold Johnson won medals with Sheffield United in 1925; their fathers, Peter Boyle and Harold Johnson sen., won medals with the same club in 1899 and 1902. Another son, Thomas Johnson, was Sheffield United's centre-half in the side beaten by Arsenal in the Final of 1936.

On the same day in April 1936, Harold Wait was Walsall's first-team goalkeeper, while his son, H. C. Wait, was Walsall's reserve team goalkeeper.

It is believed that there have been only three instances in first-class football of father and son playing together in the same club side. The first pair are J. and W. Butler who appeared together for Grimsby Town during season 1916-17. The second pair are Alec and David Herd who played inside-right and inside-left respectively for Stockport County v. Hartlepools United at Edgley Park in the last Third Division (N) game of the 1950-51 season (May 5, 1951). And in the Irish League during 1954-5 George Eastham and his son, also George, appeared regularly as the inside-forwards of Ards.

**FAST SCORING**

See under GOAL-SCORING (Individuals) Fast Scoring, GOAL-SCORING (Teams). All scored.

**FATALITIES**

See CASUALTIES and DISASTERS.

**FEDERATION INTERNATIONALE DE FOOTBALL ASSOCIATION**

In 1973 there are over 140 National Associations in membership of F.I.F.A. This body was formed in 1904 for the better control of the game on an international basis; to see that it is played in all countries under the same code of rules, and to organise an international Cup competition.

Belgium, France, Switzerland and the Netherlands originated the idea of the federation. Together with Sweden and Spain they held an inaugural meeting in Paris on May 21, 1904.

The F.A. (of England) had previously suggested that some such meeting should be held—in London—to discuss the better control of international relations. This invitation was apparently ignored and the F.A. was not represented at a meeting of the new federation until June 1906, when Mr. D. B. Woolfall of Lancashire, Honorary Treasurer of the F.A., was elected President of F.I.F.A.

In 1913, F.I.F.A. was given representation on the International Football Association Board.

An article of the Federation states that only one representative association from each country can hold membership with F.I.F.A. Therefore, in 1908, membership was refused to the Amateur Football Association and even the Associations of Ireland and Scotland. It was considered that these two national associations were subsidiaries of the English F.A.

Scotland, Ireland and Wales were, however, admitted in 1910. The F.A. of Ireland (Eire) followed in 1923.

The United Kingdom associations have twice since ceased membership of the Federation.

After World War I, the United Kingdom associations, Belgium, France and Luxembourg, refused to be associated with Austria, Germany or Hungary. It was suggested that they should form a separate federation. Neutral countries such as Denmark and Norway were opposed to this and eventually the trouble was satisfactorily ironed out. The U.K. associations returned to F.I.F.A. in 1924.

The second withdrawal took place in 1928, following disagreement over the Federation's definition of amateurism and, more particularly, the question of broken time payments. This time the U.K. associations remained outside the Federation until 1946.

One of the most important aspects of F.I.F.A. is its control over the movement of players from one member country to another. No player may transfer from a club in one country to a club in another country in the Federation without the permission of the Federation. This rule prevents the poaching of valuable players without agreement or the paying of transfer fees.

The executive committee of F.I.F.A. consists of a President elected by Congress (since Sept. 1961 Sir Stanley Rous C.B.E. has held this post), eight vice-presidents and twelve members, each nominated by different associations or groups of associations.

The headquarters of F.I.F.A. is at 11, Hitzigweg, Zurich 8032, Switzerland.

Results of games with England:
Oct. 26, 1938    England 3, F.I.F.A. 0; Highbury
Oct. 21, 1953    England 4, F.I.F.A. 4; Wembley
Oct. 23, 1963    England 2, F.I.F.A. 1; Wembley

# FINES
See also SUSPENSION.

Liverpool was fined £7,500 by the Football League for failing to field a full strength team v. Manchester City in April 1971. For a similar offence Leeds United was fined £5,000 in May 1970, while Everton was fined £2,000 in 1966.

Derby County was fined £10,000 in April 1970 and banned from Europe for a year following allegations of irregularities in their books. Manchester United was fined £7,000 in July 1969 after similar allegations, while Leyton Orient was fined £2,000 in 1857-8.

In October 1970 Birmingham City was fined £5,000 for employing W. J. Bell as a coach while he was still registered as a profeessional with Brighton and Hove Albion.

In Nov. 1967 Peterborough United was fined £500 and demoted from the Third Division for alleged irregularities, and in 1968 Port Vale was fined £4,000 and expelled from the League for alleged breaches of regulations but the club was re-elected the following season.

Another club accused of playing a weak team in the Football League is Burnley. In Mar. 1961 this club was fined £1,000 following a game with Chelsea in which they included 10 of their reserves. Despite this they drew the game 4—4.

Tottenham Hotspur was fined £350 after their home F.A. Cup tie with Astton Villa (1903-4) had to be abandoned because the crowd had invaded the pitch. The Villa was leading 1—0 at the time, but Spurs won the replay which the F.A. ordered to be played at Villa Park.

Liverpool was fined £250 in Aug. 1911 for poaching R. R. Pursell, full-back, from Queen's Park. A director of Liverpool was also suspended for two years.

Stockport County was fined £125 and two points were deducted from its record for playing J. (Joe) Smith, whose transfer had been secured from Bolton Wanderers on Mar. 16, 1927, without permission.

Sunderland was fined £50 and two points deducted from its record for playing J. Doig, Scottish international goalkeeper, in a Football League match against West Bromwich Albion on Sept. 20, 1890, before the player had completed the qualifying period of 14 days registration—the rule at that time.

In April 1957, a joint commission of the F.A. and the Football League fined Sunderland £5,000 and ordered the club to pay the expenses of an inquiry. The commission found the club guilty of making illegal payments contrary to the regulations of the Football League.

# FINLAND
Football in Finland is amateur, and due largely to the climate and the lack of suitable pitches the game has been slow to develop since its was first introduced by Englishmen in 1890.

As will be seen below, Finland was resoundingly beaten in her first game with England's full international team, all five England forwards scoring in an eight goal victory.

Their F.A. was formed in 1907 and its membership today is just over 600 clubs. The address: Suomen Pallo Liitto-Finlands Bollförbund, Stadion, 00250 Helsinki 25. Colours: White shirts, blue shorts, white stockings.

Results of international matches:

| | | |
|---|---|---|
| May 20, 1937 | Finland 0, England 8; Helsingfors |
| Sept. 8, 1949* | Eire 3, Finland 0; Dublin |
| Oct. 9, 1949* | Finland 1, Eire 1; Helsinki |
| May 25, 1954 | Finland 1, Scotland 2; Helsinki |
| May 20, 1956 | Finland 1, England 5; Helsinki |
| Oct. 21, 1964* | Scotland 3, Finland 1; Glasgow |
| May 27, 1965* | Finland 1, Scotland 2; Helsinki |
| June 26, 1966 | Finland 0, England 3; Helsinki |
| May 26, 1971† | Finland 0, Wales 1; Helsinki |
| Oct. 13, 1971† | Wales 3, Finland 0; Swansea |

\* World Cup
† European Championship

# FINNEY, Thomas, O.B.E. (1922-    )
Elected "Footballer of the Year" twice (1953-4 and 1956-7), a regular international for 12 years, over 600 games in first-class football, and generally acknowledged as one of the best wingers of the immediate post-war era, it is an astonishing fact that this brilliant footballer cannot number either a League Championship medal or an F.A. Cup winners medal among his trophies.

Tom Finney first joined Preston North

End as an amateur in 1937, signed professional in 1940, and remained with the club until a persistent groin injury forced him to retire in 1960 when still a regular first-team player and their top scorer. Played mostly at outside-right but switched to centre-forward late in his career. Born Preston.

Preston North End 1946-60, 433 apps. (187 goals). England internationals 76. Inter-League games 17. England "B" games 2. F.A. Cup runners-up 1954.

## FIXTURES

For many years after the formation of the Football League the arrangement of fixtures was left in the hands of the clubs, but as the numbers increased it became evident that some master plan for the compilation of a fixture list would have to be adopted and this work was subsequently brought to a fine art by Mr. Charles Sutcliffe who produced the League's list for many years. Today the fixtures are produced with the aid of a computer.

For five seasons after World War I it was the practice for clubs to play each other both at home and away in successive matches. But this system was abandoned, because it presented many difficulties, such as clashes of the home fixtures of neighbouring clubs and the travelling of long distances during the Christmas and Easter holidays.

Clubs are given the opportunity of appealing against the arrangement of their fixtures at the League's annual fixture meeting. Any disputes are then referred to the Management Committee. Any club in the Football League which fails to carry out a fixture on the allotted day without good reason is liable to expulsion from the League and/or such other punishment as the Management Committee may determine.

See also under BETTING and MATCHES.

## FLOODLIT FOOTBALL

The first-ever game by floodlight took place at Bramall Lane, Sheffield, Oct. 14, 1878. The teams taking part were chosen by Sheffield Association from local clubs. The game attracted a great deal of attention for electric light was still something of a novelty in the provinces. The official attendance was given as 12,000, but it was estimated that at least another 7,000 gained admission without paying. Bearing in mind the fact that the F.A. Cup Final in 1878 attracted only 5,000 people, it will be appreciated that a crowd of nearly 20,000 was quite extraordinary. The lighting itself was considered to be a great success. The electric power was generated on the ground by two portable engines—one behind each goal—driving Siemens dynamos. The lamps—one in each corner of the ground—were erected on wooden towers, 30 ft. high. The power of each lamp was 8,000 standard candles.

The result of the match was a 2—0 victory for the team captained by W. E. Clegg, an England international, later Sir William Clegg and Lord Mayor of Sheffield. The losing side was captained by his brother, J. C. Clegg, also an England international, and who later became Sir Charles Clegg, President of the F.A.

Birmingham was beaten by only two weeks for the distinction of staging the first floodlit football match. At the Lower Aston Grounds, Aston, on Oct. 28, 1878, a Birmingham representative side beat Nottingham Forest 2—1, and the illumination was provided by 12 electric lights spaced out around the pitch.

Unfortunately, this was only a partial success, as wind and rain interfered with the lights and there were a number of stoppages while the breakdowns were put right.

A week later football by floodlight was played in London. At Kennington Oval on Nov. 4, 1878, the Wanderers met Clapham Rovers under lights. But, according to Press reports, this match was not as successful as the Sheffield match.

I am indebted to the Editor of *Sport and Country* for the following quotations which appeared in its forerunner, *Illustrated Sporting and Dramatic News* during Nov. 1878.

"The result of the light, as applied to the purpose of steadily illuminating so large a field was not, as arranged on this occasion, satisfactory . . . Although in itself wonderfully powerful, pure and brilliant, the light was in this case to be tested in its management rather than in itself, and remembering that the attempt was of necessity an experiment, its comparative failure, is no very important matter. Besides who wants to play football by artificial light? As a novelty, now and then, or to attract wandering shillings after dark, it may be all very well, but for the real purpose of the game daylight is quite good enough and long enough."

In 1887 the F.A. gave permission for two floodlit games to be played in Sheffield and another early floodlit game took place at Belle Vue Gardens, Manchester, Feb. 26, 1889. On this occasion the illumination was not supplied by electricity but by Wells lights (naphtha flares with air pressure forcing the oil to the burners). The game, which was staged in aid of the Hyde Colliery Explosion Fund, was between Ardwick (later Manchester City) and Newton Heath (later Manchester United). A profit of £140 was made.

Floodlit football under more modern conditions became popular about 1929, but the F.A. refused to give its sanction. In Aug. 1930 the F.A. passed a resolution prohibiting clubs in membership from taking part in such games.

Thereafter, certain charity matches were played under lights but the resolution was not rescinded until Dec. 1950, but this was followed by the adoption of a motion, in Jan. 1951, which stated that NO competitive matches were to be played under artificial light without permission of the F.A. or the County Association and the Competition concerned.

The first competitive fixture to be played under floodlights in Great Britain was Southampton v. Tottenham Hotspur in a Football Combination "B" match at The Dell, Oct. 1,1951.

Although progress was slow or almost nil between 1878 and 1955, tremendous strides forward in the acceptance of floodlit football in Britain were taken in 1955 and 1956. Both the F.A. and the Football League were forced to accord more official recognition to this branch of the game. The first step towards general recognition of competition football under floodlights was made in Feb. 1955 when the F.A. decided that, as from season 1955-6, replays of F.A. Cup-ties, up to an including the Second Round, might be played under lights.

The first F.A. Cup replay to be so played was between Kidderminster Harriers and Brierley Hill Alliance, Preliminary Round, Sept. 14, 1955. The first F.A. Cup replay between Football League clubs was between Carlisle United and Darlington, 1st Round (2nd replay), at Newcastle, Nov. 28, 1955.

The next official move was made by the Football League at its annual meeting in June 1955, when it adopted a Sunderland proposal that postponed League games might be played by floodlight if both clubs agreed. The first Football League game to be played under lights was between Portsmouth and Newcastle United, at Fratton Park, Feb. 22, 1956.

A further relaxation of the ban on floodlight competition games was made by the F.A. in Dec. 1955 when it decided that 3rd Round F.A. Cup-ties, due to be played on Jan. 7, might be played under lights, or might be started in daylight and lights turned on during the game if necessary. On Jan. 7, 1956, lights were turned on during the following 3rd Round ties: Arsenal v. Bedford Town, Portsmouth v. Grimsby Town, Sheffield Wednesday v. Newcastle United, Tottenham Hotspur v. Boston United, and West Ham United v. Preston North End.

The England international side had already played under floodlights abroad in a match against the United States in New York on June 8, 1953. The first international match in England of which any part was played under lights was England v. Spain, at Wembley, Nov. 30, 1955. The lights were turned on as fog reduced visibility towards the end of this game.

The introduction of floodlights to so many grounds brought an increase in matches and following disputes over payment for these the Players' Union decided to ban all floodlight games, the ban to come into force on Mar. 13, 1956. But two days before the date, the ban was lifted when the League promised to consider the Union's demands.

In June 1956 Floodlit football really came into its own when it got the blessing of the Football League at their annual meeting. It was decided that floodlit League games would be permitted providing that both clubs agree. At the same time it was also agreed that a payment of from £2 to £3 could be made to each player taking part in games extra to normal League and Cup fixtures.

It was at their annual meeting in June 1958, that the Football League made the final move which freed floodlit games from any conditions apart from the obvious one that the lights should be up to a certain standard. At this meeting they decided that it would not be necessary for both clubs to agree before a game could be played under lights.

The first Scottish F.A. Cup ties to be played under floodlights were Hibernian v. Raith Rovers, and East Fife v. Stenhousemuir, Feb. 8, 1956.

## FOOTBALL, The Game
See TACTICS and TEAM EVOLUTION. See also OFFSIDE.

## FOOTBALL ASSOCIATION, THE
The Football Association is the ruling body of the game in England. As the father of all Football Associations, its influence is felt all over the world where soccer is played.

The F.A. is made up of 87 affiliated units which include 43 English County Associations, the three Services, and the various Commonwealth countries and Protectorates overseas. The major competition in England, the Football League, is an important member of the F.A. Since 1929, it has been allowed a say in the Association's affairs by having eight of its representatives sitting on the F.A. Council which controls the work of the Association.

At one time, in the early part of the century, certain foreign countries were also in membership with the F.A. The Californian Association, and the Associations of America, Argentina and Chile were among them. Subsequently they withdrew to become members of F.I.F.A. In addition to the Associations which are members of the F.A. there are also 254 clubs in full membership, plus another 115 associate members. These associate members may qualify for full membership after a period of five years and provided certain other stipulations are complied with.

All footballers in this country who play for recognised clubs must be registered with the F.A. in addition to any registration they may have to make with local leagues or competitions.

The F.A. has been a Limited Company since 1903. This is a formality to provide certain protection for its members and does not mean that it is a profit-making business concern. None of the shareholders is entitled to receive any bonus or dividends or any profit from membership. The whole of the profits is ploughed back into the game.

The F.A. is a democratic body governed by a Council which is freely elected by its members. In addition to the officers of the Association the Council includes 10 Divisional Representatives from all parts of the country; about 50 County, Service, University, English and Public School representatives, as well as those of the Football League and the Associations of Australia, New Zealand, Canada, the British West Indies and Guyana.

### The Beginning

The original meeting convened to discuss the formation of a football association took place at the Freemason's Tavern, Great Queen Street, London, on Oct. 26, 1863. Apart from a number of independent persons interested in the scheme, the following clubs were represented at this meeting: Barnes, Blackheath, Charterhouse, Perceval House (Blackheath), Kensington School, War Office, Crystal Palace, Blackheath Proprietary School, The Crusaders, Forest (Epping Forest), No Names' (Kilburn).

It had been hoped that a larger number of the public schools, which were the most important centres of football at that time, would join the Association so that a uniform code of Charterhouse and Westminster, rules could be drawn up, but Harrow decided, for the time being, to retain their

independence and their own rules.

There was a considerable difference of opinion among the original members as to the laws of the game. These were not passed until the fifth meeting. (See LAWS OF THE GAME). Shortly after the laws were published, Blackheath withdrew from membership mainly because they resented the rule banning hacking. Their withdrawal marks the separation of Rugby from Soccer. (See RUGBY).

The original rules adopted by the F.A. were brief and to the point:

1. That the Association be called "The Football Association."

2. That all clubs of one year's standing be eligible for membership.

3. That the subscription for each club be 5s. per annum payable in advance.

4. That the officers be a president, a treasurer, a secretary, with a committee comprising the before-mentioned officers and four other members.

5. That the officers be elected at the annual meeting by the majority of the representatives of clubs present, the retiring officers to be eligible for re-election.

6. That the general meetings be held in the month of February.

7. That each club be entitled to send two representatives to all meetings of the Association.

8. That in the event of any alteration being deemed necessary in the rules or the laws established by the Association, notice shall be sent in writing to the secretary of the proposed alteration on or before the 1st of February in each year; and the terms of the proposed alteration shall be advertised in such sporting newspapers as the committee may direct, at least 14 days prior to the annual meeting.

9. That each club shall forward to the secretary a statement of its distinguishing colours and costumes.

The biggest controversy over the Laws, apart from the abolition of hacking, concerned the "strict offside" rule, and it was not until this was altered in 1867 that the rules were more generally accepted.

In 1870 members of the Association numbered 39:

Amateur Athletic Club, Barnes, Brixton, Bramham College (York), Clapham Rovers, Cowley School (Oxford), Crystal Palace, Donington Grammar School (Lincoln), 21st Essex R.V., Forest School, Garrick (Sheffield), Hampstead Heathens, Harrow Pilgrims, Hitchin, Holt (Wilts.), Hull College, Kensington School, Leamington College, Lincoln, London Scottish R.V., C.C.C. (Clapham), Charterhouse School, Chesterfield, Civil Service, London

Athletic Club, Milford College, No Names' (Kilburn), Newark, Nottingham, Oxford University, Royal Engineers (Chatham), Reigate, Sheffield, Totteridge Park (Herts), Upton Park, Wanderers, Westminster School, West Brompton College, Worlabye House (Roehampton).

The move which probably did most to broaden the outlook of the F.A. and spread its influence over a greater field was made on July 20, 1871 when it was proposed that a Challenge Cup be established for competition among its members. (See FOOTBALL ASSOCIATION CHALLENGE CUP.)

After this membership increased by leaps and bounds, until in 1881 clubs and associations under the wing of the F.A. numbered 128.

Professionalism entered the game around 1881. At first the F.A. was definitely opposed to the payment of players, maintaining a strictly amateur outlook. Its attitude caused many upsets in its relations with other bodies, especially with the Football League, and the authority of the F.A. remained in the balance for a number of years until it decided to legalise professionalism in July 1885. (SEE PROFESSIONALISM.)

In April 1887, the rules of the Association were revised and the Association was re-constituted so as to be governed by a Council consisting originally of six officers.

As already mentioned, the F.A. became a Limited Company in 1903. The share capital consists of £100 in 2,000 shares of five pence each.

In 1907, certain amateur clubs and associations affiliated to the F.A. objected to a new ruling insisting that all associations must permit all clubs, professional or amateur to become members. The amateurs felt that the F.A. was now becoming too professional in its outlook. They decided to break away and form their own governing body, the Amateur Football Association. (See AMATEUR FOOTBALL ALLIANCE). It was not until 1914 that this new body agreed to recognise the authority of the Football Association.

The one important quarrel that the F.A. had with bodies outside the F.A. concerned the question of "broken time" payments to amateurs. The F.A.'s definition of amateurism has always been a much stricter one than that of the *foreign* members of F.I.F.A. And, in 1928, the British Associations withdrew from membership of F.I.F.A. on this account and did not return until 1946.

The F.A. functions to see that wherever football is played in this country and in the Commonwealth, it is played according to the Laws of the Game, and is controlled in an orderly and organised fashion. It protects the rights of the player, the club, the authority of the Football Association.

To deal with all the many aspects of the game the F.A. has a number of committees. Some deal with disciplinary matters, others deal with the competitions which are the immediate concern of the F.A. (i.e. the Challenge Cup, the Amateur Cup Challenge Trophy, the Youth Cup, County Youth Cup, and the Sunday Cup). There is a committee which concerns itself with the rules and regulations governing the game. Another takes care of the organisation and expansion of youth football. One of the most important committees is the international committee which deals with the arrangements for international matches.

**F.A. Headquarters**

The headquarters of the Football Association were originally in Holborn Viaduct. In 1890 the Association moved to 61, Chancery Lane. 1902 found it at 104, High Holborn, and in 1910 its address was 42, Russell Square.

The next move was in 1929 to 22 Lancaster Gate, and the most recent was only a short one made in 1972 to 16 Lancaster Gate, London, W2 3LW. Colours: White shirts, navy blue shorts, white stockings.

**FOOTBALL ASSOCIATION AMATEUR CHALLENGE CUP**

See also CUP MEDALS.

The Amateur Cup was inaugurated in 1893. In its earliest years it did not meet with the wholehearted support and approval of many of the leading amateur clubs who resented the fact that such a competition should come under the control of the F.A., an organisation which many amateurs at that time believed to have a bias towards professional football.

The rules have been tightened since those days and the competition is now governed by an all-amateur committee. Whereas, in its early days, the competition included former professional players who had been re-instated as amateurs, this is no longer permitted.

The only club to win both the F.A. Cup and the F.A. Amateur Cup was Old Carthusians. They defeated Old Etonians, 3—0, to win the F.A. Cup in 1881, and won the F.A. Amateur Cup on two occasions, v. Casuals, 2—1, in 1894, and v. Stockton, 4—1 (after draw 1—1), in 1897.

The only former professional player to secure an F.A. Amateur Cup winner's medal after gaining a winner's medal in the F.A. Cup competition was R. Chatt. In 1895 he was inside-right in the Aston Villa team which defeated West Bromwich Albion, 1—0. Later, when he was reinstated as an amateur, he appeared in the Stockton team which won the Amateur Cup Final of 1899, beating Harwich and Parkeston, 1—0.

Approximately 400 clubs enter for the F.A. Amateur Cup. The competition is open to all wholly amateur clubs who are members or affiliated members of the F.A. or are playing in a senior competition as members of an Association affiliated to the F.A. The closing date for entries each year is June 1.

The clubs which have won this competition the most times in the 70 seasons to 1973 are: Bishop Auckland 10, Clapton 5, Crook Town 5, Dulwich Hamlet 4, Stockton 3, Leytonstone 3 and Bromley 3.

Bishop Auckland won the trophy three times in succession 1955-6-7, the only club to perform this feat.

## FOOTBALL ASSOCIATION CHALLENGE CUP

At a meeting held in the offices of the *Sportsman*, London July 20, 1871, a proposal by C. W. Alcock (Hon. Sec. of The F.A. and of the Wanderers F.C.) 'That it is desirable that a Challenge Cup should be established in connection with the Association, for which all clubs belonging to the Association should be invited to compete' met with favour and was finally approved at a subsequent meeting on October 16, 1871.

### Amateurs

Only three amateurs have gained F.A. Cup winners medals this century:

S. B. Ashworth. left-half, Manchester City, 1904; H. P. Hardman, outside-left, Everton, 1906; Rev. K. R. G. Hunt, right-half, Wolverhampton Wanderers, 1908.

In the same period the following amateurs have appeared in an F.A. Cup Final on the losing side:

C. B. Fry, r.b., Southampton, 1902. D. Davies, g., Bolton Wanderers, 1904. H. P. Hardman, o.l., Everton, 1907 (also a winners medal 1906). J. F. Mitchell, g., Preston North End, 1922. Dr. V. E. Milne, c.h., Aston Villa, 1924. A. Turner, c.f., Charlton Athletic, 1946. F. P. Kippax, o.l., Burnley, 1947. W. J. Slater, i.l., Blackpool, 1951.

### Appearances

See PLAYERS in this section, TRANSFERS (F.A. Cup), and CUP MEDALS.

### The Cup

The present trophy is the third to be played for in the history of the competition. It was made for the F.A. early in 1911 by Messrs.

Fattorini and Sons of Bradford. In its first year it returned to Bradford after Bradford City beat Newcastle United in the Cup Final. The cost of this trophy was 50 gns. It weighs 175 oz., and stands 19 in. high, exclusive of the ebony plinth which has a silver band around it upon which are inscribed the names of the winners.

The original trophy, which was much smaller and cost about £20, was made early in 1872 by Messrs. Martin, Hall & Co. In 1895, after Aston Villa had won the competition, the cup was stolen from the window of a firm of football outfitters in Newton Row, Birmingham, where it had been placed on display. It was never recovered, and Aston Villa were fined £25 by the F.A.

A second trophy was ordered by the F.A. to be an exact replica of the original. This was possible because of the existence of silver replicas of the trophy which had been presented to Wolverhampton Wanderers, the winners of 1893, by the club's chairman. This second trophy was the work of Messrs. Vaughtons Ltd. It was retained for competition until 1910, when, prompted by the fact that the design had been duplicated for another competition, the F.A. withdrew it and presented it to Lord Kinnaird, as a token of respect, on his completing 21 years as President of the F.A.

### Extra Time

According to the rules of the competition an extra half-hour may be played in all ties before the semi-final round, if, after 90 minutes, the result is a draw.

However, except during the earliest seasons of the competition and the first four seasons after World War II, an extra half-hour has rarely been played in the first meeting between competing clubs. If a replay ends in a draw then the two sides are compelled by the rules to play the extra half-hour. This rule was introduced by the F.A. Council in 1896.

In the semi-finals, an extra half-hour must be played in a replayed match ending in a draw. The rule (introduced in 1912) calling for an extra half an hour if necessary in the final tie was revoked in 1973. Extra time has been played in the following finals:
1919-20—
Aston Villa 1, Huddersfield Town 0
1937-8—
Preston North End 1, Huddersfield Town 0
1945-6—
Derby County 4, Charlton Athletic 1
1946-7—
Charlton Athletic 1, Burnley 0
1964-5—
Liverpool 2, Leeds United 1

1967-8—                                        Chelsea 2, Leeds United 1.
  West Bromwich Albion 1, Everton 0     1970-71—
1969-70—                                      Arsenal 2, Liverpool 1
  Chelsea 2, Leeds United 2, and replay—

## The Finals

| | | | Score | Attendance | Receipts |
|---|---|---|---|---|---|
| 1872 | Wanderers | beat Royal Engineers | 1–0 | 2,000 | |
| 1873 | Wanderers | beat Oxford University | 2–0 | 3,000 | |
| 1874 | Oxford University | beat Royal Engineers | 2–0 | 2,000 | |
| 1875 | Royal Engineers | beat Old Etonians | 2–0 | 3,000 | |
| | | (replay, after draw 1–1) | | | |
| 1876 | Wanderers | beat Old Etonians | 3–0 | 3,500 | |
| | | (replay, after draw 0–0) | | | |
| 1877 | Wanderers | beat Oxford University | *2–0 | 3,000 | |
| 1878 | Wanderers | beat Royal Engineers | 3–1 | 4,500 | |
| 1879 | Old Etonians | beat Clapham Rovers | 1–0 | 5,000 | |
| 1880 | Clapham Rovers | beat Oxford University | 1–0 | 6,000 | |
| 1881 | Old Carthusians | beat Old Etonians | 3–0 | 4,500 | |
| 1882 | Old Etonians | beat Blackburn Rovers | 1–0 | 6,500 | |
| 1883 | Blackburn Olympic | beat Old Etonians | *2–1 | 8,000 | |
| 1884 | Blackburn Rovers | beat Queen's Park (Glasgow) | 2–1 | 4,000 | |
| 1885 | Blackburn Rovers | beat Queen's Park (Glasgow) | 2–0 | 12,500 | £442 |
| 1886 | Blackburn Rovers | beat West Bromwich Albion | 2–0 | 15,000 | |
| | | (replay, after draw 0–0) | | | |
| 1887 | Aston Villa | beat West Bromwich Albion | 2–0 | 15,500 | |
| 1888 | West Bromwich Albion | beat Preston North End | 2–1 | 19,000 | |
| 1889 | Preston North End | beat Wolverhampton Wanderers | 3–0 | 22,000 | |
| 1890 | Blackburn Rovers | beat Sheffield Wednesday | 6–1 | 20,000 | |
| 1891 | Blackburn Rovers | beat Notts County | 3–1 | 23,000 | £1,454 |
| 1892 | West Bromwich Albion | beat Aston Villa | 3–0 | 25,000 | £1,757 |
| 1893 | Wolverhampton Wanderers | beat Everton | 1–0 | 45,000 | £2,559 |
| 1894 | Notts County | beat Bolton Wanderers | 4–1 | 37,000 | £1,189 |
| 1895 | Aston Villa | beat West Bromwich Albion | 1–0 | 42,560 | £1,545 |
| 1896 | Sheffield Wednesday | beat Wolverhampton Wanderers | 2–1 | 48,836 | £1,824 |
| 1897 | Aston Villa | beat Everton | 3–2 | 65,891 | £2,162 |
| 1898 | Nottingham Forest | beat Derby County | 3–1 | 62,017 | £2,312 |
| 1899 | Sheffield United | beat Derby County | 4–1 | 73,833 | £2,747 |
| 1900 | Bury | beat Southampton | 4–0 | 68,945 | £2,587 |
| 1901 | Tottenham Hotspur | beat Sheffield United | 3–1 | 110,820‡ | £3,998 |
| | | (replay, after draw 2–2) | | | |
| 1902 | Sheffield United | beat Southampton | 2–1 | 76,914 | £2,895 |
| | | (replay, after draw 1–1) | | | |
| 1903 | Bury | beat Derby County | 6–0 | 63,102 | £2,470 |
| 1904 | Manchester City | beat Bolton Wanderers | 1–0 | 61,374 | £3,000 |
| 1905 | Aston Villa | beat Newcastle United | 2–0 | 101,117 | £7,785 |
| 1906 | Everton | beat Newcastle United | 1–0 | 75,609 | £6,625 |
| 1907 | Sheffield Wednesday | beat Everton | 2–1 | 84,584 | £7,053 |
| 1908 | Wolverhampton Wanderers | beat Newcastle United | 3–1 | 74,967 | £5,988 |
| 1909 | Manchester United | beat Bristol City | 1–0 | 71,401 | £6,434 |
| 1910 | Newcastle United | beat Barnsley | 2–0 | 77,747‡ | £6,898 |
| | | (replay, after draw 1–1) | | | |
| 1911 | Bradford City | beat Newcastle United | 1–0 | 69,098‡ | £6,512 |
| | | (replay, after draw 0–0) | | | |

| 1912 | Barnsley | beat West Bromwich Albion | †1–0 | 54,556‡ | £6,057 |
|------|----------|---------------------------|------|---------|--------|
| | | (replay, after draw 0–0) | | | |
| 1913 | Aston Villa | beat Sunderland | 1–0 | 120,081 | £9,406 |
| 1914 | Burnley | beat Liverpool | 1–0 | 72,778 | £6,687 |
| 1915 | Sheffield United | beat Chelsea | 3–0 | 49,557 | £4,052 |
| 1920 | Aston Villa | beat Huddersfield Town | *1–0 | 50,018 | £9,722 |
| 1921 | Tottenham Hotspur | beat Wolverhampton Wanderers | 1–0 | 72,805 | £13,414 |
| 1922 | Huddersfield Town | beat Preston North End | 1–0 | 53,000 | £10,551 |
| 1923 | Bolton Wanderers | beat West Ham United | 2–0 | 126,047 | £27,776 |
| 1924 | Newcastle United | beat Aston Villa | 2–0 | 91,695 | £14,280 |
| 1925 | Sheffield United | beat Cardiff City | 1–0 | 91,763 | £15,941 |
| 1926 | Bolton Wanderers | beat Manchester City | 1–0 | 91,447 | £23,157 |
| 1927 | Cardiff City | beat Arsenal | 1–0 | 91,206 | £23,113 |
| 1928 | Blackburn Rovers | beat Huddersfield Town | 3–1 | 92,041 | £23,238 |
| 1929 | Bolton Wanderers | beat Portsmouth | 2–0 | 92,576 | £23,400 |
| 1930 | Arsenal | beat Huddersfield Town | 2–0 | 92,488 | £26,265 |
| 1931 | West Bromwich Albion | beat Birmingham | 2–1 | 92,406 | £23,366 |
| 1932 | Newcastle United | beat Arsenal | 2–1 | 92,298 | £24,688 |
| 1933 | Everton | beat Manchester City | 3–0 | 92,950 | £24,831 |
| 1934 | Manchester City | beat Portsmouth | 2–1 | 93,258 | £24,950 |
| 1935 | Sheffield Wednesday | beat West Bromwich Albion | 4–2 | 93,204 | £24,856 |
| 1936 | Arsenal | beat Sheffield United | 1–0 | 93,384 | £24,857 |
| 1937 | Sunderland | beat Preston North End | 3–1 | 93,495 | £24,831 |
| 1938 | Preston North End | beat Huddersfield Town | *1–0 | 93,357 | £25,723 |
| 1939 | Portsmouth | beat Wolverhampton Wanderers | 4–1 | 99,370 | £29,116 |
| 1946 | Derby County | beat Charlton Athletic | *4–1 | 98,215 | £45,000 |
| 1947 | Charlton Athletic | beat Burnley | *1–0 | 99,000 | £39,500 |
| 1948 | Manchester United | beat Blackpool | 4–2 | 99,000 | £39,500 |
| 1949 | Wolverhampton Wanderers | beat Leicester City | 3–1 | 99,500 | £39,300 |
| 1950 | Arsenal | beat Liverpool | 2–0 | 100,000 | £39,296 |
| 1951 | Newcastle United | beat Blackpool | 2–0 | 100,000 | £39,336 |
| 1952 | Newcastle United | beat Arsenal | 1–0 | 100,000 | £39,351 |
| 1953 | Blackpool | beat Bolton Wanderers | 4–3 | 100,000 | £49,900 |
| 1954 | West Bromwich Albion | beat Preston North End | 3–2 | 100,000 | £49,883 |
| 1955 | Newcastle United | beat Manchester City | 3–1 | 100,000 | £49,881 |
| 1956 | Manchester City | beat Birmingham City | 3–1 | 100,000 | £49,856 |
| 1957 | Aston Villa | beat Manchester United | 2–1 | 100,000 | £48,816 |
| 1958 | Bolton Wanderers | beat Manchester United | 2–0 | 100,000 | £49,706 |
| 1959 | Nottingham Forest | beat Luton Town | 2–1 | 100,000 | £49,708 |
| 1960 | Wolverhampton Wanderers | beat Blackburn Rovers | 3–0 | 100,000 | £49,816 |
| 1961 | Tottenham Hotspur | beat Leicester City | 2–0 | 100,000 | £49,813 |
| 1962 | Tottenham Hotspur | beat Burnley | 3–1 | 100,000 | £53,837 |
| 1963 | Manchester United | beat Leicester City | 3–1 | 100,000 | £88,882 |
| 1964 | West Ham United | beat Preston North End | 3–2 | 100,000 | £89,289 |
| 1965 | Liverpool | beat Leeds United | *2–1 | 100,000 | £89,103 |
| 1966 | Everton | beat Sheffield Wednesday | 3–2 | 100,000 | £109,691 |
| 1967 | Tottenham Hotspur | beat Chelsea | 2–1 | 100,000 | £109,649 |
| 1968 | West Bromwich Albion | beat Everton | *1–0 | 100,000 | £110,064 |
| 1969 | Manchester City | beat Leicester City | 1–0 | 100,000 | £128,238 |
| 1970 | Chelsea | beat Leeds United | *2–1 | 100,000 | £128,272 |
| | | (replay, after draw *2–2) | | | |
| 1971 | Arsenal | beat Liverpool | *2–1 | 100,000 | £187,681 |
| 1972 | Leeds United | beat Arsenal | 1–0 | 100,000 | £191,917 |
| 1973 | Sunderland | beat Leeds United | 1–0 | 100,000 | £233,800 |

\* Extra half-hour played.     † Extra half-hour played in replay
‡ The attendance shown is that of the first game. The attendance at the replays were:
1886—12,000; 1901—20,470 (£1,621); 1902—33,068 (£1,625); 1910—69,000 (£4,149);
1911—58,000 (£4,478); 1912—38,555 (£2,612); 1970—62,078 (£88,495).

## The Finals (Venues)
1872, The Oval. 1873, Lillie Bridge, West Brompton. 1874-1892, The Oval. 1893, Fallowfield, Manchester. 1894, Everton. 1895-1914, Crystal Palace. 1915, Old Trafford, Manchester. 1920-22, Stamford Bridge. 1923 onward, Wembley Stadium.

## The Finals (Replay Venues)
1875 and 1876, The Oval. 1886, Derby. 1901, Bolton. 1902, Crystal Palace. 1910, Everton. 1911, Old Trafford, Manchester. 1912, Bramall Lane, Sheffield. 1970, Old Trafford, Manchester.

## The First
The first entrants for the F.A. Cup in season 1871-2 were Barnes, Civil Service, Crystal Palace, Clapham Rovers, Donington School (Spalding), Hampstead Heathens, Harrow Chequers, Hitchen, Maidenhead, Marlow, Queen's Park (Glasgow), Reigate Priory, Royal Engineers, Upton Park, and Wanderers.

Harrow Chequers, Reigate Priory and Donington School all scratched.

Wanderers, a team formed by ex-public school and university men, won the first season's competition by defeating Royal Engineers 1—0 in the final played at The Oval. The first Cup Final goal was scored by M. P. Betts who played under the assumed name of A. H. Chequer. He was an Old Harrovian who had once played for Harrow Chequers.

## Fourth Division
Only two clubs from the Fourth Division have reached the 6th Round—Oxford United, beaten 2—1 by Preston North End, 1963-4, and Colchester United, beaten 5—0 by Everton, 1970-71.

## General
In 1890-91 Birmingham were disqualified from the F.A. Cup for playing an ineligible player. In 1921-2 they missed the competition because they omitted to submit their entry form.

Sheffield Wednesday missed the competition in 1886-7 when they were too late with their entry.

Q.P.R. failed to send in their entry for season 1926-7.

In 1888-9 Sunderland withdrew from the competition when drawn to meet bitter rivals Sunderland Albion.

Both Charlton Athletic and Halifax Town withdrew in 1921-2.

There has never been a case of a club not turning up for the Cup Final, although this has happened in the Scottish Cup (q.v.).

The record number of times that the same clubs have met each other in consecutive seasons' cup-ties is four. Brighton and Hove Albion and Watford met in the F.A. Cup Competition in four consecutive seasons 1924-1928, and so did Manchester City and Leicester City 1965-1969.

In 1947-8 Manchester United were drawn in turn against six First Division clubs in the season's F.A. Cup competition, the first and only time this has happened to any club. The teams met were Aston Villa, Liverpool, Charlton Athletic, Preston North End, Derby County, and Blackpool. Manchester United beat Blackpool in the final, 4—2.

Since the formation of the Football League in 1888, all but six F.A. Cup winners have been First Division clubs. The six —Notts County (1894), Wolverhampton Wanderers (1908), Barnsley (1912), West Bromwich (1931), Sunderland (1973)—all of them Second Division sides—and Tottenham Hotspur, who were a Southern League club when they won the Cup in 1901.

## "Giant Killers"
First Division clubs knocked out by non-league clubs in the period since World War I:

1919-20 Sheffield Wednesday 0, Darlington (N.E.League) 2, (after 0—0 draw), 1st Round.

1923-4 Corinthians 1, Blackburn Rovers 0, 1st Round.

1947-8 Colchester United (Southern League) 1, Huddersfield Town 0.

1948-9 Yeovil Town (Southern League) 2, Sunderland 1.

1971-2 Hereford United (Southern League) 2, Newcastle United 1, (after 2—2 draw), 3rd Round.

## Goal Records
See GOAL-SCORING (Individuals) F.A. Cup; GOAL-SCORING (Teams and General) Highest Score.

## Ireland
Three Irish clubs have appeared in the F.A. Cup Competition Proper: Cliftonville reached the 3rd Round in 1886-7 before being beaten 11—1 by Partick Thistle; Linfield Athletic scratched after drawing, 2—2, with Nottingham Forest in 1888-9; Belfast Distillery lost 10—2 to Bolton Wanderers in the 1st Round of 1889-90.

## Medals
F.A. Cup medals are 9-carat gold, the winners' medals being slightly heavier.

See also CUP MEDALS in separate section.

**Non-League Clubs**
See also GIANT KILLERS in this section.

Since the formation of the Football League in 1888 the following non-League clubs have reached the last eight in the F.A. Cup:

| | Last Eight | Semi-final | Final |
|---|---|---|---|
| Birmingham St. George's | 1889 | | |
| Bootle | 1890 | | |
| Chatham | 1889 | | |
| Coventry City | 1910 | | |
| Crystal Palace | 1907 | | |
| Fulham | 1905 | | |
| Middlesbrough Ironopolis | 1893 | | |
| Millwall | | 1900, 1903 | |
| Nottingham Forest | 1891 | 1892 | |
| Portsmouth | 1902 | | |
| Queen's Park Rangers | 1910, 1914 | | |
| Reading | 1901 | | |
| Sheffield Wednesday | 1889, 1891, 1892 | | 1890 |
| Southampton | 1899, 1905, 1906, 1908 | 1898 | 1900, 1902 |
| Stoke | 1891 | | |
| Swindon | 1911 | 1910, 1912 | |
| Tottenham Hotspur | 1899, 1903, 1904 | | *1901 |
| West Ham United | 1911 | | |

* Tottenham Hotspur are the only non-League club to win the Cup since 1888.

Since the Football League was expanded to 86 clubs in 1921 the following non-League clubs have reached the 4th Round (last 32) or the old 2nd Round equivalent in the Cup Competition Proper:

1923-4—Corinthians: 1st Round, beat Blackburn Rovers (H) 1—0; 2nd Round, lost, West Bromwich Albion (A) 5—0.

1926-7—*Corinthians: 3rd Round, beat Walsall (A) 4—0; 4th Round, lost, Newcastle United (H) 3—1.

1928-9—*Corinthians: 3rd Round, beat Norwich City (A) 5—0; 4th Round, lost West Ham United (A) 3—0. Mansfield Town; 1st Round, beat Shirebrook (A) 4—2; 2nd Round, beat Barrow (A) 2—1; 3rd Round, beat Wolves (A) 1—0; 4th Round, lost Arsenal (H) 3—1.

1933-4—Workington: 1st Round, beat Southport (H) 1—0; 2nd Round, beat Newport County (H) 3—1; 3rd Round, beat Gateshead (H) 4—1; 4th Round, lost, Preston North End (H) 2—1.

1938-9—Chelmsford City: 1st Round beat Kidderminster (H) 4—0; 2nd Round, beat Darlington (H) 3—1; 3rd Round, beat Southampton (H) 4—1; 4th Round, lost, Birmingham (A) 6—0.

1947-8—Colchester United: 1st Round, beat Banbury Spencer (H) 2—1; 2nd Round, beat Wrexham (H) 1—0; 3rd Round, beat Huddersfield Town (H) 1—0; 4th Round, beat Bredford (H) 3—2; 5th Round, lost, Blackpool (A) 5—0.

1948-9—Yeovil Town: 1st Round, beat Runcorn (H) 2—1; 2nd Round, beat Weymouth (A) 4—0; 3rd Round, beat Bury (H)

3—1; 4th Round, beat Sunderland (H) 2—1 after extra time; 5th Round, lost, Manchester United (A) 8—0.

1952-3—Walthamstow Avenue: 1st Round, beat Wimbledon (A) 3—0 after draw 2—2; 2nd Round, beat Watford (A) 2—1 after draw 1—1; 3rd Round, beat Stockport County (H) 2—1; 4th Round, lost, Manchester United (H) 5—2 after draw 1—1.

1953-4—Headington United: 1st Round, beat Harwich and Parkeston (A) 3—2; 2nd Round, beat Millwall (A) 1—0 after draw 3—3; 3rd Round, beat Stockport County (H) 1—0 after draw 0—0; 4th Round, lost, Bolton Wanderers (H) 4—2.

1954-5—Bishop Auckland: 1st Round, beat Kettering (H) 5—1; 2nd Round, beat Crystal Palace (A) 4—2; 3rd Round, beat Ipswich Town (H) 3—0 after draw 2—2; 4th Round, lost, York City (H) 3—1.

1956-7—Rhyl: 1st Round, beat Scarborough (H) 3—2; 2nd Round, beat Bishop Auckland (H) 3—1; 3rd Round, beat Notts County (A) 3—1; 4th Round, lost, Bristol City (A) 3—0. New Brighton: 1st Round, beat Stockport County (A) 3—2 after draw 3—3; 2nd Round, beat Derby County (A) 3—1; 3rd Round, beat Torquay United (H) 2—1; 4th Round, lost, Burnley (A) 9—0. Peterborough United: 1st Round, beat Yeovil Town (A) 3—1; 2nd Round, beat Bradford (H) 3—0; 3rd Round, beat Lincoln City (A) 5—4 after draw 2—2; 4th Round, lost, Huddersfield Town (A) 3—1.

1958-9—Worcester City: 1st Round, beat Chelmsford City (H) 3—1 after draw 0—0;

2nd Round, beat Millwall (H) 5—2; 3rd Round, beat Liverpool (H) 2—1; 4th Round, lost, Sheffield United (H) 2—0.

1959-60—Peterborough United: 1st Round, beat Shrewsbury Town (H) 4—3; 2nd Round, beat Walsall (A) 3—2; 3rd Round, beat Ipswich Town (A) 3—2; 4th Round, lost, Sheffield Wednesday (A) 2—0.

1961-2—Weymouth: 1st Round, beat Barnet (H) 1—0; 2nd Round, beat Newport County (H) 1—0; 3rd Round, beat Morecombe (A) 1—0; 4th Round, lost, Preston North End (A) 2—0.

1962-3—Gravesend: 1st Round, beat Exeter City (H) 3—2; 2nd Round, beat Wycombe (H) 3—1; 3rd Round, beat Carlisle United (A) 1—0; 4th Round, lost, Sunderland (A) 5—2 after 1—1 draw.

1963-4—Bedford Town: 1st Round, beat Weymouth (H) 1—0 after draw 1—1; 2nd Round, beat Chelmsford (A) 1—0; 3rd Round, beat Newcastle United (A) 2—1; 4th Round, lost Carlisle United (H) 3—0.

1965-6—Bedford Town: 1st Round, beat Exeter City (A) 2—1; 2nd Round, beat Brighton (H) 2—1 after draw 1—1; 3rd Round, beat Hereford (H) 2—1; 4th Round, lost Everton (H) 0—3.

1969-70: Sutton United: 1st Round, beat Dagenham (A) 1—0; 2nd Round, beat Barnet (A) 2—0; 3rd Round beat Hillingdon (H) 4—1 after 0—0 draw; 4th Round, lost, Leeds United (H) 0—6.

1971-2: Hereford United: 1st Round, beat King's Lynn (H) 1—0 after 0—0 draw; 2nd Round, beat Northampton Town (at West Bromwich) 2—1 after draws 0—0, 2—2; 3rd Round, beat Newcastle United (H) 2—1 after 2—2 draw; 4th Round, lost, West Ham United (A) 1—3 after 0—0 draw.

*Corinthians were exempt until the 3rd Round.

## Players

Nine men have played in and also managed F.A. Cup winning teams:

M. Busby: Right-half in Manchester City's Cup-winning team of 1934, and manager of Manchester United, Cup-winners of 1948 and 1963.

P. McWilliam: Left-half in Newcastle United's winning team of 1910, and manager of Tottenham Hotspur, winners in 1921.

J. Mercer: Left-half in Arsenal's Cup-winning team of 1950, and manager of Manchester City, winners in 1969.

D. Revie: Centre-forward in Manchester City's Cup-winning team of 1956, and manager at Leeds United, winners in 1972.

J. Seed: Inside-right in the Tottenham Hotspur Cup-winning side of 1921, and manager of Charlton Athletic, winners in 1947.

W. Shankly: Right-half for Preston North End, Cup-winners 1938, and manager of Liverpool winners 1965. He also appeared for Preston in the 1937 final.

J. (Joe) Smith: Inside-left for Bolton Wanderers when they won the Cup in 1923 and again in 1926, and manager of Blackpool, winners in 1953 when they beat Smith's old club, Bolton Wanderers.

R. Stokoe: Centre-half for Newcastle United, Cup-winner 1955, and manager of Sunderland, winners 1973.

W. Walker: Captain of Aston Villa, Cup-winners in 1920, manager of Sheffield Wednesday, winners in 1935, and of Nottingham Forest, 1959.

Most appearances in F.A. Cup winning teams: J. H. Forrest (Blackburn Rovers) 1884, 1885, 1886, 1890, 1891. Hon. A. F. Kinnaird (Wanderers) 1873, 1877, 1878, (Old Etonians) 1879, 1882, C. H. R. Wollaston (Wanderers) 1872, 1873, 1876, 1877, 1878.

Since 1900 the most appearances in F.A. Cup-winning teams is three: C. Stephenson (Aston Villa) 1913, 1920, (Huddersfield Town) 1922. W. Butler, R. Haworth, H. Nuttall, R. Pym, and J. Seddon (all Bolton Wanderers) 1923, 1926, 1929. D. Jack (Bolton Wanderers) 1923, 1926, (Arsenal) 1930. G. Cowell, J. Milburn and R. Mitchell (all Newcastle United) 1951, 1952, 1955. D. Mackay (Tottenham Hotspur) 1961, 1962, 1967.

The record for most appearances in F.A. Cup Finals at Wembley is shared by J. Hulme and J. Giles. Hulme was outside-right for Arsenal when they were winners in 1930 and 1936, and losers in 1927 and 1932. He made his fifth appearance at outside-right for Huddersfield Town, losers in 1938. Giles got a winners' medal with Manchester United in 1963 and has since made four appearances with Leeds United—runners-up in 1965, 1970 and 1973, and winners 1972.

The record for the most players in a Cup Final team who had already had Cup Final experience is 10—Preston North End 1889, Newcastle United 1906, Everton 1907, Bolton Wanderers 1926, and Arsenal 1972.

The first club to win the F.A. Cup with an all-English side was West Bromwich Albion in 1888.

There was only one Englishman in Cardiff City's F.A. Cup winning team in 1927. W. Hardy, the left-half. The rest of the team comprised four Irishmen, three Scotsmen, and three Welshmen.

The most Scots in a F.A. Cup winning team was eight in Bradford City's team in

1911.

Only two men have won both F.A. Cup and F.A. Amateur Cup winners' medals. R. Chatt was in Aston Villa's team of 1895, and was later re-instated as an amateur and appeared in the Stockton side which won the Amateur Final of 1899. T. Morren was Middlesbrough's centre-half in 1895, and Sheffield United's centre-half when they won the F.A. Cup in 1899.

## Replays

Five replays (six games)—the most games played in a single tie of the F.A. Cup competition—were needed before Alvechurch beat Oxford City 1—0, 4th Qualifying Round, 1971-72. Total playing time 11 hr.

Four replays (five games) have occurred in the following ties:

New Brompton (now known as Gillingham) defeated Woolwich Arsenal 1—0 at Gravesend, season 1899-1900, after drawing 1—1 at Plumstead, 0—0 at New Brompton, 2—2 at Millwall, and 1—1 at Tottenham. The total playing time was 9 hr. 30 min.

In 1924-25 Gillingham and Barrow met 5 times in the 6th Qualifying Round. Barrow won 2—1 at New Cross after drawing 0—0 at Gillingham, 1—1 at Barrow, 1—1 at Wolverhampton, and 1—1 at Highbury. Total 9 hr. 30 min.

Also in season 1924-25, Leyton defeated Ilford after 5 games, lasting a record time of 9 hr. 40 min. A double period of extra time was played in two of the games.

The record time of 9 hr. 22 min. in the Competition Proper was played in a 3rd Round tie between Stoke City and Bury in 1954-5. They met at Bury, Stoke (abandoned eight minutes from the end of extra time with the home side leading 1—0), Goodison Park, Anfield and Old Trafford before Stoke City won 3—2.

Doncaster Rovers defeated Aston Villa 3—1 at The Hawthorns, West Bromwich, in the 4th replay of a 4th Round tie, 1954-5. Total playing time: 9 hr.

Chelsea defeated Burnley 2—0 at White Hart Lane, Tottenham, after four drawn games, 4th Round, 1955-6. Total playing time 9 hr.

Hull City defeated Darlington 3—0 at Middlesbrough, after four drawn games in 2nd Round, 1960-1.

Three replays (four games) have been played in the following ties:

1898-9. Sheffield United defeated Liverpool, 1—0 in the Semi-final after 2 drawn games and a game abandoned as a goalless draw after the crowd invaded the field.

1911-12. Barnsley beat Bradford City, 3—2 in the 4th Round, after three drawn games.

1922-3. Sheffield United beat Nottingham Forest, 1—0 in the 1st Round after three drawn games. In the four games only three goals were scored in a total of seven hours play.

1923-4. Newcastle United beat Derby County, 5—3 in the 2nd Round after three drawn games.

1923-4. Crystal Palace beat Notts County, 2—1 in the 2nd Round after three drawn games. Only three goals were scored in the seven hours' play.

1925-6. Blyth Spartans beat Hartlepools United 2—1 at Sunderland in the 1st Round after three drawn games.

1938-9. Halifax Town beat Mansfield Town 2—1 in 2nd Round after three drawn games. Total playing time 7 hrs. 30 min.

1951-2. Tranmere Rovers beat Blyth Spartans, 5—1 in the 2nd Round at Everton after three drawn games. The first replay was abandoned after only 15 min. extra time owing to bad light.

1952-3. Chelsea beat West Bromwich Albion, 4—0 in the 4th Round at Highbury after three drawn games.

1953-4. Blackpool beat Luton Town, 2—0 in the 3rd Round at Wolverhampton after three drawn games.

1969-70. Barrow beat Alfreton 2—0 at Preston after three drawn games in 1st Round.

## Results

For results of Finals see under FINALS in this section.

See also under separate sections DEFEATS (Undefeated) and WITHOUT A WIN.

Only 2 clubs have won the Cup three times in succession. Blackburn Rovers 1884, 1885, 1886, and Wanderers, 1876, 1877, 1878.

The highest number of consecutive F.A. Cup ties played by a single club without defeat is 24 by Blackburn Rovers, Dec. 1883 to Dec. 1886.

Huddersfield Town were unbeaten at home in 26 F.A. Cup ties from 1913 to 1932.

## Scotland

The last season in which Scottish Clubs entered the F.A. Cup competition was 1886-7. In that season Rangers reached the semi-finals in which they were beaten 1—3 by Aston Villa. Thereafter the Scottish F.A. made a rule preventing clubs from entering any national competition other than its own. Scottish clubs who have competed in the competition are Heart of Midlothian,

Cowlairs, Renton, Queen's Park, Rangers, Partick Thistle.

Queen's Park reached the Final twice but were beaten by Blackburn Rovers on both occasions.

A semi-final tie in the F.A. Cup was played in Scotland in 1885 when Queen's Park defeated Nottingham Forest, 3—0 at Merchiston Castle, Edinburgh, after drawing 1—1 at Derby.

For list of players who have gained both Scottish F.A. Cup winners' medals see separate section CUP MEDALS.

For most Scots in an F.A. Cup winning team see under PLAYERS in this section.

## Second Division

For Division II Cup winners see GENERAL in this section.

There has never been a Final between two Second Division sides.

## Third Division

Clubs which have reached the 6th Round (or its earlier equivalent) whilst in Division III are:

| | |
|---|---|
| Bournemouth and Boscombe Athletic | 1956-57 |
| Bristol Rovers | 1950-51 |
| Charlton Athletic | 1922-23 |
| Coventry City | 1962-63 |
| Exeter City | 1930-31 |
| Gateshead | 1952-53 |
| Hull City | 1948-49, 1965-66 |
| Leyton Orient | 1953-54 |
| Luton Town | 1932-33 |
| Mansfield Town | 1968-69 |
| Millwall | 1921-22, 1926-27, 1936-37 |
| Norwich City | 1958-59 |
| Peterborough United | 1964-65 |
| Port Vale | 1953-54 |
| Queen's Park Rangers | 1922-23, 1947-48 |
| Southport | 1930-31 |
| Swindon Town | 1923-24 |
| Watford | 1931-32 |
| York City | 1937-38, 1954-55 |

Only four clubs have reached the Semi-final of the F.A. Cup while members of Division III: Millwall in 1936-7, Port Vale in 1953-4, York City in 1954-5, and Norwich City in 1958-9. York City and Norwich City each drew their first game but were beaten in the replay.

## Wales

The entry of Welsh clubs unto the F.A. Cup competition is restricted to 14. Their entries must be submitted by Mar. 1, not May 1, the deadline for all other accepted entries.

The only occasion when the F.A. Cup was won by a club from outside of England was in 1927 when Cardiff City beat Arsenal 1—0.

## Winners

The club that has won the F.A. Cup the greatest number of times is Aston Villa who have carried off the trophy on seven occasions.

Next to the Villa come Blackburn Rovers and Newcastle United—six times each.

## FOOTBALL ASSOCIATION CHALLENGE TROPHY

In 1969 the F.A. decided to introduce a new national competition for non-League clubs —the F.A. Challenge Trophy—with the incentive of an appearance at Wembley for the finalists.

Winners: 1970—Macclesfield Town. 1971—Telford United. 1972—Stafford Rangers. 1973—Scarborough.

## FOOTBALL ASSOCIATION CHARITY SHIELD

The annual F.A. Charity Shield match was inaugurated in 1908.

The first game was played at Stamford Bridge, April 27, 1908, between the Champions of the Football League, Manchester United, and the Champions of the Southern League, Queen's Park Rangers.

The champions of these two Leagues met in this match for the next four years. Subsequently, the game was played between teams chosen by the F.A., usually the Amateurs v. Professionals, or the F.A. Cup holders v. the League Champions. In recent years the matches have more often than not been between the Cup holders and the League Champions.

| | | | | |
|---|---|---|---|---|
| 1908–09 | Manchester United | 4 | Queen's Park Rangers | 0 |
| | (after drawn game 1—1) | | | |
| 1909–10 | Newcastle United | 2 | Northampton Town | 0 |
| 1910–11 | Brighton and Hove Albion | 1 | Aston Villa | 0 |
| 1911–12 | Manchester United | 8 | Swindon Town | 4 |
| 1912–13 | Blackburn Rovers | 2 | Queen's Park Rangers | 1 |
| 1913–14 | Professionals | 7 | Amateurs | 2 |
| 1919–20 | West Bromwich Albion | 2 | Tottenham Hotspur | 0 |
| 1920–21 | Tottenham Hotspur | 2 | Burnley | 0 |
| 1921–22 | Huddersfield Town | 1 | Liverpool | 0 |

| 1922–23 | No match | | | |
|---|---|---|---|---|
| 1923–24 | Professionals | 2 | Amateurs | 0 |
| 1924–25 | Professionals | 3 | Amateurs | 1 |
| 1925–26 | Amateurs | 6 | Professionals | 1 |
| 1926–27 | Amateurs | 6 | Professionals | 3 |
| 1927–28 | Cardiff City | 2 | Corinthians | 1 |
| 1928–29 | Everton | 2 | Blackburn Rovers | 1 |
| 1929–30 | Professionals | 3 | Amateurs | 0 |
| 1930–31 | Arsenal | 2 | Sheffield Wednesday | 1 |
| 1931–32 | Arsenal | 1 | West Bromwich Albion | 0 |
| 1932–33 | Everton | 5 | Newcastle United | 3 |
| 1933–34 | Arsenal | 3 | Everton | 0 |
| 1934–35 | Arsenal | 4 | Manchester City | 0 |
| 1935–36 | Sheffield Wednesday | 1 | Arsenal | 0 |
| 1936–37 | Sunderland | 2 | Arsenal | 1 |
| 1937–38 | Manchester City | 2 | Sunderland | 0 |
| 1938–39 | Arsenal | 2 | Preston North End | 1 |
| 1948–49 | Arsenal | 4 | Manchester United | 3 |
| 1949–50 | Portsmouth | 1 | Wolverhampton Wanderers | 1 |
| 1950–51 | World Cup XI | 4 | Canadian Tourists | 2 |
| 1951–52 | Tottenham Hotspur | 2 | Newcastle United | 1 |
| 1952–53 | Manchester United | 4 | Newcastle United | 2 |
| 1953–54 | Arsenal | 3 | Blackpool | 1 |
| 1954–55 | Wolverhampton Wanderers | 4 | West Bromwich Albion | 4 |
| 1955–56 | Chelsea | 3 | Newcastle United | 0 |
| 1956–57 | Manchester United | 1 | Manchester City | 0 |
| 1957–58 | Manchester United | 4 | Aston Villa | 0 |
| 1958–59 | Bolton Wanderers | 4 | Wolverhampton Wanderers | 1 |
| 1959–60 | Wolverhampton Wanderers | 3 | Nottingham Forest | 1 |
| 1960–61 | Burnley | 2 | Wolverhampton Wanderers | 2 |
| 1961–62 | Tottenham Hotspur | 3 | F.A. Selection XI | 2 |
| 1962–63 | Tottenham Hotspur | 5 | Ipswich Town | 1 |
| 1963–64 | Everton | 4 | Manchester United | 0 |
| 1964–65 | Liverpool | 2 | West Ham United | 2 |
| 1965–66 | Liverpool | 2 | Manchester United | 2 |
| 1966–67 | Liverpool | 1 | Everton | 0 |
| 1967–68 | Manchester United | 3 | Tottenham Hotspur | 3 |
| 1968–69 | Manchester City | 6 | West Bromwich Albion | 1 |
| 1969–70 | Leeds United | 2 | Manchester City | 1 |
| 1970–71 | Everton | 2 | Chelsea | 1 |
| 1971–72 | Leicester City | 1 | Liverpool | 0 |
| 1972–73 | Manchester City | 1 | Aston Villa | 0 |

## FOOTBALL ASSOCIATION OF IRELAND
See under EIRE

## FOOTBALL ASSOCIATION SUNDAY CUP
From a refusal to recognise Sunday football to the inauguration of a national cup competition for bona-fide amateur Sunday clubs in the space of 10 years. It was certainly a sign of the times when the F.A. completed their change of outlook and introduced this competition in 1964.

In the first season it was played at County level with London the winners. Since then, however, club sides have competed.

## FOOTBALL ASSOCIATIONS (VARIOUS)
The title and address of the governing football body of each foreign country is given under the name of each country.

The first football association to be formed was the F.A. in London in 1863 (see under FOOTBALL ASSOCIATION, The).

The next oldest in chronological order are: Sheffield 1867, Scotland 1873, Birmingham 1875, Wales 1876, Sheffield New, Staffordshire, Surrey (reformed 1882) 1877, Berks and Bucks, Cheshire, Lancashire 1878, Northumberland and Durham 1879, Ireland 1880, Cleveland (North Riding), Lincolnshire, Norfolk 1881.

The Sheffield New was re-named Hallamshire in 1881 and subsequently amalgamated with the original Sheffield Association. Northumberland and Durham split in 1883.

The first of the above named associations to become affiliated to the F.A. (England) were the Sheffield, Lancashire, and Birmingham associations.

The earliest football associations to be formed outside the United Kingdom, were those of Holland and Denmark 1889, New Zealand 1891, Argentine 1893, Belgium, Chile and Switzerland, 1895.

## FOOTBALL LEAGUE, The

This is the father of all league football competitions. Formed in 1888 it has proved a worthy model for all successive competitions of its kind.

The Football League is governed by a Management Committee of 9 elected members who have full power to deal with all matters requiring attention outside of the Annual General Meeting which is held usually at the beginning of June.

At the A.G.M. there are 49 members entitled to vote on all proposals: 44 members of the First and Second Divisions, four representatives of the Third and Fourth Divisions, and the President. The membership of the League is limited to the 44 clubs in the first two divisions. The Third and Fourth Division clubs are merely Associate Members, limited in number to 48, and entitled to send only one representative for every eleven of their number to the A.G.M. to vote. Even then their vote is limited to certain matters.

The limited representation of the two lower Divisions has caused much discontent among the Associate Members but it must be remembered that when the members of the old Southern League approached the Football League and applied for membership and the formation of a Third Division, they accepted the status of Associate Members without any voting power whatsoever before 1929.

The Football League owes its inception to a Scotsman, Mr. W. McGregor, an official of the Aston Villa Club. As professionalism spread throughout the North of England and the Midlands it became important for those clubs, who had to find money to pay players, to run games on business-like lines.

Football before 1888 was a carefree affair. Even when fixtures were arranged no one was certain that their opponents would turn up. When they did, it was nothing for games to be delayed an hour or so because of their late arrival. In addition, the game lacked the regular competitive element that only a league system could bring.

Mr. McGregor first wrote to five of the leading clubs, suggesting that a stricter control could be kept on the game, and more attractive fixtures arranged, if ten or twelve of the more powerful clubs formed themselves into a league. His suggested title for this organisation was The Association Football Union.

Following his circular, an informal meeting was held at Anderton's Hotel, Fleet Street, London, on Mar. 22, 1888. There the proposal to form a League was accepted. The first formal meeting of "The Football League" took place a month later, April 17, at The Royal Hotel, Manchester.

Twelve clubs formed the new League and agreed to an annual subscription of £2 2s (£2.10p). They were Accrington, Aston Villa, Blackburn Rovers, Bolton Wanderers, Burnley, Derby County, Everton, Notts County, Preston North End, Stoke, West Bromwich Albion and Wolverhampton Wanderers. Three other clubs —Sheffield Wednesday, Nottingham Forest and Halliwell—applied for membership at the time but were not accepted because of the difficulty of arranging fixtures.

A Second Division consisting of 12 clubs was formed in 1892, by which time the First Division had increased to 16 clubs. There were several subsequent additions to both divisions before they were brought up to their present strength of 22 clubs each in 1919-20.

For some time before World War I there was talk of forming a Third Division but this did not come into being until 1920 when the 22 members of the First Division of the Southern League joined en bloc, with the exception of Cardiff City, who went straight into the Second Division of the Football League in place of Grimsby Town then relegated to the new Third Division with the Southern clubs.

This Third Division became the Southern Section in 1921 when a new Third Division (Northern Section) was formed. Originally this consisted of 20 clubs but was increased to 22 clubs in 1923. The two sections of the Third Division were each increased to 24 clubs in 1950.

A proposal to reorganise the Football League with four national divisions was turned down in 1956 but accepted the following year. And so, for season 1958-9, the Northern and Southern Sections of the Third Division were abolished and the clubs formed into new Third and Fourth Divisions with four up and four down promotion and relegation between them.

In 1933 the Division III clubs introduced a Cup competition of their own, which was continued until 1939. These were the winners:

Southern Section
1934—Exeter City
1935—Bristol Rovers
1936—Coventry City
1937—*Watford and Millwall

Northern Section
1934—Darlington
1935—Stockport County
1936—Chester
1937—Chester
1938—Southport

*The final was held over until the 1937-8 season, and then, after playing two drawn games, Watford and Millwall were considered to be joint holders.

It is interesting to note that during the 85 years of its existence the Football League has been served by only four Secretaries: H. Lockett 1888-1902, T. Charnley 1902-33, F. Howarth 1933-57, and A. Hardaker 1957-

## FOOTBALL LEAGUE CHAMPIONS
### Football League
1888-9 Preston North End; 1889-90 Preston North End; 1890-91 Everton; 1891-2 Sunderland.

### First Division
1892-3 Sunderland; 1893-4 Aston Villa; 1894-5 Sunderland; 1895-6 Aston Villa; 1896-7 Aston Villa; 1897-8 Sheffield United; 1898-9 Aston Villa; 1899-1900 Aston Villa; 1900-01 Liverpool; 1901-2 Sunderland; 1902-3 Sheffield Wednesday; 1903-4 Sheffield Wednesday; 1904-5 Newcastle United; 1905-6 Liverpool; 1906-7 Newcastle United; 1907-8 Manchester United; 1908-9 Newcastle United; 1909-10 Aston Villa; 1910-11 Manchester United; 1911-12 Blackburn Rovers; 1912-13 Sunderland; 1913-14 Blackburn Rovers; 1914-15 Everton; 1919-20 West Bromwich Albion; 1920-21 Burnley; 1921-2 Liverpool; 1922-3 Liverpool; 1923-4 *Huddersfield Town; 1924-5 Huddersfield Town; 1925-6 Huddersfield Town; 1926-7 Newcastle United; 1927-8 Everton; 1928-9 Sheffield Wednesday; 1929-30 Sheffield Wednesday; 1930-31 Arsenal; 1931-2 Everton; 1932-3 Arsenal; 1933-4 Arsenal; 1934-5 Arsenal; 1935-6 Sunderland; 1936-7 Manchester City; 1937-8 Arsenal; 1938-9 Everton; 1946-7 Liverpool; 1947-8 Arsenal; 1948-9 Portsmouth; 1949-50 *Portsmouth; 1950-51 Tottenham Hotspur; 1951-2 Manchester United; 1952-3 *Arsenal; 1953-4 Wolverhampton Wanderers; 1954-5 Chelsea; 1955-6 Manchester United; 1956-7 Manchester United; 1957-8 Wolverhampton Wanderers; 1958-9 Wolverhampton Wanderers; 1959-60 Burnley; 1960-61 Tottenham Hotspur; 1961-2 Ipswich Town; 1962-3 Everton; 1963-4 Liverpool; 1964-5 *Manchester United; 1965-6 Liverpool; 1966-7 Manchester United; 1967-8 Manchester City; 1968-9 Leeds United; 1969-70 Everton; 1970-71 Arsenal; 1971-2 Derby County; 1972-3 Liverpool.

### Second Division
1892-3 Small Heath; 1893-4 Liverpool; 1894-5 Bury; 1895-6 *Liverpool; 1896-7 Notts County; 1897-8 Burnley; 1898-9 Manchester City; 1899-1900 Sheffield Wednesday; 1900-1901 Grimsby Town; 1901-2 West Bromwich Albion; 1902-3 Manchester City; 1903-4 Preston North End; 1904-5 Liverpool; 1905-6 Bristol City; 1906-7 Nottingham Forest; 1907-8 Bradford City; 1908-9 Bolton Wanderers; 1909-10 Manchester City; 1910-11 West Bromwich Albion; 1911-12 Derby County; 1912-13 Preston North End; 1913-14 Notts County; 1914-15 Derby County; 1919-20 Tottenham Hotspur; 1920-21 *Birmingham; 1921-2 Nottingham Forest; 1922-3 Notts County; 1923-4 Leeds United; 1924-5 Leicester City; 1925-6 Sheffield Wednesday; 1926-7 Middlesbrough; 1927-8 Manchester City; 1928-9 Middlesbrough; 1929-30 Blackpool; 1930-31 Everton; 1931-2 Wolverhampton Wanderers; 1932-3 Stoke City; 1933-4 Grimsby Town; 1934-5 Brentford; 1935-6 Manchester United; 1936-7 Leicester City; 1937-8 Aston Villa; 1938-9 Blackburn Rovers; 1946-7 Manchester City; 1947-8 Birmingham City; 1948-9 Fulham; 1949-50 Tottenham Hotspur; 1950-51 Preston North End; 1951-2 Sheffield Wednesday; 1952-3 Sheffield United; 1953-4 *Leicester City; 1954-5 *Birmingham City; 1955-6 Sheffield Wednesday; 1956-7 Leicester City; 1957-8 West Ham United; 1958-9 Sheffield Wednesday; 1959-60 Aston Villa; 1960-61 Ipswich Town; 1961-2 Liverpool; 1962-3 Stoke City; 1963-4 Leeds United; 1964-5 Newcastle United; 1965-6 Manchester City; 1966-7 Coventry City; 1967-8 Ipswich Town; 1968-9 Derby County; 1969-70 Huddersfield Town; 1970-71 Leicester City; 1971-2 Norwich City; 1972-3 Burnley.

### Third Division (Southern Section)
1920-21 Crystal Palace; 1921-2 *Southampton; 1922-3 Bristol City; 1923-4 Portsmouth; 1924-5 Swansea Town; 1925-6 Reading; 1926-7 Bristol City; 1927-8 Millwall; 1928-9 *Charlton Athletic; 1929-30 Plymouth Argyle; 1930-31 Notts County; 1931-2 Fulham; 1932-3 Brentford; 1933-4 Norwich City; 1934-5 Charlton Athletic;

1935-6 Coventry City; 1936-7 Luton Town; 1937-8 Millwall; 1938-9 Newport County; 1946-7 Cardiff City; 1947-8 Queen's Park Rangers; 1948-9 Swansea Town; 1949-50 Notts County; 1950-51 Nottingham Forest; 1951-2 Plymouth Argyle; 1952-3 Bristol Rovers; 1953-4 Ipswich Town; 1954-5 Bristol City; 1955-6 Leyton Orient; 1956-7 Ipswich Town; 1957-8 Brighton and Hove Albion.

**Third Division (Northern Section)**
1921-2 Stockport County; 1922-3 Nelson; 1923-4 Wolverhampton Wanderers; 1924-5 Darlington; 1925-6 Grimsby Town; 1926-7 Stoke City; 1927-8 Bradford; 1928-9 Bradford City; 1929-30 Port Vale; 1930-31 Chesterfield; 1931-2 *Lincoln City; 1932-3 Hull City; 1933-4 Barnsley; 1934-5 Doncaster Rovers; 1935-6 Chesterfield; 1936-7 Stockport County; 1937-8 Tranmere Rovers; 1938-9 Barnsley; 1946-7 Doncaster Rovers; 1947-8 Lincoln City; 1948-9 Hull City; 1949-50 Doncaster Rovers; 1950-51 Rotherham United; 1951-2 Lincoln City; 1952-3 Oldham Athletic; 1953-4 Port Vale; 1954-5 Barnsley; 1955-6 Grimsby Town; 1956-7 Derby County; 1957-8 Scunthorpe United.

**Third Division**
1958-9 Plymouth Argyle; 1959-60 Southampton; 1960-61 Bury; 1961-2 Portsmouth; 1962-3 Northampton Town; 1963-4 *Coventry City; 1964-5 Carlisle United; 1965-6 Hull City; 1966-7 Queen's Park Rangers; 1967-8 Oxford United; 1968-9 *Watford; 1969-70 Orient; 1970-71 Preston North End; 1971-2 Aston Villa; 1972-3 Bolton Wanderers.

**Fourth Division**
1958-9 Port Vale; 1959-60 Walsall; 1960-61 Peterborough United; 1961-2 Millwall; 1962-3 Brentford; 1963-4 *Gillingham; 1964-5 Brighton; 1965-6 *Doncaster Rovers; 1966-7 Stockport County; 1967-8 Luton Town; 1968-9 Doncaster Rovers; 1969-70 Chesterfield; 1970-71 Notts County; 1971-2 Grimsby Town; 1972-3 Southport.

* Won on goal average.

**Medals**
Football League Championship medals are 9 carat gold. 14 each are awarded to the winners of the four divisions, 11 for the players and one each for the manager, secretary and trainer.

**FOOTBALL LEAGUE CUP**
At the A.G.M. of the Football League in May 1960 a proposal that they should

introduce their own Cup competition was accepted and approved by 31 votes to 16.

Providing that it is a First Division club, then the winner of this competition is nominated by the League for entry into the UEFA Cup.

Results of finals:
1960-61 Aston Villa beat Rotherham United on aggregate in a two-leg final, 0—2, 3—0 after extra time.
1961-62 Norwich City beat Rochdale 3—0, 1—0.
1962-63 Birmingham City beat Aston Villa, 3—0, 0—0.
1963-64 Leicester City beat Stoke City, 1—1, 3—2.
1964-65 Chelsea beat Leicester City, 3—2, 0—0.
1965-66 West Bromwich Albion beat West Ham United, 1—2, 4—1.
1966-67 Queen's Park Rangers beat West Bromwich Albion, 3—2.
1967-68 Leeds United beat Arsenal 1—0.
1968-69 Swindon Town beat Arsenal 3—1.
1969-70 Manchester City beat West Bromwich Albion 2—1 after extra time.
1970-71 Tottenham Hotspur beat Aston Villa 2—0
1971-72 Stoke City beat Chelsea 2—1.
1972-73 Tottenham Hotspur beat Norwich City 1—0.

Season 1969-70 was the first season in which all 92 clubs took part. Whereas the competition was originally optional it has been compulsory since 1971.

The winners and runners-up each receive tankards.

For goalscoring records see under separate section.

**FOOTBALL POOLS**
See under BETTING.

**FOOTBALLER OF THE YEAR**
The Football Writers' Association annual award.
1947-48 S. Matthews, Blackpool
1948-49 J. Carey, Manchester United
1949-50 J. Mercer, Arsenal
1950-51 H. Johnston, Blackpool
1951-52 W. Wright, Wolverhampton Wanderers
1952-53 N. Lofthouse, Bolton Wanderers
1953-54 T. Finney, Preston North End
1954-55 D. Revie, Manchester City
1955-56 B. Trautmann, Manchester City
1956-57 T. Finney, Preston North End
1957-58 D. Blanchflower, Tottenham Hotspur
1958-59 S. Owen, Luton Town
1959-60 W. Slater, Wolverhampton Wanderers

1960-61  D. Blanchflower, Tottenham Hotspur
1961-62  J. Adamson, Burnley
1962-63  S. Matthews, Stoke City
1963-64  R. Moore, West Ham United
1964-65  R. Collins, Leeds United
1965-66  R. Charlton, Manchester United
1966-67  J. Charlton, Leeds United
1967-68  G. Best, Manchester United
1968-69  D. Mackay, Derby County and A. Book, Manchester City
1969-70  W. Bremner, Leeds United
1970-71  F. McLintock, Arsenal
1971-72  G. Banks, Stoke City
1972-73  P. Jennings, Tottenham Hotspur

## European

The French football weekly "France Football" conducts an annual poll among football writers in various European countries to decide the "European Footballer of the Year." These are the winners:

1956   S. Matthews (England)
1957   A. Di Stefano (Spain)
1958   R. Kopa (France)
1959   A. Di Stefano (Spain)
1960   L. Suarez (Spain)
1961   O. E. Sivori (Italy)
1962   J. Masopust (Czechoslovakia)
1963   L. Yachin (U.S.S.R.)
1964   D. Law (Scotland)
1965   Eusebio (Portugal)
1966   R. Charlton (England)
1967   F. Albert (Hungary)
1968   G. Best (Ireland)
1969   G. Rivera (Italy)
1970   G. Muller (W. Germany)
1971   J. Cruyff (Holland)
1972   F. Beckenbauer (W. Germany)

## FOREIGN PLAYERS IN FOOTBALL LEAGUE

Several foreign born players have appeared for Football League clubs. These include:

*Belgian:* M. Gaillard, Crystal Palace, Portsmouth, 1947-53.

*Chinese:* Cheung Chi Doy, Blackpool, 1960-62.

*Danish:* N. Middleboe, Chelsea, 1913-21. H. V. Jensen, Hull City, 1948-56. P. Arentoft, Newcastle United, Blackburn Rovers 1969- . P. Bartram, Crystal Palace, 1970-71.

*Dutch:* G. P. Keizer, Arsenal and Charlton Athletic 1930-32.

*Egyptian:* T. Abdullah, Derby County, 1920-22, Hartlepools United, 1923-24. H. Hegazi, Fulham, 1911-12 M. Mansour, Queen's Park Rangers, 1938-9.

*German:* M. Seeburg, Chelsea, Tottenham Hotspur, Burnley, Grimsby Town and Reading, 1907-14. A. Eisentrager, Bristol City, 1949-56. B. Trautmann, Manchester City, 1949-63. D. Bruck, Coventry City, 1960-70.

*Hungarian:* B. Olah, Northampton Town, 1960-62. M. Nagy, Swindon Town, 1951-2. J. Haasz, Swansea Town, Workington, 1960-63.

*Italian:* A. Freezia, Reading, 1913-14.

*Polish:* F. Staroscik, Northampton Town, 1953-5. S. Gerula, Leyton Orient. 1949-50.

*Spanish:* E. Aldecoa, Coventry City, 1946-7. J. Gallego, Brentford, 1946-8.

*Swedish:* H. Jeppson, Charlton Athletic, 1950-51.

## FORFAR ATHLETIC F.C.

Founded 1885. First admitted to Scottish League, Division II, 1921. Honours: None. Record attendance: 10,780 v. Rangers, Scottish Cup, 2nd Round, Feb. 2, 1970. Address: Station Park, Forfar (Tel. 0307 3576). Nickname: Loons. Colours: Sky blue and navy blue striped shirts, sky blue shorts. Record League goal-scorer: J. Kilgour, 45 goals, Division II, 1929-30. Record victory: 8—1 v. Stenhousemuir, Division II, Dec. 26, 1936 and v. Alloa Athletic, Division II, Mar. 13, 1971. Record defeat: 10—2 v. Dundee, Division II 1938-39.

## FRANCE

A football club was formed at Le Havre as long ago as 1872 following the introduction of the game to the town by English sailors in the summer of that year, but it was many years after this before the dribbling code really made any progress in France.

Rugby took a much stronger hold on the country than soccer and it was not until 1917 that widespread interest in the dribbling code was created by the introduction of a national cup competition run on similar lines to the F.A. Cup. This was the Charles Simon Cup, in memory of the founder of the Comité Français Interfédéral who had been killed in the war in 1915. After that war this competition became known simply as the Coupe de France.

France's best year in the World Cup was 1958 when with stars like Jonquet, Fontaine, Kopa and Piantoni they won 3rd place in the Finals.

The controlling body of football in France is the Fédération Française du Football, formed in 1919 out of the old Comité Francais Interfédéral which consisted of four separate organisations.

Professionalism in France was not approved until 1932 and even today most of the players among the first-class clubs are only part-time professionals.

The leading French clubs of recent years are Saint Étienne, who created a record

83

1967-70 by winning the League Championship four times in succession, and Olympique Marseille who won the title in 1971 and 1972.

The address of the governing body of football in France: Fédération Française de Football, 60bis Avenue d'Iéna 75, Paris 16e. Colours: Blue jerseys, white shorts, red stockings.

| | |
|---|---|
| May 10, 1923 | France 1, England 4; Paris |
| May 17, 1924 | France 1, England 3; Paris |
| May 21, 1925 | France 2, England 3; Paris |
| May 26, 1927 | France 0, England 6; Paris |
| May 17, 1928 | France 1, England 5; Paris |
| May 9, 1929 | France 1, England 4; Paris |
| May 18, 1930 | France 0, Scotland 2; Paris |
| May 14, 1931 | France 5, England 2; Paris |
| May 8, 1932 | France 1, Scotland 3; Paris |
| May 25, 1933 | France 1, Wales 1; Paris |
| Dec. 6, 1933 | England 4, France 1; Tottenham |
| May 23, 1937 | Eire 2, France 0; Paris |
| May 26, 1938 | France 2, England 4; Paris |
| May 20, 1939 | France 2, Wales 1; Paris |
| May 3, 1947 | England 3, France 0; Highbury |
| May 23, 1948 | France 3, Scotland 0; Paris |
| April 27, 1949 | Scotland 2, France 0; Hampden |
| May 22, 1949 | France 1, England 3; Paris |
| May 27, 1950 | France 0, Scotland 1; Paris |
| May 12, 1951 | Ireland 2, France 2; Belfast |
| May 16, 1951 | Scotland 1, France 0; Hampden |
| Oct. 3, 1951 | England 2, France 2; Highbury |
| Nov. 11, 1952 | France 3, Ireland 1; Paris |
| Nov. 16, 1952 | Eire 1, France 1; Dublin |
| May 14, 1953 | France 6, Wales 1; Paris |
| Oct. 4, 1953* | Eire 3, France 5; Dublin |
| Nov. 25, 1953* | France 1, Eire 0; Paris |
| May 15, 1955 | France 1, England 0; Paris |
| Nov. 27, 1957 | England 4, France 0; Wembley |
| June 15, 1958* | Scotland 1, France 2; Sweden |
| June 19, 1958* | Ireland 0, France 4; Sweden |
| Oct. 3, 1962 | England 1, France 1; Sheffield |
| Feb. 27, 1963† | France 5, England 2; Paris |
| July 20, 1966* | England 2, France 0; Wembley |
| Mar. 12, 1969 | England 5, France 0; Wembley |
| Nov. 15, 1972* | Eire 2, France 1; Dublin |
| May 19, 1973* | France 1, Eire 1; Paris |

\* World Cup
† Nations Cup

## FULHAM F.C.
Founded 1879 as St. Andrew's Sunday School, West Kensington. The nearest available ground was at Fulham so went under the name of Fulham St. Andrews. Elected to Football League, Division II, 1907. Honours: Champions Division II 1948-9. Runners-up, 1958-9. Champions, Division III (S), 1931-2. Runners-up, Division III, 1970-71. Best in Division I, 10th, 1959-60. Record attendance: 49,335 v. Millwall, Division II, Oct. 8, 1938. Address: Craven Cottage, Stevenage Road, S.W.6 (Tel. 01-736 5621). Nickname: Cottagers. Colours: White shirts, black shorts with two white stripes down seam, red stockings. Record League goal-scorer: F. Newton, 41 goals, Division III(S), 1931-2. Record victory: 10—1 v. Ipswich Town, Division I, Dec. 26, 1963. Record defeat 9—0 v. Wolverhampton Wanderers, Division I, Sept. 16, 1959.

84

## GALLACHER, Hugh Kilpatrick (1903-1957)

Considered by many to have been the greatest opportunist ever there was no more determined centre-forward between the two World Wars than this mercurial Scot from Bellshill, Lanarkshire. Below average height he took a lot of hard knocks but his brilliant ball control enabled him to carve a way through most defences. Always temperamental he committed suicide in 1957 when 54 years of age.

Airdrieonians 1921-25, 111 apps. (91 goals). Newcastle Utd. 1925-30, 155 apps. (133 goals). Chelsea 1930-34, 132 apps. (72 goals). Derby County 1934-36, 51 apps. (38 goals). Notts County 1936-38, 45 apps. (32 goals). Grimsby Town 1938, 11 apps. (3 goals). Gateshead 1938-39, 31 apps. (18 goals). Scottish internationals 20. Inter-League games (Scottish League) 2. Scottish Cup winners 1924. Football League Champions 1926-7.

## GALLAGHER, Patrick (1894-1953)

Nicknamed "The mighty atom" this Irishman from Donegal defied those who thought him too small for the hurly burly of League Football and graced the game for more than 20 years. At inside-right he would mesmerise the opposition with his tricky ball control and this kind of clever football brought him many memorable goals although he was principally a creator of opportunities for his centre-forward.

Glasgow Celtic 1911-26, 436 apps. (184 goals). Falkirk 1926-32, 129 apps. (19 goals). N. Ireland Internationals 11. Eire Internationals 1. Inter-League 4. Scottish Cup medals 1912, 1914, 1923, 1925. Scottish League Champions 1913-14, 1914-15, 1915-16, 1916-17, 1918-19, 1921-2.

## GAMBLING

See under BETTING.

## GAMES

Meeting same opponents or most games. See under MATCHES.

## GATE RECEIPTS

### European Cup

The record receipts for a European Cup tie were those taken in the semi-final (1st leg) between A. C. Milan and Manchester United, Milan, April 23, 1969. The figure was approximately £130,000.

### F.A. Amateur Cup

Record receipts £41,662.90, Wembley, April 14, 1973. Final tie between Walton and Hersham and Slough Town.

### F.A. Cup

For list of receipts at F.A. Cup Finals see FOOTBALL ASSOCIATION CHALLENGE CUP (Finals). The record Cup Final receipts, £233,800, were taken in 1973.

Rules for division of gate receipts are laid down by the F.A., and, briefly, are as follows:

The home club is entitled to deduct match expenses such as fees to the referee and linesmen, cost of advertising, printing, police, etc., and the travelling expenses of the visiting team are also deducted. Thereafter the division is:

All rounds prior to Round 3 of the Competition Proper (other than replays in the Competition Proper): equally between the two clubs.

Rounds 3, 4, 5 and 6: equally between the two clubs and the Cup pool.

Replays in these rounds: 5% to the F.A. and the balance divided equally between the two clubs, and the pool.

Semi-finals: the net proceeds of the two games are pooled and then divided—25% to the F.A., 25% to the Cup Pool, and the remainder equally between the four clubs.

The division is similar in replays.

The Final: 25% to the F.A., 25% to the Cup Pool, and the remainder between the two clubs.

As regards the Cup pool, this is subsequently divided equally among all the Football League clubs who entered the competition. Non-League clubs surviving Round 2 do not contribute to the Pool, but in these games the Football League club pays one third of its share to the Pool.

### Football League

After necessary expenses have been deducted the net proceeds from gate receipts is divided as follows:

4% to the Football League pool (the net amount in this case includes an appropriate proportion of receipts from the sale of season tickets); to the visiting club an amount consisting of 8p for each adult and 4p for each schoolchild, including all season ticket holders; the balance to the home club.

In all cases the visiting club's share must be at least £250.

## Football League Cup
The record League Cup Final receipts were taken in 1972 for the match Stoke City v. Chelsea—£132,000.

After paying expenses each club takes 40% of match gate receipts while the remaining 20% goes into a pool to be shared equally between all 92 clubs.

## Internationals
The record receipts for an international match played in the British Isles, £204,805, World Cup Final, Wembley, July 30, 1966.

## Scottish Association Cup
The record receipts for a single game in this competition amounted to £56,761 for the Final between Celtic and Hibernian, May 6, 1972.

In all ties of the Scottish Association Cup competition proper, excluding the semi-finals and final, the home club must guarantee their visitors a sum equivalent to the cost of 15 rail or bus fares plus £20 if the clubs are more than 100 miles apart.

Referee's and linesmen's fees and expenses and also a levy of 5% for the Cup Pool are deducted, and then, providing that the visitors receive their guarantee as first mentioned, the receipts are divided equally between the two clubs.

In the semi-finals the total receipts are pooled and, after payment of match expenses and clubs' guarantees, the Scottish F.A. takes 5% of the balance. The remainder, less allowances for use of grounds, is then divided equally between the four clubs. There are other more complex arrangements for re-played semi-finals. The Association also takes 5% of the receipts at the Final tie. The balance is then divided equally after deduction of guarantees and expenses and allowance for use of the ground.

## Scottish League
Receipts divided equally between competing clubs, providing that the visiting club receives a guarantee of £500 in the First Division and £150 in Second Division and League Cup games.

The Scottish League only takes 2% of net receipts at games played on neutral grounds and the Semi-finals and Final of the League Cup. In these games the competing clubs share the proceeds equally.

If a game is abandoned there is no guarantee for the visiting club in the replay but the proceeds are shared equally.

## World Cup
The record receipts at a football match anywhere in the world is £204,805, the amount paid to see the World Cup Final at Wembley, July 30, 1966.

## GERMANY
Germany was one of the first countries outside of the British Isles where football was played under Association rules. That would be in about 1870. A team from Oxford University visited Germany in 1875 and this was the first-ever overseas tour of a soccer team. Soon after this a number of German universities were encouraged to take up the game.

The oldest club still in existence in Germany, Hamburg S.V., was formed in 1887. Two years later the English F.A. sent over a representative side, and in 1900 the German F.A. was founded.

Aston Villa F.C. visited Berlin in 1901 and in the same year the Germans sent a side to meet England in games at White Hart Lane and Manchester. These two games are not ranked as official internationals. In the first, England, represented by amateurs, won 12—0. Professionals took over for England in the second game and won 10—0.

Germany played their first official representative international match in 1908 when they lost 5—3 to Switzerland at Basle.

The first full international between Germany and one of the home countries took place in 1929 against Scotland. England met Germany a year later.

Needless to say there are, today, two German F.A.s, the East and the West. Both are members of F.I.F.A. and it should be noted that there are more registered players in West Germany than in any country in the world apart from Russia.

It is not surprising, therefore, that West Germany is one of only two Continental countries (the other is Italy), to have won the World Cup. Their victory in 1954 was achieved with a side of super-fit men who played real down-to-earth football without any frills. It is generally acknowledged that they were not as good a side as the Hungarians whom they beat in the final, catching them on an off-day in conditions (it was pouring with rain) which suited the Germans better than the more artistic Hungarians, but there is no denying that the Germans' effort was a remarkable one.

The East German team with only about a third as many clubs from which to select their players has so far not made anything like the same impression in world soccer. Indeed, with the exception of Berlin, the part of the old Germany which now forms the German Democratic Republic had never produced clubs or players of a high standard in the same quantity as West Germany.

The East German Association was formed in 1947. Its address is: Deutscher Fussball-Verband, Storkower Strasse 118, Berlin 1055. Colours: White shirts, blue shorts, white stockings.

The West German Association, refounded in 1950, is the Deutscher Fussball Bund, Zeppelinalle 77, Postschliesstach 900260, 6 Frankfurt (main)-90. Colours: White shirts, black shorts, white stockings.

| | | |
|---|---|---|
| June 1, 1929 | Germany 1, Scotland 1; Berlin |
| May 10, 1930 | Germany 3, England 3; Berlin |
| May 8, 1935 | Germany 3, Eire 1; Dortmund |
| Dec. 4, 1935 | England 3, Germany 0; Tottenham |
| May 6, 1936 | Germany 4, Eire 1; Cologne |
| Oct. 14, 1936 | Scotland 2, Germany 2; Ibrox |
| Oct. 17, 1936 | Eire 5, Germany 2; Dublin |
| May 14, 1938 | Germany 3, England 6; Berlin |
| May 23, 1939 | Germany 1, Eire 1; Bremen |
| Oct. 17, 1951 | Eire 3, West Germany 2; Dublin |
| May 4, 1952 | West Germany 3, Eire 0; Cologne |
| Dec. 1, 1954 | England 3, West Germany 1; Wembley |
| May 28, 1955 | West Germany 2, Eire 1; Hamburg |
| May 26, 1956 | West Germany 1, England 3; Berlin |
| Nov. 25, 1956 | Eire 3, West Germany 0; Dublin |
| May 19, 1957* | East Germany 2, Wales 1; Leipzig |
| May 22, 1957 | West Germany 1, Scotland 3; Stuttgart |
| Sept. 25, 1957* | Wales 4, East Germany 1; Cardiff |
| June 15, 1958* | Ireland 2, West Germany 2; Sweden |
| May 6, 1959 | Scotland 3, West Germany 2; Hampden |
| May 11, 1960 | West Germany 0, Eire 1; Dusseldorf |
| Oct. 26, 1960* | Ireland 3, West Germany 4; Belfast |
| May 10, 1961* | West Germany 2, Ireland 1; Hamburg |
| June 2, 1963 | East Germany 1, England 2; Leipzig |
| May 12, 1964 | West Germany 2, Scotland 2; Hanover |
| May 12, 1965 | West Germany 0, England 1; Nuremberg |
| Feb. 23, 1966 | England 1, West Germany 0; Wembley |
| May 4, 1966 | Eire 0, West Germany 4; Dublin |
| May 7, 1966 | Ireland 0, West Germany 2; Belfast |
| July 30, 1966* | England 4, West Germany 2; Wembley† |
| May 8, 1968 | Wales 1, West Germany 1; Cardiff |
| June 1, 1968 | West Germany 1, England 0; Hanover |
| Mar. 26, 1969 | West Germany 1, Wales 1; Frankfurt |
| April 16, 1969* | East Germany 2, Wales 1; Dresden |
| April 16, 1969* | Scotland 1, West Germany 1; Glasgow |
| Oct. 22, 1969* | Wales 1, East Germany 3; Cardiff |
| Oct. 22, 1969* | West Germany 3, Scotland 2; Hamburg |
| May 9, 1970 | West Germany 2, Eire 1; Berlin |
| June 14, 1970* | England 2, West Germany 3; Leon† |
| Nov. 25, 1970 | England 3, East Germany 1; Wembley |
| April 29, 1972 | England 1, West Germany 3; Wembley |
| May 13, 1972 | West Germany 0, England 0; Berlin |

\* World Cup
† After extra time

## GILLINGHAM F.C.

New Brompton Excelsior met with such success in local junior football that a company was formed in 1893 and the club set on a proper footing as New Brompton. It changed its name to Gillingham in 1913. One of the original members of the Football League, Division III, 1920. Dropped out, 1938. Re-elected 1950. Honours: Champions, Division IV, 1963-4. Record attendance: 23,002 v. Queens Park Rangers, F.A. Cup 3rd Round, Jan. 10, 1948. Address: Priestfield Road, Gillingham ME7 4DD. (Tel. Medway 51854). Nickname: Gills. Colours: All blue. Record League goal-scorer: E. Morgan, 31 goals,

Division III(S), 1954-5. Record victory: 10—1 v. Gorleston, F.A. Cup, 1st Round, Nov. 16, 1957. Record defeat: 9—2 v. Nottingham Forest, Division III(S), Nov. 18, 1950.

## GOAL AVERAGE

To calculate goal average the number of goals for are divided by the number of goals against. The higher the result, the better is the goal average.

Goal average does not count in the International Championship and it should be noted that goal average is never considered in many competitions abroad. In Belgium, for instance, the team with the greater number of victories is placed highest, while many countries, including Northern Ireland, still insist on a play-off for the top places.

In the Football League and the Scottish League the championship of each division has been decided on goal average in the following instances:

| Season | Champions | Goal Average | Runners-up | Goal Average |
|---|---|---|---|---|
| | | Division I | | |
| 1923–24 | Huddersfield Town | 1.818 | Cardiff City | 1.794 |
| 1949–50 | Portsmouth | 1.947 | Wolverhampton W. | 1.551 |
| 1952–53 | Arsenal | 1.515 | Preston North End | 1.416 |
| 1964–65 | Manchester United | 2.282 | Leeds United | 1.596 |
| | | Division II | | |
| 1895–96 | Liverpool | 3.312 | Manchester City | 1.657 |
| 1911–12 | Derby County | 2.645 | Chelsea | 1.882 |
| 1920–21 | Birmingham | 2.078 | Cardiff City | 1.843 |
| 1953–54 | Leicester City | 1.616 | Everton | 1.586 |
| 1954–55 | Birmingham City | 1.972 | Luton Town | 1.660 |
| | | | (3rd) Rotherham United | 1.468 |
| | | Division III | | |
| 1963–64 | Coventry City | 1.606 | Crystal Palace | 1.431 |
| 1968–69 | Watford | 2.176 | Swindon Town | 2.028 |
| | | Division IV | | |
| 1963–64 | Gillingham | 1.966 | Carlisle United | 1.948 |
| 1965–66 | Doncaster Rovers | 1.575 | Darlington | 1.358 |
| | | Division III(S) | | |
| 1921–22 | Southampton | 3.238 | Plymouth Argyle | 2.625 |
| 1928–29 | Charlton Athletic | 1.433 | Crystal Palace | 1.208 |
| 1956–57 | Ipswich Town | 1.870 | Torquay United | 1.390 |
| | | Division III(N) | | |
| 1931–32 | Lincoln City | 2.257 | Gateshead | 1.958 |
| | | Scottish League. Division I or A | | |
| 1952–53 | Rangers | 2.051 | Hibernian | 1.823 |
| 1964–65 | Kilmarnock | 1.878 | Hearts | 1.836 |

In 1890–91 Dumbarton and Rangers finished level on points at head of the table. A deciding match between the clubs resulted in a draw 2—2. They were held to be joint champions for the season.

Celtic and Rangers finished level on points in 1904–5. A decider was won by Celtic, 2—1.

| | | Division II or B | | |
|---|---|---|---|---|
| 1929–30 | Leith Athletic | 2.190 | East Fife | 1.965 |
| 1931–32 | East Stirling | 2.018 | St. Johnstone | 1.961 |
| 1948–49 | Raith Rovers | 1.818 | Stirling Albion | 1.510 |
| 1950–51 | Queen of South | 1.971 | Stirling Albion | 1.772 |
| 1969–70 | Falkirk | 2.764 | Cowdenbeath | 2.314 |

Goal difference rather than goal average is used to determine the order of teams finishing level on points in the World Cup and Olympic Games, and this system is now used by the Scottish League where it was first applied in 1971–2 to place Dumbarton ahead of Arbroath at the top of Division II.

## GOALKEEPERS
See also DEBUTS

The goalkeeper, as we know him today, came into being about 1870. The word "goalkeeper" appeared in the Sheffield Rules before then, but not in reference to a particular individual.

The relevant passage occurs in the rule concerning "offside." It reads:

"The goalkeeper is that player on the defending side who, for the time being, is nearest his own goal."

The first mention of a goalkeeper as a player who is permitted to use his hands was made in the Football Association Rules of 1870.

### Four Goalkeepers
Four goalkeepers were called upon to take part in the England v. Wales game at Wrexham, Mar. 16, 1908. England's goalkeeper was H. Bailey (Leicester Fosse). The Welsh goalkeeper, L. R. Roose (Sunderland) was injured in the first half and his place was taken by full-back C. Morris (Derby County). In the second half England agreed to D. Davies (Bolton Wanderers) substituting in goal, and Morris returned to his original position.

### Goalkeepers' Jerseys
At the annual meeting of the Football League, June 8, 1909, it was decided that goalkeepers must play in distinctive colours of either scarlet, royal blue or white, to assist the referee. Royal green was added on June 3, 1912.

On June 3, 1921, it was ruled that goalkeepers in international matches should wear jerseys of deep yellow.

### Goalkeeper Goal-scorers
The Football League goalscoring record for a goalkeeper was set up in season 1923-24 by A. Birch of Chesterfield. He played in every one of Chesterfield's Division III(N) matches that season and scored five goals, all from penalties.

C. Williams, playing in goal for Manchester City, scored with a goal kick against Sunderland in a Division I game, April 14, 1900. The Sunderland goalkeeper, E. Doig, touched the ball as it entered the net. Sunderland won 3—1. In those days the full-back (in this instance, D. Jones) tapped the ball into the goalkeeper's hands to enable him to take a drop kick.

Three other goalkeepers who have scored with long kicks are P. Jennings (Tottenham Hotspur) v. Manchester United, Charity Shield, Aug. 12, 1967; P. Shilton (Leicester City) v. Southampton, Division I, Oct. 14, 1967 and R. Woods (East Stirling) v. Queen of the South, Scottish League, Division II, Jan. 9, 1971.

A goalkeeper's "own goal" was scored at Home Park, Plymouth, 16 minutes after the start of a Division II game between Plymouth Argyle and Fulham, on Oct. 2, 1954, when F. Elliott, the Fulham goalkeeper, in trying to cut out a cross shot while the Plymouth Argyle centre-forward Langman, challenged him, fell as he smothered the ball and rolled over on his back, injured. As he lay on the ground he threw the ball back over his head and it rolled gently into his own goal.

Other goalkeepers who have suffered the misfortune of scoring in their own goal include: H. G. Williamson (England) v. Ireland, Feb. 25, 1905; H. Brown (Queen's Park Rangers) v. Northampton Town, Dec. 27, 1954; J. Cumbes (West Bromwich Albion) v. Wolverhampton Wanderers, Nov. 7, 1970; R. Drinkwater (Queen's Park Rangers) v. Brentford, Nov. 22, 1958; G. Wright (Colchester United) v. Torquay United, Feb. 16, 1952; H. Gregg (Manchester United) v. Tottenham Hotspur, Nov. 9, 1963; G. Sprake (Leeds United) v. Liverpool, Dec. 9, 1967; M. Gibson (Bristol City) v. Manchester City, Aug. 28, 1965; F. Lane (Liverpool) v. Derby County, Sept. 2, 1972; R. Wilson (Exeter City) v. Torquay United, Dec. 26, 1972.

There have been several instances of goalkeepers giving up their position during a game because of injury, continuing in another position and scoring. Examples include T. Adlington (Torquay United) v. Barnet, F.A. Cup, 1st Round, Nov. 16, 1963; I. Black (Fulham) v. Leicester City, Division II, Aug. 25, 1952; G. Bradley (Notts County) v. Leicester City, Division II, Sept. 22, 1956; H. Dowd (Manchester City) v. Bury, Division II, Feb. 8, 1964; G. Farm (Blackpool) v. Preston North End, Division I, Oct. 20, 1955; M. Granger (Halifax Town) v. Workington, F.A. Cup, 1st Round, Nov. 16, 1963; D. Herod (Stoke City) v. Aston Villa, Division I, Feb. 16, 1952; F. Moss (Arsenal) v. Everton, Division I, Mar. 16, 1935; E. Scattergood (Bradford) v. Clapton Orient, Division II, Dec. 26, 1921; B. Singleton (Exeter City) v. Aldershot, Division III(S), Dec. 25, 1950; J. Savage (Halifax Town) v. Bradford, Division III(N), Dec. 27, 1952; C. Tinsley (Exeter City) v. Workington, Division IV, Sept. 20, 1962; A. Wilkie (Reading) v. Halifax Town (2 goals), Division III, Aug. 31, 1962.

E. Scattergood scored 8 goals during his league career with Derby County and Bradford, 1907-25, 7 of them from the penalty spot.

J. Maidment, Newport County goal-keeper, scored 3 goals from the penalty spot in Division III(S), seasons 1927-8 (2) and 1928-9 (1).

J. A. Read, who kept goal for Sheffield Wednesday, Peterborough United, and Luton Town, also made several appearances as a forward and once scored three goals for Luton Town v. Notts County, Division IV, Nov. 20, 1965.

## GOAL NETS
Goal nets were invented and patented by J. A. Brodie of Liverpool in 1890. The first important game in which nets were used was North v. South, at Nottingham, Jan. 1891. Nets were first used in the F.A. Cup Final in 1891 at the Oval.

## GOAL-SCORING (INDIVIDUALS)
**Aggregate Record for Single Season**
Football League:
Division I:

| | | Goals | Games |
|---|---|---|---|
| W. R. Dean (Everton) | 1927-28 | 60 | 39 |
| T. Waring (Aston Villa) | 1930-31 | 49 | 39 |

Division II:

| | | Goals | Games |
|---|---|---|---|
| G. Camsell (Middlesbrough) | 1926-27 | 59 | 37 |
| D. Dooley (Sheffield Wednesday) | 1951-52 | 46 | 30 |

Division III(S):

| | | | |
|---|---|---|---|
| J. Payne (Luton Town) | 1936-37 | 55 | 39 |
| C. Bourton (Coventry City) | 1931-32 | 49 | 40 |

Division III(N):

| | | | |
|---|---|---|---|
| E. Harston (Mansfield Town) | 1936-37 | 55 | 41 |
| A. Lythgoe (Stockport County) | 1933-34 | 46 | 39 |

Division III:

| | | | |
|---|---|---|---|
| D. Reeves (Southampton) | 1959-60 | 39 | 46 |

Division IV:

| | | | |
|---|---|---|---|
| T. Bly (Peterborough United) | 1960-61 | 52 | 46 |

Scottish League:
Division I:

| | | | |
|---|---|---|---|
| W. McFadyen (Motherwell) | 1931-32 | 52 | 34 |

Division II:

| | | | |
|---|---|---|---|
| J. Smith (Ayr United) | 1927-28 | 66 | 38 |

Highest aggregate of goals in a single season of first-class football in any of the home countries is 96 by F. Roberts, Glentoran centre-forward, in season 1930-31.

| Irish League | 55 |
|---|---|
| Irish Cup | 4 |
| Belfast City Cup | 28 |
| County Antrim Shield | 7 |
| Belfast Charity Cup | 2 |
| | 96 |

J. Bambrick, Linfield centre-forward, scored 94 goals in season 1929-30:

| Irish League | 50 |
|---|---|
| Irish Cup | 7 |
| Belfast City Cup | 10 |
| County Antrim Shield | 5 |
| Belfast Charity Cup | 9 |
| Inter-League games | 5 |
| Irish Gold Cup | 1 |
| Conder Cup | 1 |
| International games | 6 |
| | 94 |

J. Smith, Ayr United centre-forward scored 84 goals in season 1927-8.

| Scottish League, Division II | 66 |
|---|---|
| Scottish F.A. Cup | 2 |
| Ayr Charity Cup | 1 |
| Other Games | 15 |
| | 84 |

W. Dean, Everton centre-forward scored 82 goals in season 1927-8.

| Football League, Division I | 60 |
|---|---|
| F.A. Cup | 3 |
| Inter-League games | 6 |
| International trial games | 8 |
| Internationals | 5 |
| | 82 |

G. Camsell, Middlesbrough centre-forward, scored 79 goals in season 1926-7.

| Football League, Division II | 59 |
|---|---|
| F.A. Cup | 5 |
| North-Eastern League | 12 |
| International trial games | 3 |
| | 79 |

Top League scorers in post-war seasons in European countries:
J. Deak (FTC), Hungary, 59 goals, 1948-49
J. Deak (SZAC), Hungary, 54 goals, 1945-46
F. Puskas (Kispest), Hungary, 50 goals, 1947-48
R. Bonyhadi (Arad), Rumania, 49 goals, 1947-48
J. Deak (SZAC), Hungary, 48 goals 1946-47
J. Humpal (Sochaux), France, 45 goals, 1946-47

H. Schlienz (VFB Stuttgart), West Germany, 45 goals, 1945-46
J. Skoblar (Marseille), France, 44 goals, 1970-71
Top goal-scorers in each division for every season since World War I:

### Division I

| | | |
|---|---|---|
| 1919-20 | F. Morris, West Bromwich Albion | 37 |
| 1920-21 | J. Smith, Bolton Wanderers | 38 |
| 1921-22 | A. Wilson, Middlesbrough | 31 |
| 1922-23 | C. Buchan, Sunderland | 30 |
| 1923-24 | W. Chadwick, Everton | 28 |
| 1924-25 | F. Roberts, Manchester City | 31 |
| 1925-26 | E. Harper, Blackburn Rovers | 43 |
| 1926-27 | J. Trotter, Sheffield Wednesday | 37 |
| 1927-28 | W. Dean, Everton | 60 |
| 1928-29 | D. Halliday, Sunderland | 43 |
| 1929-30 | V. Watson, West Ham United | 41 |
| 1930-31 | T. Waring, Aston Villa | 49 |
| 1931-32 | W. Dean, Everton | 44 |
| 1932-33 | J. Bowers, Derby County | 35 |
| 1933-34 | J. Bowers, Derby County | 35 |
| 1934-35 | E. Drake, Arsenal | 42 |
| 1935-36 | E. Glover, Grimsby Town | 31 |
| | H. Carter, Sunderland | 31 |
| | R. Gurney, Sunderland | 31 |
| 1936-37 | F. Steel, Stoke City | 33 |
| 1937-38 | T. Lawton, Everton | 38 |
| 1938-39 | T. Lawton, Everton | 35 |
| 1946-47 | D. Westcott, Wolverhampton Wanderers | 37 |
| 1947-48 | R. Rooke, Arsenal | 33 |
| 1948-49 | W. Moir, Bolton Wanderers | 25 |
| 1949-50 | D. Davis, Sunderland | 25 |
| 1950-51 | S. Mortensen, Blackpool | 30 |
| 1951-52 | G. Robledo, Newcastle United | 33 |
| 1952-53 | C. Wayman, Preston North End | 24 |
| 1953-54 | J. Glazzard, Huddersfield Town | 29 |
| 1954-55 | R. Allen, West Bromwich Albion | 27 |
| 1955-56 | N. Lofthouse, Bolton Wanderers | 33 |
| 1956-57 | J. Charles, Leeds United | 38 |
| 1957-58 | R. Smith, Tottenham Hotspur | 36 |
| 1958-59 | J. Greaves, Chelsea | 33 |
| 1959-69 | D. Viollet, Manchester United | 32 |
| 1960-61 | J. Greaves, Chelsea | 41 |
| 1961-62 | R. Crawford, Ipswich Town | 33 |
| | D. Kevan, West Bromwich Albion | 33 |
| 1962-63 | J. Greaves, Tottenham Hotspur | 37 |
| 1963-64 | J. Greaves, Tottenham Hotspur | 35 |
| 1964-65 | A. McEvoy, Blackburn Rovers | 29 |
| | J. Greaves, Tottenham Hotspur | 29 |
| 1965-66 | W. Irvine, Burnley | 29 |
| 1966-67 | R. Davies, Southampton | 37 |
| 1967-68 | G. Best, Manchester United | 28 |
| | R. Davies, Southampton | 28 |
| 1968-69 | J. Greaves, Tottenham Hotspur | 27 |
| 1969-70 | J. Astle, West Bromwich Albion | 25 |
| 1970-71 | A. Brown, West Bromwich Albion | 28 |
| 1971-72 | F. Lee, Manchester City | 33 |
| 1972-73 | B. Robson, West Ham United | 28 |

### Division II

| | | |
|---|---|---|
| 1919-20 | S. Taylor, Huddersfield Town | 35 |
| 1920-21 | S. Puddefoot, West Ham United | 29 |
| 1921-22 | J. Broad, Stoke City | 25 |
| 1922-23 | H. Bedford, Blackpool | 32 |
| 1923-24 | H. Bedford, Blackpool | 34 |
| 1924-25 | A. Chandler, Leicester City | 33 |
| 1925-26 | J. Trotter, Sheffield Wednesday | 37 |
| 1926-27 | G. Camsell, Middlesbrough | 59 |
| 1927-28 | J. Cookson, West Bromwich Albion | 38 |
| 1928-29 | J. Hampson, Blackpool | 40 |
| 1929-30 | J. Hampson, Blackpool | 45 |
| 1930-31 | W. Dean, Everton | 39 |
| 1931-32 | C. Pearce, Swansea Town | 35 |
| 1932-33 | E. Harper, Preston North End | 37 |
| 1933-34 | E. Glover, Grimsby Town | 42 |
| 1934-35 | J. Milsom, Bolton Wanderers | 31 |
| 1935-36 | R. Finan, Blackpool | 34 |
| | E. Dodds, Sheffield United | 34 |
| 1936-37 | J. Bowers, Leicester City | 33 |
| 1937-38 | G. Henson, Bradford | 27 |
| 1938-39 | H. Billington, Luton Town | 28 |
| 1946-47 | C. Wayman, Newcastle United | 30 |
| 1947-48 | E. Quigley, Sheffield Wednesday | 23 |
| 1948-49 | C. Wayman, Southampton | 32 |
| 1949-50 | T. Briggs, Grimsby Town | 35 |
| 1950-51 | J. McCormack, Barnsley | 33 |
| 1951-52 | D. Dooley, Sheffield Wednesday | 46 |
| 1952-53 | A. Rowley, Leicester City | 39 |
| 1953-54 | J. Charles, Leeds United | 42 |
| 1954-55 | T. Briggs, Blackburn Rovers | 33 |
| 1955-56 | W. Gardiner, Leicester City | 34 |
| 1956-57 | A. Rowley, Leicester City | 44 |
| 1957-58 | B. Clough, Middlesbrough | 40 |
| 1958-59 | B. Clough, Middlesbrough | 42 |
| 1959-60 | B. Clough, Middlesbrough | 39 |
| 1960-61 | R. Crawford, Ipswich Town | 39 |
| 1961-62 | R. Hunt, Liverpool | 41 |
| 1962-63 | R. Tambling, Chelsea | 35 |
| 1963-64 | R. Saunders, Portsmouth | 33 |
| 1964-65 | G. O'Brien, Southampton | 34 |
| 1965-66 | M. Chivers, Southampton | 30 |
| 1966-67 | R. Gould, Coventry City | 24 |
| 1967-68 | J. Hickton, Middlesbrough | 24 |
| 1968-69 | J. Toshack, Cardiff City | 22 |
| 1969-70 | J. Hickton, Middlesbrough | 24 |
| 1970-71 | J. Hickton, Middlesbrough | 25 |
| 1971-72 | R. Latchford, Birmingham City | 23 |
| 1972-73 | D. Givens, Queen's Park Rangers | 23 |

### Division III(S)

| | | |
|---|---|---|
| 1920-21 | J. Connor, Crystal Palace | 28 |

|  |  |
|---|---|
| E. Simms, Luton Town | 28 |
| G. Whitworth, Northampton Town | 28 |
| 1921-22 F. Richardson, Plymouth Argyle | 30 |
| 1922-23 F. Pagnam, Watford | 30 |
| 1923-24 W. P. Haines, Portsmouth | 28 |
| 1924-25 J. Fowler, Swansea Town | 28 |
| 1925-26 J. Cock, Plymouth Argyle | 32 |
| 1926-27 D. Morris, Swindon Town | 47 |
| 1927-28 D. Morris, Swindon Town | 38 |
| 1928-29 A. Rennie, Luton Town | 43 |
| 1929-30 G. Goddard, Queen's Park Rangers | 37 |
| 1930-31 P. Simpson, Crystal Palace | 46 |
| 1931-32 C. Bourton, Coventry City | 49 |
| 1932-33 C. Bourton, Coventry City | 40 |
| 1933-34 A. Dawes, Northampton Town and Crystal Palace | 27 |
| 1934-35 R. Allen, Charlton Athletic | 32 |
| 1935-36 A. Dawes, Crystal Palace | 38 |
| 1936-37 J. Payne, Luton Town | 55 |
| 1937-38 H. Crawshaw, Mansfield Town | 25 |
| 1938-39 G. Morton, Swindon Town | 28 |
| 1946-47 D. Clarke, Bristol City | 36 |
| 1947-48 L. Townsend, Bristol City | 29 |
| 1948-49 D. McGibbon, Bournemouth and Boscome United | 30 |
| 1949-50 T. Lawton, Notts County | 31 |
| 1950-51 W. Ardron, Nottingham Forest | 36 |
| 1951-52 R. Blackman, Reading | 39 |
| 1952-53 G. Bradford, Bristol Rov. | 33 |
| 1953-54 J. English, Northampton Town | 28 |
| 1954-55 E. Morgan, Gillingham | 31 |
| 1955-56 R. Collins, Torquay United | 40 |
| 1956-57 E. Phillips, Ipswich Town | 42 |
| 1957-58 S. McGrory, Southend United | 31 |
| D. Reeves, Southampton | 31 |

## Division III(N)

|  |  |
|---|---|
| 1921-22 J. Carmichael, Grimsby Town | 37 |
| 1922-23 G. Beel, Chesterfield | 23 |
| J. Carmichael, Grimsby Town | 23 |
| 1923-24 D. Brown, Darlington | 27 |
| 1924-25 D. Brown, Darlington | 39 |
| 1925-26 J. Cookson, Chesterfield | 44 |
| 1926-27 A. Whitehurst, Rochdale | 44 |
| 1927-28 J. Smith, Stockport County | 38 |
| 1928-29 J. McConnell, Carlisle United | 43 |
| 1929-30 F. Newton, Stockport County | 36 |
| 1930-31 J. McConnell, Carlisle United | 37 |
| 1931-32 B. Hall, Lincoln City | 42 |
| 1932-33 W. McNaughton, Hull City | 39 |
| 1933-34 A. Lythgoe, Stockport County | 46 |
| 1934-35 G. Alsop, Walsall | 39 |
| 1935-36 R. Bell, Tranmere Rovers | 33 |
| 1936-37 E. Harston, Mansfield Town | 55 |
| 1937-38 J. Roberts, Port Vale | 28 |
| 1938-39 S. Hunt, Carlisle United | 32 |
| 1946-47 C. Jordan, Doncaster Rovers | 41 |
| 1947-48 J. Hutchinson, Lincoln City | 32 |
| 1948-49 W. Ardon, Rotherham United | 29 |

|  |  |
|---|---|
| 1949-50 R. Phillips, Crewe Alexandra | 26 |
| P. Doherty, Doncaster Rovers | 26 |
| 1950-51 J. Shaw, Rotherham United | 37 |
| 1951-52 A. Graver, Lincoln City | 36 |
| 1952-53 J. Whitehouse, Carlisle United | 29 |
| 1953-54 G. Ashman, Carlisle United | 30 |
| 1954-55 A. Bottom, York City | 30 |
| D. Travis, Oldham Athletic | 30 |
| J. Connor, Stockport County | 30 |
| 1955-56 R. Crossbie, Grimsby Town | 36 |
| 1956-57 R. Straw, Derby County | 37 |
| 1957-58 A. Ackerman, Carlisle United | 35 |

## Division III

|  |  |
|---|---|
| 1958-59 E. Towers, Brentford | 32 |
| 1959-60 D. Reeves, Southampton | 39 |
| 1960-61 A. Richards, Walsall | 36 |
| 1961-62 C. Holton, Watford and Northampton | 37 |
| 1962-63 G. Hudson, Coventry City | 30 |
| 1963-64 A. Biggs, Bristol Rovers | 30 |
| 1964-65 K. Wagstaff, Mansfield Town and Hull City | 34 |
| 1965-66 L. Allen, Queen's Park Rangers | 30 |
| 1966-67 R. Marsh, Queen's Park Rangers | 30 |
| 1967-68 D. Rogers, Swindon Town | 25 |
| 1968-69 D. Rogers, Swindon Town | 22 |
| 1969-70 G. Jones, Bury | 26 |
| 1970-71 G. Ingram, Preston North End | 22 |
| D. Roberts, Mansfield Town | 22 |
| 1971-72 E. MacDougall, Bournemouth | 35 |
| 1972-73 A. Horsfield, Charlton Athletic | 26 |

## Division IV

|  |  |
|---|---|
| 1958-59 A. Rowley, Shrewsbury Town | 37 |
| 1959-60 C. Holton, Watford | 42 |
| 1960-61 T. Bly, Peterborough United | 52 |
| 1961-62 R. R. Hunt, Colchester United | 37 |
| 1962-63 K. Wagstaff, Mansfield Town | 34 |
| 1963-64 H. McIlmoyle, Carlisle United | 39 |
| 1964-65 A. Jeffrey, Doncaster Rovers | 36 |
| 1965-66 K. Hector, Bradford | 44 |
| 1966-67 E. Phythian, Hartlepools United | 23 |
| 1967-68 L. Massie, Halifax Town | 25 |
| R. Chapman, Port Vale | 25 |
| 1968-69 G. Talbot, Chester | 22 |
| 1969-70 A. Kinsey, Wrexham | 27 |
| 1970-71 E. MacDougall, Bournemouth | 42 |
| 1971-72 P. Price, Peterborough United | 28 |
| 1972-73 F. Binney, Exeter City | 27 |

## Scottish League

## Division I

|  |  |
|---|---|
| 1919-20 H. Ferguson, Motherwell | 33 |
| 1920-21 H. Ferguson, Motherwell | 43 |
| 1921-22 D. Walker, St. Mirren | 45 |
| 1922-23 J. White, Hearts | 30 |
| 1923-24 D. Halliday, Dundee | 38 |

| | | |
|---|---|---|
| 1924-25 | W. Devlin, Cowdenbeath | 33 |
| 1925-26 | W. Devlin, Cowdenbeath | 37 |
| 1926-27 | J. McGrory, Celtic | 49 |
| 1927-28 | J. McGrory, Celtic | 47 |
| 1928-29 | E. Morrison, Falkirk | 43 |
| 1929-30 | B. Yorston, Aberdeen | 38 |
| 1930-31 | B. Battles, Hearts | 44 |
| 1931-32 | W. McFadyen, Motherwell | 52 |
| 1932-33 | W. McFadyen, Motherwell | 45 |
| 1933-34 | J. Smith, Rangers | 41 |
| 1934-35 | D. McCulloch, Hearts | 38 |
| 1935-36 | J. McGrory, Celtic | 50 |
| 1936-37 | D. Wilson, Hamilton Academicals | 34 |
| 1937-38 | A. Black, Hearts | 40 |
| 1938-39 | A. Venters, Rangers | 34 |
| 1946-47 | R. Mitchell, Third Lanark | 22 |
| 1947-48 | A. Aikman, Falkirk | 20 |
| 1948-49 | A. Stott, Dundee | 30 |
| 1949-50 | W. Bauld, Hearts | 30 |
| 1950-51 | L. Reilly, Hibernian | 22 |
| 1951-52 | L. Reilly, Hibernian | 27 |
| 1952-53 | C. Fleming, East Fife | 30 |
| | L. Reilly, Hibernian | 30 |
| 1953-54 | J. Wardhaugh, Hearts | 27 |
| 1954-55 | W. Bauld, Hearts | 21 |
| 1955-56 | J. Wardhaugh, Hearts | 30 |
| 1956-57 | H. Baird, Airdrieonians | 33 |
| 1957-58 | J. Wardhaugh, Hearts | 28 |
| 1958-59 | J. Baker, Hibernian | 25 |
| 1959-60 | J. Baker, Hibernian | 42 |
| 1960-61 | J. Harley, Third Lanark | 42 |
| 1961-62 | A. Gilzean, Dundee | 24 |
| 1962-63 | J. Millar, Rangers | 25 |
| 1963-64 | A. Gilzean, Dundee | 32 |
| 1964-65 | J. Forrest, Rangers | 30 |
| 1965-66 | J. McBride, Celtic | 31 |
| 1966-67 | S. Chalmers, Celtic | 23 |
| 1967-68 | R. Lennox, Celtic | 32 |
| 1968-69 | K. Cameron, Dundee United | 27 |
| 1969-70 | C. Stein, Rangers | 24 |
| 1970-71 | H. Hood, Celtic | 22 |
| 1971-72 | J. Harper, Aberdeen | 33 |
| 1972-73 | A. Gordon, Hibernian | 27 |

**Aggregate Record in League Career**

Here are listed the men who have scored 250 or more goals in Football League and Scottish League games:

| | | | | |
|---|---|---|---|---|
| A. G. Rowley | c.f. | West Bromwich Albion, Fulham, Leicester City, Shrewsbury Town | 1946–65 | 434 |
| J. McGrory | c.f. | Celtic, Clydebank | 1922–38 | 410 |
| H. Gallacher | c.f. | Airdreonians, Newcastle United, Chelsea, Derby County, Notts County, Grimsby Town, Gateshead | 1921–39 | 387 |
| W. R. Dean | c.f. | Tranmere Rovers, Everton, Notts County | 1923–37 | 379 |
| H. Ferguson | c.f. | Motherwell, Cardiff City, Dundee | 1916–30 | 361 |
| S. Bloomer | i.r. | Derby County (twice), Middlesbrough | 1892–1914 | 357 |
| J. Greaves | i.f. | Chelsea, Tottenham Hotspur, West Ham United | 1957–71 | 352 |
| G. Camsell | c.f. | Durham City, Middlesbrough | 1923–39 | 346 |
| D. Halliday | c.f. | St. Mirren, Dundee, Sunderland, Arsenal, Manchester City, Clapton Orient | 1920–35 | 338 |
| V. Watson | c.f. | West Ham United, Southampton | 1920–36 | 317 |
| J. Atyeo | c.f. | Bristol City | 1951–66 | 315 |
| Joe Smith | i.l. | Bolton Wanderers, Stockport County | 1908–29 | 314 |
| H. Johnson | c.f. | Sheffield United, Mansfield Town | 1919–36 | 309 |
| H. Bedford | c.f. or i.f. | Nottingham Forest, Blackpool, Derby County, Newcastle United, Sunderland, Bradford, Chesterfield | 1919–34 | 309 |
| R. McPhail | i.l. | Airdrieonians, Rangers | 1923–39 | 305 |
| G. Hodgson | c.f. or i.f. | Liverpool, Aston Villa, Leeds United | 1925–39 | 296 |
| C. Holton | c.f. | Arsenal, Watford (twice), Northampton Town, Crystal Palace, Charlton Athletic, Leyton Orient | 1950–68 | 295 |
| D. H. Morris | c.f. | Fulham, Brentford, Millwall, Swansea Town, Swindon Town, Clapton Orient | 1920–34 | 294 |
| R. Crawford | c.f. | Portsmouth, Ipswich Town (twice), Wolverhampton Wanderers, W.B.A., Charlton Athletic, Colchester United | 1957–72 | 290 |
| J. Hampson | i.f. | Nelson, Blackpool | 1925–38 | 289 |
| E. Hine | i.r. | Barnsley (twice), Leicester City, Huddersfield Town, Manchester United | 1921–38 | 287 |
| J. H. Baker | c.f. | Hibernian (twice), Arsenal, Nottingham Forest, Sunderland, Raith Rovers | 1957–73 | 282 |
| A. Chandler | c.f. | Queen's Park Rangers, Leicester City | 1920–35 | 278 |

| | | | | |
|---|---|---|---|---|
| T. Keetley | c.f. | Bradford, Doncaster Rovers, Notts County | 1919–33 | 277 |
| R. Allen | c.f. | Port Vale, West Bromwich Albion, Crystal Palace | 1946–65 | 274 |
| W. McFadyen | c.f. | Motherwell, Huddersfield Town | 1923–39 | 269 |
| R. Hunt | i.f. | Liverpool, Bolton Wanderers | 1960–72 | 269 |
| G. Brown | c.f. | Huddersfield Town, Aston Villa, Burnley, Leeds United, Darlington | 1921–38 | 268 |
| D. B. N. Jack | i.f. | Plymouth Argyle, Bolton Wanderers, Arsenal | 1920–34 | 261 |
| E. C. Harper | c.f. | Blackburn Rovers (twice), Sheffield Wednesday, Tottenham Hotspur, Preston North End | 1923–35 | 260 |
| J. McColl | c.f. | Celtic, Stoke, Partick Thistle, Hibernian, Leith Athletic | 1913–32 | 260† |
| C. M. Buchan | i.r. | Sunderland, Arsenal | 1910–28 | 258 |
| R. T. Davies | c.f. | Chester, Luton Town, Norwich City, Southampton | 1959–73 | 257* |
| R. Ferrier | o.l. | Motherwell | 1918–37 | 256 |
| J. Cookson | c.f. | Chesterfield, West Bromwich Albion, Plymouth Argyle, Swindon Town | 1925–39 | 256 |
| T. Briggs | c.f. | Grimsby Town (twice), Coventry City, Birmingham City, Blackburn Rovers | 1947–59 | 255 |
| N. Lofthouse | c.f. | Bolton Wanderers | 1946–61 | 255 |
| C. Wayman | c.f. | Newcastle United, Southampton, Preston North End, Middlesbrough, Darlington | 1946–58 | 254 |
| B. Clough | c.f. | Middlesbrough, Sunderland | 1955–64 | 252 |
| I. Allchurch | i.f. | Swansea Town (twice), Newcastle United, Cardiff City | 1949–68 | 250 |
| J. A. Bradford | c.f. | Birmingham, Bristol City | 1920–36 | 250 |
| K. Wagstaff | i.f. | Mansfield Town, Hull City | 1960–73 | 250* |

\* May still add to this total in 1973–74.
† Total of goals scored season 1917–18 not known.

**Aggregate Record in League Career for a single club**
Here are listed the men who have scored 200 or more goals *for a single club* in either the Football League or the Scottish League. Only league games are included.

| | | | | |
|---|---|---|---|---|
| J. McGrory | c.f. | Celtic | 1922–38 | 397 |
| W. R. Dean | c.f. | Everton | 1925–37 | 349 |
| G. Camsell | c.f. | Middlesbrough | 1925–39 | 326 |
| J. Atyeo | c.f. | Bristol City | 1951–66 | 315 |
| V. Watson | c.f. | West Ham United | 1920–35 | 306 |
| S. Bloomer | i.r. | Derby County | 1892–1906, 1910–14 | 291 |
| H. Ferguson | c.f. | Motherwell | 1916–25 | 283 |
| A. Chandler | c.f. | Leicester City | 1923–35 | 262 |
| R. Ferrier | o.l. | Motherwell | 1918–37 | 256 |
| N. Lofthouse | c.f. | Bolton Wanderers | 1946–61 | 255 |
| Joe Smith | i.l. | Bolton Wanderers | 1908–26 | 254 |
| A. G. Rowley | c.f. | Leicester City | 1950–58 | 251 |
| J. A. Bradford | c.f. | Birmingham | 1920–35 | 250 |
| W. McFadyen | c.f. | Motherwell | 1923–37 | 249 |
| J. Hampson | i.f. | Blackpool | 1927–38 | 247 |
| D. Wilson | c.f. | Hamilton Academicals | 1928–39 | 246 |
| G. Bradford | c.f. | Bristol Rovers | 1949–64 | 245 |
| R. Hunt | i.f. | Liverpool | 1960 69 | 245 |
| G. Turner | i.f. | Luton Town | 1949–64 | 243 |
| R. McPhail | i.l. | Rangers | 1927–39 | 233 |
| G. Hodgson | c.f. or i.f. | Liverpool | 1925–26 | 233 |
| J. Smith | c.f. | Rangers | 1929–39 | 224 |

| D. McCrae | c.f. | St. Mirren | 1923–34 | 223 |
|---|---|---|---|---|
| J. Greaves | i.f. | Tottenham Hotspur | 1961–70 | 220 |
| D. H. Morris | c.f. | Swindon Town | 1926–33 | 216 |
| W. Liddell | o.l. or c.f. | Liverpool | 1946–60 | 216 |
| H. Hampton | c.f. | Aston Villa | 1904–20 | 213 |
| W. Walker | i.f. | Aston Villa | 1919–34 | 213 |
| C. M. Buchan | i.r. | Sunderland | 1911–25 | 209 |
| J. Wardhaugh | i.l. | Hearts | 1946–59 | 206 |
| R. Allen | c.f. | West Bromwich Albion | 1950–61 | 206 |
| H. Johnson | c.f. | Sheffield United | 1919–30 | 205 |
| R. Gurney | c.f. | Sunderland | 1925–39 | 205 |
| R. Collins | o.l. or c.f. | Torquay United | 1948–58 | 204 |
| G. W. Elliott | c.f. | Middlesbrough | 1909–25 | 202 |
| C. R. Eyre | c.f. | Bournemouth and Boscombe | 1924–33 | 202 |
| J. Patterson | i.f. or c.f. | Queen of the South | 1949–63 | 201 |
| A. Wilson | c.f. | Sheffield Wednesday | 1900–19 | 200 |

## Averages

Averages are not normally associated with soccer but readers may be interested to see how the players who have scored over 300 League goals in the Football League or Scottish League figure in such a list. The figures quoted are the average of goals per game.

J. McGrory (Celtic, Clydebank) 1·004, W. R. Dean (Everton, etc.) ·867, H. Ferguson (Motherwell, Cardiff City, Dundee) ·855, G. Camsell (Durham City, Middlesbrough) ·784, D. Halliday (Dundee, Sunderland, etc.) ·751, H. Gallacher (Airdrie, Newcastle United, etc.) ·712, A. G. Rowley (West Bromwich Albion, Fulham, etc.) ·701, J. Greaves (Chelsea, Spurs, West Ham) ·691, H. Johnson (Sheffield United, Mansfield Town), ·653, R. McPhail (Airdrie, Rangers) ·650, V. Watson (West Ham United, Southampton) ·636, H. Bedford (Nottingham Forest, Blackpool, etc.) ·634, S. Bloomer (Derby County, Middlesbrough) ·586, Joe Smith (Bolton Wanderers, Stockport County) ·582, J. Atyeo (Portsmouth, Bristol City) ·525.

## Both Sides

The only player to score two goals for each side in a single Football League game—S. Wynne, Oldham Athletic v. Manchester United, Division II, Oct. 6, 1923. He scored with a free kick and a penalty kick for his own side but also put two through his own goal.

## Consecutive Games

A. Chandler created a record in 1924-25 by scoring in 16 consecutive Football League games for Leicester City in Division II.

## Debuts, Goal-scoring

The record number of goals scored by a player making his debut in first-class football is eight by J. Dyet, making his first appearance for King's Park v. Forfar Athletic in the Scottish League, Division II, Jan. 2, 1930. Result 12—2.

In the Football League the goal-scoring record for a player making his first appearance is five. G. Hilsdon scored that number for Chelsea v. Glossop, Division II, Sept. 1, 1906.

Five players have each scored four goals in League debut:

A. Gardiner, centre-forward for Leicester City v. Portsmouth, Feb. 21, 1934.

T. Hall, for Rotherham v. Wigan Borough, Nov. 5, 1927.

F. Howard, centre-forward for Manchester City v. Liverpool, Jan. 18, 1913.

J. Shepherd, centre-forward for Millwall v. Leyton Orient (A.), Oct. 25, 1952.

R. Turnbull, centre-forward for Sunderland v. Portsmouth, Nov. 29, 1947.

One other player scored four goals when making his debut for a Football League club, but this was in the F.A. Cup, 3rd Round, Jan. 5, 1957. Seventeen-year-old Ian Lawson scored four goals for Burnley v. Chesterfield.

Many players have scored three goals when making their Football League debut. They include:

M. Daniel, Luton Town v. Sheffield Wednesday, Aug. 31, 1946.

J. Downing, Darlington v. Carlisle United, April 29, 1933.

W. Hales, Gillingham v. Port Vale (A), Mar. 31, 1951.

R. Hollis, Norwich City v. Queen's Park Rangers, April 21, 1948.

T. Francis, Hartlepools United v. Bradford, Nov. 30, 1963.

R. Graham, Liverpool v. Aston Villa, Sept. 26, 1964.

W. C. Jordan, West Bromwich Albion v. Gainsborough Trinity, Feb. 16, 1907.

J. Kendall, Barrow v. Rotherham United, May 31, 1947.

P. Laraman, Torquay United v. Barnsley, Sept. 7, 1961.

T. Lowder, Rotherham United v. Carlisle United, Dec. 4, 1948.

H. Nash, Aston Villa v. Liverpool, April 3, 1915.

N. O'Halloran, Cardiff City v. Charlton Athletic, Dec. 10, 1955.

M. Owen, Swindon Town v. Watford, Jan. 11, 1947.

D. Pearson, Oldham Athletic v. Halifax Town, Aug. 21, 1956.

J. Pye, Notts County, 1945. War-time League.

G. Robledo, Barnsley v Nottingham Forest, Aug. 31, 1946.

A. Rowles, Bristol City v. Exeter City, Jan. 15, 193338.

D. Thompson, Hull City, v. Accrington Stanley. Apl. 26, 1947.

K. Tucker, West Ham United v. Chesterfield, Oct. 4, 1947.

C. Vilijoen, Ipswich Town v. Portsmouth, Mar. 25, 1967.

R. Wainscoat, Barnsley v. Fulham, Mar. 6, 1920.

J. Welsh (3 in 6 min.) Queen of the South v. Cowdenbeath, Nov. 16, 1968.

A. Whittaker, Blackburn Rovers v. Preston North End, Oct. 14, 1899.

C. Wilson, Tottenham Hotspur v. South Shields, Sept. 20, 1919.

A. Withers, Blackpool v. Huddersfield Town, Nov. 18, 1950.

## European Cup

Individual match record—5 goals:

Albert, Ferencvaros v. IB Keflavik, Sept. 8, 1965.

Altafini, Milan v. Union Luxembourg, Sept. 12, 1962.

Crawford, Ipswich Town v. Floriana Malta, Sept. 25, 1962.

Kotkov, Lokomotiv Sofia v. FF Malmo, Sept. 10, 1964.

Lofquist, BK 1913 Odense v. CA Spora, Sept. 13, 1961.

Muller, Bayern Munich v. Oomonia Nicosia, Oct. 24, 1972.*

Ohlsson, OFK Gothenberg v. Linfield, Sept. 23, 1959.

Van Himst, Anderlecht v. Haka Valkeakoski (away), Sept. 14, 1966.

* This was a 2nd Round game. All others listed were in Preliminary Round.

## European Cup-winners' Cup

Individual match record—6 goals by Emmerich, Borussia Dortmund v. Floriana Malta, 1st Round, 1965-6.

## Fast Scoring

See also CUP SCORING in this section.

Four goals in five minutes were scored by:

J. McIntyre for Blackburn Rovers v. Everton, at Ewood Park, Division I, Sept. 16, 1922.

W. Richardson, West Bromwich Albion, centre-forward, at West Ham, Division I, Nov. 7, 1931.

Three goals in 2½ minutes were scored by E. Dodds in a war-time Cup game for Blackpool v. Tranmere Rovers, Feb. 28, 1943.

Three goals in three minutes were scored by:

W. Best, Southend United v. Brentwood, F.A. Cup, 2nd Round, Dec. 7, 1968.

J. Hartburn, Leyton Orient v. Shrewsbury Town, Division III(S), Jan. 22, 1955.

W. Lane, Watford v. Clapton Orient, Division III(S), Dec. 12, 1933.

G. Leggatt, Fulham v. Ipswich Town, Division I, Dec. 26, 1963.

J. Lindsay, Southport v. Scunthorpe United, Division III(N), Feb. 9, 1952.

J. McGrory, Celtic v. Motherwell, Scottish League, Division I, Mar. 14, 1936.

I. St. John, Motherwell v. Hibernian, Scottish League Cup, Aug. 15, 1959.

J. Scarth, Gillingham v. Leyton Orient, Division III(S), Nov. 1, 1952.

C. Stein, Rangers v. Arbroath, Scottish League, Division I, Nov. 2, 1968.

J. Swindells, Altrincham v. Scarborough, F.A. Cup, 1st Round, Nov. 13, 1965.

G. Talbot, Chester v. Crewe Alexandra, F.A. Cup, 1st Round, Nov. 14, 1964.

Six goals were scored in 21 min. by F. Keetley Lincoln City v. Halifax Town, Division III(N), Jan. 16, 1932.

The record of having scored the quickest goal in first-class football is credited to J. Fryatt who is considered to have scored only four seconds after the kick-off for Bradford v. Tranmere Rovers, April 25, 1964. This time is fantastic but it was confirmed by referee R. J. Simon.

Three men have each scored only six seconds after the kick-off: A. Mundy for Aldershot at Hartlepools, Division IV, Oct. 25, 1958: B. Jones for Notts County v. Torquay United, Division III, Mar. 31, 1962. Jones was making his League debut; K. Smith for Crystal Palace v. Derby County, at Derby, Division II, Dec. 12, 1964.

Other quick goals:

7 sec. W. Sharp for Partick Thistle v. Queen of the South, Scottish League, Division A, Dec. 20, 1947; R. Langton for Preston North End v. Manchester City, Division I, Aug. 25, 1948; R. Drake for

Stockport County v. Accrington Stanley, Division III(N), Dec. 25, 1956.

8 sec. K. East for Bournemouth v. Shrewsbury Town, Division III, at Bournemouth Aug. 31, 1968. G. Hudson, Tranmere Rovers v. Bury, Division III Dec. 2, 1967. V. Lambden, Bristol Rovers v. Aldershot, F.A. Cup, 3rd Round, Jan 6, 1951.

### F.A. Cup

The record individual score in an F.A. Cup tie is 9 goals by E. MacDougall, Bournemouth v. Margate, 1st Round, Nov. 20, 1971.

Scorers of 6 or more goals in F.A. Cup ties are listed in this section under MATCH RECORDS.

The highest number of goals scored by any player during this century, in one F.A. Cup-tie, in or after the third round (or the old first round equivalent) is six: G. Hilsdon for Chelsea v. Worksop Town, 1st Round, Jan. 11, 1908; R. Rooke, Fulham v. Bury, 3rd Round, Jan. 7, 1939; G. Best, Manchester United v. Northampton Town (A), 5th Round, Feb. 7, 1970.

D. Law also scored six goals in a cup-tie, Manchester City v. Luton Town, 4th Round, Jan. 28, 1961, but this game had to be abandoned.

The most goals for a defeated side was scored by W. H. Minter of St. Albans City who scored seven goals v. Dulwich Hamlet in a replayed 4th Qualifying Round tie of the F.A. Cup, Nov. 22, 1922. Result 8—7. Minter's side lost.

The following players have scored in every round of the F.A. Cup competition in a single season:

A. Brown, Tottenham Hotspur, 1900-01; E. Rimmer, Sheffield Wednesday 1934-35; F. O'Donnell, Preston North End 1936-37; S. Mortensen, Blackpool 1947-48; J. Milburn, Newcastle United 1950-51; N. Lofthouse, Bolton Wanderers 1952-53; C. Wayman, Preston North End 1953-54; J. Astle, West Bromwich Albion 1967-68; P. Osgood, Chelsea, 1969-70.

A. Brown scored the record number of 15 goals in the F.A. Cup, 1900-1901.

The individual F.A. Cup Final goalscoring record is held jointly by three players. Each scored three Cup Final goals:

| | |
|---|---|
| W. Townley, Blackburn Rovers | 1890 |
| J. Logan, Notts County | 1894 |
| S. Mortensen, Blackpool* | 1953 |

*One of his goals went in off a Bolton defender and is given as "Hassell, own goal" in some records.

The first full-back to score in an F.A. Cup Final at Wembley was E. Shimwell who scored with a penalty kick for Blackpool against Manchester United in 1948.

The quickest goal scored in an F.A. Cup Final occurred 40 sec. after the start of the Aston Villa v. West Bromwich Albion Final in 1895. It was scored by J. Devey although it is sometimes credited to R. Chatt.

J. Milburn scored for Newcastle United 45 sec. after the start of the 1955 Final v. Manchester City.

Blackburn Rovers' centre-forward, J. Roscamp, scored inside a minute against Huddersfield Town in the 1928 Cup Final.

### Fewest Goals

W. Milne, Swansea Town full-back, 1919-37, played in 500 Football League games before scoring his first League goal.

### Football League

The individual match record is ten goals by J. Payne (Luton Town).

See under MATCH RECORDS in this section for details of this feat and other scorers of six or more goals.

Various other scoring records in the Football League appear under individual headings in this section.

### Football League Cup

The highest individual score in a Football League Cup tie, five goals by D. Reeves, Southampton v. Leeds United, 4th Round, 1960-61, and also by R. Wilks, Queen's Park Rangers v. Oxford United, 3rd Round, 1967-68.

Highest individual aggregate in a single season, 11 goals by G. Hitchens (Aston Villa) 1960-61, G. Hurst (West Ham United), and A. Brown (West Bromwich Albion) 1965-66, R. Marsh (Queen's Park Rangers) 1966-67.

### Full-Backs

The probable record number of goals netted by a full-back in a Football League game is four, scored by S. Wynne, left-back of Oldham Athletic v. Manchester United, Division II, Oct. 6, 1923. Wynne scored once with a penalty, once with a free kick, and also put the ball twice into his own goal.

In season 1921-2, J. Evans, Southend United full-back, scored a total of 10 goals in the Football League, Division III(S). All the goals were scored from penalties. In season 1964-5, S. Lynn, Birmingham City's full-back also scored 10 goals (8 penalties).

C. Lawler scored 10 goals for Liverpool in Division I, 1969-70, all from open play as a full-back. Evans and Lynn ended the season as their club's top League goalscorer (Lynn actually shared top) and are the only full-backs who have achieved this distinction with Football League clubs.

## Goalkeepers, Goal-scoring
See GOALKEEPERS in separate section.

## Half-Backs
The record number of Football League goals scored by any player other than a forward in a single season is 15, by J. Lewis for Reading, Division III(S), 1951-2, and by A. Brown, West Bromwich Albion, Division I, 1968-9. Both players were at right-half. Brown actually scored two more League goals in this season but these were obtained while playing at inside-right.

Runner-up is A. Grimsdell who scored 14 goals from left-half for Tottenham Hotspur in Division II, 1919-20.

The record number of goals scored by a half-back in a single game in the Football League is three, by Robertson for Small Heath v. Luton Town, Division II, Nov. 12, 1898; T. McDonald for Newcastle United v. Cardiff City, Division I, Dec. 25, 1926; by W. Imrie for Newcastle United v. Wolverhampton Wanderers, Division I, April 21, 1934; J. Muir for Bristol Rovers v. Crystal Palace, Division III(S), Sept. 5, 1931; D. Mackay, Tottenham Hotspur v. West Ham United, Division I, Dec. 22, 1962; R. Rooks, Middlesbrough v. Cardiff City, Division II, May 3, 1966; D. Webb, Chelsea v. Ipswich Town (A.), Division I, Dec. 26, 1968; E. Winstanley, Barnsley v. Watford, Division III, April 22, 1969.

All three Chesterfield half-backs, H. Wass, H. Wightman, and R. Duckworth scored v. Accrington Stanley, Division III(N), Jan. 4, 1930.

In the Football Combination, May 1, 1961. Swindon Town's left half-back, P. Chamberlain, scored five goals against Crystal Palace.

## "Hat-Tricks"
The record number of "hat-tricks" scored in the Football League is 37 by W. Dean in 18 seasons.

The record number of "hat-tricks" in a season of League Football is nine by G. Camsell for Middlesbrough in Division II, 1926-7.

T. Keetley scored three goals in each of three consecutive Football League, Division II matches, away from home with Notts County, 1931: v. Plymouth Argyle, Oct. 10, 1931; v. Manchester United, Oct. 24, 1931; v. Chesterfield, Nov. 7, 1931.

J. Balmer scored three (or more) goals for Liverpool in each of three consecutive Football League, Division I, games: v. Portsmouth (H). Nov. 9, 1946, v. Derby County (A) (4 goals), Nov. 16, 1946, v. Arsenal (H), Nov. 23, 1946.

T. Holford scored "hat-tricks" for Manchester City in three out of four consecutive matches at Hyde Road in Jan. 1909: v. Bradford City, League, Division I. Jan. 9, 1909; v. Tottenham Hotspur, Cup, 1st Round, Jan. 16, 1909; v. Everton, League, Division I, Jan. 30, 1909.

## Heading Goals
The following are reckoned to be the record long-distance goal-scoring headers in the Football League:

In Division I, Sept. 1, 1952, P. Aldis, Aston Villa full-back, headed a goal against Sunderland from 35yd. This was his first goal in League football.

On Boxing Day, 1921, the winning goal for Aston Villa against Sheffield United in a Division I match, was headed from 30yd. by centre-half F. Barson.

## Internationals and Inter-League
The individual goal-scoring record in international matches is held by G. Fuchs, who scored 10 goals for Germany v. Russia in the Consolation Tournament of the Olympic Games of 1912. Germany won 16—0.

When Denmark beat France 'A' 17—1 in 1908 S. Nielsen scored seven goals.

International and Inter-League records of British players are as follows:

*Eight Goals:*
V. J. Woodward, England v. France (Amateur), Paris, Nov. 1, 1906.
*Seven Goals:*
H. G. Bache, England (Amateur F.A.) v. France, Ipswich, Mar. 12, 1910.
*Six Goals:*
J. Bambrick, Ireland v. Wales, Belfast, Feb. 1, 1930.
R. E. Foster, England v. Germany, Tottenham, Sept. 1901.
(N.B. This game is not recognised as an official international match).
W. C. Jordan, England v. France (Amateur) at Park Royal, London, Mar. 23, 1908.
N. Lofthouse, Football League v. League of Ireland, Wolverhampton, Sept. 24, 1952.
H. A. Walden, England v. Hungary (Amateur), Olympic Games, Stockholm, July 1, 1912.
V. J. Woodward, England v. Holland (Amateur), Stamford Bridge, Chelsea, Dec. 11, 1909.
*Five Goals:*
B. Battles, Scottish League v. Irish League, Firhill Park, Glasgow, Oct. 31, 1928.
J. Bradford, Football League v. Irish League, Goodison Park, Liverpool, Sept.

25, 1929.

B. Clough, Football League v. Irish League, Windsor Park, Belfast, Sept. 23, 1959.

R. Flavell, Scottish League v. Irish League, Windsor Park, Belfast, April 30, 1947.

H. Gallacher, Scottish League v. Irish League, Belfast, Nov. 11, 1925.

G. W. Hall, England v. Ireland, Old Trafford, Manchester, Nov. 16, 1938 (including three goals in 3½ min.).

C. Heggie, Scotland v. Ireland, Belfast, Mar. 20, 1886.

G. O. Smith, England v. Ireland at Sunderland, Feb. 18, 1899.

A. Stubbins, Football League v. Irish League, Bloomfield Road, Blackpool, Oct. 18, 1950.

Four goals is the individual record for England v. Scotland, scored by D. Wilshaw in the 7—2 England victory at Wembley, April 2, 1955.

Leading International goal-scorers:

*England:*

| | *I.C. | V.I. | O. | T. |
|---|---|---|---|---|
| R. Charlton (Manchester United) | 16 | — | 33 | 49 |
| J. Greaves (Chelsea, Tottenham Hotspur) | 19 | — | 25 | 44 |
| N. Lofthouse (Bolton Wanderers) | 10 | — | 20 | 30 |
| T. Finney (Preston North End) | 10 | — | 20 | 30 |
| V. J. Woodward (Tottenham Hotspur, Chelsea) | 14 | — | 15 | 29 |
| S. Bloomer (Derby County, Middlesbrough) | 28 | — | — | 28† |
| S. Mortensen (Blackpool) | 8 | 1 | 15 | 24 |
| G. Hurst (West Ham United) | 9 | — | 15 | 24 |
| T. Lawton (Everton, Chelsea, Notts County) | 7 | 1 | 15 | 23[1] |

*Scotland:*

| | | | | |
|---|---|---|---|---|
| D. Law (Huddersfield Town, Manchester City, Torino, Manchester United) | 13 | — | 17 | 30 |
| H. Gallacher (Airdrieonians, Newcastle United, Chelsea, Derby County) | 21 | — | 2 | 23 |
| L. Reilly (Hibernian) | 11 | — | 11 | 22 |
| A. N. Wilson (Dunfermline, Middlesbrough) | 13 | 4 | — | 17 |
| R. C. Hamilton (Rangers, Dundee) | 15 | — | — | 15 |
| R. S. McColl (Queen's Park, Newcastle United, Rangers) | 13 | — | — | 13 |
| W. Steel (Morton, Derby County, Dundee) | 7 | — | 6 | 13[2] |
| A. Gilzean (Dundee, Tottenham Hotspur) | 7 | — | 5 | 12 |

*Ireland:*

| | | | | |
|---|---|---|---|---|
| W. Gillespie (Sheffield United) | 7 | — | 6 | 13 |
| J. Bambrick (Linfield, Chelsea) | 11 | — | — | 11 |

*Wales:*

| | | | | |
|---|---|---|---|---|
| T. Ford (Swansea Town, Aston Villa, Sunderland, Cardiff City) | 11 | — | 12 | 23 |
| I. Allchurch (Swansea Town, Newcastle United, Cardiff City) | 9 | — | 13 | 22 |
| C. Jones (Swansea Town, Tottenham Hotspur) | 10 | — | 6 | 16 |
| W. J. Charles (Leeds United, Juventus) | 13 | — | 2 | 15[3] |

[1] Also scored 2 for Great Britain v. Rest of Europe, 1947.

[2] Also scored 1 for Great Britain v. Rest of Europe, 1947.

[3] Also scored 1 (own goal) for England, 1956.

* I.C.—International Championship. V.I.—Victory Internationals (not ranked as full internationals. O.—Overseas countries.

† Bloomer also scored two goals v. Germany, Sept. 25, 1901. But this is not ranked as a full international.

## Long-distance Goals

Full-backs who have scored goals with big kicks from their own half or the field, include:

S. Barkas, Bradford City v. West Ham United, Division II, Sept. 7, 1932.

A. Black, Leicester City v. Sunderland, Division I, April 22, 1933.

D. Burnett, West Ham United v. Oldham Athletic, F.A. Cup, 3rd Round, Jan. 22, 1966.

W. J. Charles, Cardiff City v. Norwich City, Division II, Aug. 24, 1963.

A. Chalkley, West Ham United v. Manchester City, Division I, Mar. 2, 1932.

T. Garrett, Blackpool v. Huddersfield Town, F.A. Cup, 4th Round, Jan. 31, 1953.

A. Ingham, Queen's Park Rangers v. Gillingham, Division III(S), Jan. 31, 1953.

R. Kirk, Coventry City v. Northampton

Town, F.A. Cup, 1st Round, Nov. 20, 1954.

W. Lowton, Wolverhampton Wanderers v. Nottingham Forest, Division II, Nov. 16, 1929.

P. Roscoe, Halifax Town v. Gateshead, F.A. Cup, 1st Round, Nov. 14, 1959.

**Match Records (United Kingdom)**
The individual goal-scoring record for a single game in British first-class football was set up by J. Petrie who scored 13 for Arbroath v. Bon Accord in the Scottish Cup, Sept. 5, 1885.

Next to Petrie the top goal-scoring feats by British players are as follows:

*Ten Goals:*
G. Baker, St. Mirren v. Glasgow University, Scottish Cup, 1st Round, Jan. 30, 1960.

J. Payne, Luton Town v. Bristol Rovers, Division III(S), April 13, 1936.

*Nine Goals:*
J. Baker, Hibernian v. Peebles Rovers, Scottish Cup, 2nd Round, Feb. 11, 1961.

R. Bell, Tranmere Rovers v. Oldham Athletic, Division III(N), Dec. 26, 1935.

E. MacDougall, Bournemouth v. Margate, F.A. Cup, 1st Round, Nov. 20, 1971.

J. Simpson, Partick Thistle v. Royal Albert, Scottish Cup, 1st Round, Jan. 17, 1931.

J. Smith, Rangers v. Blairgowrie, Scottish Cup, 1st Round, Jan. 20, 1934.

*Eight Goals:*
J. Calder, Morton v. Raith Rovers, Scottish League, Division II, April 18, 1936.

J. Dyet, King's Park v. Forfar Athletic, Scottish League, Division II, Jan. 2, 1930.

J. McGrory, Celtic v. Dunfermline, Scottish League, Division I, Jan. 14, 1928.

O. McNally, Arthurlie v. Armadale, Scottish League, Division II, Oct. 1, 1927.

W. Walsh, Hearts v. King's Park, Scottish Cup, 2nd Round, Feb. 13, 1937.

*Seven Goals:*
T. Briggs, Blackburn Rovers v. Bristol Rovers, Division II, Feb. 5, 1955.

A. Brown, Southampton v. Northampton Town, Southern League, Dec. 28, 1901.

N. J. Coleman, Stoke City v. Lincoln City, Division II, Feb. 23, 1957.

E. Drake, Arsenal v. Aston Villa, at Villa Park, Division I. Dec. 14, 1935.

E. Gemmell, Oldham Athletic v. Chester, Division III(N), Jan. 19, 1952.

A. Gilzean, Dundee v. Queen of the South, Scottish League, Division I, Dec. 1, 1962.

E. Harston, Mansfield Town v. Hartlepools United, Division III(N), Jan. 12, 1937.

A. Juliussen, Dundee v. Dunfermline, Scottish League, Division B, Mar. 22, 1947.

C. Lello, Lincoln City v. Notts County, war-time North Regional League, Dec. 18, 1943.

H. Maxwell, Falkirk v. Clyde, Scottish League, Division 1, Dec. 8, 1962.

W. H. Minter, St. Albans City v. Dulwich Hamlet, replayed F.A. Cup-tie, 4th Qualifying Round, Nov. 22, 1922.

J. Ross (jnr.), Preston North End v. Stoke, Division I, Oct. 6, 1888.

R. Thompson, Chelsea v. Luton Town, London Combination, Mar. 3, 1916.

D. Weir, Halliwell v. Notts County, March 24, 1888.

A. J. Whitehurst, Bradford City v. Tranmere Rovers, Division III(N), Mar. 6, 1929.

*Six Goals:*
E. Addison, Berwick Rangers v. Dundee United, Scottish League, Division II, Feb. 21, 1959.

M. Armstrong, Aberdeen v. Ayr United, Scottish League, Division I, Feb. 16, 1935.

H. Atkinson, Tranmere Rovers v. Ashington, F.A. Cup, 1st Round, Nov. 22, 1952.

A. Bacon, Reading v. Stoke City, Division II, April 3, 1931.

J. Bambrick, Ireland v. Wales, Feb. 1, 1930.

G. Best, Manchester United v. Northampton Town (A.), F.A. Cup, 5th Round, Feb. 7, 1970.

S. Bloomer, Derby County v. Sheffield Wednesday, Division I, Jan. 21, 1899.

A. Brown, Swindon Town v. Watford, Southern League, April 6, 1915.

D. F. Brown, Dundee v. Raith Rovers, Scottish League, Dec. 9, 1916.

F. Cheesemuir, Gillingham v. Merthyr Town, Division III(S), April 26, 1930.

S. Curran, Belfast Celtic v. Newry Town, Dec. 18, 1926.

A. Chandler, Leicester City v. Portsmouth, Division I, Oct. 20, 1928.

J. Cookson, West Bromwich Albion v. Blackpool (including two penalties), Division II, Sept. 17, 1927.

C. Dickson, Dunfermline v. St. Mirren, Scottish League, Division I, Dec. 30, 1961.

J. Duncan, Leicester City v. Port Vale, Division II, Dec. 25, 1924.

J. Fleming, Rangers v. Clyde, Glasgow Cup, Sept. 26, 1927.

R. E. Foster, England v. Germany, White Hart Lane, Sept. 1901 (not a full international).

J. W. Glover, Southport v. Grimsby Town, Division III(N), Oct. 22, 1921.

A. Graver, Lincoln City v. Crewe Alexandra, Division III(N), Sept. 29, 1951.

G. Henson, Bradford v. Blackburn Rovers, Division II, Jan. 29, 1938.

D. Hunt, Sheffield Wednesday v. Norwich City, Division II, Nov. 19, 1938.

H. Halse, Manchester United v. Swindon Town, F.A. Charity Shield, Sept. 25, 1911.

G. Hilsdon, Chelsea v. Worksop, F.A. Cup, 1st Round, Jan. 11, 1908.

W. Humphries, Motherwell v. Dundee United, Scottish League, Division B, Jan. 23, 1954.

G. Hurst, West Ham United v. Sunderland, Division I, Oct. 19, 1968.

W. C. Jordan, England v. France (Amateur), Park Royal, Mar. 23, 1908.

A. Juliussen, Dundee v. Alloa Athletic, Scottish League, Division B, Mar. 8, 1947. Juliussen scored 13 goals in two successive League games at this time.

F. Keetley, Lincoln City v. Halifax Town (six in 21 min.) Division III(N), Jan. 19, 1932.

T. Keetley, Doncaster Rovers v. Ashington, Division III(N), Feb. 16, 1929.

D. Law, Manchester City v. Luton Town (at Luton), F.A. Cup, 4th Round, Jan. 28, 1961. Match abandoned.

D. Lindsay, Cowdenbeath v. St. Johnstone, Scottish Cup, 1st Round, Jan. 21, 1928.

H. Lister, Oldham Athletic v. Southport, Division IV, Dec. 26, 1962.

S. Littlewood, Port Vale v. Chesterfield, Division II, Sept. 24, 1932.

N. Lofthouse, Football League v. Irish League, Sept. 24, 1952.

R. S. McColl, Queen's Park v. Port Glasgow Athletic, Scottish League, April 26, 1910.

L. McBain, Queen's Park v. Partick Thistle, Scottish League, Feb. 8, 1927.

E. MacDougall, Bournemouth v. Oxford City, F.A. Cup, 1st Round (replay), Nov. 24, 1970.

H. Melrose, Dunfermline Athletic v. Partick Thistle, Scottish League, Division I, April 18, 1959.

J. Miller, Sunderland v. Fairfield, F.A. Cup, 1st Round, 1894-95.

J. Milsom, Bolton Wanderers v. Burnley, Division II, Jan. 2, 1935.

L. Page, Burnley v. Birmingham, at St. Andrews, Division I, April 10, 1926.

J. Patterson, Queen of the South v. Cowdenbeath, Scottish League, Division II, Dec. 16, 1961.

R. Rooke, Fulham v. Bury, F.A. Cup, 3rd Round, Jan. 7, 1939.

L. Shackleton, Newcastle United v. Newport County, Division II, Oct. 5, 1946.

P. Simpson, Crystal Palace v. Exeter City, Division III(S), Oct. 4, 1930.

R. Smith, Newton Heath v. Walsall Town Swifts, Division II, Mar. 9, 1895.

J. Southworth, Everton v. West Bromwich Albion, Division I, Dec. 30, 1893.

T. Tippett, Rochdale v. Hartlepools United, Division III(N), April 21, 1930.

H. A. Walden, Great Britain v. Hungary, (Olympic Games, Stockholm), July 1, 1912.

T. Walsh, Bristol City v. Gillingham, Division III(S), Jan. 15, 1927.

T. Waring, Tranmere Rovers v. Durham City, Division III(N), Jan. 7, 1928.

G. Watson, Motherwell v. Falkirk, Scottish League, Oct. 27, 1928.

V. Watson, West Ham United v. Leeds United, Division I, Feb. 9, 1929.

D. Wilson, Rangers v. Falkirk, Scottish League, Mar. 17, 1962.

V. J. Woodward, England v. Holland (Amateur), Chelsea, Dec. 11, 1909.

**Own Goal**

See also GOALKEEPERS (Goal-scorers).

Goals which are shared between two players are rare, but an "own goal" shared in a First Division game at Stamford Bridge, Dec. 18, 1954, is unique. Leicester City defenders, Milburn and Froggatt, were involved in a misunderstanding in front of their own goal. Going for the ball together, they connected with it simultaneously and sent it into their own net. The players themselves confirmed that each had got his boot to the ball at the same time. The result was a 3—1 win for Chelsea and one of their goals is entered in the records as "Milburn and Froggatt, shared one own goal."

A most remarkable "own goal" was scored by D. Evans, the Arsenal left-back in a Division I game at Highbury, Dec. 17, 1955. The game appeared to be running over time and an agitated spectator blew a whistle. Thinking it was the referee's signal to end the game, Evans kicked the ball into his own net and several players began to leave the field. But the referee, F. B. Coultas, pointed to the centre spot, signalling for a goal.

The record for the quickest "own goal" probably belongs to A. Mullery (Fulham) who scored for Sheffield Wednesday within 30 seconds of the start and before any Sheffield player had touched the ball. Jan. 21, 1961.

T. Wright (Everton) scored an "own goal" v. Liverpool in 33 seconds and v. Manchester City in 32 seconds on consecutive Saturdays in March 1972.

**Penalty Goals**

See PENALTIES in separate section.

## Scottish Cup and Scottish League
See under MATCH RECORDS in this section.

## Wingmen Scoring
The record aggregates of goals scored by wing forwards is as follows:

Football League: 33 goals, C. Bastin, outside-left, Arsenal, Division I, 1932-3. C. Taylor, outside-left, Walsall Division III, 1960-61.

Scottish League: 39 goals, K. Dawson, outside-left, Falkirk, Division II, 1935-6.

32 goals, T. McCall, Queen of the South, Division II, 1932-3; also 32 goals, R. Ferrier, outside-left, Motherwell, Division I, 1929-30.

The record number of goals by a wing-forward in a single match is 13, scored by J. Petrie, Arbroath v. Bon Accord, Scottish Cup, Sept. 5, 1885.

The Football League record: N. J. Coleman, seven goals for Stoke City v. Lincoln City, Division II, Feb. 23, 1957.

The Scottish League record: H. Melrose, six goals for Dunfermline Athletic v. Partick Thistle, Scottish League, Division I, April 18, 1959.

The following wing-forwards have scored five goals in a match:

R. Auld, Celtic v. Airdrie (A), Scottish League, Division I, Mar. 10, 1965. Included two penalties.

T. Eglington, Everton v. Doncaster Rovers, Football League, Division II, Sept. 27, 1952.

P. Harris, Portsmouth v. Aston Villa, Division I, Sept. 3, 1958 (including a penalty).

H. Melrose, Dunfermline Athletic v. Falkirk, Scottish League, Division I, Sept. 5, 1964.

W. Robbins, Cardiff City v. Thames Association, Division III(S), Feb. 6, 1932.

G. Smith, Hibernian v. Third Lanark, Scottish League, Division A, Nov. 8, 1947.

J. Summers, Charlton Athletic v. Huddersfield Town, Division II, Dec. 21, 1957, and v. Portsmouth, Division II, Oct. 1, 1960.

R. Tambling, Chelsea v. Aston Villa, at Villa Park, Division I, Sept. 17, 1966.

A. Turner, Doncaster Rovers v. New Brighton, Division III(N), Feb. 16, 1935.

## UEFA Cup (formerly Fairs Cup)
Individual match record: 5 goals by Brundi (1 pen.), Eintracht Braunschweig v. Glentoran, 1st Round, 1971-2; Capkovic, Slovan Bratislava v. Vojvodina, 1st Round, 1972-3; Lohr, IFC Cologne v. Viking Stavanger, 2nd Round, 1972-3, and by Zaldua, Barcelona v. DOS Utrecht, 1st Round, 1965-6.

## GOAL-SCORING (TEAMS and GENERAL)

### All Scored
In season 1912-13 every one of the Greenock Morton players who appeared in the Scottish League, Division I, scored a goal. The goalkeeper scored from a penalty.

Several times each member of a team's forward-line has scored in a single game, but the outstanding example was when all the Everton forwards scored against Charlton Athletic at The Valley in an 18 min. spell. The Everton forwards were Stein, Dean, Dunn, Critchley and Johnson. Everton won 7—0 in Division II, Feb. 7, 1931.

### Away Wins
See Under HIGHEST SCORE (Record Away Wins) in this section.

### Defensive Records
See separate section.

### Double Figures
Here are listed all the clubs who have scored double figures in peacetime Football League games:

*Five times*
Birmingham City (originally known as Small Heath): v. Walsall Town Swifts 12—0, Division II, Dec. 17, 1892; v. Ardwick 10—2, Division II, Mar. 17, 1894; v. Blackpool 10—1, Division II, Mar. 2, 1901; v. Doncaster Rovers 12—0, Division II, April 11, 1903; v. Glossop 11—1, Division II, Jan. 6, 1915.

*Four times*
Hull City: v. Wolverhampton Wanderers 10—3, Division II, Dec. 12, 1919; v. Halifax Town 10—0, Division III(N), Dec. 26, 1930; v. Southport 10—1, Division III(N), Jan. 13, 1938; v. Carlisle United 11—1, Division III(N), Jan. 14, 1939.

Aston Villa: v. Accrington 12—2, Division I, March 12, 1892; v. Sheffield Wednesday 10—0, Division I, Oct. 5, 1912; v. Burnley 10—0, Division I, Aug. 29, 1925; v. Charlton Athletic 11—1, Division II, Nov. 14, 1959.

*Three Times*
Sheffield United: v. Burslem Port Vale 10—0*, Division II, Dec. 10, 1892; v. Cardiff City 11—2, Division I, Jan. 1, 1926; v. Burnley 10—0, Division I, Jan. 19, 1929.

*Twice*
Darwen: v. Rotherham Town 10—2, Division II, Jan. 13, 1896; v. Walsall 12—0, Division II, Dec. 26, 1896.

Fulham: v. Torquay United 10—2, Division III(S), Sept 7, 1931; 10—1 v. Ipswich Town, Division I, Dec. 26, 1963.

Luton Town: v. Torquay United 10—2,

Division III(S), Sept. 2, 1933; v. Bristol Rovers 12—0, Division III(S), April 13, 1936.

Manchester City: v. Lincoln City 11—3, Division II, Mar. 23, 1895; v. Darwen 10—0, Division II, Feb. 4, 1899.

Notts County: v. Burslem Port Vale 10—0, Division II, Feb. 26, 1895; v. Newport County 11—1, Division III(S), Jan. 15, 1949.

Oldham Athletic: v. Chester 11—2, Division III(N), Jan. 19, 1952; v. Southport 11—0, Division IV, Dec. 26, 1962.

Tranmere Rovers: v. Durham City 11—1, Division III(N), Jan. 7, 1928; v. Oldham Athletic 13—4, Division III(N), Dec. 26, 1935.

*Once*

Barrow: v. Gateshead 12—1, Division III(N), May 5, 1934.

Bournemouth and Boscombe Athletic: v. Northampton Town 10—0, Division III(S), Sept. 2, 1939.

Bradford City: v. Rotherham United 11—1, Division III(N), Aug. 25, 1928.

Chester v. York City 12—0, Division III(N), Feb. 1, 1936.

Chesterfield: v. Glossop 10—0, Division II, Jan. 17, 1903.

Doncaster Rovers: v. Darlington 10—0, Division IV, Jan. 25, 1964.

South Shields†: v. Rotherham United 10—1, Division III(N), Mar. 16, 1929.

Hartlepools: v. Barrow 10—1, Division IV, April 4, 1959.

Huddersfield Town: v. Blackpool 10—1, Division I, Dec. 13, 1930.

Leicester City: v. Portsmouth 10—0, Division I, Oct. 20, 1928.

Lincoln City: v. Crewe Alexandra 11—1, Division III(N), Sept. 29, 1951.

Liverpool: v. Rotherham Town 10—1, Division II, Feb. 18, 1896.

Loughborough Town: v. Darwen 10—0, Division II, April 1, 1899.

Newton Heath‡: v. Wolverhampton Wanderers 10—1, Division I, Oct. 15, 1892.

Middlesbrough: v. Sheffield United 10—3, Division I, Nov. 18, 1933.

Newcastle United: v. Newport County 13—0, Division II, Oct. 5, 1946.

Newport County: v. Merthyr Town 10—0, Division III(S), April 10, 1930.

Northampton Town: v. Walsall 10—0, Division III(S), Nov. 5, 1927.

Norwich City: v. Coventry City 10—2, Division III(S), Mar. 15, 1930.

Nottingham Forest: v. Leicester Fosse 12—0, Division I, April 21, 1909.

Preston North End: v. Stoke 10—0, Division I, Sept. 14, 1889.

Reading: v. Crystal Palace 10—2, Division III(S), Sept 4, 1946.

Stockport County: v. Halifax Town 13—0, Division III(N), Jan. 6, 1934.

Stoke City: v. West Bromwich Albion 10—3, Division I, Feb. 4, 1937.

Tottenham Hotspur: v. Everton 10—4, Division I, Oct. 11, 1958.

Walsall: v. Darwen 10—0, Division II, Mar. 4, 1899.

West Bromwich Albion: v. Darwen 12—0, Division I, April 4, 1892.

Wolverhampton Wanderers: v. Leicester City 10—1, Division I, April 15, 1938.

Woolwich Arsenal: v. Loughborough Town 12—0, Division II, Mar. 12, 1900.

Wrexham v. Hartlepools United 10—1, Division IV, Mar. 3, 1962.

*All the above matches resulted in home wins with the exception of this game which stands as the record away win in the Football League.

† Now known as Gateshead.

‡Now known as Manchester United.

**Failed to Score**

After losing at home 1—2 to Leicester City, Oct. 4, 1919, Coventry City did not score another goal in Division II until Dec. 25, 1919 when they defeated Stoke 3—2 at home. In the interim period they played 11 games without scoring.

In 1923-4 Exeter City created a Football League record by playing 14 consecutive away games without scoring.

Mansfield Town failed to score in their first nine home Third Division games of season 1971-2.

**Fast Scoring**

Preston North End scored six goals in seven minutes when they defeated Hyde 26—0, F.A. Cup, Oct. 15, 1887.

Nottingham Forest scored three goals within five minutes of kick-off v. Clapton (away), F.A. Cup, 1st Round, Jan. 17, 1891.

Ipswich Town scored two goals within two minutes of the kick-off v. Brentford, Division II (S), Sept. 22, 1956.

In a First Division game, Dec. 4, 1909, Liverpool and Newcastle United were 1—1 after only 2 minutes play.

**Highest Score in Cup Games**

*European Cup*
Feyenoord 12, Reykjavik 2, 1st Round, Sept. 17, 1969.

*European Cup-winners' Cup*
Sporting Lisbon 16, Apoel (Nicosia) 1, 1st Round, 1963-4.

*F.A. Cup*
The record score in an F.A. Cup-tie: Preston North End 26, Hyde 0, 1st Series, 1st

103

Round, Oct. 15, 1887. Every player except the goalkeeper scored. This game is believed to have run more than half an hour over time because of an error by the referee.

Other big scores in the F.A. Cup Competition Proper are:

| | | | | | |
|---|---|---|---|---|---|
| Preston North End | 18 | Reading | 0 | 1st Round | 1893–94 |
| Wanderers | 16 | Farningham | 0 | 1st Round | 1874–75 |
| Royal Engineers | 15 | High Wycombe | 0 | 1st Round | 1875–76 |
| Darwen | 15 | Romford | 0 | 5th Round | 1880–81 |
| Notts County | 15 | Thornhill United | 0 | 1st Round | 1885–86 |
| Aston Villa | 14 | Derby Midland | 0 | 2nd Round | 1886–87 |
| Wolverhampton Wanderers | 14 | Crosswells Brewery | 0 | 2nd Round | 1886–87 |
| Clapton | 0 | Nottingham Forest | 14 | 1st Round | 1890–91 |
| Bolton Wanderers | 13 | Sheffield United | 0 | 2nd Round | 1889–90 |
| Aston Villa | 13 | Casuals | 1 | 1st Round | 1890–91 |
| Aston Villa | 13 | Wednesbury Old Athletic | 0 | 1st Round | 1886–87 |
| Darwen | 13 | Kidderminster | 0 | 1st Round | 1890–91* |
| Tottenham Hotspur | 13 | Crewe Alexandra | 2 | 4th Round | 1959–60* |
| Clapham Rovers | 12 | Leyton | 0 | 2nd Round | 1875–76 |
| Bury | 12 | Stockton | 1 | 1st Round | 1896–97* |
| Sheffield Wednesday | 12 | Halliwell | 0 | 1st Round | 1890–91 |

 * Replay

The record F.A. Cup Final victory: Bury 6, Derby County 0, April 18, 1903. Semi-finals: Newcastle United 6, Fulham 0, 1908; West Bromwich Albion 6, Nottingham Forest 2, 2nd replay, 1892.

*Football League Cup*
Workington 9, Barrow 1; 1st Round, Sept. 2, 1964.

| | | | | | |
|---|---|---|---|---|---|
| Queen's Park | 16 | St. Peter's | 0 | 1st Round | 1885–86 |
| Partick Thistle | 16 | Royal Albert | 0 | 1st Round | 1930–31 |
| St. Mirren | 15 | Glasgow United | 0 | 1st Round | 1959–60 |
| Hearts | 15 | King's Park | 0 | 2nd Round | 1936–37 |
| Vale of Leven | 15 | Jamestown | 0 | 3rd Round | 1878–79 |
| Hibernian | 15 | Peebles Rovers | 1 | 2nd Round | 1960–61 |
| Queen's Park | 15 | Hurlford | 1 | 5th Round | 1879–80 |
| Queen's Park | 15 | Shotts | 0 | 6th Round | 1881–82 |

The record victory in a Scottish Association Cup Final: Renton 6, Cambuslang 1, Hampden Park, Feb. 4, 1888.
Celtic 6, Hibernian 1, Hampden Park, May 6, 1972.

*Scottish League Cup*
The record victory in a Scottish League Cup Final: Celtic 7, Rangers 1, Hampden Park, Oct. 19, 1957.

*UEFA Cup (formerly Fairs Cup)*
F.C. Cologne 13, Union Luxembourg 0, 1st Round, 1965-6.

**Highest Score in Internationals**
See also INTERNATIONALS (ENGLAND, IRELAND, SCOTLAND, WALES).
Record victory in the International Championship: England 13, Ireland 0, Belfast, Feb. 18, 1882.
Record victory for any international match which included at least one of the home countries: Australia 0, England 17,

*Scottish Association Cup*
The record score in a Scottish Association Cup-tie: Arbroath 36, Bon Accord 0; Dundee Harp 35, Aberdeen Rovers 0. Both were 1st Round ties played on the same day, Sept. 5, 1885.
Other high scores:

Sydney, June 30, 1951.
Record victory in an amateur international match between any two of the home countries: England 9, Wales 0, Merthyr Tydfil, Jan. 24, 1920. England 9, Wales 1, Plymouth, Feb. 2, 1914.
Record victory in any amateur international match which included at least one of the home countries: England 15, France 0, Paris, Nov. 1, 1906.
In 1910 at Ipswich England beat France 20—0, but this was under the auspices of the breakaway A.F.A.
Other big scores in internationals:
Denmark 17, France 1 (Olympic Games), 1908. Germany 16, Russia 0 (Olympic Games), 1912. Germany 13, Finland 0, 1940. Spain 13, Bulgaria 0, 1933. England 13, Ireland 2, Sunderland, 1899. Hungary 13, France 1, 1927.
Record victory in world cup: West Germany 12, Cyprus 0, May 21, 1969.

## Highest Score in League Games

**Division I**

| | | | | | |
|---|---|---|---|---|---|
| West Bromwich Albion | 12 | Darwen | 0 | Mar. 4, 1892 |
| Nottingham Forest | 12 | Leicester Fosse | 0 | April 21, 1909 |
| Aston Villa | 12 | Accrington | 2 | Mar. 12, 1892 |

**Division II**

| | | | | | |
|---|---|---|---|---|---|
| Newcastle United | 13 | Newport County | 0 | Oct. 5, 1946 |
| Small Heath | 12 | Walsall Town Swifts | 0 | Dec. 17, 1892 |
| Small Heath | 12 | Doncaster Rovers | 0 | April 11, 1903 |
| Darwen | 12 | Walsall | 0 | Dec. 26, 1896 |
| Woolwich Arsenal | 12 | Loughborough Town | 0 | Mar. 12, 1900 |

**Division III(S)**

| | | | | | |
|---|---|---|---|---|---|
| Luton Town | 12 | Bristol Rovers | 0 | April 13, 1936 |

**Division III(N)**

| | | | | | |
|---|---|---|---|---|---|
| Stockport County | 13 | Halifax Town | 0 | Jan. 6, 1934 |
| Tranmere Rovers | 13 | Oldham Athletic | 4 | Dec. 26, 1935 |
| Barrow | 12 | Gateshead | 1 | May 5, 1934 |
| Chester | 12 | York City | 0 | Feb. 1, 1936 |

**Division III**

| | | | | | |
|---|---|---|---|---|---|
| Tranmere Rovers | 9 | Accrington Stanley | 0 | April 18, 1959 |
| Brentford | 9 | Wrexham | 0 | Oct. 15, 1963 |
| Brighton | 9 | Southend United | 1 | Nov. 27, 1965 |
| Queen's Park Rangers | 9 | Tranmere Rovers | 2 | Dec. 3, 1960 |

**Division IV**

| | | | | | |
|---|---|---|---|---|---|
| Oldham Athletic | 11 | Southport | 0 | Dec. 26, 1962 |

*Scottish League*

**Division I (A)**

| | | | | | |
|---|---|---|---|---|---|
| Celtic | 11 | Dundee | 0 | Oct. 26, 1895 |
| Airdrieonians | 11 | Falkirk | 1 | April 28, 1951 |
| Airdrieonians | 1 | Hibernian | 11 | Oct. 24, 1959 |
| Hibernian | 11 | Hamilton Academicals | 1 | Nov. 6, 1965 |

**Division II (B)**

| | | | | | |
|---|---|---|---|---|---|
| East Fife | 13 | Edinburgh City | 2 | Dec. 11, 1937 |

## Highest Score (Record Away Wins)

**FOOTBALL LEAGUE**

| | |
|---|---|
| Division I | Cardiff City 1, Wolverhampton Wanderers 9; Sept. 3, 1955 |
| | Newcastle United 1, Sunderland 9; Dec. 5, 1908 |
| Division II | Burslem Port Vale 0, Sheffield United 10; Dec. 10, 1892 |
| Division III (South) | Northampton Town 0, Walsall 8; Feb. 2, 1947 |
| Division III (North) | Accrington Stanley 0, Barnsley 9; Feb. 3, 1934 |
| Division III | Halifax Town 0, Fulham 8; Sept. 16, 1969 |
| Division IV | Darlington 0, Southport 7; Jan. 6, 1973 |

**SCOTTISH LEAGUE:**

| | |
|---|---|
| Division I | Airdrieonians 1, Hibernian 11; Oct. 24, 1959 |
| | Partick Thistle 2, Hibernian 10; Dec. 19, 1959 |
| Division II | Alloa Athletic 0, Dundee 10; Mar. 8, 1947 |

| | |
|---|---|
| F.A. Cup (Proper) | Clapton 0, Nottingham Forest 14; Round 1, 1890–91 |
| Scottish Cup | Coldstream 1, Raith Rovers 10; 2nd Round, Feb. 13, 1954 |
| | St. Johnstone 1, Third Lanark 10, 1st Round, Jan. 24, 1903 |
| Football League Cup | Coventry City 1, Leicester City 8; 5th Round, Dec. 1, 1964 |

## Highest Score in a League Season

The record aggregate of goals in a single season:

**Football League**

Division I: 128 goals, 42 games, Aston Villa, 1930-31.

Division II: 122 goals, 42 games, Middlesbrough, 1926-7.

Division III(S): 127 goals, 42 games, Millwall, 1927-8.

Division III(N): 128 goals, 42 games, Bradford City, 1928-9.

Division III: 111 goals, 46 games, Queen's Park Rangers, 1961-2.

Division IV: 134 goals, 46 games, Peterborough United, 1960-61.

Scottish League
Division I: 132 goals, 34 games, Heart of Midlothian, 1957-8.
Division II: 142 goals, 34 games, Raith Rovers, 1937-8.

**Lowest Score (aggregate) in a League season**
Season of at least 42 games:
Division I: Huddersfield Town, 27 goals, 42 games, 1971-2.
Division II: Orient, 29 goals, 42 games, 1970-71.
Division III(S): Crystal Palace, 33 goals, 42 games, 1950-51.
Division III(N): Crewe Alexandra, 32 goals, 42 games, 1923-4.
Division III: Stockport County, 27 goals, 46 games, 1969-70.
Division IV: Bradford, 30 goals, 46 games, 1967-8.
Lowest Aggregates in seasons with fewer games than above:
Division I: Stoke, 26 goals, 22 games, 1888-9.
Woolwich Arsenal, 26 goals, 38 games, 1912-13.
Division II: Loughborough Town, 18 goals, 34 games, 1899-1900
Division III(N): Southport, 32 goals, 38 games, 1922-3.

**Own Goals**
Three "own goals" for the same side in a single Football League game were registered when Carlisle defeated Rochdale, 7—2, on Dec. 25, 1954. Three of Carlisle United's goals were scored by Rochdale players—Underwood, Boyle and Murphy.

West Bromwich Albion's score included three "own goals" by Sheffield Wed. players (Kenny, Curtis, and Gannon) at Hillsborough, Division I, Dec. 26, 1952. Albion won 5-4.

**GOODALL, John (1863-1942)**
A gentleman both on and off the field and a master tactician, known affectionately as "Johnny Allgood". John Goodall was an England International but one schooled in the traditional Scottish style.

Born in London but brought up in Kilmarnock this player's name has gone down in history as one of the pioneers of scientific football. Like any truly great footballer he was capable of playing in any position but was generally noted as a centre or inside-forward. The "brains" of the Preston side that won the "double" in 1888-89.

Kilmarnock 1882-83, Great Lever 1883-86. Preston North End 1886-89, 21 apps. Derby County 1889-1900, 240 apps. Glossop 1900-03, 20 apps. In 1903 he became

player-manager of Watford. England internationals 14. Inter-League games 4. F.A. Cup winners 1889, finalists 1888 and 1898. League Champions 1888-9.

**GREAVES, James Peter (1940-    )**
This master marksman scored more First Division goals than any player in Football League history. He found the net when making his League debut with Chelsea in 1957 and when making his debut for England in 1959, as well as his first match for Tottenham Hotspur (1961) and for West Ham United (1970). Greaves headed his club's scoring list in each of his first 12 seasons in the Football League and became the first player to top the First Division scoring list in as many as six seasons.

Like Steve Bloomer—the man whose First Division scoring record he broke—Greaves had the knack of being able to shoot from any angle without even looking for the goal.

Chelsea 1957-61, 157 apps. (124 goals). A.C. Milan 1961, 14 apps. (9 goals). Tottenham Hotspur 1961-70, 321 apps. (220 goals). West Ham United 1970-71, 36 (2) apps. (13 goals). England internationals 57. England Under-23 games 12. Inter-League games 10. Rest of Europe XI 1. F.A. Cup winners 1962, 1967. European Cup-winners' Cup winners 1963.

**GREECE**
Panathinaikos, coached by former Hungarian star, Ferenc Puskas, put Greek football on the international soccer map by reaching the Final of the European Cup in 1971. They were beaten 2-0 by Ajax but the enthusiasm for the game which this club's efforts engendered at home was unprecedented in that country.

Football had been played in Greece ever since the 1890s and the Greek F.A. was formed in November 1926, but their international side have had very little success until the last decade or two when a small number of victories have included those over both Wales and N. Ireland.

Address of the governing body: Elliniki Podosferiki Omodpondia, 93 Rue de l'Academie, Athens I. Colours: White shirts, blue shorts, blue stockings with white tops.
Results of internationals:
May 3, 1961* Greece 2, N. Ireland 1; Athens.
Oct. 17, 1961* N. Ireland 2, Greece 0; Belfast.
Dec. 9, 1964* Greece 2, Wales 0; Athens.
Mar. 17, 1965* Wales 4, Greece 1; Cardiff.
April 21, 1971† England 3, Greece 0; Wembley.

Dec. 1, 1971† Greece 0, England 2; Athens.
*World Cup  †Nations Cup

## GREN, Gunnar (1920-    )

One of the world's highest paid players in the early 1950s when he starred in Italian football. Born Gothenberg, Sweden, he attracted world-wide attention as inside-right in Sweden's victorious Olympic team of 1948, scoring twice in the final, once from the penalty spot. The following year he turned professional with A.C. Milan. A clever, constructive type of inside-forward his experience and brainy football helped Sweden win through to the Final of the 1958 World Cup when Gren starred in their side at the age of 38. Was still playing in the Swedish Second Division at the age of 48.

I.F.K. Gothenburg 1936-49. A.C. Milan 1949-53, Fiorentina 1953-55, Genoa 1955-56, Orebro 1956-58. Oergryte 1958-62. Redberslid 1967-68. Italian League champions 1951. Swedish internationals 57. World Cup runners-up 1958.

## GRIMSBY TOWN F.C.

Founded as Grimsby Pelham 1878. Dropped the name "Pelham" 1879. One of the original members of the Football League, Division II, 1892. Honours: Champions, Division II, 1900-1901, 1933-4. Runners-up, 1928-9. Champions, Division III(N), 1925-6, 1955-6. Runners-up, 1951-2. Runners-up, Division III, 1961-2. Champions, Division IV, 1971-2. Best in Division I, 5th, 1934-5. Record attendance: 31,651 v. Wolverhampton Wanderers, F.A. Cup, 5th Round, Feb. 20, 1937. Address: Blundell Park, Cleethorpes (Tel. Cleethorpes 61420). Nickname: Mariners. Colours: Black and white striped shirts, black shorts, red stockings. Record League goal-scorer: E. Glover, 42 goals, Divison II, 1933-4. Record victory: 9—2 v. Darwen, Division II, April 15, 1899. Record defeat: 9—1 v. Arsenal, Division I, Jan. 28, 1931.

## GROUNDS

The club grounds in the U.K. with the greatest capacities are:

England: The Valley, London (Charlton Athletic), 73,500.

N. Ireland: Windsor Park, Belfast (Linfield), 60,000.

Scotland: Hampden Park, Glasgow (Queen's Park), 135,000.

Wales: Ninian Park, Cardiff (Cardiff City), 60,000.

The largest football stadia abroad are in Brazil—Maracana, Rio (220,000), Pinheirao, Curitiba (180,000), and Morumbi, São Paulo (160,000).

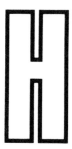

## HALF-BACKS
See GOAL-SCORING, TACTICS AND TEAM EVOLUTION, OFFSIDE.

## HALIFAX TOWN F.C.
Founded 1911 and played in the Yorkshire Combination. Eventually joined the Midland League. Joined Football League, Division III(N), on its formation, 1921. Honours: Runners-up, Division III(N), 1934-5. Runners-up, Division IV, 1968-9. Address: The Shay Ground, Halifax, HX1 2YS (Tel. 53423). Record attendance: 36,995 v. Tottenham Hotspur, F.A. Cup, 5th Round, Feb. 14, 1953. Colours: White shirts with tangerine and blue trim, white shorts with tangerine and blue stripes down seams, white stockings with blue tops. Record League goal-scorer: A. Valentine, 34 goals, Division III(N), 1934-5. Record victory: 7—0 v. Bishop Auckland, F.A. Cup, 2nd Round (replay), Jan. 10, 1967. Record defeat: 13—0 v. Stockport County, Division III(N), Jan. 6, 1934.

## HAMILTON ACADEMICALS F.C.
Founded 1870. Joined Scottish League, Division II, 1898. Honours: Champions, Division II, 1903-4. Runners-up (B), 1952-3. Runners-up, Division II, 1964-5. Scottish Cup: Finalists, 1911, 1935. Address: Douglas Park, Hamilton (Tel. 42 23108). Record attendance: 28,281 v. Hearts, Scottish Cup, 3rd Round, Mar. 3, 1937. Nickname: Accies. Colours: Red and white hooped shirts, white shorts. Record League goal-scorer in Division I: D. Wilson, 34 goals, 1936-7. Record victory: 10—2 v. Cowdenbeath, Division I, 1932-3. Record defeat: 11—1 v. Hibernian, Division I, Nov. 6, 1965.

## HANAPPI, Gerhardt (1929-    )
An architect by profession this talented player, who excelled at wing-half, enjoyed a run of 55 consecutive international appearances for Austria during the 1950's. In 1953 he played right-back for the Rest of the World v. England and eventually created an Austrian international appearance record

before a row with the team manager brought his international career to an end. Wacker S.C. 1945-50. S.K. Rapid 1950-64. Austrian internationals 96. League champions 1951, 1952, 1954, 1956, 1957, 1960. Rest of World v. England 1953.

## HAPGOOD, Edris (Eddie) Albert (1908-1973)
After refusing an offer to sign for Bristol Rovers this Bristolian joined Kettering from where he was soon snapped up by Arsenal developing into one of the finest left-backs ever to pull on an England shirt. Cool and calculating, no defender ever displayed a finer positional sense than this player who is also remembered for the perfection with which he timed his tackles.

He first captained England in the infamous "Battle of Highbury" when Italy were beaten 3—2. Hapgood received a broken nose in that game. He subsequently captained England in another 33 games, including war-time internationals.

Arsenal 1927-44, 396 apps. England internationals 30 (plus 13 war-time). Inter-League games 4. League Championship medals 1930-31, 1932-3, 1933-4, 1934-5, 1937-8. F.A. Cup (winners) 1930, 1936, (runners-up) 1932.

## HARDY, Samuel (1883-1966)
With an uncanny sense of anticipation Sam Hardy always made goalkeeping look easy and it was rare to see him make a full length dive to save a shot because he knew all there was to know about narrowing angles. Hardy's consistency was such that his international career extended over a period of 13 years from April 1907 to April 1920. It is claimed that in a first-class career of 22 years he probably saved more penalties than any goalkeeper in the game's history.

Born at Newbold, nr. Chesterfield he began playing football as a centre-forward with Newbold White Star before graduating to the local League club where he was paid 18s (90p) per week.

Chesterfield 1903-05, 71 apps. Liverpool 1905-12, 218 apps. Aston Villa 160 apps. Nottingham Forest 1921-5, 103 apps. England internationals 24 (including 3 Victory games). Inter-League games 8. League Champions 1905-6. F.A. Cup winners 1913, 1920.

## HARTLEPOOL F.C.
Founded 1908. One of the original members of Division III(N) on its formation, 1921. Honours: Runners-up, Division III(N), 1956-7. Record attendance: 17,426 v. Manchester United, F.A. Cup, 3rd Round, Jan. 5, 1957. Address: Victoria

Ground, West Hartlepool (Tel. 3492). Nickname: Pool. Colours: Blue shirts, white shorts blue and white hooped stockings. Record League goal-scorer: W. Robinson, 28 goals, Division III(N), 1927-8. Record victory: 10—1 v. Barrow, Division IV, April 4, 1959. Record defeat: 10—1 v. Wrexham, Division IV, Mar. 3, 1962.

## HAT-TRICKS
See also GOAL-SCORING (INDIVIDUALS), Hat-tricks.

The term "hat-trick," used in football to denote three consecutive goals for a team scored by the same player, originates from cricket. It dates back to the days when a bowler was presented with a new hat by his club whenever he succeeded in taking three wickets with three balls.

Strictly speaking, it is not correct to credit a player with a "hat-trick" in football if his sequence of three goals is broken by a goal from another player for the same side.

## HAYNES, John Norman (1934-    )
The outstanding England inside-forward of thhe post-war era, this immaculate footballer was the master of the long pass, delivered with such accuracy and timing that he could usually split a defence with ease.

Born at Kentish Town, London, Haynes became the first player to appear for England in every international class —schoolboy, youth, under-23, "B", and full international, making his debut in a full international before his 20th birthday and establishing himself as one of England's most consistent performers until leg injuries suffered in a car crash put him out of the game for several months and ended his international career.

Haynes, however, resumed his career with Fulham, his only League club, before being given a free transfer in 1970 and going to South Africa.

Fulham 1952-70, 598 apps. (159 goals). England internationals 56. England "B" games 5. Under-23 games 8. Inter-League games 13.

## HEADING
See GOAL-SCORING (INDIVIDUALS), Heading.

## HEART OF MIDLOTHIAN F.C.
Founded 1873. Moved to present headquarters, 1886. One of the original members of the Scottish League in 1890. Honours: Champions, Division I, 1894-5, 1896-7, 1957-8, 1959-60. Runners-up, 1893-4, 1898-9, 1903-4, 1905-6, 1914-15, 1937-8, 1953-4, 1955-6, 1956-7, 1958-9, 1964-5. Scottish Cup: Winners, 1891, 1896, 1901, 1906, 1956. Finalists, 1903, 1907, 1968. Scottish League Cup: winners, 1955, 1959, 1960, 1963. Finalists, 1962. Record attendance: 53,490 v. Rangers, Scottish Cup, 3rd Round, Feb. 13, 1932. Address: Tynecastle Park, Edinburgh (Tel. 031-3376132). Colours: Maroon shirts with white centre panel, white shorts. Record League goal-scorer: B. Battles, 44 goals, 1930-31. Record victory: 15—0 v. King's Park, Scottish Cup, 2nd Round, Feb. 13, 1937. Record defeat: 7—1 v. Dundee (H), Division I, Feb. 27, 1965.

## HEIGHT
### Shortest
The shortest player to appear in Football League matches is outside-right F. le May. He was 5 ft. high. He played for Thames 1930-31, Watford 1931-2, and Clapton Orient 1932-3.

C. Nastri, an outside-right, made two Football League appearances for Crystal Palace in 1958-9 when he was 5ft. 1in.

The shortest goalkeeper to play for England is E. Davison (Sheffield Wednesday) v. Wales, Mar. 13, 1922. Height: 5ft. 7in.

The shortest full-back to play for England is H. Burgess (Manchester City) who made four appearances between 1904 and 1906. Height: 5ft. 5in.

The shortest centre-half for England, J. Holt (Everton) who appeared in the 1890s, and W. Wedlock (Bristol City) who appeared in the early 1900s up to World War I. Both were 5ft. 4½in.

The shortest wing-half to appear in an England side is T. Magee of West Bromwich Albion. He was 5ft. 3in. A right-half, he was capped five times in the 1920s.

The shortest England international forward is probably F. Walden, Tottenham Hotspur's 5ft. 3in. outside-right who was capped once before, and once after World War I.

S. Tufnell, who played for Blackpool from 1927 to 1934, was the shortest half-back ever to apppear in Football League matches. Height 5ft. 2½in.

J. Talks of Lincoln was probably the shortest referee seen in first-class football. On the Football League and Southern League lists immediately before World War I he was 4ft. 9½in. tall.

### Tallest
The tallest players to appear in Football League matches include:

S. Taylor, centre-half, Bristol Rovers, 1966-73; 6ft. 5in.

A Iremonger, goalkeeper, Notts County and Lincoln City, 1904-27; 6ft. 5in.

G. Ephgrave, goalkeeper, Aston Villa,

Swindon Town, Southampton, Norwich City and Watford, 1938-53; J. Corrigan, goalkeeper, Manchester City, 1967—6ft. 4½in.

H. Liley, goalkeeper, Bristol Rovers, 1946-51; 6ft. 4½in.

N. Middleboe, half-back, Chelsea, 1913-21; J. Nicholls, goalkeeper, Tottenham Hotspur, Bristol Rovers, 1926-39; M. Deacy, half-back, Newport County, 1968-70; 6ft. 4in.

Ivan Horrath, Dynamo (Zagreb) and Yugoslavian international centre-half of the post-war era stands 6ft. 5in. tall.

## HEREFORD UNITED F.C.
Founded: 1924. Elected to Football League 1972. Honours: Runners-up, Division IV, 1972-3. Record attendance: 18,114 v. Sheffield Wednesday, F.A. Cup, 3rd Round, Jan. 4, 1958. Address: Edgar Street, Hereford (Tel. 4037). Colours: White shirts with black trim, black shorts, white stockings.

## HIBBS, Henry E. (1905-    )
Joining Birmingham from Tamworth in July 1924 Harry Hibbs was on the small side for a goalkeeper and was never spectacular, but after succeeding Dan Tremelling as first choice he developed into one of the safest custodians in the game. Quiet, even shy, Hibbs concentrated on his profession to such a degree that he made goalkeeping an exact science.

It has been suggested that Hibbs was seldom at his best in internationals, but even if this was true he still enjoyed an England career spread over seven seasons before being succeeded by Ted Sagar in 1936. Born Wilnecote, Staffs.

Birmingham 1929-40, 340 apps. England internationals 25. Inter-League games 3. F.A. Cup, runners-up 1931.

## HIBERNIAN F.C.
Founded 1875 by Irishmen in Edinburgh. One of the original members of the Scottish League, Division II, 1893. Honours: Champions, Division I, 1902-3, 1947-8, 1950-51, 1951-2. Runners-up, 1896-7, 1946-7, 1949-50, 1952-3. Champions, Division II, 1893-4, 1894-5, 1932-3. Scottish Cup: Winners, 1887, 1902. Finalists, 1896, 1914, 1923, 1924, 1947, 1972. Scottish League Cup: Winners, 1973. Finalists, 1951, 1969. Record attendance: 65,850 v. Hearts, Division A, Jan. 2, 1950. Address: Easter Road Park, Edinburgh (Tel. 031-6612159). Nickname: Hibs. Colours: Green shirts, white sleeves, white shorts. Record League goalscorer: J. Baker, 42 goals, Division I, 1959-60. Record victory: 15—1 v. Peebles Rovers, Scottish Cup, 2nd Round, Feb. 11, 1961. Record defeat: 9—2 v. Greenock Morton, Division I, Feb. 15, 1919.

## HOLLAND
See under NETHERLANDS.

## HOME DEFEATS
The record number of consecutive home defeats in one season in the Football League is 13 by Rochdale. After defeating New Brighton, 3—2 on Nov. 7, 1931, they were beaten in all 13 remaining home matches that season.

Rochdale also suffered defeat in their first home game of the following season and it was not until their second home game that they broke the spell by drawing 0—0 with Barrow.

Barrow lost a total of 15 home matches in Division III(N)), 1925-6.

## HOME WINS
The record for home wins in a single season of Football League matches is held by Brentford. In Division III(S) in 1929-30, Brentford won all 21 of their home matches.

Brentford Reserves won all their 23 home matches in the London Combination in 1932-3. In fact, they won 44 successive home games in that competition from Nov. 1931 to Nov. 1933.

Five other clubs in addition to Brentford have won all of their home matches in the Football League during a single season:

| | | | |
|---|---|---|---|
| Sunderland | Division I | 1891–2 | 13 games |
| Liverpool | Division II | 1893–4 | 15 ,, |
| Bury | Division II | 1894–5 | 16 ,, |
| Sheffield Wednesday | Division II | 1899–1900 | 18 ,, |
| Small Heath (Birmingham) | Division II | 1902–3 | 18 ,, |

The smallest number of home wins obtained by any club in a single season of Football League matches is one —Loughborough Town, 1899-1900; Notts County, 1904-5; Woolwich Arsenal, 1912- 13; Blackpool, 1966-7. All Division I except Loughborough in Division II.

Since World War I all 11 matches in a single division of the Football League have resulted in home wins on four occasions:

Division I: Feb. 13, 1926; Dec. 10, 1955.

Division III(N), April 3, 1926; Mar. 14, 1931.

In Division I on Christmas Day, 1936, 10 of the 11 games resulted in home wins. The remaining game was a draw. This also occurred Sept. 1, 1956, and Sept. 12, 1964.

## HUDDERSFIELD TOWN F.C.

Founded 1908. Played one season in North-Eastern League, then joined Midland League. Elected to Football League, Division II, 1910. The club nearly went out of existence in 1919 but local supporters collected a substantial amount of money and the club was kept going. Honours: Champions, Division I, 1923-4, 1924-5, 1925-6. Runners-up, 1926-7, 1927-8, 1933-4. Champions, Division II, 1969-70. Runners-up, 1919-20, 1952-3. F.A. Cup: winners, 1922. Finalists, 1920, 1928, 1930, 1938. Record attendance: 67,037 v. Arsenal, F.A. Cup, 6th Round, Feb. 27, 1932. Address: Leeds Road, Huddersfield HD1 6PE (Tel. 20335). Nickname: Terriers. Colours: Blue and white striped shirts, white shorts and stockings. Record League goal-scorer: S. J. Taylor, 35 goals, Division II, 1919-20, and G. Brown, 35 goals, Division I, 1925-6. Record victory: 10—1 v. Blackpool, Division I, Dec. 13, 1930. Record defeat: 7—1 v. Bolton Wanderers, Division I, Jan. 1, 1930, and v. Wolverhampton Wanderers, Division I, Oct. 2, 1948.

## HULL CITY F.C.

Founded 1904. Formed into a limited company, 1905. Elected to Football League, Division II, 1905. Honours: Champions, Division III, 1965-6. Champions, Division III(N), 1932-3, 1948-9. Runners-up, Division III, 1958-9. Best in Division II, 3rd, 1909-10. Record attendance: 55,019 v. Manchester United, F.A. Cup, 6th Round, Feb. 26, 1949. Address: Boothferry Park, Hull HU4 6EU (Tel 0482 52195). Nickname: Tigers. Colours: Amber with black edgings, black shorts, black stockings with amber ring. Record League goal-scorer: W. F. McNaughton, 39 goals, Division III(N), 1932-3. Record victory: 11—1 v. Carlisle United, Division III(N), Jan. 14, 1939. Record defeat: 8—0 v. Wolverhampton Wanderers, Division II, Nov. 4, 1911.

## HUNGARY

The Hungarian national team of the 1950s will never be forgotten. They were, undoubtedly, the finest national soccer combination ever seen up to that time. Unfortunately, however, all the more recent performances of Hungarian XIs are judged by the standard set by those Mighty Magyars of that earlier decade and one is apt to miss the fact that although they have slipped from that once high pinnacle they are still not far behind the most powerful nations in world soccer.

Hungary went 13 years undefeated at home in international games—from their 7—2 defeat by Sweden in 1943 to their 4—2 defeat by Czechoslovakia in 1956. At home and away their crack team of the 1950s played 29 matches without defeat over a period of more than four years. The defeat which ended that run was the one suffered in the final of the World Cup of 1954 when they lost 3—2 to West Germany.

The defeat of England, 6—3 at Wembley in Nov. 1953, is a game that shook British football to the core. Not only because it was England's first-ever home defeat by a continental side, but because of the immaculate display of the Hungarians which proved how far the old masters had slipped behind.

Here are details of that historic match:

Nov. 25, 1953, at Wembley Stadium.

Referee: Mr. L. Horn of Holland.

Hungary 6 (scorers—Hidegkuti 3, Puskas 2, Bozsik).

England 3 (scorers—Sewell, Mortensen, Ramsey—penalty).

England: Merrick; Ramsey, Eckersley; Wright, Johnston, Dickinson; Matthews, Taylor, Mortensen, Sewell, Robb.

Hungary: Grosics; Buzansky, Lantos; Bozsik, Lorant, Zakarias; Budai, Kocsis, Hidegkuti, Puskas, Czibor.

Apart from the precision of the Hungarian team and the power of its shooting, one of the features of their play was the terrific speed and anticipation of its wing-men. As soon as a wing-half or inside-forward gained possession, the winger immediately raced away up the touch-line and gained several yards before the ball was lobbed ahead of him. This running into position to receive the ball was carried out with great success by every man in the side.

As if to prove that this was no flash in the pan Hungary gave England an even bigger beating six months later, winning 7—1 in Budapest, May 23, 1954.

In case one is led to believe that Hungarian football begins and ends with this brilliant national team of the 1950s perhaps it should be pointed out that Hungary first beat England in 1934 in Budapest, and were World Cup finalists in 1938 when they lost 4—2 to Italy. Indeed, Hungarian footballers have long been respected for their ability and Hungarian soccer coaches have been accepted in many parts of the world and acknowledged as among the finest the game has ever produced.

The Hungarian F.A. was formed in 1901, the same year as a National League was inaugurated, and now there are more than 110,000 players registered.

Hungarian football reecovered quickly from the 1956 Revolution which sent several of their players fleeing abroad, for many returned and they won through to the Final Tournament of the 1958 World Cup only to be eliminated by Wales (2—1) in a play-off.

They reached the quarter-finals in 1962 and 1966 before being eliminated by Czechoslovakia and Russia respectively.

Clinging to their brand of amateurism Hungary won both the 1964 and 1968 Olympic Tournaments, and finished runners-up in Munich in 1972.

The address of the governing body of football in Hungary is the Magyar Labdarugók Szövetsége, Népköztarsaság utja 47, 1393 Budapest VI. Colours: Red shirts, white shorts, green stockings.

Results of internationals:

| | |
|---|---|
| June 10, 1908 | Hungary 0, England 7; Budapest |
| May 29, 1909 | Hungary 2, England 4; Budapest |
| May 31, 1909 | Hungary 2, England 8; Budapest |
| May 10, 1934 | Hungary 2, England 1; Budapest |
| Dec. 15, 1934 | Eire 2, Hungary 4; Dublin |
| May 3, 1936 | Hungary 3, Eire 3; Budapest |
| Dec. 2, 1936 | England 6, Hungary 2; Highbury |
| Dec. 6, 1936 | Eire 2, Hungary 3; Dublin |
| Dec. 7, 1938 | Scotland 3, Hungary 1; Ibrox Park |
| Mar. 19, 1939 | Eire 2, Hungary 2; Cork |
| May 18, 1939 | Hungary 2, Eire 2; Budapest |
| Nov. 25, 1953 | England 3, Hungary 6; Wembley |
| May 23, 1954 | Hungary 7, England 1; Budapest |
| Dec. 8, 1954 | Scotland 2, Hungary 4; Hampden Park |
| May 29, 1955 | Hungary 3, Scotland 1; Budapest |
| May 7, 1958 | Scotland 1, Hungary 1; Hampden Park |
| June 8, 1958* | Wales 1, Hungary 1; Sweden |
| June 17, 1958* | Wales 2, Hungary 1; Sweden |
| May 22, 1960 | Hungary 2, England 0; Budapest |
| June 5, 1960 | Hungary 3, Scotland 3; Budapest |
| May 28, 1961 | Hungary 3, Wales 2; Budapest |
| May 31, 1962* | Hungary 2, England 1; Chile |
| Nov. 7, 1962† | Hungary 3, Wales 1; Budapest |
| Mar. 20, 1963† | Wales 1, Hungary 1; Cardiff |
| May 5, 1965 | England 1, Hungary 0; Wembley |
| June 8, 1969* | Eire 1, Hungary 2; Dublin |
| Nov. 5, 1969* | Hungary 4, Eire 0; Budapest |

* World Cup
† Nations Cup

EUROPEAN CUP. Manchester United, winners 1967-68. Back row (*left to right*): Foulkes, Aston, Rimmer, Stepney, Gowling, Herd; middle row, Sadler, Dunne, Brennan, Crerand, Best, Burns, Jack Crompton (trainer); front row, Ryan, Stiles, Law, Sir Matt Busby (Manager), Charlton, Kidd, Fitzpatrick. (*Photo*: United Press International).

EUROPEAN CUP. The 1963 final at Wembley. Eusebio, famous for the power and accuracy of his shooting, scores Benfica's only goal against AC Milan's Ghezzi. Milan won 2-1. (*Photo*: Otto Metelmann).

EUROPEAN CUP WINNERS' CUP. Greaves scoring for Tottenham Hotspur in the 1963 final at Rotterdam against Atletico Madrid. By winning 5-1 Tottenham became the first English club to win a major European Trophy. (*Photo:* Planet News Ltd.).

FINNEY, TOM. The Preston star in action, 1955. (*Photo:* Radio Times Hulton Picture Library)

FOOTBALL ASSOCIATION CHALLENGE CUP. (*above*) Harold Hampton (fourth from right) seen scoring the first of his two goals for Aston Villa when they beat Newcastle United 2-0 in the 1905 Cup Final. (*Photo*: Radio Times Hulton Picture Library) (*below*) The 1927 Final when Cardiff beat Arsenal to take the trophy out of England for the first and only time. The picture shows the ball going into the Arsenal net after their own keeper, Lewis, had attempted to throw it clear. (*Photo*: Topix).

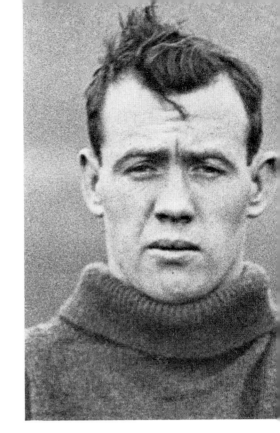

GOAL SCORERS (INDIVIDUALS). (*top facing*) Two record-breakers, W. R. " Dixie " Dean and Hughie Gallacher. (*Photos*: P.A. Reuter and Central Press Photos): (*bottom facing*) Record International goal scorers: Bobby Charlton and Denis Law (*Photos*: Central Press Photos and United Press International); and (*above*) Billy Gillespie and Trevor Ford (*Photos*: *The Morning Telegraph*, Sheffield, and Central Press Photos).

GREAVES, JIMMY. Greaves challenges the great Russian goalkeeper, Lev Yashin at Wembley in October 1963 when England beat the rest of the World 2-1. (*Photo:* Central Press)

HUDDERSFIELD TOWN F.C. This group includes twelve players who helped the club win the Championship three years in succession between 1923 and 1926. Johnston appeared in only one of these seasons. Back row, Wilson, Smith, (A.), Shaw, Taylor, Wadsworth, Cook, Chaplin (trainer), Watson; front row, Steele, Johnston, Stephenson, Brown, Smith (W. H.), Cawthorne. (*Photo*: A. J. Winder).

KOPA, RAYMOND. (*Photo*: Associated Press).　　　　LAWTON, TOMMY. (*Photo*: P.A. Reuter).

LEEDS UNITED F. C. This is the side that created a First Division record of 67 points when winning the Championship in season 1968-69. Back row, Reaney, Hunter, Clarke, O'Grady, Harvey, Sprake, Madeley, Gray, Belfitt, Charlton; front row, Jones, Cooper, Hibbitt, Bremner, Giles, Bates, Lorimer. (*Photo*: Provincial Press Agency).

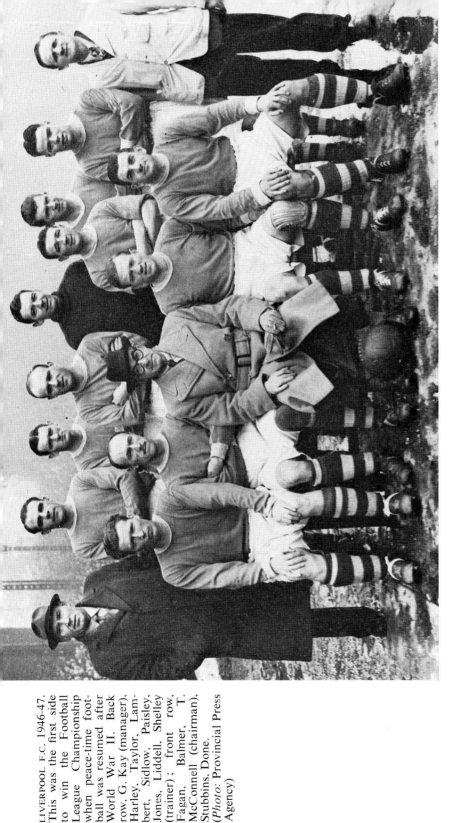

LIVERPOOL F.C. 1946-47. This was the first side to win the Football League Championship when peace-time football was resumed after World War II. Back row. G. Kay (manager), Harley, Taylor, Lambert, Sidlow, Paisley, Jones, Liddell, Shelley (trainer); front row, Fagan, Balmer, T. McConnell (chairman), Stubbins, Done. (Photo: Provincial Press Agency)

## ICELAND

An island with a population only roughly equivalent to that of a town the size of Southend or Wolverhampton could not be expected to make much of an impression in international soccer, but the Republic of Iceland have not been without their success, beating such countries as Finland, Sweden, Norway and U.S.A.

The first club was formed in 1899 and a national league was inaugurated in 1912. But it was not until after World War II that Icelandic football really began to develop. In 1946 they played their first International —with Denmark, and that same year they sent a touring side to play amateur clubs in England. That team's star inside-forward, Albert Gudmundsson, subsequently made two First Division appearances for Arsenal. He later became President of the Icelandic F.A. which had been formed in 1947.

Iceland's first application for entry into the World Cup Competition in 1953-4 arrived too late for acceptance, and when they were grouped with France and Belgium in the 1958 Qualifying Competition they were outclassed. They did not enter again until the 1974 competition when they finished bottom of their group.

The address of the governing body: Knattspyrnusamband Islands—K.S.I., P.O. Box 1011, Reykjavik. Colours: Blue shirts, white shorts, blue and white stockings.

Results of international matches:
Aug. 12, 1962 Eire 4, Iceland 2; Dublin
Sept. 2, 1962 Iceland 1, Eire 1; Reykjavik
Both Nations Cup games

## INJURIES

The only five Football League players who have fractured a leg as many as four times during their playing careers are L. Ritson, Leyton Orient f.b., 1946-9; A. Evans, Aston Villa and West Bromwich Albion, f.b., 1896-1908; D. Smith, Burnley, Brighton and Bristol City f.b., 1950-63 (five times); A. Davidson, Hull City f.b., 1950-68; L. Leslie, Airdrie, West Ham United, Stoke City, Millwall, Southend United, gl., 1959-72.

In a Division IV game at Chester, Jan. 1, 1966, the home side lost both of their full-backs, R. Jones and B. Jones, with broken legs. Even so, Chester beat Aldershot 3—2.

In September 1964 D. Mackay of Tottenham Hotspur was unlucky enough to break a leg for the second time in nine months.

See also under CASUALTIES

## INTER-LEAGUE

The first Inter-League game took place on April 20, 1891, at Sheffield, between the Football League and the Football Alliance.

Next came the Football League's first game with the Scottish League, played at Bolton, April 11, 1892, ending in a draw 2—2. The Football League side included four Scots, T. McInnes (Lincoln City), D. Gow (Sunderland), W. Groves (West Bromwich Albion), and H. Gardiner (Bolton Wanderers). It was the last time that the Football League knowingly included Scottish players until D. Mackay (Tottenham Hotspur) played against the Scottish League in Mar. 1960. On one other occasion a Scottish-born player, A. Maitland (South Shields) unwittingly was chosen to play against the Irish League, at Bolton, in Oct. 1922. The selectors discovered their error before the match, but decided to let Maitland play.

The first game between the Football League and the Irish League was played at Belfast, Feb. 10, 1894.

The first game between the Football League and the League of Ireland (Eire), took place at Dalymount Park, Dublin, April 30, 1947.

Before World War I, the old Southern League also entered into competition with the three other big leagues. They met the Football League six times between 1909 and 1915, and the Scottish and Irish Leagues five times each during the same period.

The Football League enjoyed a record run of 24 games without defeat 1914-29. After losing 3—2 to the Scottish League at Burnley, Mar. 21, 1914 the Football League was not beaten again in an official peacetime match until they lost 2—1 to the Scottish League, Glasgow, Nov. 2, 1929. Between those dates the Football League met the Scottish League 11 times, Irish League 11 times, The Army once, and the Southern League once.

Here is a summary of the results of Inter-League games correct to c.s. 1973.

Football League v. Scottish League: Played 70, Football League won 38, Scottish League won 18, drawn 14.

Football League v. Irish League: Played 61, Football League won 54, Irish League won 3, drawn 4.

Football League v. League of Ireland (Eire): Played 21, Football League won 18, League of Ireland won 1, drawn 2.

Football League v. Southern League: Played 6, Football League won 4, Southern League won 1, drawn 1.

Scottish League v. Irish League: Played 60, Scottish League won 55, Irish League won 5, drawn 0.

Scottish League v. Southern League: Played 5, Scottish League won 2, Southern League won 2, drawn 1.

Scottish League v. League of Ireland (Eire): Played 22, Scottish League won 18, League of Ireland won 1, drawn 3.

Irish League v. Southern League: Played 5, Irish League won 0, Southern League won 3, drawn 2.

Football League v. International Football Combination of Denmark: Played 1, Football League won 1.

Football League v. Italian League; Played 4, Football League won 1, Italian League won 3, drawn 0.

Football League v. Belgian League: Played 1, drawn 1.

Scottish League v. Italian League: Played 2, Scottish League won 0, Italian League won 1, drawn 1.

Irish League v. Italian League: Played 1, Irish League won 1, Italian League won 0, drawn 0.

## INTERNATIONAL CHAMPIONSHIP
See under INTERNATIONALS.

## INTERNATIONAL FOOTBALL ASSOCIATION BOARD
In 1882 the Football Association proposed that there should be a meeting between the four national associations of the United Kingdom to agree on the Laws of the Game.

At first the Scottish F.A. was reluctant to participate at such a meeting. They preferred to retain their own version of the rules and would not tolerate any interference with their independence. The English F.A. threatened to discontinue international matches with Scotland and a serious breakdown of negotiations seemed imminent before the Scottish F.A. relented and agreed to the meeting.

This was held at Manchester, Dec. 6, 1882, and was attended by two members of each of the four Associations of England, Scotland, Ireland and Wales. It was an immediate success. A uniform code of rules was drawn up, being subsequently agreed upon by all four countries, and the International Association Board came into being.

At the present time the Board meets at least once a year and in addition to four representatives from each of the four United Kingdom Associations, four members of the Fédération Internationale de Football Association are entitled to attend.

The prime object of the Board is the same today as it was originally, that is, to discuss alterations to the Laws of the Game. They reserve the right alone to make any such alterations as they may agree upon from time to time. Furthermore, in accordance with present agreements, no single Association can themselves make any alterations to the Laws of the Game unless these are passed by the Board.

## INTERNATIONAL FOOTBALL LEAGUE BOARD
This was formed in 1897 when the Football League and the Scottish League agreed to meet to draw up some uniform code of rules regarding the rights of clubs to retain players, and in particular, the recognition of these rights by each League, so that "poaching" of players by one League from another could be prevented.

The board is made up of twelve representatives, four each from the Football League and the Scottish League, and two each from the Irish Football League and the Football League of Ireland.

It is because of the agreements drawn up by this board that no player retained or transfer-listed by any club in any one of those four Leagues can play for any other club in the Leagues without a proper transfer.

## INTERNATIONALS
See also AMATEURS (INTERNATIONALS), APPEARANCES (INTERNATIONALS), ATTENDANCES, AGE (of players), GOAL-SCORING, and also various International

Cup Competitions.

International Championships data concerning England, Ireland, Scotland and Wales appear in this section. Details of other countries including results of international matches with the home countries and Eire are to be found under the respective names of those foreign countries.

## Club Records

Rangers have supplied more international players to any one of the home countries than any other club. 102 of their players have been honoured by Scotland.

This number has not been exceeded by any other club, even when internationals to all four home countries are included, and the Rangers' record figure in this respect is increased to 110 with the addition of eight Irish internationals.

Torino had 10 players in the Italian side v. Hungary, May 11, 1947. This is a world record. The fact that Queen's Park provided all the players for Scotland v. England in the first official international of 1872 could not be considered a genuine record as no attempt was made to choose a representative team.

The greatest number of players from one club appearing in the International Championship on the same day is eight. Leeds United had this number playing on May 15, 1971: Madeley, Cooper, and Clarke for England v. Ireland; Lorimer, Bremner, and Gray for Scotland v. Wales; and Sprake and Yorath for Wales.

Arsenal had seven players in the England team v. Italy, Nov. 14, 1934: Moss, Male, Hapgood, Copping, Bowden, Drake and Bastin. This is a record for the home countries.

Arsenal had six players in the England team v. Wales, Feb. 5, 1936, and also v. Austria, May 6, 1936.

Blackburn Rovers supplied five men for the England team v. Ireland, Mar. 15, 1890: Forrest, Lofthouse, Townley, Barton and Walton. Arsenal also provided five men for this match, Feb. 6, 1935: Male, Hapgood, Copping, Drake and Bastin.

Manchester United supplied five men for the Scottish team v. England, Feb. 14, 1973: Forsyth, Buchan, Macari, Graham and Morgan.

W. Rowley, T. Clare, A. Underwood, all of Stoke, formed the England defence v. Ireland, Mar. 5, 1892.

Other instances of a one-club-defence in an England team was v. Wales, in a wartime international, May 9, 1942. Marks, Scott and Hapgood of Arsenal were the players, and v. Ireland, Oct. 2, 1954, when

Manchester United provided R. Wood, W. Foulkes and R. Byrne.

Wolverhampton Wanderers provided England's half-back line v. Russia (twice), Brazil and Austria, in May and June, 1958. The players were E. Clamp, W. Wright and W. Slater.

Here are instances of all three half-backs being provided by one club in home International Championship games: H. McKeown, S. Johnston, and S. Torrans (Linfield), Ireland v. Scotland, Mar. 25, 1893; J. Darling, R. G. Milne, and H. Maginnis (Linfield), Ireland v. Scotland, Mar. 21, 1903; T. Muirhead, D. Meiklejohn, and T. Craig (Rangers), Scotland v. Ireland, Feb. 25, 1928; T. Smith, L. Lloyd, E. Hughes (Liverpool), England v. Wales, May 19, 1971.

Tottenham Hotspur had four men in the England team v. Scotland, April 9, 1921: B. Smith, A. Grimsdell, B. Bliss, and J. H. Dimmock.

Huddersfield Town had four men in the England team v. Scotland, Mar. 31, 1928: F. R. Goodall, T. Wilson, R. Kelly, and W. H. Smith, while their winger, A. Jackson appeared for Scotland in the same game.

Sheffield Wednesday had four men in the England team v. Scotland, April 5, 1930: E. Blenkinsop, A. Strange, W. Marsden, and E. Rimmer.

The England team v. Scotland has included as many as three forwards from the same club on four occasions: 1875—C. H. Wollaston, C. W. Alcock and H. E. Heron (Wanderers). 1878—H. Wace, J. G. Wylie and H. E. Heron (Wanderers). 1891—F. Geary, E. Chadwick and A. Milward (Everton). 1937—S. Matthews, F. C. Steele and J. A. Johnson (Stoke).

The England team which met Hungary at Wembley, Nov. 25, 1953, included three forwards from Blackpool: S. Matthews, E. Taylor and S. Mortensen. In addition, H. Johnston of Blackpool was at centre-half in the same side.

The England team which defeated Wales 5—1 at Wrexham, Mar. 5, 1894, and also that which drew with the Principality, 1—1, at Queen's Club, London, Mar. 18, 1895, consisted entirely of Corinthian players. This cannot be considered a club record in the ordinary way, because the Corinthian team was for the most part a combined eleven made up of players from various schools, colleges and universities, who also played for other clubs.

Scotland's side which beat England, 2—1, at Sheffield, April 4, 1903, included a one-club defence, Doig, McCombie and Watson, from an English club —Sunderland.

Arsenal's best season for internationals on their books was 1936-7. By the end of the season, 13 Arsenal players had been capped by their respective countries. The selection of A. Kirchen for England v. Norway, May 14, 1937, brought the total to 14. C. Bastin, R. Bowden, W. Copping, J. Crayston, E. Drake, E. Hapgood, J. Hulme, B. Joy, A. Kirchen, G. Male, F. Moss and H. Roberts were the England internationals. A. James (Scotland) and R. John (Wales) brought up the total.

Cardiff City had 14 players towards the end of the 1925-6 season, who had all been capped. They were: Keenor, Davies (W.), Davies (L.), Beadles, Evans (J.), Evans (H.), for Wales. Cassidy, Nelson, Blair and Lawson for Scotland. Farquharson, McIlvenny, Watson and Sloan for Ireland.

In 1933-4, Aston Villa possessed 15 men who had played for their respective countries: Beresford, Brown, Cunliffe, Gardener, Houghton, Mort, Tate, Smart, Walker and Waring for England. Blair, Gibson and Nibloe for Scotland, and Astley for Wales.

At the start of season 1965-6 Manchester United had 15 internationals on their books including Amateur cap, D. Sadler. The other full internationals were P. Dunne, H. Gregg, S. Brennan, N. Cantwell, A. Dunne, P. Crerand, W. Foulkes, N. Stiles, G. Best, R. Charlton, J. Connelly, D. Herd, D. Law and G. Moore. United had as many as 13 internationals for a long spell in the 1960s.

In May 1973 Leeds United had 14 internationals. Charlton, Clarke, Cooper, Hunter, Jones, Madeley and Reaney of England; Bremner, Gray, Jordan and Lorimer of Scotland; Sprake and Yorath of Wales; Giles of Eire.

Towards the end of the season 1932-33, Rangers possessed 13 international players. Archibald, Brown, Craig, Fleming, Gray, Hamilton (T.), McPhail, Marshall, Meiklejohn and Morton for Scotland; English, Hamilton (R.), and McDonald for Ireland.

Rangers also had 13 international players near the end of the previous season. But R. McAuley, a Scottish international was transferred during the summer of 1932 to Chelsea. However the total of 13 was maintained, by the capping of English for Ireland v. Scotland in Sept. 1932.

When Wales and Scotland met in the International Championship at Ninian Park, Feb. 16, 1924, Wales were captained by F. Keenor of Cardiff City, and Scotland were captained by J. Blair, also of Cardiff City. This is a club record.

**Consecutive Appearances**
See APPEARANCES (INTERNATIONALS).

**Eire**
See separate section.

**England**
England's first home defeat by an international team from abroad took place on Sept. 21, 1949 at Goodison Park. Result, England 0, Eire 2. Teams:
*England:* Williams (Wolverhampton Wanderers); Mozley (Derby County), Aston (Manchester United); Wright (Wolverhampton Wanderers), (capt.), Franklin (Stoke City), Dickinson (Portsmouth); Harris (Portsmouth), Morris (Derby County), Pye (Wolverhampton Wanderers), Mannion (Middlesbrough), Finney (Preston North End).
*Eire:* Godwin (Shamrock Rovers); Carey (Manchester United) (capt.), Aherne (Luton Town); Walsh (W.), (Manchester City), Martin (Aston Villa), Moroney (West Ham United); Corr (Everton), Farrell (Everton), Walsh (D.), (West Bromwich Albion), Desmond (Middlesbrough), O'Conner (Shamrock Rovers). Scorers: Martin and Farrell.

However, as some may not consider Eire to be foreign it must be noted that the first Continental team to beat England on English soil was Hungary. Details are given under the heading, HUNGARY.

England's first defeat abroad was against Spain at Madrid, May 15, 1929. Result 3—4. In fact, this was the first defeat abroad of an England team including professionals, for an England all-amateur side was beaten abroad at Copenhagen, May 5, 1910, Denmark winning 2—1. The teams in England's first professional defeat were:
*England:* Hufton (West Ham United); Cooper (Derby County), Blenkinsop (Sheffield Wednesday); Kean (Bolton Wanderers), Hill (Newcastle United), Peacock (Middlesbrough); Adcock (Leicester City), E. Kail (Dulwich Hamlet), Carter (West Bromwich Albion), Bradford (Birmingham), Barry (Leicester City).
*Spain.* Zamora (Club Deportive Espanol of Barcelona); Quesada (Real Madrid), Quincoces (Club Deportive Alaves of Vittoria); Prats (Real Madrid), Marculeta (Real Sociedad of San Sebastian), J. M. Pena (Real Madrid); Lazcano (Real Madrid), Goiburu (Osasuna Club of Pampona), Rubio (Real Madrid), Padron (Club Deportive of Barcelona), Yurrita (Real Sociedad of San Sebastian).
Scorers: Spain—Rubio, Lazcano 2, Goiburu. England—Carter 2, Hill.

The highest individual score for England in an International Championship match is five by G. W. Hall v. Ireland. Nov. 16, 1938, and by G. O. Smith v. Ireland, Feb.

18, 1899.

England have won the International Championship outright 29 times—more times than any other country.

v. Scotland. Played 90, won 33, lost 35, drawn 22.
Biggest win: 9—3 at Wembley, April 15, 1961.
Biggest defeat: 2—7 at Old Hampden, Mar. 2, 1878.
v. Ireland. Played 80, won 62, lost 6 drawn 12.
Biggest win: 13—0 at Belfast, Feb. 18,1882.
Biggest defeat: 0—3 at Middlesbrough, Feb. 14, 1914.
v. Wales. Played 83, won 55, lost 11, drawn 17.
Biggest win 9—1 at Cardiff, Mar. 16, 1896.
Biggest defeat: 3—5 at Wrexham, Mar. 13, 1882.

**First**

The first international matches were those played between England and Scotland in 1870, although these games and others played in 1871 and 1872 are not accorded official recognition as full internationals. The series owes its beginning to the enterprise of Mr. C. W. Alcock who, shortly after his appointment as Honorary Secretary of the Football Association, wrote a letter to *The Sportsman* newspaper.

This letter, published on Feb. 5, 1870, announced that a match between "the leading representatives of the Scotch and English sections" was to be played under the auspices of the Football Association and it invited players to submit their names for selection.

The match was played at Kennington Oval on Mar. 5, 1870, resulting in a draw 1—1, and it created such interest that another game was arranged to take place at the same venue later in the year.

On Nov. 1, 1870 Mr. Alcock wrote a letter which was published in the *Glasgow Herald* inviting applications from or nomination of Scottish players for this series of matches and the Queen's Park club took an immediate interest. Indeed, one of their players, R. Smith, figured in the second game which was played at The Oval on November 19th and also in the third and fourth games played during 1871.

As a matter of record the results of these games which are no longer considered as official internationals were as follows:

Mar. 5, 1870   England 1, Scotland 1
Nov. 19, 1870   England 1, Scotland 0
Feb. 28, 1871   England 1, Scotland 1
Nov. 18, 1871   England 2, Scotland 1
Feb. 24, 1872   England 1, Scotland 0
All were played at Kennington Oval and

it is the first of the series to be played North of the Border—at the ground of the West of Scotland Cricket Club at Partick, near Glasgow, on Saturday, Nov. 30, 1872, that is now accepted as being the first official international.

This first international to be played in Scotland was an obvious follow-up to the earlier games in London, but the definite plans had been set in motion following discussions between leading members of the Queen's Park Club, the F.A., and the Wanderers F.C., when the Scottish enthusiasts had travelled down to London to meet the Wanderers in the first semi-final of the new F.A. Cup Competition in Feb. 1872. The F.A. at a meeting on Oct 3, 1872, formally agreed to send a representative team "in order to further the interests of the Association in Scotland."

As may be seen in this section under RESULTS the game ended in a goalless draw. Bell's Life described it as "one of the jolliest, one of the most spirited and most pleasant matches that have ever been played according to Association Rules . . . and each member of the two sides was greeted with a volley of applause as he entered the pavilion." The spectators numbered about 4,000.

The dates of the earliest internationals between the other home countries are as follows:

Mar. 25, 1876, Scotland v. Wales at Glasgow.

Jan. 18, 1879, England v. Wales at The Oval.

Feb. 18, 1882, England v. Ireland at Belfast.

Feb. 25, 1882, Wales v. Ireland at Wrexham.

Jan. 28, 1884, Ireland v. Scotland at Belfast.

The first official international between any of the home countries and a foreign country was that between England and Austria, in Vienna, June 6, 1908. Two earlier games between England and a visiting German side which were played in Sept. 1901 are not ranked as official.

The first international played in Europe —Austria 5, Hungary 0, Oct. 12, 1902.

The first international played in South America—Argentine 1, Uruguay 1, 1905.

**Fourth Division**

The first player to win a full international cap while on the books of a Fourth Division club—V. Rouse of Crystal Palace, who kept goal for Wales v. Ireland, April 22, 1959.

## General

In 1955-6 all four countries in the International Championship finished level with three points each, the first time that this has happened.

The only instances of International Championship games being played outside the two countries concerned were at Shrewsbury, Feb. 8, 1890, and at Goodison Park, Liverpool, May 19, 1973. Both games were between Ireland and Wales.

Ireland played a "home" European Championship Cup game with Spain at Hull, Feb. 16, 1972, and "home" World Cup games v. Portugal, at Coventry, Mar. 28, 1973, and v. Cyprus, at Fulham, May 9, 1973.

The only non-British-born player to appear in the International Championship was W. Andrews the Glentoran and Grimsby Town half-back. Born Kansas City, U.S.A., he made three appearances for Ireland: 1907-8, v. Scotland, 1912-13 v. England and Scotland.

The only gipsy ever to play for England was R. Howell, Sheffield United and Liverpool half-back, who made two appearances in the 1890s. He was born in a caravan near Sheffield.

## Goal-scoring

See GOAL-SCORING (INTERNATIONALS).

## Individual Appearances

See APPEARANCES (INTERNATIONALS).

## Ireland

This section refers to Northern Ireland. International matches concerning the Football Association of Ireland (Dublin) appear under the heading, EIRE.

The Irish Football Association (Belfast) are entitled by F.I.F.A. ruling to include players from Eire in International Championship matches with either England, Scotland or Wales, but must restrict their choice to players born in Northern Ireland for all other international matches. In June 1954, F.I.F.A. ruled that the official designation for international teams under the jurisdiction of the Irish F.A. should be "Northern Ireland".

Ireland gained her only outright International Championship title in 1913-14, although in 1902-3, 1955-6, 1957-8, 1958-9 and 1963-4 she shared the Championship.

In that Championship winning season of 1913-14 Ireland defeated Wales 2—1 at Wrexham, and England 3—0 at Middlesbrough, and drew with Scotland 1—1 at Belfast.

The men who took part in Ireland's most successful season were:

Goal: McKee (Belfast Celtic) v. W. E. S.

Full-backs: McConnell (Bohemians) v. W. E. S., Craig (Morton) v. W. E. S.

Half-backs: Harris (Everton) v. W. S., Hampton (Bradford City) v. E., O'Connell (Hull City) v. W. E. S., Rollo (Linfield, v. W., Hamill (Manchester United) v. E. S.

Forwards: Seymour (Bohemians) v. W., Rollo (Linfield) v. E., Houston (Everton) v. S., Young (Linfield) v. W. E. S., Nixon (Linfield) v. S., Gillespie (Sheffield United) v. W. E., Lacey (Liverpool) v. W. E. S., Brookman (Bradford City) v. W., Thompson (Clyde) v. E. S.

Goal-scorers: v. Wales, Gillespie (2). v. England, Gillespie and Lacey (2). v. Scotland, Young.

v. *Scotland*. Played 78, won 12, lost 55, drawn 11.

Biggest win: 2—0 at Glasgow, Mar. 21, 1903. Also at Belfast, Oct. 4, 1947. Biggest defeat: 0—11 at Glasgow, Feb. 23, 1901.

v. *Wales*. Played 79, won 25, lost 37, drawn 17.

Biggest win: 7—0 at Belfast, Feb. 1, 1930. Biggest defeat: 0—11 at Wrexham, Mar. 3, 1888.

v. *England*. Played 80, won 6, lost 62, drawn 12.

Biggest win: 3—0 at Middlesbrough, Feb. 14, 1914. Biggest defeat: 0—13 at Belfast, Feb. 18, 1882.

The highest individual scorer for Ireland in a single game is J. Bambrick who scored six goals v. Wales at Belfast, Feb. 1, 1930.

## Qualifications

For many years the qualification of players appearing for any of the home countries was birth within the area of the National Association, or, in the case of British subjects born abroad, they could claim their father's nationality. In 1971 it was decided to allow players to appear for the country of their father's birth.

For cases of players appearing for countries other than that for which they were rightly qualified, see APPEARANCES (INTERNATIONALS); General.

## Results

Here follow the results of internationals between the home countries. Results of internationals with all foreign countries are given under those countries.

*England v. Scotland*

| *Year | Venue | E. | S. |
|---|---|---|---|
| 1873 | Glasgow | 0 | 0 |
| 1873 | Kennington Oval | 4 | 2 |
| 1874 | Glasgow | 1 | 2 |
| 1875 | Kennington Oval | 2 | 2 |
| 1876 | Glasgow | 0 | 3 |

| Year | Venue | | | Year | Venue | | |
|---|---|---|---|---|---|---|---|
| 1877 | Kennington Oval | 1 | 3 | 1949 | Wembley | 1 | 3 |
| 1878 | Glasgow | 2 | 7 | 1950 | Glasgow | 1 | 0 |
| 1879 | Kennington Oval | 5 | 4 | 1951 | Wembley | 2 | 3 |
| 1880 | Glasgow | 4 | 5 | 1952 | Glasgow | 2 | 1 |
| 1881 | Kennington Oval | 1 | 6 | 1953 | Wembley | 2 | 2 |
| 1882 | Glasgow | 1 | 5 | 1954 | Glasgow | 4 | 2 |
| 1883 | Sheffield | 2 | 3 | 1955 | Wembley | 7 | 2 |
| 1884 | Glasgow | 0 | 1 | 1956 | Glasgow | 1 | 1 |
| 1885 | Kennington Oval | 1 | 1 | 1957 | Wembley | 2 | 1 |
| 1886 | Glasgow | 1 | 1 | 1958 | Glasgow | 4 | 0 |
| 1887 | Blackburn | 2 | 3 | 1959 | Wembley | 1 | 0 |
| 1888 | Glasgow | 5 | 0 | 1960 | Glasgow | 1 | 1 |
| 1889 | Kennington Oval | 2 | 3 | 1961 | Wembley | 9 | 3 |
| 1890 | Glasgow | 1 | 1 | 1962 | Glasgow | 0 | 2 |
| 1891 | Blackburn | 2 | 1 | 1963 | Wembley | 1 | 2 |
| 1892 | Glasgow | 4 | 0 | 1964 | Glasgow | 0 | 1 |
| 1893 | Richmond | 5 | 2 | 1965 | Wembley | 2 | 2 |
| 1894 | Glasgow | 2 | 2 | 1966 | Glasgow | 4 | 3 |
| 1895 | Everton | 3 | 0 | 1967 | Wembley | 2 | 3 |
| 1896 | Glasgow | 1 | 2 | 1968 | Glasgow | 1 | 1 |
| 1897 | Crystal Palace | 1 | 2 | 1969 | Wembley | 4 | 1 |
| 1898 | Glasgow | 3 | 1 | 1970 | Glasgow | 0 | 0 |
| 1899 | Birmingham | 2 | 1 | 1971 | Wembley | 3 | 1 |
| 1900 | Glasgow | 1 | 4 | 1972 | Glasgow | 1 | 0 |
| 1901 | Crystal Palace | 2 | 2 | 1973 | § Glasgow | 5 | 0 |
| 1902 | Birmingham | 2 | 2 | 1973 | Wembley | 1 | 0 |
| 1903 | Sheffield | 1 | 2 | | | | |
| 1904 | Glasgow | 1 | 0 | *England v. Ireland* | | | |

| Year | Venue | | | *Year | Venue | E. | I. |
|---|---|---|---|---|---|---|---|
| 1905 | Crystal Palace | 1 | 0 | 1882 | Belfast | 13 | 0 |
| 1906 | Glasgow | 1 | 2 | 1883 | Liverpool | 7 | 0 |
| 1907 | Newcastle | 1 | 1 | 1884 | Belfast | 8 | 1 |
| 1908 | Glasgow | 1 | 1 | 1885 | Manchester | 4 | 0 |
| 1909 | Crystal Palace | 2 | 0 | 1886 | Belfast | 6 | 1 |
| 1910 | Glasgow | 0 | 2 | 1887 | Sheffield | 7 | 0 |
| 1911 | Everton | 1 | 1 | 1888 | Belfast | 5 | 1 |
| 1912 | Glasgow | 1 | 1 | 1889 | Everton | 6 | 1 |
| 1913 | Chelsea | 1 | 0 | 1890 | Belfast | 9 | 1 |
| 1914 | Glasgow | 1 | 3 | 1891 | Wolverhampton | 6 | 1 |
| 1919 | ‡Everton | 2 | 2 | 1892 | Belfast | 2 | 0 |
| 1919 | ‡Glasgow | 4 | 3 | 1893 | Birmingham | 6 | 1 |
| 1920 | Sheffield | 5 | 4 | 1894 | Belfast | 2 | 2 |
| 1921 | Glasgow | 0 | 3 | 1895 | Derby | 9 | 0 |
| 1922 | Villa Park | 0 | 1 | 1896 | Belfast | 2 | 0 |
| 1923 | Glasgow | 2 | 2 | 1897 | Nottingham | 6 | 0 |
| 1924 | Wembley | 1 | 1 | 1898 | Belfast | 3 | 2 |
| 1925 | Glasgow | 0 | 2 | 1899 | Sunderland | 13 | 2 |
| 1926 | Manchester | 0 | 1 | 1900 | Dublin | 2 | 0 |
| 1927 | Glasgow | 2 | 1 | 1901 | Southampton | 3 | 0 |
| 1928 | Wembley | 1 | 5 | 1902 | Belfast | 1 | 0 |
| 1929 | Glasgow | 0 | 1 | 1903 | Wolverhampton | 4 | 0 |
| 1930 | Wembley | 5 | 2 | 1904 | Belfast | 3 | 1 |
| 1931 | Glasgow | 0 | 2 | 1905 | Middlesbrough | 1 | 1 |
| 1932 | Wembley | 3 | 0 | 1906 | Belfast | 5 | 0 |
| 1933 | Glasgow | 1 | 2 | 1907 | Everton | 1 | 0 |
| 1934 | Wembley | 3 | 0 | 1908 | Belfast | 3 | 1 |
| 1935 | Glasgow | 0 | 2 | 1909 | Bradford | 4 | 0 |
| 1936 | Wembley | 1 | 1 | 1910 | Belfast | 1 | 1 |
| 1937 | Glasgow | 1 | 3 | 1911 | Derby | 2 | 1 |
| 1938 | Wembley | 0 | 1 | 1912 | Dublin | 6 | 1 |
| 1939 | Glasgow | 2 | 1 | 1913 | Belfast | 1 | 2 |
| 1946 | ‡Glasgow | 0 | 1 | 1914 | Middlesbrough | 0 | 3 |
| 1947 | Wembley | 1 | 1 | 1920 | Belfast | 1 | 1 |
| 1948 | Glasgow | 2 | 0 | | | | |

| Year | Venue | | |
|------|-------|---|---|
| 1921 | Sunderland | 2 | 0 |
| 1922 | Belfast | 1 | 1 |
| 1923 | West Bromwich | 2 | 0 |
| 1924 | Belfast | 1 | 2 |
| 1925 | Everton | 3 | 1 |
| 1926 | Belfast | 0 | 0 |
| 1927 | Liverpool | 3 | 3 |
| 1928 | Belfast | 0 | 2 |
| 1929 | Everton | 2 | 1 |
| 1930 | Belfast | 6 | 2 |
| 1931 | Sheffield | 5 | 1 |
| 1932 | Belfast | 6 | 2 |
| 1933 | Blackpool | 1 | 0 |
| 1934 | Belfast | 3 | 0 |
| 1935 | Everton | 2 | 1 |
| 1936 | Belfast | 3 | 1 |
| 1937 | Stoke | 3 | 1 |
| 1938 | Belfast | 5 | 1 |
| 1939 | Manchester | 7 | 0 |
| 1946 | ‡Belfast | 1 | 0 |
| 1947 | Belfast | 7 | 2 |
| 1948 | Everton | 2 | 2 |
| 1949 | Belfast | 6 | 2 |
| 1950 | Manchester | 9 | 2 |
| 1951 | Belfast | 4 | 1 |
| 1952 | Villa Park | 2 | 0 |
| 1953 | Belfast | 2 | 2 |
| 1954 | Liverpool | 3 | 1 |
| 1955 | Belfast | 2 | 0 |
| 1956 | Wembley | 3 | 0 |
| 1957 | Belfast | 1 | 1 |
| 1958 | Wembley | 2 | 3 |
| 1959 | Belfast | 3 | 3 |
| 1960 | Wembley | 2 | 1 |
| 1961 | Belfast | 5 | 2 |
| 1962 | Wembley | 1 | 1 |
| 1963 | Belfast | 3 | 1 |
| 1964 | Wembley | 8 | 3 |
| 1965 | Belfast | 4 | 3 |
| 1966 | Wembley | 2 | 1 |
| 1967 | Belfast | 2 | 0 |
| 1968 | Wembley | 2 | 0 |
| 1969 | Belfast | 3 | 1 |
| 1970 | Wembley | 3 | 1 |
| 1971 | Belfast | 1 | 0 |
| 1972 | Wembley | 0 | 1 |
| 1973 | Everton | 2 | 1 |

*England v. Wales*

| *Year | Venue | E. | W. |
|-------|-------|----|----|
| 1879 | Kennington Oval | 2 | 1 |
| 1880 | Wrexham | 3 | 2 |
| 1881 | Blackburn | 0 | 1 |
| 1882 | Wrexham | 3 | 5 |
| 1883 | Kennington Oval | 5 | 0 |
| 1884 | Wrexham | 4 | 0 |
| 1885 | Blackburn | 1 | 1 |
| 1886 | Wrexham | 3 | 1 |
| 1887 | Kennington Oval | 4 | 0 |
| 1888 | Crewe | 5 | 1 |
| 1889 | Stoke-on-Trent | 4 | 1 |
| 1890 | Wrexham | 3 | 1 |
| 1891 | Sunderland | 4 | 1 |
| 1892 | Wrexham | 2 | 0 |
| 1893 | Stoke-on-Trent | 6 | 0 |
| 1894 | Wrexham | 5 | 1 |
| 1895 | London | 1 | 1 |
| 1896 | Cardiff | 9 | 1 |
| 1897 | Sheffield | 4 | 0 |
| 1898 | Wrexham | 3 | 0 |
| 1899 | Bristol | 4 | 0 |
| 1900 | Cardiff | 1 | 1 |
| 1901 | Newcastle | 6 | 0 |
| 1902 | Wrexham | 0 | 0 |
| 1903 | Portsmouth | 2 | 1 |
| 1904 | Wrexham | 2 | 2 |
| 1905 | Liverpool | 3 | 1 |
| 1906 | Cardiff | 1 | 0 |
| 1907 | Fulham | 1 | 1 |
| 1908 | Wrexham | 7 | 1 |
| 1909 | Nottingham | 2 | 0 |
| 1910 | Cardiff | 1 | 0 |
| 1911 | Millwall | 3 | 0 |
| 1912 | Wrexham | 2 | 0 |
| 1913 | Bristol | 4 | 3 |
| 1914 | Cardiff | 2 | 0 |
| 1920 | ‡Cardiff | 1 | 2 |
| 1920 | ‡Stoke | 2 | 0 |
| 1920 | Highbury | 1 | 2 |
| 1921 | Cardiff | 0 | 0 |
| 1922 | Liverpool | 1 | 0 |
| 1923 | Cardiff | 2 | 2 |
| 1924 | Blackburn | 1 | 2 |
| 1925 | Swansea | 2 | 1 |
| 1926 | London (Selhurst) | 1 | 3 |
| 1927 | Wrexham | 3 | 3 |
| 1928 | Burnley | 1 | 2 |
| 1929 | Swansea | 3 | 2 |
| 1930 | Stamford Bridge | 6 | 0 |
| 1931 | Wrexham | 4 | 0 |
| 1932 | Liverpool | 3 | 1 |
| 1933 | Wrexham | 0 | 0 |
| 1934 | Newcastle | 1 | 2 |
| 1935 | Cardiff | 4 | 0 |
| 1936 | Wolverhampton | 1 | 2 |
| 1937 | Cardiff | 1 | 2 |
| 1938 | Middlesbrough | 2 | 1 |
| 1939 | Cardiff | 2 | 4 |
| 1946 | ‡West Bromwich | 0 | 1 |
| 1947 | Manchester | 3 | 0 |
| 1948 | Cardiff | 3 | 0 |
| 1949 | Villa Park | 1 | 0 |
| 1950 | Cardiff | 4 | 1 |
| 1951 | Sunderland | 4 | 2 |
| 1952 | Cardiff | 1 | 1 |
| 1953 | Wembley | 5 | 2 |
| 1954 | Cardiff | 4 | 1 |
| 1955 | Wembley | 3 | 2 |
| 1956 | Cardiff | 1 | 2 |
| 1957 | Wembley | 3 | 1 |
| 1958 | Cardiff | 4 | 0 |
| 1959 | Villa Park | 2 | 2 |
| 1960 | Cardiff | 1 | 1 |
| 1961 | Wembley | 5 | 1 |
| 1962 | Cardiff | 1 | 1 |
| 1963 | Wembley | 4 | 0 |

| Year | Venue | | |
|------|-------|---|---|
| 1964 | Cardiff | 4 | 0 |
| 1965 | Wembley | 2 | 1 |
| 1966 | Cardiff | 0 | 0 |
| 1967 | Wembley | 5 | 1 |
| 1968 | Cardiff | 3 | 0 |
| 1969 | Wembley | 2 | 1 |
| 1970 | Cardiff | 1 | 1 |
| 1971 | Wembley | 0 | 0 |
| 1972 | Cardiff | 3 | 0 |
| 1973 | †Cardiff | 1 | 0 |
| 1973 | Wembley | 3 | 0 |

*Scotland v. Wales*

| *Year | Venue | S. | W. |
|-------|-------|----|----|
| 1876 | Glasgow | 4 | 0 |
| 1877 | Wrexham | 2 | 0 |
| 1878 | Glasgow | 9 | 0 |
| 1879 | Wrexham | 3 | 0 |
| 1880 | Glasgow | 5 | 1 |
| 1881 | Wrexham | 5 | 1 |
| 1882 | Glasgow | 5 | 0 |
| 1883 | Wrexham | 3 | 0 |
| 1884 | Glasgow | 4 | 1 |
| 1885 | Wrexham | 8 | 1 |
| 1886 | Glasgow | 4 | 1 |
| 1887 | Wrexham | 2 | 0 |
| 1888 | Edinburgh | 5 | 1 |
| 1889 | Wrexham | 0 | 0 |
| 1890 | Paisley | 5 | 0 |
| 1891 | Wrexham | 4 | 3 |
| 1892 | Edinburgh | 6 | 1 |
| 1893 | Wrexham | 8 | 0 |
| 1894 | Kilmarnock | 5 | 2 |
| 1895 | Wrexham | 2 | 2 |
| 1896 | Dundee | 4 | 0 |
| 1897 | Wrexham | 2 | 2 |
| 1898 | Motherwell | 5 | 2 |
| 1899 | Wrexham | 6 | 0 |
| 1900 | Aberdeen | 5 | 2 |
| 1901 | Wrexham | 1 | 1 |
| 1902 | Greenock | 5 | 1 |
| 1903 | Cardiff | 1 | 0 |
| 1904 | Dundee | 1 | 1 |
| 1905 | Wrexham | 1 | 3 |
| 1906 | Edinburgh | 0 | 2 |
| 1907 | Wrexham | 0 | 1 |
| 1908 | Dundee | 2 | 1 |
| 1909 | Wrexham | 2 | 3 |
| 1910 | Kilmarnock | 1 | 0 |
| 1911 | Cardiff | 2 | 2 |
| 1912 | Tynecastle | 1 | 0 |
| 1913 | Wrexham | 0 | 0 |
| 1914 | Glasgow | 0 | 0 |
| 1920 | Cardiff | 1 | 1 |
| 1921 | Aberdeen | 2 | 1 |
| 1922 | Wrexham | 1 | 2 |
| 1923 | Paisley | 2 | 0 |
| 1924 | Cardiff | 0 | 2 |
| 1925 | Tynecastle | 3 | 1 |
| 1926 | Cardiff | 3 | 0 |
| 1927 | Glasgow | 3 | 0 |
| 1928 | Wrexham | 2 | 2 |
| 1929 | Glasgow | 4 | 2 |
| 1930 | Cardiff | 4 | 2 |
| 1931 | Glasgow | 1 | 1 |
| 1932 | Wrexham | 3 | 2 |
| 1933 | Edinburgh | 2 | 5 |
| 1934 | Cardiff | 2 | 3 |
| 1935 | Aberdeen | 3 | 2 |
| 1936 | Cardiff | 1 | 1 |
| 1937 | Dundee | 1 | 2 |
| 1938 | Cardiff | 1 | 2 |
| 1939 | Edinburgh | 3 | 2 |
| 1946 | ‡Glasgow | 2 | 0 |
| 1947 | Wrexham | 1 | 3 |
| 1948 | Glasgow | 1 | 2 |
| 1949 | Cardiff | 3 | 1 |
| 1950 | Glasgow | 2 | 0 |
| 1951 | Cardiff | 3 | 1 |
| 1952 | Glasgow | 0 | 1 |
| 1953 | Cardiff | 2 | 1 |
| 1954 | Glasgow | 3 | 3 |
| 1955 | Cardiff | 1 | 0 |
| 1956 | Glasgow | 3 | 0 |
| 1957 | Cardiff | 2 | 2 |
| 1958 | Glasgow | 1 | 1 |
| 1959 | Cardiff | 3 | 0 |
| 1960 | Glasgow | 1 | 1 |
| 1961 | Cardiff | 0 | 2 |
| 1962 | Glasgow | 2 | 0 |
| 1963 | Cardiff | 3 | 2 |
| 1964 | Glasgow | 2 | 1 |
| 1965 | Cardiff | 2 | 3 |
| 1966 | Glasgow | 4 | 1 |
| 1967 | Cardiff | 1 | 1 |
| 1968 | Glasgow | 3 | 2 |
| 1969 | Wrexham | 5 | 3 |
| 1970 | Glasgow | 0 | 0 |
| 1971 | Cardiff | 0 | 0 |
| 1972 | Glasgow | 1 | 0 |
| 1973 | Wrexham | 2 | 0 |

*Scotland v. Ireland*

| *Year | Venue | S. | I. |
|-------|-------|----|----|
| 1884 | Belfast | 5 | 0 |
| 1885 | Glasgow | 8 | 2 |
| 1886 | Belfast | 7 | 2 |
| 1887 | Glasgow | 4 | 1 |
| 1888 | Belfast | 10 | 2 |
| 1889 | Glasgow | 7 | 0 |
| 1890 | Belfast | 4 | 1 |
| 1891 | Glasgow | 2 | 1 |
| 1892 | Belfast | 3 | 2 |
| 1893 | Glasgow | 6 | 1 |
| 1894 | Belfast | 2 | 1 |
| 1895 | Glasgow | 3 | 1 |
| 1896 | Belfast | 3 | 3 |
| 1897 | Glasgow | 5 | 1 |
| 1898 | Belfast | 3 | 0 |
| 1899 | Glasgow | 9 | 1 |
| 1900 | Belfast | 3 | 0 |
| 1901 | Glasgow | 11 | 0 |
| 1902 | Belfast | 5 | 1 |
| 1903 | Glasgow | 0 | 2 |
| 1904 | Dublin | 1 | 1 |
| 1905 | Glasgow | 4 | 0 |

| Year | Venue | | | Year | Venue | | |
|------|-------|---|---|------|-------|---|---|
| 1906 | Dublin | 1 | 0 | 1883 | Belfast | 1 | 1 |
| 1907 | Glasgow | 3 | 0 | 1884 | Wrexham | 6 | 0 |
| 1908 | Dublin | 5 | 0 | 1885 | Belfast | 8 | 2 |
| 1909 | Glasgow | 5 | 0 | 1886 | Wrexham | 5 | 0 |
| 1910 | Belfast | 0 | 1 | 1887 | Belfast | 1 | 4 |
| 1911 | Glasgow | 2 | 0 | 1888 | Wrexham | 11 | 0 |
| 1912 | Belfast | 4 | 1 | 1889 | Belfast | 3 | 1 |
| 1913 | Dublin | 2 | 1 | 1890 | Shrewsbury | 5 | 2 |
| 1914 | Belfast | 1 | 1 | 1891 | Belfast | 2 | 7 |
| 1919 | ‡Glasgow | 2 | 1 | 1892 | Bangor | 1 | 1 |
| 1919 | ‡Belfast | 0 | 0 | 1893 | Belfast | 3 | 4 |
| 1920 | Glasgow | 3 | 0 | 1894 | Swansea | 4 | 1 |
| 1921 | Belfast | 2 | 0 | 1895 | Belfast | 2 | 2 |
| 1922 | Glasgow | 2 | 1 | 1896 | Wrexham | 6 | 1 |
| 1923 | Belfast | 1 | 0 | 1897 | Belfast | 3 | 4 |
| 1924 | Glasgow | 2 | 0 | 1898 | Llandudno | 0 | 1 |
| 1925 | Belfast | 3 | 0 | 1899 | Belfast | 0 | 1 |
| 1926 | Glasgow | 4 | 0 | 1900 | Llandudno | 2 | 0 |
| 1927 | Belfast | 2 | 0 | 1901 | Belfast | 1 | 0 |
| 1928 | Glasgow | 0 | 1 | 1902 | Cardiff | 0 | 3 |
| 1929 | Belfast | 7 | 3 | 1903 | Belfast | 0 | 2 |
| 1930 | Glasgow | 3 | 1 | 1904 | Bangor | 0 | 1 |
| 1931 | Belfast | 0 | 0 | 1905 | Belfast | 2 | 2 |
| 1932 | Glasgow | 3 | 1 | 1906 | Wrexham | 4 | 4 |
| 1933 | Belfast | 4 | 0 | 1907 | Belfast | 3 | 2 |
| 1934 | Glasgow | 1 | 2 | 1908 | Aberdare | 0 | 1 |
| 1935 | Belfast | 1 | 2 | 1909 | Belfast | 3 | 2 |
| 1936 | Edinburgh | 2 | 1 | 1910 | Wrexham | 4 | 1 |
| 1937 | Belfast | 3 | 1 | 1911 | Belfast | 2 | 1 |
| 1938 | Aberdeen | 1 | 1 | 1912 | Cardiff | 2 | 3 |
| 1939 | Belfast | 2 | 0 | 1913 | Belfast | 1 | 0 |
| 1946 | ‡Belfast | 3 | 2 | 1914 | Wrexham | 1 | 2 |
| 1947 | Glasgow | 0 | 0 | 1920 | Belfast | 2 | 2 |
| 1948 | Belfast | 0 | 2 | 1921 | Swansea | 2 | 1 |
| 1949 | Glasgow | 3 | 2 | 1922 | Belfast | 1 | 1 |
| 1950 | Belfast | 8 | 2 | 1923 | Wrexham | 0 | 3 |
| 1951 | Glasgow | 6 | 1 | 1924 | Belfast | 1 | 0 |
| 1952 | Belfast | 3 | 0 | 1925 | Wrexham | 0 | 0 |
| 1953 | Glasgow | 1 | 1 | 1926 | Belfast | 0 | 3 |
| 1954 | Belfast | 3 | 1 | 1927 | Cardiff | 2 | 2 |
| 1955 | Glasgow | 2 | 2 | 1928 | Belfast | 2 | 1 |
| 1956 | Belfast | 1 | 2 | 1929 | Wrexham | 2 | 2 |
| 1957 | Glasgow | 1 | 0 | 1930 | Belfast | 0 | 7 |
| 1958 | Belfast | 1 | 1 | 1931 | Wrexham | 3 | 2 |
| 1959 | Glasgow | 2 | 2 | 1932 | Belfast | 0 | 4 |
| 1960 | Belfast | 4 | 0 | 1933 | Wrexham | 4 | 1 |
| 1961 | Glasgow | 5 | 2 | 1934 | Belfast | 1 | 1 |
| 1962 | Belfast | 6 | 1 | 1935 | Wrexham | 3 | 1 |
| 1963 | Glasgow | 5 | 1 | 1936 | Belfast | 2 | 3 |
| 1964 | Belfast | 1 | 2 | 1937 | Wrexham | 4 | 1 |
| 1965 | Glasgow | 3 | 2 | 1938 | Belfast | 0 | 1 |
| 1966 | Belfast | 2 | 3 | 1939 | Wrexham | 3 | 1 |
| 1967 | Glasgow | 2 | 1 | 1946 | ‡Cardiff | 0 | 1 |
| 1968 | Belfast | 0 | 1 | 1947 | Belfast | 1 | 2 |
| 1969 | Glasgow | 1 | 1 | 1948 | Wrexham | 2 | 0 |
| 1970 | Belfast | 1 | 0 | 1949 | Belfast | 2 | 0 |
| 1971 | Glasgow | 1 | 0 | 1950 | Wrexham | 0 | 0 |
| 1972 | Glasgow | 2 | 0 | 1951 | Belfast | 2 | 2 |
| 1973 | Glasgow | 1 | 2 | 1952 | Swansea | 3 | 0 |
| | | | | 1953 | Belfast | 3 | 2 |
| | | | | 1954 | Wrexham | 1 | 2 |

*Wales v. Ireland*

| *Year | Venue | W. | I. |
|-------|-------|----|----|
| 1882 | Wrexham | 7 | 1 |
| 1955 | Belfast | 3 | 2 |
| 1956 | Cardiff | 1 | 1 |

| 1957 | Belfast | 0 | 0 |
|------|---------|---|---|
| 1958 | Cardiff | 1 | 1 |
| 1959 | Belfast | 1 | 4 |
| 1960 | Wrexham | 3 | 2 |
| 1961 | Belfast | 5 | 1 |
| 1962 | Cardiff | 4 | 0 |
| 1963 | Belfast | 4 | 1 |
| 1964 | Cardiff | 2 | 3 |
| 1965 | Belfast | 5 | 0 |
| 1966 | Cardiff | 1 | 4 |
| 1967 | Belfast | 0 | 0 |
| 1968 | Wrexham | 2 | 0 |
| 1969 | Belfast | 0 | 0 |
| 1970 | Swansea | 1 | 0 |
| 1971 | Belfast | 0 | 1 |
| 1972 | Wrexham | 0 | 0 |
| 1973 | Everton | 0 | 1 |

\* The year is the last year of the season, i.e. 1959 means season 1958-9.

‡ Victory international.

† World Cup.

§ Centenary match.

## Rules

By a law drawn up in 1921, every goal-keeper appearing in an International Championship game has to wear a jersey of deep yellow.

It has been agreed that any National Association wishing to utilise the services of a Football League player for an international match must insure the players' club against permanent total disablement in an amount of not less than £25,000.

Football League clubs still retain the right to refuse to release players for international matches to any National Association except the F.A.

## Scotland

Scotland has won the International Championship outright 22 times including a run of five Championships in six seasons from 1920 to 1926.

The 1920s were halcyon years for Scottish international football when such great players as goalkeeper W. Harper; full-backs W. McStay and D. Meiklejohn; wing-half J. McMullan and outside-left A. Morton were at the peak of their careers.

v. *England.* Played 90, won 35, lost 33, drawn 22. Biggest win: 7—2 at Old Hampden, Mar. 2, 1878. Biggest defeat: 3—9 at Wembley, April 15, 1961.

v. *Ireland.* Played 78, won 55, lost 12, drawn 11. Biggest win: 11—0 at Hampden Park, Feb. 23, 1901. Biggest defeat: 0—2 at Hampden Park, Mar. 21, 1903, and also at Belfast, Oct. 4, 1947.

v. *Wales.* Played 86, won 52, lost 15, drawn 19. Biggest win: 9—0 at Old Hampden, Mar. 23, 1878. Biggest defeat: 2—5 at Edinburgh, Oct. 26, 1932.

The highest individual score for Scotland in an International Championship match is five by C. Heggie v Ireland, Mar. 20, 1886.

Scotland's first defeat by a foreign country took place on May 16, 1932, at Vienna when Austria won 5—0.

The record number of Anglo-Scots in a Scottish international team is nine, when Scotland played England on April 6, 1907. The Scotland team on that occasion was: McBride (Preston North End); Thomson (Hearts), Sharp (Woolwich Arsenal); Aitken (Middlesbrough), Raisbeck (Liverpool), McWilliam (Newcastle United); Stewart (Manchester City), Walker (Hearts), A. Wilson (Sheffield Wednesday), White (Bolton Wanderers) and G. Wilson (Everton).

## Substitutes

See separate section.

## Third Division

Only three players from the Third Division have played for England in the International Championship since World War II: T. Lawton, who was with Notts County when he played centre-forward against Scotland at Hampden Park, April 10, 1948; R. Matthews of Coventry City, played in goal v. Scotland, at Hampden Park, April 14, 1956, and v. Ireland at Windsor Park, Oct. 6, 1956; and J. Byrne of Crystal Palace, inside-right v. Ireland, at Wembley, Nov. 22, 1961.

While still in the Third Division Lawton also played against Sweden, Italy and Denmark; and Matthews played against Brazil, Sweden and Germany.

## Wales

Wales have won the International Championship outright seven times, but never since 1937.

The outstanding period in the history of Welsh international football was in the 1930s. From 1932 to 1934 a great Welsh side won the Championship two seasons running being undefeated throughout.

The following players represented Wales during that time:

Goal: R. John (Stoke City), L. Evans (Birmingham).

Full backs: B. Williams (Everton), B. Ellis (Motherwell), R. John (Arsenal), S. Lawrence (Swansea Town), D. Jones (Leicester City).

Half-backs: J. Murphy (West Bromwich Albion), F. Keenor (Crewe Alexandra), A. Day (Tottenham Hotspur), T. Griffiths (Bolton Wanderers and Middlesbrough), H. Hanford (Swansea Town), D. Richards (Wolverhampton Wanderers).

Forwards: F. Warren (Middlesbrough),

C. Phillips (Wolverhampton Wanderers), W. Richards (Fulham), E. O'Callaghan (Tottenham Hotspur), D. Astley (Aston Villa), E. Glover (Grimsby Town), W. Robbins (West Bromwich Albion), T. Mills (Clapton Orient), D. Lewis (Swansea Town), W. Evans (Tottenham Hotspur), E. Curtis (Birmingham).

The highest individual scorer in a single Championship match for Wales is four goals: J. Price (Wrexham) v. Ireland at Wrexham, Feb. 25, 1882, and M. Charles (Cardiff City), v. Ireland at Cardiff, April 11, 1962.

v. *England.* Played 83, won 11, lost 55, drawn 17. Biggest win: 5—3 at Wrexham, Mar. 13, 1882. Biggest defeat: 1—9 at Cardiff, Mar. 16, 1896.

v. *Ireland.* Played 79, won 37, lost 25, drawn 17. Biggest win: 11—0 at Wrexham, Mar. 3, 1888. Biggest defeat: 0—7 at Belfast, Feb. 1, 1930.

v. *Scotland.* Played 86, won 15, lost 52, drawn 19. Biggest win: 5—2 at Edinburgh, Oct. 26, 1932. Biggest defeat: 0—9 at Glasgow, Mar. 23, 1878.

## IPSWICH TOWN F.C.

Founded 1880. Adopted professionalism, 1936. Elected to Football League, Division III(S), 1938. Honours: Champions, Division I, 1961-2. Champions, Division II, 1960-61, 1967-8. Champions, Division III(S), 1953-4, 1956-7. Record attendance: 33,525 v. Arsenal, Division I, Mar. 10, 1973. Address: Portman Road, Ipswich (Tel. 51306). Colours: Royal blue shirts, white shorts. Record League goal-scorer: E. Phillips, 41 goals. Division III(S), 1956-7. Record victory: 7—0 v. Portsmouth, Division II, Nov. 7, 1964. Record defeat: 10—1 v. Fulham, Division I, Dec. 26th, 1963.

## IRAN

The Persian F.A. (now Iran) was formed in 1922 but it was not until 1972 that any country from the British Isles met them in an international match.

The trophy presented to the winners of the Football Association Sunday Cup Competition is one that was given to the F.A. by the Shah of Persia to mark the Association's centenary.

The address of the governing body of football in Iran: Iranian Football Federation, Sports Federation Joint Bureau, Park-e-Shahr Khiabian Varzesh, P.O. Box 11-1642, Teheran. Colours: Green shirts, white shorts, red stockings.

Result of international match: June 11, 1972 Eire 2, Iran 1: Recife, Brazil

## IRELAND

See under IRISH FOOTBALL ASSOCIATION, IRISH FOOTBALL ASSOCIATION CUP, IRISH LEAGUE, INTERNATIONALS (IRELAND) and (RESULTS).

The oldest club in Ireland is Cliftonville formed in 1879 by Mr. J. M. McAlery who introduced the game into Ireland and also formed the Irish F.A. (q.v.).

Cliftonville played their first match on the ground of the local cricket club on Oct. 11, 1879, but, sad to relate, these enterprising sportsmen were defeated 2—1 by a team consisting largely of rugby players.

Other clubs formed almost immediately after Cliftonville included Banbridge Academy, Ulster, Ardee, Knock, Portland and Moyola Park, but none of these has maintained a continuous existence as a senior club.

## IRELAND, FOOTBALL ASSOCIATION OF
See EIRE.

## IRISH REPUBLIC
See EIRE.

## IRISH FOOTBALL ASSOCIATION

The "father" of Association Football in Ireland was Mr. J. M. McAlery, a keen Belfast sportsman. He was so impressed by what he saw of the game on a visit to Scotland in 1877 that he determined to introduce it to his home town.

After calling a meeting of other sporting personalities, Mr. McAlery wrote to Mr. J. Allen, the honorary secretary of Glasgow Caledonian F.C., with an invitation to stage an exhibition match in Belfast.

Mr. Allen liked the idea and contacted the neighbouring Queen's Park club asking them to provide the opposition for such a game.

Association Football came to Ireland on Oct. 24, 1878, when, on the ground of the Ulster Cricket Club, Belfast, Queen's Park defeated Caledonian F.C. by three goals to two.

Soon after this, another Scottish club, Lenzie F.C., visited Ireland and met the newly formed Ulster F.C.

These games were sufficient to arouse enthusiasm for the dribbling code, and despite the strength of the established Rugby game, Soccer clubs begaan to form in Ireland.

In 1880 Mr. McAlery called meetings to organise the formation of an Irish F.A. and this was established Nov. 18 of that year. Mr. McAlery was made the first Honorary Secretary, and the first President was Major (afterwards Lord) Spencer Chichester.

The Association became a limited company in 1909. Three years later such serious disputes arose between this governing body and a large number of the senior clubs that the Association's authority and existence was threatened. Agreement, however, was reached and differences settled before the final break was made a few years later.

This break came in 1921 when clubs in the South of Ireland formed what was then known as the Irish Free State F.A. (For details of this and other matters which concern both the Belfast and Dublin Association, see Eire).

When the country was split politically in 1923, a meeting of the four home Associations was held at Liverpool. The I.F.S.A. received official recognition, and it was agreed that the Irish F.A.'s jurisdiction should be restricted to Northern Ireland. The Irish F.A. (Northern Ireland), however, is the only one of the two Irish Associations to be a member of the International Board and take part in the International Championship.

The address of the Irish F.A. is 20 Windsor Avenue, Belfast. 9. Colours: Green shirts, white shorts, green stockings.

## IRISH FOOTBALL ASSOCIATION CUP

This trophy was purchased for £55 18s. 6d. and put up for competition for the first time in 1880 when seven clubs took part after paying an entrance fee of 10s. each. Those seven clubs were Alexander (Limavady), Avoniel, Cliftonville, Distillery, Knock, Oldpark, and Moyola Park, and the latter became the first winners defeating Cliftonville 1—0.

Linfield are by the far the most successful club, winning the trophy on 30 occasions. Next comes Distillery with 11 wins. Linfield also hold the record for the highest score in the Cup Final, 10—1 v. Bohemians, 1895.

No Final tie was played in season 1911-12 because of the football split in the country at that time, but the Cup was awarded to Linfield. Similarly there was no Final in season 1919-20 when it was decided not to play the game because of the riots at the replayed semi-final tie between Belfast

Celtic and Glentoran on the Cliftonville ground. Shelbourne, who had qualified for the Final, were awarded the trophy.

## IRISH INTERNATIONALS
See INTERNATIONALS (IRELAND), APPEARANCES (INTERNATIONAL).

## IRISH LEAGUE
Eight clubs formed the Irish League in 1890. They were Clarence, Cliftonville, Distillery, Glentoran, Linfield, Milford, Old Park and Ulster. The first President was Mr. McNiece of Cliftonville.

In 1911-12 season the Belfast clubs withdrew their reserve teams from the Irish Junior League after a dispute with the F.A. and formed a Second Division of the Irish League as well as instituting the Irish Gold Cup competition.

In 1921 the Southern clubs, Shelbourne and the Bohemians, broke away from the Irish League and together with other clubs in the South formed their own Association and League.

The Irish League has enjoyed a continuous existence since its inaugural season of 1890-91 with the exception of three seasons during World War I when it was suspended and substituted by the Belfast League competition, and during the second World War from season 1940-41 to 1946-7 inclusive when the competition was known as the Northern Ireland Regional League.

Linfield are the outstanding club of this League having won the Championship 29 times.

## ISRAEL
The Israel F.A.—Hitachdut Lekadrugel Beisrael—was founded in 1928 and now has a membership of more than 80 clubs, all amateur.

The address of the Israel F.A. is 12 Carlebach Street, P.O. Box 88, Tel-Aviv. Colours: Blue shirts, white shorts, blue and white stockings.

Israel first appeared in the World Cup Final Tournament in 1970 but finished bottom of their group.

Results of international matches:
Jan. 15, 1958*  Israel 0, Wales 2; Tel-Aviv
Feb. 5, 1958*  Wales 2, Israel 0; Cardiff
May 16, 1967  Israel 1, Scotland 2; Tel-Aviv
Sept. 10, 1968  Israel 2, Ireland 3; Jaffa
* World Cup

## ITALY
Italian footballers have long been among the highest-paid players in the world. Such are the bonuses that the Italian clubs have attracted many stars from foreign countries, and, in all, over 300 overseas players signed for Italian clubs after World War II

before the F.A. placed a ban on new arrivals.

Many of the leading clubs are sponsored by wealthy industrialists who appear to have unlimited supplies of money for the purchase of star players and the payment of top bonuses, but with such extravagance Italian League clubs ran up debts said to exceed £24 million, and in 1967 the Italian F.A. obtained a loan from the state run football pools with which to settle all the interest payments that were then crippling so many clubs.

On the other hand, however, as these wealthy club presidents are prepared to pay so well to get the best they are less tolerant of sub-standard performances, and the constant striving to satisfy their masters means that Italian professionals must be exceptionally dedicated to the game and prepared to work and play under a strict disciplinary code.

The Italians won the World Cup in 1934 when the competition was held in their country, and, two years later, they won the soccer tournament of the Olympic Games in Berlin. They confirmed their supremacy in 1938 by retaining the World Cup, defeating Hungary 4—2 in the Final.

At international level Italy went through a bad spell after World War II. Their failure to qualify for the World Cup in 1958 caused quite a commotion, and their defensive complex showed up in the 1962 and 1966 tournaments. The side returned home in disgrace after a 1—0 defeat by North Korea in 1966.

Lost prestige was restored in 1970 when they reached the Final before losing 4—1 to Brazil, but their defensive complex still showed through and they have yet to recapture the all-round brilliance of pre-war days when they produced such grand attackers as Meazza, Piola, Ferrari and Schiavio.

The Italian F.A. was formed in 1898, and today it has a membership of over 5,000 clubs. The oldest of these is Genoa, formed in 1893.

The address of the governing body is: Federazione Italiana Giuoco Calcio, Via Gregorio Allegri 14, C.P. 2450, 00198—Roma. Colours: Blue shirts, white shorts, blue and white stockings.

Results of international matches:

| | |
|---|---|
| Mar. 21, 1926 | Italy 3, Eire 0; Turin |
| May 20, 1931 | Italy 3, Scotland 0; Rome |
| May 13, 1933 | Italy 1, England 1; Rome |
| Nov. 14, 1934 | England 3, Italy 2; Highbury |
| May 13, 1939 | Italy 2, England 2; Milan |
| May 16, 1948 | Italy 0, England 4; Turin |
| Nov. 30, 1949 | England 2, Italy 0; Tottenham |
| May 18, 1952 | Italy 1, England 1; Florence |
| April 25, 1957* | Italy 1, Ireland 0; Rome |
| Dec. 4, 1957 | Ireland 2, Italy 2; Belfast |
| Jan. 15, 1958* | Ireland 2, Italy 1; Belfast |
| May 6, 1959 | England 2, Italy 2; Wembley |
| April 25, 1961 | Italy 3, Ireland 2; Bologna |
| May 24, 1961 | Italy 2, England 3; Rome |
| May 1, 1965 | Italy 4, Wales 1; Florence |
| Nov. 9, 1965* | Scotland 1, Italy 0; Hampden Park |
| Dec. 7, 1965* | Italy 3, Scotland 0; Naples |
| Oct. 23, 1968* | Wales 0, Italy 1; Cardiff |
| Nov. 4, 1969* | Italy 4, Wales 1; Rome |
| Dec. 8, 1970† | Italy 3, Eire 0; Rome |
| May 10, 1971† | Eire 1, Italy 2; Dublin |
| June 14, 1973 | Italy 2, England 0; Turin |

* World Cup    † European Championship

**JACK, David Bone Nightingale (1899-1958)**
This tall inside-forward was one of the most elegant footballers of the period between the two world wars. A great opportunist and noted for his body swerve it was not unusual to see him beat three or four opponents in a run for goal. He collected more League and Cup medals than any other England inside-right.

David Jack began with Plymouth Argyle when his father was manager of that club. With Bolton he had the distinction of scoring the first-ever goal in a Wembley Cup Final. Transfer discussions lasted for 11 hours before Arsenal persuaded Bolton to part with him for a fee of £10,890 in 1928, the first four-figure fee and one that was 50% higher than any previously paid. Born Bolton.

Plymouth Argyle 1919-20, 14 apps. (3 goals). Bolton Wanderers 1920-28, 295 apps. (143 goals). Arsenal 1928-34, 181 apps. (112 goals). England internationals 9. Inter-League games 5. League Champions 1930-31, 1932-3. F.A. Cup winners 1923, 1926, 1930, runners-up 1932.

**JAMES, Alex (1902-1953)**
A ball artist with a baffling body swerve this Scot was undoubtedly one of the outstanding characters in the game's history. Born Mossend, near Glasgow, his first senior club was Raith Rovers, and he became a goalscoring inside-forward with them and later with Preston North End, but when he joined Arsenal he was switched to a really deep lying position and became one of the finest schemers ever seen. A natural showman he will always be remembered for his long baggy pants.

Raith Rovers 1922-25, 110 apps. (27 goals). Preston North End 1925-29, 147 apps. (53 goals). Arsenal 1929-37, 231 apps. (26 goals). Scottish Internationals 8. League Champions 1930-31, 1932-3, 1933-4, 1934-5. F.A. Cup winners 1930, 1936.

## KEENOR, Frederick C. (1892-1972)

This Welshman (born Cardiff) may not rank among the all-time greats as a centre or right half-back, but there has never been a finer captain. Possessed of a seemingly inexhaustible store of energy Keenor rallied his team by his own example and those fortunate enough to be present never forgot his display in 1930 when a Welsh team which included three amateurs and several other nonentities held Scotland to a 1—1 draw at Ibrox. He also captained Cardiff City on the only occasion that the F.A. Cup was taken out of England.

Cardiff City 1913-31, 369 apps. (12 goals). Crewe Alexandra 1931-34, 116 apps. (5 goals). He also made 61 Southern League apps. (4 goals) for Cardiff City before they joined the Football League. Welsh Internationals 32. F.A. Cup winners 1927, runners-up 1925.

## KICKING

See GOAL-SCORING (INDIVIDUALS), Long-distance goals; GOALKEEPERS (GOAL-SCORING).

R. Whiting, a 6ft. goalkeeper who played with Chelsea and Brighton immediately before World War I, could kick a ball from his goal-line over the bar of the goal at the other end.

## KILMARNOCK F.C.

Founded 1869. The club originally played rugby (hence the name of their ground) but when rugby fixtures became difficult to arrange the club changed to soccer. Became a limited company in 1906. Admitted to Scottish League, Division II, 1896. Honours: Champions, Division I, 1964-5. Runners-up, Division I, 1959-60, 1960-61, 1962-3, 1963-4, Champions, Division II, 1898-9, Runners-up 1953-4. Scottish Cup Winners, 1920, 1929. Finalists, 1898, 1932, 1938, 1957, 1960. Scottish League Cup: Finalists, 1953, 1961, 1963. Record attendance: 33,545 v. Rangers, Scottish Cup, 2nd Round (replay), Feb. 17, 1954. Address: Rugby Park, Kilmarnock (Tel. 0563 25184). Nickname: Killies. Colours: Royal blue shirts with white facings, white shorts. Record League goal-scorer: H. Cunningham, 35 goals, Division I, 1927-8. Record victory: 11—1 v. Paisley Academicals, Scottish Cup, 1st Round, Jan. 18, 1930. Record defeat: 8—0 v. Hibernian, Division I, 1925-6, and v. Rangers, Division I, 1936-7.

## KOPA, Raymond (1931-    )

Real name Kopaszewski, he was born at Noeux-les-Mines, northern France, of a Polish father and a French mother and made debut as a winger with SCO Angers in 1949. On the small side but perfectly balanced he developed into the outstanding player in French football history, being a superb dribbler especially noted for his control at speed. Played in almost any position in the forward line but is remembered best as a centre-forward. In the 1960s he campaigned for better conditions among French professional footballers.

European Footballer of the Year 1958.

SCO Angers 1949-51. Rheims 1951-57, 1959-63. Real Madrid 1956-59. 45 French Internationals. Rest of World 1963. Rest of Europe v. G.B. 1955. European Cup, Finalists 1956, winners 1957, 1958, 1959. French League champions 1953, 1955, 1960, 1962. Spanish League champions 1957, 1958.

## LAW, Denis (1940-    )

The razor sharp reflexes of this Scotsman helped make him one of the most dangerous inside-forwards of the post-war era. Fast and clever on the ground and brilliant in the air he has long been one of the game's most entertaining personalities.

Law might well have created a new F.A. Cup scoring record had not the game in which he scored six goals for Manchester City at Luton in 1961 been abandoned with 21 minutes still to go. Born Aberdeen and made initial international appearance when still only 18 years of age.

Huddersfield Town 1956-60, 81 apps. (18 goals). Manchester City 1960-61, 44 apps. (21 goals). Torino 1961-2. Manchester United 1962-73, 305 apps. (172 goals). Scottish Internationals, 49. F.I.F.A. v. England 1963. Rest of Europe v. Scandinavia 1964. Football League Champions 1964-5, 1966-7. F.A. Cup winners 1963.

## LAW, THE, and FOOTBALL

The validity of the Football League's retain and transfer system was put to the test in law in 1912 when L. J. Kingaby and the Players' Union brought an action against Aston Villa.

Details of this case appear under the heading TRANSFERS, but the outcome of it was that the League's regulations were upheld.

In 1963, however, when G. Eastham brought a case against his old club, Newcastle United, the F.A., and the Football League, he was successful in so far as a declaration was made to the effect that the system of retaining a player after the expiration of his contract was not binding in law.

Since then, of course, certain alterations and additions have been made to the wording of players' contracts, but the system remains very much the same.

## LAWS OF THE GAME

Football of sorts was played at the public schools as long ago as the middle of the 18th century. Each school, however, had its own rules and these often varied considerably from school to school. None bore much resemblance to the modern game.

It is generally considered that it was at Cambridge University that the first code of rules was compiled which closely resembles that we know today.

The date of these first rules is believed to be 1848. But although the existence of these rules has been definitely established, no copy of them has ever been traced.

Enough of them is known, however, to judge that the major differences between them and the original Football Association rules, published in 1863, were that at Cambridge handling was permitted to a greater degree, and the offside rule was more severely applied.

The earliest set of Cambridge University rules still in existence is dated 1856 and the reference to handling the ball and to "offside" make interesting reading:

"When a player catches the ball directly from the foot, he may kick it as he can without running with it. In no other case may the ball be touched with the hands, except to stop it.

"If the ball has passed a player and has come from the direction of his goal, he may not touch it till the other side have kicked it, unless there are more than three of the other side before him. No player is allowed to loiter between the ball and the adversaries' goal."

Another of the earliest set of rules, details of which have been traced, were those drawn up by a master at Uppingham School, Mr. J. C. Thring. They are dated June 1862, and are worth a close examination:

1. A goal is scored whenever the ball is forced through the goal and under the bar, except it be thrown by the hand.
2. Hands may be used only to stop the ball and place it on the ground before the feet.
3. Kicks must be aimed only at the ball.
4. A player may not kick the ball whilst in the air.
5. No tripping up or heel kicking is allowed.
6. Whenever a ball is kicked beyond the side-flags, it must be returned by the player who kicked it, from the spot it passed the flag-line in a straight line towards the middle of the ground.
7. When a ball is kicked behind the line of goal, it shall be kicked off from that line by one of the side whose goal it is.
8. No player may stand within six paces of the kicker when he is kicking off.
9. A player is "out of play" immediately he is in front of the ball, and must return

behind the ball as soon as possible. If the ball is kicked by his own side past a player, he may not touch it, kick it, or advance, until one of the other side has first kicked it, or one of his own side, having followed up, has been able, when in front of him, to kick it.

10. No charging allowed when a player is out of play, i.e. immediately the ball is behind him.

Clubs other than those drawn from the public schools became more numerous about this time, and each had their own code of rules. A further effort was made at Cambridge to draw up a uniform code of rules more acceptable to all clubs. The result of this effort was published in Oct. 1863:

1. The length of the ground should not be more than 150yd. and the breadth not more than 100yd. The ground shall be marked out by posts, and two posts shall be placed on each side line, at distance 25yd. from each goal-line.

2. The goals shall consist of two upright poles at a distance of 15ft. from each other.

3. The choice of goals and kick-off shall be determined by tossing, and the ball shall be kicked off from the middle of the ground.

4. In a match, when half the time agreed upon has elapsed, the sides shall change goals when the ball is next out of play. After a change or a goal obtained, the kick-off shall be from the middle of the ground in the same direction as before. The time during which the match shall last, and the number on each side, are settled by the heads of the sides.

5. When a player has kicked the ball, any one of the same side who is nearer to the opponents' goal-line is out of play, and may not touch the ball himself, nor in any way whatsoever prevent any other player from doing so.

6. When the ball goes out of the ground by crossing the side lines, it is out of play, and shall be kicked straight into the ground again from the point where it first stopped.

7. When a player has kicked the ball beyond the opponents' goal-line, whoever first touches the ball when it is on the ground with his hand may have a free-kick, bringing the ball 25yd. straight out from the goal-line.

8. No player may touch the ball behind his opponent's goal-line, who is behind it when the ball is kicked there.

9. If the ball is touched down behind the goal-line and beyond the line of the side posts, the free-kick shall be from the 25yd. post.

10. When a player has a free-kick no one of his own side may be between him and his opponents' goal-line, and no one of the opposite side may stand within 10yd. of him.

11. A free-kick may be taken in any manner the player may choose.

12. A goal is obtained when the ball goes out of the ground by passing between the poles, or in such a manner that it would have passed between them had they been of sufficient height.

13. The ball when in play may be stopped by any part of the body, but may not be held or hit by the hands, arms or shoulders.

14. All charging is fair; but holding, pushing with the hands, tripping up and shinning are forbidden.

These rules were published about the time the Football Association was holding its inaugural meeting and drafting its own rules for the game.

There is no doubt it was greatly influenced by the Cambridge rules, but the fact that these rules did not permit "hacking", nor handling the ball while in play, caused much argument in the newly-formed Association. Although there was a majority vote in favour of the ban on "hacking" the F.A. did not feel inclined to dispense entirely with the use of the hands.

It was not without more than one resignation that the F.A. rules were eventually agreed upon and published in Dec. 1863. Here they are:

1. The maximum length of the ground shall be 200yd.; the maximum breadth shall be 100yd.; the length and breadth shall be marked off with flags; and the goals shall be defined by two upright posts, 8yd. apart, without any tape or bar across them.

2. The winners of the toss shall have the choice of goals. The game shall be commenced by a place-kick from the centre of the ground by the side losing toss. The other side shall not approach within 10yd. of the ball until it is kicked off.

3. After a goal is won, the losing side shall kick off, and goals shall be changed.

4. A goal shall be won when the ball passes between the posts or over the space between the posts (at whatever height), not being thrown, knocked on, or carried.

5. When the ball is in touch, the first player who touches it shall throw it from the point on the boundary-line where it left the ground in a direction at right angles with the boundary-line, and it shall not be in play until it has touched the ground.

6. When a player has kicked the ball, any one of the same side who is nearer the opponents' goal-line is out of play, and may not touch the ball himself nor in any way

whatever prevent any other player from doing so until the ball has been played; but no player is out of play when the ball is kicked from behind the goal-line.

7. In case the ball goes behind the goal-line, if a player on the same side to whom the goal belongs first touches the ball, one of his side shall be entitled to a free-kick from the goal-line at the point opposite the place where the ball shall be touched. If a player of the opposite side first touches the ball, one of his side shall be entitled to a free-kick (but at the goal only) from a point 15yd. from the goal-line opposite the place where the ball is touched; the opposing side shall stand behind the goal-line until he has had his kick.

8. If a player makes a fair catch,* he shall be entitled to a free-kick, provided he claims it by making a mark with his heel at once; and in order to take such a kick he may go as far back as he pleases, and no player on the opposite side shall advance beyond his mark until he has kicked.

9. No player shall carry the ball.

10. Neither tripping nor hacking shall be allowed, and no player shall use his hands to hold or push an adversary.

11. A player shall not throw the ball or pass it to another.

12. No player shall take the ball from the ground with his hands while it is in play under any pretence whatever.

13. A player shall be allowed to throw the ball or pass it to another if he made a fair catch or catches the ball on the first bounce.

14. No player shall be allowed to wear projecting nails, iron plates or gutta percha on the soles or heels of his boots.

For the sake of brevity and easy reference the principal alterations in the Laws of the Game from the original F.A. laws, are set out below in chronological order:

1865: Tape to be stretched across the goals 8ft. from the ground.

1866: Offside rule altered to allow a player to be onside when three of the opposing team are nearer their own goal-line.

1866: Fair catch rule omitted.

1869: Kick-out rule altered and goal-kicks introduced.

1871: Goalkeepers mentioned in the laws for the first time.

1872: Corner kick adopted.

1874: Umpires first mentioned.

1875: Tapes may be replaced by crossbar.

1877: The London Association and the Sheffield Association agreed to use the same rules.

A player may be charged if he is facing his own goal.

1880: Referees mentioned. The referee was empowered to give a goal against a player who handled in attempting to prevent the ball crossing the goal-line.

1882: Handling rule of 1881 rescinded. Two-handed throw-in introduced.

1883: The four home countries' F.A.s agreed on uniform set of rules.

1890: Penalty-kick introduced after suggestion of the Irish F.A. Accepted by English F.A. Sept. 1891.

1891: Linesmen replaced umpires.

1892: Penalty kicker must not play ball twice.

Extra time allowed for taking of penalty.

1894: Referee given complete control of the game. No longer necessary for players to appeal to him for a decision.

Goalkeeper could only be charged when "playing the ball or obstructing opponent".

1895: Goalposts and cross bars must not exceed 5in. in width.

Player taking throw-in must stand on touch-line. (No run-up.)

1897: The word "intentional" introduced into the law on handling.

1912: Goalkeeper not permitted to handle the ball outside his own penalty area.

1913: Opposing players not to approach within 10yd. (instead of 6yd.) of ball when free-kick is being taken.

1914: Above alteration applied to corner kicks.

1920: Players cannot be offside at a throw-in.

1924: Goal may be scored direct from a corner kick.

1925: Following proposal of the Scottish F.A., the offside rule was changed so that a player could not be offside when two opponents instead of three were between himself and the opposing goal-line.

Player taking throw-in must have both feet on the touch-line.

1929: Goalkeeper compelled to stand still on his goal-line when penalty-kick is being taken.

1931: Goalkeeper permitted to carry ball four steps instead of two.

Instead of a free-kick for foul throw-in, reverts to opposing side.

1936: Defending players no longer permitted to tap ball into goalkeeper's hands when goal-kick is being taken.

* A Fair Catch is when the ball is caught after it has touched the person of an adversary, or has been kicked or knocked on by an adversary, and before it has touched the ground or one of the side catching it; but if the ball is kicked from behind the goal-line, a fair catch cannot be made.

1937: Defending player no longer permitted to tap ball into goalkeeper's hands when a free-kick is being taken inside the penalty area.

Weight of ball increased from 13-15oz. to 14-16oz.

Arc of circle 10yd. radius from penalty spot to be drawn outside the penalty area.

1951: Obstruction included as one of the offences punishable by an indirect free-kick.

Studs may project three-quarters of an inch instead of half an inch.

1954: Ball shall not be changed during the game unless authorised by the Referee.

The Laws of the Game as they stand in 1973 are as follows:

## Law 1 The Field of Play

The Field of Play and appurtenances shall be:

(1) *Dimensions.* The field of play shall be rectangular, its length being not more than 130 yards nor less than 100 yards and its breadth not more than 100 yards nor less than 50 yards. (In International Matches the length shall be not more than 120 yards nor less than 110 yards and the breadth not more than 80 yards nor less than 70 yards.) The length shall in all cases exceed the breadth.

(2) *Marking.* The field of play shall be marked with distinctive lines, not more than 5 inches in width, not by a V-shaped rut, in accordance with the plan, the longer boundary lines being called the touch lines and the shorter the goal-lines. A flag on a post not less than 5 feet high and having a non-pointed top, shall be placed at each corner; a similar flagpost may be placed opposite the half-way line on each side of the field of play, not less than 1 yard outside the touch-line. A halfway-line shall be marked out across the field of play. The centre of the field of play shall be indicated by a suitable mark and a circle with a 10-yards radius shall be marked round it.

(3) *The Goal-Area.* At each end of the field of play two lines shall be drawn at right-angles to the goal-line, 6 yards from each goal-post. These shall extend into the field of play for a distance of 6 yards and shall be joined by a line drawn parallel with the goal-line. Each of the spaces enclosed by these lines and the goal-line shall be called a goal-area.

(4) *The Penalty-Area.* At each end of the field of play two lines shall be drawn at right-angles to the goal-line, 18 yards from each goal-post. These shall extend into the field of play for a distance of 18 yards and shall be joined by a line drawn parallel with the goal-line. Each of the spaces enclosed by these lines and the goal-line shall be called a penalty-area. A suitable mark shall be made within each penalty area, 12 yards from the mid-point of the goal-line, measured along an undrawn line at right angles thereto. These shall be the penalty-kick marks. From each penalty-kick mark an arc of a circle, having a radius of 10 yards, shall be drawn outside the penalty-area.

(5) *The Corner-Area.* From each corner-flag post a quarter circle, having a radius of 1 yard, shall be drawn inside the field of play.

(6) *The Goals.* The goals shall be placed on the centre of each goal-line and shall consist of two upright posts, equidistant from the corner-flags and 8 yards apart (inside measurement), joined by a horizontal cross-bar the lower edge of which shall be 8 feet from the ground. The width and depth of the goal-posts and the width and depth of the cross-bars shall not exceed 5 inches (12 cm). The goal-posts and the cross-bars shall have the same width.

Nets may be attached to the posts, cross-bars and ground behind the goals. They should be appropriately supported and be so placed as to allow the goalkeeper ample room.

## Law 2 The Ball

The ball shall be spherical; the outer casing shall be of leather or other approved materials. No material shall be used in its construction which might prove dangerous to the players.

The circumference of the ball shall not be more than 28 inches and not less than 27 inches. The weight of the ball at the start of the game shall not be more than 16 oz. nor less than 14 oz. The pressure shall be equal to one atmosphere, which equals 15 lb/sq. in. $(= 1 \text{ kg/cm}^2)$ at sea level. The ball shall not be changed during the game unless authorised by the Referee.

## Law 3 Number of Players

(1) A match shall be played by two teams, each consisting of not more than eleven players, one of whom shall be goalkeeper.

(2) Substitutes may be used in any match played under the rules of a competition, subject to the following conditions:

(a) that the authority of the International Association(s) or National Association(s) concerned, has been obtained.

(b) that, subject to the restriction contained in the following paragraph (c) the rules of a competition shall state how many, if any, substitutes may be used, and

(c) that a team shall not be permitted to use more than two substitutes in any match.

(3) Substitutes may be used in any other match, provided that the two teams concerned reach agreement on a maximum number, not exceeding five, and that the terms of such agreement are intimated to the referee, before the match. If the referee is not informed, or if the teams fail to reach agreement, no more than two substitutes shall be permitted.

(4) Any of the other players may change places with the goalkeeper, provided that the referee is informed before the change is made, and provided also, that the change is made during a stoppage in the game.

(5) When a goalkeeper or any other player is to be replaced by a substitute, the following conditions shall be observed:

(a) the referee shall be informed of the proposed substitution, before it is made,

(b) the substitute shall await a signal from the referee before entering the field of play,

(c) he shall enter the field during a stoppage in the game, and at the half-way line, and

(d) play shall not be re-started until the player who has been replaced has left the field.

*PUNISHMENT. Any player who infringes this Law shall be cautioned.*

## Law 4  Players' Equipment

A player shall not wear anything which is dangerous to another player. Boots must conform to the following standard:

(a) Bars shall be made of leather or rubber and shall be transverse and flat, not less than half an inch in width and shall extend the total width of the boot and be rounded at the corners.

(b) Studs shall be made of leather, rubber, aluminium, plastic or similar material and shall be solid. With the exception of that part of the stud forming the base, which shall not protrude from the sole, more than one quarter of an inch, studs shall be round in plan and not less than half an inch in diameter. Where studs are tapered, the minimum diameter of any section of the stud must not be less than half an inch. Where metal seating for the screw type is used, this seating must be embedded in the sole of the boot and any attachment screw shall be part of the stud. Other than the metal seating for the screw type of stud, no metal plates even though covered with leather or rubber shall be worn, neither studs which are threaded to allow them to be screwed on to a base screw that is fixed by nails or otherwise to the soles of boots, nor studs which, apart from the base, have any form of protruding edge rim, or relief marking, or ornament, should be allowed.

(c) Combined bars and studs may be worn, provided the whole conforms to the general requirements of this law. Neither bars nor studs on the soles or heels shall project more than three-quarters-of-an-inch. If nails are used they shall be driven in flush with the surface.

(N.B.—The usual equipment of a player consists of a jersey or shirt, shorts, stockings and boots. A goalkeeper shall wear colours which distinguish him from the other players.)

*PUNISHMENT. For any infringement of this Law, the player at fault shall be sent off the field of play to adjust his equipment and he shall not return without first reporting to the Referee, who shall satisfy himself that the player's equipment is in order: the player shall only re-enter the game at a moment when the ball has ceased to be in play.*

## Law 5  Referees

A Referee shall be appointed to officiate in each game. His jurisdiction shall begin from the time he signals for the kick-off, and his power of penalising shall extend to offences committed when play has been temporarily suspended or when the ball is out of play. His decision on points of fact connected with the play shall be final, so far as the result of the game is concerned. He shall:

(a) Enforce the Laws and decide any disputed point.

(b) Refrain from penalising in cases where he is satisfied that by doing so he would be giving an advantage to the offending team.

(c) Keep a record of the game; act as timekeeper and allow the full or agreed time, adding thereto all time lost through accident or other cause.

(d) Have discretionary power to stop the game for any infringement of the Laws and to suspend or terminate the game whenever, by reason, of the elements, interference by spectators, or other cause, he deems such stoppage necessary. In such a case he shall submit a detailed report to the competent authority, within the stipulated time, and in accordance with the provisions set up by the National Association under whose jurisdiction the match was played. Reports will be deemed to be made when received in the ordinary course of post.

(e) From the time he enters the field of play, caution any player guilty of misconduct or ungentlemanly behaviour and, if he persists, to suspend him from further participation in the game. In such cases the Referee shall send the name of the offender to the competent authority, within the stipulated time, and in accordance with the provisions set up by the National Association under whose jurisdiction the match was played. Reports will be deemed to be made when received in the ordinary course of post.

(f) Allow no person other than the players and Linesmen to enter the field of play without his permission.

(g) Stop the game if, in his opinion, a player has been seriously injured; have the player removed as soon as possible from the field of play, and immediately resume the game. If a player is slightly injured, the game shall not be stopped until the ball has ceased to be in play. A player who is able to go to the touch- or goal-line for attention of any kind, shall not be treated on the field of play.

(h) Send off the field of play, any player who, in his opinion, is guilty of violent conduct, serious foul play, or the use of foul and abusive language.

(i) Signal for recommencement of the game after all stoppages.

(j) Decide that the ball provided for a match meets with the requirements of Law 2.

## Law 6   Linesmen

Two Linesmen shall be appointed, whose duty (subject to the decision of the Referee) shall be to indicate when the ball is out of play and which side is entitled to the corner-kick, goal-kick, or throw-in. They shall also assist the Referee to control the game in accordance with the Laws. In the event of undue interference or improper conduct by a Linesman, the Referee shall dispense with his services and arrange for a substitute to be appointed. (The matter shall be reported by the Referee to the competent authority).

The Linesmen should be equipped with flags by the Club on whose ground the match is played.

## Law 7   Duration of the Game

The duration of the game shall be two equal periods of 45 minutes, unless otherwise mutually agreed upon, subject to the following:

(a) Allowance shall be made in either period for all time lost through accident or other cause, the amount of which shall be a matter for the discre-

tion of the Referee.

(b) Time shall be extended to permit of a penalty kick being taken at or after the expiration of the normal period in either half.

At half-time the interval shall not exceed five minutes except by consent of the Referee.

## Law 8   The Start of Play

(a) *At the beginning of the game*, choice of ends and the kick-off shall be decided by the toss of a coin. The team winning the toss shall have the option of choice of ends or the kick-off.

The Referee, having given a signal, the game shall be started by a player taking a place-kick (i.e., a kick at the ball while it is stationary on the ground in the centre of the field of play) into his opponents' half of the field of play. Every player shall be in his own half of the field and every player of the team opposing that of the kicker shall remain not less than 10 yards from the ball until it is kicked-off; it shall not be deemed in play until it has travelled the distance of its own circumference. The kicker shall not play the ball a second time until it has been touched or played by another player.

(b) *After a goal has been scored*, the game shall be restarted in like manner by a player of the team losing the goal.

(c) *After half-time*; when restarting after half-time, ends shall be changed and the kick-off shall be taken by a player of the opposite team to that of the player who started the game.

*PUNISHMENT. For any infringement of this Law, the kick-off shall be retaken, except in the case of the kicker playing the ball again before it has been touched or played by another player; for this offence, an indirect free-kick shall be taken by a player of the opposing team from the place where the infringement occurred. A goal shall not be scored direct from a kick-off.*

(d) *After any other temporary suspension*; when restarting the game after a temporary suspension of play from any cause not mentioned elsewhere in these Laws, provided that immediately prior to the suspension the ball has not passed over the touch or goal-lines, the Referee shall drop the ball at the place where it was when play was suspended and it shall be deemed in play when it has touched the ground; if, however, it goes over the touch- or goal-lines after it has been dropped by the Referee, but before it is touched by a player, the Referee shall again drop it. A player shall not play the ball until it has touched the ground. If this section of the Law is not complied with the Referee shall again drop the ball.

## Law 9   Ball in and out of play

The ball is out of play:
(a) When it has wholly crossed the goal-line or touch-line, whether on the ground or in the air.
(b) When the game has been stopped by the Referee.

The ball is in play at all other times from the start of the match to the finish including:
(a) If it rebounds from a goal-post, cross-bar or corner-flag post into the field of play.
(b) If it rebounds off either the Referee or Linesmen when they are in the field of play.
(c) In the event of a supposed infringement of the Laws, until a decision is given.

## Law 10   Method of Scoring

Except as otherwise provided by these Laws, a goal is scored when the whole of the ball has passed over the goal-line, between the goal-posts and under the cross-bar, provided it has not been thrown, carried or propelled by hand or arm, by a player of the attacking side, except in the case of a goalkeeper, who is within his own penalty area.

The team scoring the greater number of goals during a game shall be the winner; if no goals, or an equal number of goals are scored, the game shall be termed a "draw".

## Law 11   Off-Side

A player is off-side if he is nearer his opponents' goal-line than the ball *at the moment the ball* is *played unless.*
(a) He is in his own half of the field of play.
(b) There are two of his opponents nearer to their own goal-line than he is.
(c) The ball last touched an opponent or was last played by him.
(d) He receives the ball direct from a goal-kick, a corner-kick, a throw-in, or when it was dropped by the Referee.

*PUNISHMENT. For an infringement of this Law, an indirect free kick shall be taken by a player of the opposing team from the place where the infringement occurred.*

*A player in an off-side position shall not be penalised unless, in the opinion of the Referee, he is interfering with the play or with an opponent, or is seeking to gain an advantage by being in an off-side position.*

## Law 12   Fouls and Misconduct

A player who intentionally commits any of the following nine offences:
(a) Kicks or attempts to kick an opponent;
(b) Trips an opponent, i.e., throwing or attempting to throw him by the use of the legs or by stooping in front of or behind him;
(c) Jumps at an opponent;
(d) Charges an opponent in a violent or dangerous manner;
(e) Charges an opponent from behind unless the latter be obstructing;
(f) Strikes or attempts to strike an opponent;
(g) Holds an opponent with his hand or any part of his arm;
(h) Pushes an opponent with his hand or any part of his arm;
(i) Handles the ball, i.e., carries, strikes or propels the ball with his hand or arm. (this does not apply to the goalkeeper within his own penalty-area);
shall be penalised by the award of a *direct free-kick* to be taken by the opposing side from the place where the offence occurred.

Should a player of the defending side intentionally commit one of the above nine offences within the penalty-area he shall be penalised by a *penalty-kick*.

A penalty-kick can be awarded irrespective of the position of the ball, if in play, at the time an offence within the penalty-area is committed.

A player committing any of the five following offences:
1 Playing in a manner considered by the Referee to be dangerous, e.g., attempting to kick the ball while being held by the goalkeeper.
2 Charging fairly, i.e., with the shoulder, when the ball is not within playing distance of the players concerned and they are definitely not trying to play it;
3 When not playing the ball, intentionally obstructing an opponent, i.e., running between the opponent and the ball, or interposing the body so as to form an obstacle to an opponent.
4 Charging the goalkeeper except when he
    (a) is holding the ball;
    (b) is obstructing an opponent;
    (c) has passed outside his goal-area;
5 When playing as goalkeeper
    (a) takes more than 4 steps whilst holding, bouncing or throwing the ball in the air and catching it again without releasing it so that it is played by another player, or
    (b) indulges in tactics which, in the opinion of the Referee, are designed merely to hold up the game and thus waste time and so give an unfair advantage to his

135

own team
shall be penalised by the award of an *indirect free-kick* to be taken by the opposing side from the place where the infringement occurred.

A player shall be *cautioned* if:

(j)  he enters or re-enters the field of play to join or re-join his team after the game has commenced, or leaves the field of play during the progress of the game (except through accident) without, in either case, first having received a signal from the Referee showing him that he may do so. If the Referee stops the game to administer the caution the game shall be restarted by an indirect free-kick taken by a player of the opposing team from the place where the offending player was when the Referee stopped the game. If, however, the offending player has committed a more serious offence he shall be penalised according to that section of the law he infringed.

(k)  he persistently infringes the Laws of the Game.

(l)  he shows by word or action, dissent from any decision given by the Referee;

(m)  he is guilty of ungentlemanly conduct.

For any of these last three offences, in addition to the caution, an *indirect free-kick* shall also be awarded to the opposing side from the place where the offence occurred unless a more serious infringement of the Laws of the Game was committed.

A player shall be *sent off* the field of play if:

(n)  in the opinion of the Referee, he is guilty of violent conduct or serious foul play.

(o)  he used foul or abusive language;

(p)  he persists in misconduct after having received a caution.

If play be stopped by reason of a player being ordered from the field of play for an offence without a separate breach of the Law having been committed, the game shall be resumed by an *indirect free-kick* awarded to the opposing side from the place where the infringement occurred.

## Law 13   Free-Kick

Free-kicks shall be classified under two heads "Direct" (from which a goal can be scored direct against the *offending side)*, and "Indirect" (from which a goal cannot be scored unless the ball has been played or touched by a player other than the kicker before passing through the goal).

When a player is taking a direct or an indirect free-kick inside his own penalty-area, all of the opposing players shall

remain outside the area, and shall be at least ten yards from the ball whilst the kick is being taken. The ball shall be in play immediately it has travelled the distance of its own circumference and is beyond the penalty-area. The goalkeeper shall not receive the ball into his hands, in order that he may thereafter kick it into play. If the ball is not kicked direct into play, beyond the penalty-area, the kick shall be retaken.

When a player is taking a direct or an indirect free-kick outside his own penalty area, all of the opposing players shall be at least ten yards from the ball, until it is in play, unless they are standing on their own goal-line, between the goal-posts. The ball shall be in play when it has travelled the distance of its own circumference.

If a player of the opposing side encroaches into the penalty-area, or within ten yards of the ball, as the case may be, before a free-kick is taken, the Referee shall delay the taking of the kick, until the Law is complied with.

The ball must be stationary when a free-kick is taken, and the kicker shall not play the ball a second time, until it has been touched or played by another player.

*PUNISHMENT. If the kicker after taking the free-kick, plays the ball a second time before it has been touched or played by another player an indirect free-kick shall be taken by a player of the opposing team from the spot where the infringement occurred.*

## Law 14   Penalty-Kick

A penalty-kick shall be taken from the penalty-mark and, when it is being taken, all players with the exception of the player taking the kick, and the opposing goalkeeper, shall be within the field of play but outside the penalty-area, and at least 10 yards from the penalty-mark. The opposing goalkeeper must stand (without moving his feet) on his own goal-line, between the goal-posts, until the ball is kicked. The player taking the kick must kick the ball forward; he shall not play the ball a second time until it has been touched or played by another player. The ball shall be deemed in play directly it is kicked, i.e., travelled the distance of its own circumference, and a goal may be scored direct from such a penalty-kick. If the ball touches the goalkeeper before passing between the posts, when a penalty-kick is being taken at or after the expiration of half-time or full-time, it does not nullify a goal. If necessary, time of play shall be extended at half-time or full-time to allow a penalty-kick to be taken.

*PUNISHMENT: For any infringement of this Law:*

(a)  by the defending team, the kick shall

be retaken if a goal has not resulted;
(b) by the attacking team, other than by the player taking the kick, if a goal is scored it shall be disallowed and the kick retaken.
(c) by the player taking the penalty-kick, committed after the ball is in play, a player of the opposing team shall take an indirect free kick from the spot where the infringement occurred.

## Law 15   Throw-In
When the whole of the ball passes over a touch-line, either on the ground or in the air, it shall be thrown in from the point where it crossed the line, in any direction, by a player of the team opposite to that of the player who last touched it. The thrower at the moment of delivering the ball must face the field of play and part of each foot shall be either on the touch-line or on the ground outside the touch-line. The thrower shall use both hands and shall deliver the ball from behind and over his head. The ball shall be in play immediately it enters the field of play, but the thrower shall not again play the ball until it has been touched or played by another player. A goal shall not be scored direct from a throw-in.
*PUNISHMENT:*
(a) If the ball is improperly thrown in the throw-in shall be taken by a player of the opposing team.
(b) If the thrower plays the ball a second time before it has been touched or played by another player, an indirect free-kick shall be taken by a player of the opposing team from the place where the infringement occurred.

## Law 16   Goal-Kick
When the whole of the ball passes over the goal-line excluding that portion between the goal-posts, either in the air or on the ground, having last been played by one of the attacking team, it shall be kicked direct into play beyond the penalty-area from a point within that half of the goal-area nearest to where it crossed the line, by a player of the defending team. A goalkeeper shall not receive the ball into his hands from a goal-kick in order that he may thereafter kick it into play. If the ball is not kicked beyond the penalty-area, i.e., direct into play, the kick shall be retaken. The kicker shall not play the ball a second time until it has touched or been played by another player. A goal shall not be scored direct from such a kick. Players of the team opposing that of the player taking the goal-kick shall remain outside the penalty-area whilst the kick is being taken.
*PUNISHMENT: If a player taking a*

*goal-kick plays the ball a second time after it has passed beyond the penalty-area, but before it has touched or been played by another player, an indirect free-kick shall be awarded to the opposing team, to be taken from the place where the infringement occurred.*

## Law 17   Corner-Kick
When the whole of the ball passes over the goal-line, excluding that portion between the goal-posts, either in the air or on the ground, having last been played by one of the defending team, a member of the attacking team shall take a corner-kick, i.e., the whole of the ball shall be placed within the quarter circle at the nearest corner flag-post, which must not be moved, and it shall be kicked from that position.
A goal may be scored direct from such a kick. Players of the team opposing that of the player taking the corner-kick shall not approach within 10 yards of the ball until it is in play, i.e., it has travelled the distance of its own circumference, nor shall the kicker play the ball a second time until it has been touched or played by another player.
*PUNISHMENT: For an infringement of this Law, an indirect free-kick shall be awarded to the opposing team, to be taken from the place where the infringement occurred.*
The introduction of other rules which may be of some interest were made as follows:
1896: An extra half-hour to be played in all replayed cup ties, if drawing at the end of 90 min.
1912: An extra half-hour must be played in the Cup Final if the sides are drawing at full time.
1924: Where colours clash, visitors must change.
1927: Professionals reinstated as amateurs not permitted to play in amateur international matches.
1931: Two years' residential qualification for non-British born subjects registering as professionals in the Football League.
1939: Watering pitches permitted except during November, December, January and February. Players in Football League matches must be numbered.

## LAWTON, Thomas (1919-    )
Tall and well built for the job Tommy Lawton was one of the most accomplished centre-forwards in the game's history being supremely accurate with head or foot. A master in the air he picked his spot with his head or would nod the ball down to either

137

of his inside-forwards. Lawton always commanded attention throughout his 20 years as a professional, scoring a hat-trick when making his debut as a professional for Burnley and being the subject of a £6,500 transfer to Everton fee when still only 17. Notts County later caused a sensation as a Third Division club by paying a record £20,000 fee to take him from Chelsea.

Born Bolton he might well have created goalscoring records but for the war interrupting his career.

Burnley 1935-36, 25 apps. (16 goals). Everton 1936-45, 87 apps. (66 goals). Chelsea 1945-47, 42 apps. (30 goals). Notts County 1947-52, 151 apps. (94 goals). Brentford 1952-53, 50 apps. (17 goals). Arsenal 1953-56, 35 apps. (13 goals). England internationals 23 (plus 23 war-time and victory games). Inter-League games 3. League Champions 1938-9.

## LEEDS UNITED F.C.

Founded 1920 after Leeds City club was wound up. (Leeds City had been in existence since 1904, and was a member of the Football League, Division II, from 1905.) Leeds United was elected to the Football League, Division II, in 1920. Honours: Champions Division I, 1968-9. Runners-up, 1964-5, 1965-6, 1969-70, 1970-71, 1971-2. Champions, Division II, 1923-4, 1963-4. Runners-up, 1927-8, 1931-2, 1955-6. F.A. Cup: Winners, 1972. Finalists, 1965, 1970, 1973. League Cup Winners, 1968. Fairs Cup: Winners, 1968, 1971. Finalists, 1967. European Cup-winners' Cup: Finalists, 1973. Record attendance: 57,892 v. Sunderland, F.A. Cup, 5th Round (replay), Mar. 15, 1967. Address: Elland Road, Leeds LS11 0ES (Tel. 76037). Nickname: Peacocks. Colours: All white. Record League goalscorer: J. Charles, 42 goals, Divison II, 1953-4. Record victory: 8—0 v. Leicester City, Division I, April 7, 1934; (as Leeds City) v. Nottingham Forest, Division II, Nov. 29, 1913. In a European Cup game, Sept. 17, 1969. Leeds United beat Lynn Oslo, 10—0. Record defeat: 8—1 v. Stoke City, Division I, Aug. 27, 1934.

## LEICESTER CITY F.C.

Founded 1884 by old boys of Wyggeston School and adopted the name Leicester Fosse. Changed to Leicester City, 1919. Elected to Football League, Division II, 1894. Honours: Runners-up, Division I, 1928-9. Champions, Division II, 1924-5, 1936-7, 1953-4, 1956-7, 1970-71. Runners-up, 1907-8. F.A. Cup: Finalists, 1949, 1961, 1963, 1969. F.L. Cup: Winners, 1964. Finalists, 1965. Record attendance: 47,298 v. Tottenham Hotspur, F.A. Cup, 5th Round,

Feb. 18, 1928. Address: Filbert Street Ground, Leicester (Tel. 57111). Nickname: Filberts. Colours: White shirts with blue trim, white shorts and stockings. Record League goal-scorer: A. Rowley, 44 goals, Division II, 1956-7. Record victory: 10—0 v. Portsmouth, Division I, Oct. 20, 1928. Record defeat: 12—0 (as Leicester Fosse) v. Nottingham Forest, Division I, April 21, 1909.

## LIDDELL, Billy (1922-    )

Born Townhill, near Dunfermline, Billy Liddell joined Liverpool in April 1939, but due to the war he did not make his Football League debut until August 1946, although, by that time he had become recognised as one of the finest outside-lefts in the country. From the time he established himself in the Liverpool side in 1946 he was not dropped for 12 years and went on to make well over 500 appearances before hanging up his boots in 1961. He also figured at centre-forward for a long spell later in his career, being fast and direct with few frills and a deadly shot in either foot.

Liverpool 1939-60, 492 apps. (216 goals). Scottish Internationals 28. Great Britain v. Rest of Europe 1947 and 1955. League Championship medal 1946-7. F.A. Cup runners-up 1950.

## LIMITED COMPANIES

The first football club to become a Limited Liability Company was Small Heath (now Birmingham City) in 1888.

All of the present members of the Football League are limited companies with the exception of Nottingham Forest.

F.A. regulations applying to club companies restrict the dividend payable in respect of any year to a maximum of $7\frac{1}{2}\%$, or in the case of tax free dividends—5%.

Preference shares may be issued with cumulative preference dividend not exceeding £7.50 per cent for a period not exceeding three years, but the company may not issue more Preference Shares than its subscribed Ordinary Shares.

## LINCOLN CITY F.C.

Founded 1883. One of the original members of the Football League, Division II, 1892. Lincoln City failed to gain immediate re-election to the League on three separate occasions, 1908, 1911 and 1920. Each time, however, the club has been out of the League for only one season before regaining admission. On the last occasion (after dropping out of Division II in 1920), the club returned a year later as a member of the newly-formed Division III(N). Honours: Champions, Division III(N), 1931-2,

1947-8, 1951-2. Runners-up, 1927-8, 1930-31, 1936-7. Best in Division II, 5th, 1901-2. Record attendance: 23,196 v. Derby County, F. League Cup, 4th Round, Nov. 15, 1967. Address: Sincil Bank, Lincoln LN5 8LD (Tel. 21912). Nickname: Imps. Colours: Red shirts with white trim, red shorts with white trim, red stockings with white tops. Record League goal-scorer: A. Hall, 42 goals, Division III(N), 1931-2. Record victory: 11—1 v. Crewe Alexandra, Division III(N), Sept. 29, 1951. Record defeat: 11—3 v. Manchester City, Division II, Mar. 23, 1895.

## LINDLEY, Dr. Tinsley, O.B.E. (1865–1940)

A centre-forward of the true blue amateur school who played a tremendous amount of football and all for the love of the game. Just look at this list of the sides with whom he appeared after making his debut with Nottingham Forest at the age of 16. England, North, South, Oxford, Cambridge, Corinthians, Nottinghamshire, Sheffield & District, London & Middlesex, Preston North End, Notts County, Swifts, Casuals, Crusaders, and for the Gentlemen v. Players. Born in Nottingham he also played both cricket and rugby for his county.

Led the Corinthians to a 5—0 defeat of the Preston side that had won the League and Cup double. He concentrated on speed and generally chose to play in ordinary shoes rather than boots, but he only failed to score in two of his 13 England games. A Doctor of Law he became a County Court Judge.

The periods in which he served his principal clubs – Corinthians 1884-94. Nottingham Forest 1883-92. England Internationals 13.

## LINESMEN

See REFEREES AND LINESMEN.

## LIVERPOOL F.C.

Founded 1892 after the majority of the members of Everton F.C. left their ground at Anfield Road for Goodison Park following a rent dispute. Those who remained behind formed a new club, Liverpool. Elected to the Football League, Division II, 1893. Honours: Champions Division I, 1900-1901, 1905-6, 1921-2, 1922-3, 1946-7, 1963-4, 1965-6, 1972-3. Runners-up, 1898-9, 1909-10, 1968-9. Champions Division II, 1893-4, 1895-6, 1904-5, 1961-2. F.A. Cup: Winners, 1965. Finalists, 1914, 1950, 1971. European Cup Winners Cup: Finalists, 1966. UEFA Cup, Winners, 1973. Record attendance: 61,905 v. Wolverhampton Wanderers, F.A. Cup, 4th Round, Feb. 2,

1952. Address: Anfield Road, Liverpool L4 0TH (Tel. Anfield 051-263 2361). Nickname: Reds. Colours: All red. Record League goal-scorer: R. Hunt, 41 goals, Division II, 1961-2. Record victory: 10—1 v. Rotherham United, Division II, Feb. 18, 1896. Record defeat: 9—1 v. Birmingham City, Division II, Dec. 11. 1954.

## LONG SERVICE
### Managers

It is difficult to establish the record for long service as manager with a single club for in the old days the men who were managers were not accorded that title and there is some confusion between men who would now be regarded simply as secretaries and those who had anything at all to do with team management.

However, if we restrict our choice to men who have managed Football League clubs since World War II and not include secretary-Managers then the record belongs to Sir Matt Busby, C.B.E., who was manager or General Manager of Manchester United from Oct. 1945 until June 1971 when he was appointed to the Board of Directors.

Next comes J. Seed who was manager of Charlton Athletic from May 1933 to Sept. 1956.

J. (Joe) Smith was appointed manager of Blackpool in the summer of 1935 and remained with them until May 1958.

W. H. Walker was manager at Nottingham Forest from 1939 to 1960.

J. E. Davison was manager of Sheffield United for 20 years, from June 1932 until the summer of 1952.

Another post-war manager with a distinguished record including 18 years as manager of West Ham United is C. Paynter. In all, Mr. Paynter served West Ham United for 50 years. Joining them as a player in 1900, he became assistant trainer in 1902, trainer 1912, team-manager 1932, and secretary-manager during World War II. He retired in 1950.

E. W. Taylor has been with Sheffield Wednesday since August 1929 and was Assistant Secretary until just before World War II. He became Team Manager in February 1942, Secretary-Manager 1945, and has been General Manager and Secretary since September 1958.

### Other Officials

Here are some details of long service among club, F.A. and League officials.

Sir Charles Clegg (b. June 1850; d. June 1937) was connected with the administration of the F.A. for 51 years. He became a member of the F.A. Council in 1886. In 1889 he was elected a Vice-President of the

F.A. The following year he became Chairman. In 1923 he became President, a position he held until his death.

Mr. W. C. Cuff became a director of Everton F.C. in 1895 and—with the exception of one short break—was connected with the club's affairs until 1948. He was a leading figure in the management of the Football League. He was elected a member of the League's committee in 1925 and became Vice-President in 1937. Two years later Mr. Cuff was elected President, a position he held until his death in Feb. 1949.

Mr. Fred Everiss was appointed secretary of West Bromwich Albion in 1902 and retained the position for 46 years. He then became a director of the club and was still on the board when he died three years later in 1951. Prior to his appointment as secretary he had been office boy, so that his service to the club extended over more than 50 years. He was succeeded as secretary in 1948 by his brother-in-law Ephriam Smith, who had been with the club since 1906 and who held the post until 1960 when Alan Everiss (Fred's son) took over. The job has, therefore, been in the family for over 70 years.

Another West Bromwich Albion stalwart with over 50 years service is Mr. T. W. Glidden. He joined the club as an outside-right in 1922 and played until 1936, subsequently joining the Board.

Mr. H. J. Huband, founder of the Isthmian League, was a member of the F.A. Council for 45 years. He was for several years a member of the International Selection Committee. In addition, Mr. Huband gave more than 50 years' service to the London F.A. He died in 1952.

Lord Kinnaird, the famous Old Etonian, served the F.A. for 55 years. Elected to the Committee in 1868, he became Honorary Treasurer in 1877, and President in 1890. Lord Kinnaird was President of the F.A. until his death at the age of 75, on Jan. 30, 1923. In his younger days, Lord Kinnaird won five F.A. Cup-winners' medals with the Wanderers and Old Etonians.

Mr. John K. McDowall was Secretary of the Scottish Football League for over 46 years—from April 26, 1882, until he died on Sept. 6, 1928.

Mr. John McKenna, founder and chairman of Liverpool F.C. was connected with Football League administration for 34 years. He was elected a member of the Management Committee in 1902. He became a Vice-President in 1908 and President in 1910. He was President until his death in Mar. 1937. Mr. McKenna was also a Vice-President of the F.A.

Mr. William Pickford of Bournemouth was elected a member of the F.A. Council in 1888 and continued his association with the game until his death in Nov. 1938. He became President of the F.A. in 1937, and was also one of the men responsible for the early development of the Referees' Association.

Mr. George B. Ramsay served Aston Villa for 59 years. Joining them in 1876 he was in turn player, captain, member of the committee and secretary. Finally he was consulting adviser to the club.

Mr. Ted Robbins of Wrexham was Secretary of the F.A. of Wales from 1910 until his death in Jan. 1946.

Mr. Charles E. Sutcliffe of Rawtenstall who died in Jan. 1939, first became a member of the Football League Management Committee in 1898. He was a Vice-President from 1927 until he became President in 1937.

Sir Frederick Wall: Secretary of the F.A. for 39 years, 1895-1934. He was the man chiefly responsible for the formation of the Referees' Association and was also for many years one of the leading figures in the London Football Association and the Middlesex Association. He died in 1944.

## Players

The long-service record for a player with a single club goes to E. Sagar who joined Everton, Mar. 26, 1929, and retired May 1953. This represents 24 years 1 month's service.

The previous long-service record for a player was held by R. Crompton who was a Blackburn Rovers' full-back for 23 years 7 months. Crompton, one of England's greatest defenders, signed for Blackburn Rovers in Oct. 1896, and remained with them as a player until May 1920.

In the Scottish League the record was set up by outside-left A. Smith. He made his debut for the Rangers in April 1894 and his playing career with them extended over 21 seasons.

Right back A. McNair equalled this record completing 21 seasons with Celtic to 1925.

## LONGEST GAME

The longest game on record in first-class football was that between Stockport County and Doncaster Rovers on Mar. 30, 1946. This was a 2nd leg tie in the Third Division (N) Cup, and in an effort to reach a decisive result the game lasted for 205 min. before bad light forced them to stop play.

In the 2nd Round, Football League North, War Cup, 2nd leg match, at Ninian Park, Cardiff, April 14, 1945, Cardiff City and Bristol City played for 3hr. 22min. before a deciding goal was scored. The teams were drawing 2—2 after 90min., and, in accordance with war-time rules, they played an extra 10min. each way, but still without a winning goal. They then continued to play until a goal was scored (by Cardiff City).

A Western Hemisphere club championship game between Santos (Brazil) and Penarol (Uruguay) at Santos, Aug. 2-3, 1962 began at 9.30 p.m. and finished $3\frac{1}{2}$ hours later with the score 3—3, but the actual playing time was less than the games mentioned above.

## LOSING RUN
See under DEFEATS AND WITHOUT A WIN

## LUTON TOWN F.C.
Founded 1885 by the amalgamation of Wanderers and Excelsior. Luton Town were the pioneers of professional football in the South of England, employing paid players as early as 1890. Elected to the Football League, Division II, 1897. Failed to gain re-election 1900. Re-entered Football League as members of Division III, 1920. Honours: Runners-up, Division II, 1954-5, Champions, Division III(S), 1936-7. Runners-up, 1935-6. Champions, Division IV, 1967-8. Runners-up, Division III, 1969-70. F.A. Cup: Finalists, 1959. Record attendance: 30,069 v. Blackpool, F.A. Cup, 6th Round (replay), Mar. 4, 1959. Address:

Kenilworth Road, Luton LU1 1DH (Tel. 0582 23151). Nickname: Hatters or Straw-plaiters. Colours: White shirts, black shorts, white stockings. Record League goal-scorer: J. Payne, 55 goals, Division III(S), 1936-7 (this is a record for the Southern Section). Record victory: 12—0 v. Bristol Rovers, Division III(S), April 13, 1936. Record defeat: 9—1 v. Swindon Town, Division III(S), Aug. 28, 1921.

## LUXEMBOURG
Considering that Luxembourg has a population of only about 300,000 it is not surprising that they have not had much success in international matches.

Their Football Federation, however, was founded as long ago as 1908 and has been a member of F.I.F.A. since 1910.

Luxembourg has never beaten any of the home countries in a full international but their finest win, undoubtedly, was that obtained in a World Cup game in 1961 when they beat Portugal 4—2.

They are as keen about football in Luxembourg as anywhere on the Continent and their leading clubs compete regularly in the principal international cup competitions. All players in Luxembourg are amateur and at the present time the Federation has a membership of 178 clubs.

Address of governing body: Fédération Luxembourgeoise de Football, 50 Rue de Strasbourg, Luxembourg. Colours: Red shirts, white shorts, blue stockings.

Results of international matches:
| | | |
|---|---|---|
| May 21, 1927 | Luxembourg 2, England 5; Luxembourg |
| May 9, 1936 | Luxembourg 1, Eire 5; Luxembourg |
| May 24, 1947 | Luxembourg 0, Scotland 6; Luxembourg |
| Oct. 28, 1953* | Eire 4, Luxembourg 0; Dublin |
| Mar. 7, 1954* | Luxembourg 0, Eire 1; Luxembourg |
| Oct. 19, 1960* | Luxembourg 0, England 9; Luxembourg |
| Sept. 28, 1961* | England 4, Luxembourg 1; Highbury |

* World Cup

## McCRACKEN, William (1883-    )

This Irishman from Belfast has gone down in history as one of the greatest exponents of the offside "trap" at a time when these tactics were so much in evidence that they eventually led to the alteration in the rules because goals were becoming increasingly difficult to score. McCracken was one of the fastest full-backs of his day and Newcastle United beat a number of clubs to obtain his transfer in 1904 after he had already been capped a half dozen times and collected an Irish Cup winners' medal while with Distillery.

McCracken's total of caps was restricted to 15 only because he was often at loggerheads with the Irish F.A. demanding more appearance money, and he refused to play for them on more than one occasion. Made last international appearance when manager of Hull City.

Distillery 1901-04. Newcastle United 1904-23, 377 apprs. (6 goals). Irish internationals 15. Irish Cup medals 1902 (runners-up),1903 (winners). Football League Championship 1906-07, 1908-09. F.A. Cup runners-up 1908, 1911, winners 1910.

## McGRORY, James Edward

No player ever scored as many goals for a British club in first-class football as this Glaswegian who netted 397 League goals for Celtic. Add to these the number he netted in internationals and Cup games as well as those scored while on loan to Clydebank early in his career and his grand total came to 550.

Powerfully built and possessed of a great turn of speed, as well as superb heading ability, McGrory topped the Scottish First Division scoring list three times, his best figure being 50 in season 1935-6.

Surprisingly enough McGrory made only seven appearances for his country. Pride in his club spurred him on to his greatest deeds.

Celtic 1922-3, 1924-38, 378 apprs. (397 goals). Clydebank 1923-4, 30 apprs. (13 goals). Scottish internationals 7. Inter-League games 6. Scottish Cup runners-up 1926, 1928, winners 1925, 1931, 1933, 1937. Scottish League Champions 1925-6, 1935-6.

## McILROY, James (1931-    )

Born Lambeg, N. Ireland he first made his mark with Glentoran before developing into a brilliant inside-forward with Burnley, who paid £7,000 for his transfer in 1950. A clever strategist he was one of the stars of the Northern Ireland side that reached the finals of the World Cup in 1958.

After making over 400 First Division appearances for Burnley he was surprisingly transferred to Stoke in 1963 and helped that club regain First Division status before becoming player-manager of Oldham Athletic.

An immaculate footballer McIlroy had the personality, skill and judgement to be able to control the pace of a game. A creator of chances rather than a scorer.

Glentoran 1949-50. Burnley 1950-63, 436 apprs. (116 goals). Stoke City 1963-66, 98 apprs. (16 goals). Oldham Athletic 1966-68, 35 (4) apprs. (1 goal). N. Ireland internationals 55. G.B. v. Rest of Europe 1955. Inter-League games (Football League) 2. F.A. Cup runners-up 1962. League Champions 1959-60.

## McMENEMY, James

One of the talented footballers who helped Celtic win the Scottish League championship 11 times between the turn of the century and 1919. An inside-forward who so stamped his personality on the game and was such a master strategist that the fans nicknamed him 'Napoleon'.

When Celtic thought he was finished they gave him a free transfer in 1920 and he joined Partick. At the end of his first season with that club he was still good enough to scheme their Cup Final victory over Rangers.

Glasgow Celtic 1901-20, over 450 apprs. Partick Thistle 1920-22, 56 apprs. Scottish Internationals 12. Inter-League games 13. Scottish Cup winners 1904, 1907, 1908, 1911, 1912, 1914, 1921. Also appeared in Final in 1909 when Cup was withheld after two drawn games. Scottish League Champions 1904-05, 1905-06, 1906-07, 1907-08, 1908-09, 1909-10, 1913-14, 1914-15, 1915-16, 1916-17, 1918-19.

## McPHAIL, Robert

This powerful inside-forward won seven Scottish Cup medals, his first in his initial season with Airdrie in 1924 and the others with Rangers for whom he made 466 League and Cup appearances and scored 281 goals. Born Barrhead, Glasgow, he attracted the attention of several English clubs soon after making his debut with Airdrie but refused to cross the border and Rangers got him in 1927 for £4,500. A clever footballer as well as possessing a great shot his international career spread over 12 seasons. Indeed, 10 years after making his debut against England he scored two goals in Scotland's 3—1 victory over the Sassenachs at Hampden Park in 1937.

Airdrie 1923-27, 109 apprcs. (72 goals). Rangers 1927-39, 354 apprcs. (233 goals). Scottish Internationals 17. Inter-League games 6. Scottish Cup medals, 1924, 1928, 1930, 1932, 1934, 1935, 1936. Scottish League Championship 1927-8, 1928-9. 1929-30, 1930-31, 1932-3, 1933-4, 1934-5, 1936-7, 1938-9.

## McWILLIAM, Peter

Injury cut short this player's career in 1911 but in nine seasons with Newcastle United he became acknowledged as one of the finest wing-halves in the country and helped his club win the League Championship three times as well as playing in four F.A. Cup Finals—winning once. He also played for Scotland against England in four out of five successive seasons 1905-09.

Born at Inverness he was snapped up by Newcastle when on his way to pay a visit to his former Inverness Thistle team-mate, Andy McCombie, who was then with Sunderland. A colourful character his standard of play was so high that he became known as 'Peter the Great.'

After a spell as manager of Tottenham Hotspur he became the first manager to draw a four-figure salary when appointed to Middlesbrough.

Newcastle United 1902-11, 198 apprcs. (7 goals). Scottish Internationals 8. F.A. Cup runners-up 1905, 1906, 1908, winners 1910. League Champions 1904-05, 1906-07, 1908-09.

## MALTA

An island with a population of 300,000 cannot be expected to make much of an impression in the International field, although England was only able to win by a single goal in their first appearance on the island in 1971, and at club level the Maltese part-timers have been able to surprise quite a few visiting teams.

The Maltese play on bone-hard or sanded pitches and these surfaces have often been used as an excuse by visitors who have not done as well as expected against the local enthusiasts.

The Malta F.A. was formed in 1900 and has a membership of 36 clubs. The address is 84 Old Mint Street, Valletta. Colours:

Red shirts, white shorts, red stockings.

Feb. 3, 1971† Malta 0, England 1; Valletta

May 12, 1971† England 5, Malta 0; Wembley.     † Nations Cup.

## MANAGERS

For the names of individuals who have both played in and managed F.A. Cup winning teams see FOOTBALL ASSOCIATION CHALLENGE CUP (PLAYERS).

Only four men have both played for and subsequently managed Football League championship winning sides. E. Drake, Arsenal, centre-forward, 1933-4, 1934-5, 1937-8; Chelsea, manager, 1954-5. W. Nicholson, Tottenham Hotspur, right half-back, 1950-51; manager, 1960-61. A. E. Ramsey, right-back, Tottenham Hotspur, 1950-51, manager, Ipswich Town, 1961-2. J. Mercer left-half, Everton 1938-9, Arsenal 1947-8, 1952-3; manager, Manchester City, 1967-8.

The late W. McCandless set up a managers' record for promoting teams from the Third Division. He managed three—all Welsh: 1938-9 Newport County, 1946-7 Cardiff City, and 1948-9 Swansea Town. Mr. McCandless was himself an Irishman from Ballymena.

Managers of Football League clubs today hold extremely precarious positions. Since World War II over 700 have been sacked or left their clubs in the Football League.

The shortest time anyone has served as manager with a Football League club is 13 days. Mar. 31, 1939 to April 13, 1939 was the duration of J. Cochrane's managership at Reading.

J. McIlroy was team-manager of Bolton Wanderers for only 18 days before resigning in Nov. 1970.

T. Ward was appointed manager of Exeter City in Mar. 1953 but became manager of Barnsley (his former club) 25 days later. He was actually at Exeter only seven days before returning to Barnsley.

W. Lambton was appointed manager of Scunthorpe United, April 21, 1959, but the agreement was only a verbal one and the appointment was cancelled three days later.

In Scotland R. Flavell was manager of Ayr United for only 17 days in Dec. 1961 before returning to St. Mirren as that club's manager. He had previously been coach at St. Mirren.

For manager with longest service see under separate section LONG SERVICE (Managers).

One of the most famous managers of all time was Herbert Chapman. No manager met with greater success. He was the only one who has managed four different Football League clubs when they won either the League Championship or the F.A. Cup. Here is his record:

Manager of Northampton Town, Southern League Champions, 1908-09.

Manager of Leeds City, Champions of the Midland Section of the Football League, 1916-17, 1917-18.

Manager of Huddersfield Town when they won the F.A. Cup, 1922, and the League Championship, 1923-4, 1924-5.

Manager of Arsenal, F.A. Cup winners, 1930. League Champions, 1930-31, 1932-3.

Mr. Chapman died after a short illness, Jan. 6, 1934. leaving £6,780.

When Andrew Beattie was appointed General Manager of Notts County in Mar. 1967 he created a record by managing his eighth Football League club. He had previously managed Barrow, Stockport County, Huddersfield Town, Carlisle United, Nottingham Forest, Plymouth Argyle and Wolverhampton Wanderers.

Major Frank Buckley was manager of seven different clubs—Norwich City, Blackpool, Wolverhampton Wanderers, Notts County, Hull City, Leeds United, and Walsall, before he retired in Sept. 1955.

## MANCHESTER CITY F.C.

Founded 1894. The club is descended from the West Gorton club (1880-83), Gorton Athletic (1884-7) and Ardwick (1887-94). Ardwick had been one of the original members of the Football League, Division II in 1892. A limited company was formed and the title changed to Manchester City in 1894. Honours: Champions, Division I, 1936-7, Runners-up Division I, 1903-4, 1920-21. Champions, Division II, 1898-9, 1902-3, 1909-10, 1927-8, 1946-7, 1965-6. Runners-up Division II, 1895-6, 1950-51. F.A. Cup: Winners, 1904, 1934, 1956, 1969. Finalists, 1926, 1933, 1955. League Cup: Winners, 1970. European Cup Winners Cup: Winners, 1970. Record attendance: 84,569 v. Stoke City, F.A. Cup, 6th Round, Mar. 3, 1934. Address: Maine Road, Manchester M14 7WN (Tel. 061-226 1191). Nickname: The Blues or Citizens. Colours: Sky blue shirts with white trim, white shorts, sky blue stockings with maroon and white rings at top. Record League goalscorer: T. Johnson, 38 goals, Division I, 1928-9. Record victory: 11—3 v. Lincoln City, Division II, Mar. 23, 1895. Record defeat: 9—1 v. Everton, Division I, Sept. 3, 1906.

## MANCHESTER UNITED F.C.

Founded by workmen employed by the Lancashire and Yorkshire Railway Company, probably in 1878. First known as Newton Heath but re-formed under its present title in 1902. Elected to Football League, Division I, 1892. Honours: Champions, Division I, 1907-8, 1910-11, 1951-2, 1955-6, 1956-7, 1964-5, 1966-7. Runners-up, 1946-7. 1947-8, 1948-9, 1950-51, 1958-9, 1963-4, 1967-8. Champions, Division II, 1935-6. Runners-up, 1897-8, 1905-6, 1924-5, 1937-8. F.A. Cup: Winners, 1909, 1948, 1963. Finalists, 1957, 1958. European Cup: Winners, 1968. Record attendance: 76,962, Wolverhampton Wanderers v. Grimsby Town, F.A. Cup Semi-Final, Mar. 25, 1939. Manchester United game, 70,504 v. Aston Villa, Division I, Dec. 27, 1920. Address: Old Trafford, Manchester M16 0RA (Tel. 061-872 1661). Colours: Red shirts with white collars, white shorts, black stockings with red and white band. Record League goal-scorer: D. Viollet, 32 goals, Division I, 1959-60. Record victory: 10—1 v. Wolverhampton Wanderers, Division I, Oct. 15, 1892. In a European Cup Preliminary Round, Sept. 26, 1956, United beat Anderlecht 10—0. Record defeat: 7—0 v. Aston Villa, Division I, Dec. 27, 1930.

## MANSFIELD TOWN F.C.

Founded 1910. Elected to Football League, Division III(S), 1931. Honours: Runners-up, Division III(N), 1950-51. Record attendance: 24,467 v. Nottingham Forest, F.A. Cup 3rd Round, Jan. 10, 1953. Address: Field Mill, Mansfield (Tel. 23567). Nickname: Stags. Colours: White shirts with blue and amber collar and cuffs, royal blue shorts with amber stripe, white stockings. Record league goal-scorer: E. Harston, 55 goals, Division III(N), 1936-7 (this is a record for the Northern Section). Record victory: 9—2 v. Rotherham United, Division III(N), Dec. 27, 1932, and v. Hounslow Town, F.A. Cup, 1st Round (replay), Nov. 5, 1962. Record defeat: 8—1 v. Walsall, Division III(N), Jan. 19, 1933.

## MATCHES

A number of clubs have met the same opponents in the Football League, League Cup, and F.A. Cup, in the one season, but including replays Plymouth Argyle and Huddersfield Town met six times in these three competitions during 1963-4.

In season 1911-12 West Bromwich Albion played in two F.A. Cup Finals and five Division I games in 10 days: April 20, Cup Final, 0—0 v. Barnsley; April 22, 0—3(A) Everton; April 24, Cup Final (replay), 0—1 (after half-hour extra time) v. Barnsley; April 25, 1—4(A) Blackburn Rovers; April 26, 0—0(H) Bradford City;

April 27, 1—5(H) Sheffield Wednesday; April 29, 0—0(H) Oldham Athletic.

Leeds United played 66 major competition matches in season 1967-8: 42 League, 5 F.A. Cup, 7 Football League Cup, and 12 Fairs Cup.

Stoke City also played 66 matches in 1971-72: 42 League, 8 F.A. Cup, 12 Football League Cup, and 4 Texaco Cup.

See SCOTTISH ASSOCIATION CUP (replays) and SCOTTISH LEAGUE for details of clubs that played two matches in a day.

## MATTHEWS, Sir Stanley, C.B.E. (1915- )

This football genius from Hanley, Staffordshire, was already being acclaimed as 'the finest dribbler in the country' before he made his international debut for England (v. Wales in 1934) and was still making rings around First Division full-backs nearly 30 years later. Indeed, he did not make his final First Division appearance until he had celebrated his 50th birthday.

Always supremely fit Stanley Matthews was the outstanding crowd puller of his day, no wonder that he became the first footballer to receive a knighthood while still a registered player. As an outside-right he was sometimes criticised for holding the ball too long and slowing the game down, but he was one of the finest goal-providers in the game's history.

Stoke City 1931-47, 1961-65, 322 apprcs. (54 goals). Blackpool 1947-61, 379 apprcs. (17 goals). England internationals 54 (plus 29 war-time and Victory games). Great Britain v. Rest of Europe 1947 and 1955. Inter-League games 13. F.A. Cup runners-up 1948, 1951, winners 1953.

## MEDALS

See CUP MEDALS, F.A. CUP (Medals), and TROPHIES.

## MERCER, Joseph (1914- )

England's half-back line during World War II, Cliff Britton, Stan Cullis and Joe Mercer, is widely considered to have been the finest ever fielded by the home country and Mercer enjoyed a First Division career spread over 22 years until it ended in April 1954 when he broke his leg.

Coming from a football family and born in Ellesmere Port Mercer began his professional career with Everton and helped them win the League Championship. Using the short pass to turn defence into attack, Mercer was a wing-half with amazing stamina. He was wiry and a fierce tackler and when, after 15 years, Everton thought he was finished, because of a knee injury, they sold him to Arsenal, Mercer made an amazing recovery to appear in another 247

League games with the Gunners, helping them win the Championship twice as well as collecting a couple of Cup medals.

Subsequently managed Sheffield United, Aston Villa, Manchester City and Coventry City.

Everton 1932-46, 173 apprcs (1 goal). Arsenal 1946-54, 247 apprcs. (2 goals). England International 6 (plus 27 war-time and Victory games). Inter-League games 1. League Champions 1938-9, 1947-8, 1952-3. F.A. Cup runners-up 1952, winners 1950.

## MEREDITH, William (1874-1958)

It is more than 50 years since this brilliant Welsh winger made his last international appearance—against England at Highbury in March 1920—yet his total of 48 appearances in the Home International Championship still stands as a record today! Meredith was nearly 46 years of age when he played in that game and that is also a record.

Joining Manchester City from Northwich Victoria in October 1894 he became known as 'The Prince of wingers.' When, in 1906, the City were found guilty of making illegal payments to their players and it was decreed that those involved should not be allowed to remain with the club, Meredith was one of four who moved to Manchester United. He rejoined the City in 1921 and rounded off his illustrious career by playing in an F.A. Cup semi-final in 1924 when he was nearly 50 years of age. Born Chirk.

Northwich Victoria 1893-94, 12 apprcs. (goals unknown). Manchester City 1894-1906, 1921-24, 367 apprcs. (146 goals). Manchester United 1906-21, 303 apprcs. (35 goals). Welsh Internationals 48. F.A. Cup winners 1904, 1909. League Champions 1907-08, 1910-11.

## MEXICO

Considering that Mexico have appeared in seven of the World Cup final tournaments they must at least be ranked as the soccer champions of North America. Possibly their finest performance in this competition was their surprise 3—1 victory over Czechoslovakia in Chile in 1962. In the 1970 Finals they held Russia to a goalless draw and had victories over El Salvador and Belgium.

The Mexican F.A. was founded in 1927 and now has a membership of about 360 clubs including a limited number of professionals.

The address of the governing body: Federación Mexicana de Futbol Asociación, Abraham Gonzalez 74, Mexico D.F. Z.P.6. Colours: Green shirts, white shorts, green stockings.

Results of international matches:

| | | |
|---|---|---|
| June 11, 1958* | Wales 1, Mexico 1; Sweden | |
| May 24, 1959 | Mexico 2, England 1; Mexico City | |
| May 10, 1961 | England 8, Mexico 0; Wembley | |
| May 22, 1962 | Mexico 2, Wales 1; Mexico City | |
| June 22, 1966 | Ireland 4, Mexico 1; Belfast | |
| July 16, 1966* | England 2, Mexico 0; Wembley | |
| June 1, 1969 | Mexico 0, England 0; Mexico City | |

* World Cup

## MIDDLESBROUGH F.C.
Founded 1876. Adopted professionalism 1889. Reverted to amateur status 1892 but turned professional again in 1899. Elected to Football League, Division II, 1899. Honours: Champions, Division II, 1926-7, 1928-9. Runners-up, Division II, 1901-2. Runners-up, Division III, 1966-7. Best in Division I, 3rd, 1913-14. F.A. Amateur Cup: Winners, 1895, 1898. Record attendance: 53,596 v. Newcastle United, Division I, Dec. 27, 1949. Address: Ayresome Park, Middlesborough TS1 4PB (Tel. 89659). Nickname: Ironsides or Borough. Colours: Red shirts,red shorts with white stripe down seam, red stockings. Record League goalscorer: G. Camsell, 59 goals, Division II, 1926-7 (a record for this Division). Record victory: 10—3 v. Sheffield United, Division I, Nov. 18, 1933. Record defeat: 9—0 v. Blackburn Rovers, Division II, Nov. 6, 1954.

## MILLWALL F.C.
Founded 1885 as Millwall Rovers. One of the original members of Division III, 1920. Honours: Champions, Division III(S), 1927-8, 1937-8. Runners up, Division III, 1965-6. Champions, Division IV, 1961-2. Runners-up, 1964-5. Best Division II, 7th, 1932-3. F.A. Cup: Semi-finalists, 1900, 1903, 1937. Record attendance: 48,672 v. Derby County, F.A. Cup, 5th Round, Feb. 20, 1937. Address: The Den, Cold Blow Lane, New Cross, London SE14 5RH (Tel. 01-639 3143). Nickname: Lions. Colours: All white. Record League goal-scorer: R. Parker, 37 goals, Division III(S), 1926-7. Record victory: 9—1 v. Torquay United, Division III(S), Aug. 29, 1927, and v. Coventry City, Division III(S), Nov. 19, 1927. Record defeat: 9—1 v. Aston Villa, F.A. Cup 4th Round, Jan. 28, 1946.

## MONTROSE F.C.
Founded: 1879. Elected to Scottish League, Division II, 1929. Honours: none. Record attendance: 6,389 v. Celtic, Scottish Cup, 2nd Round, Feb. 4, 1939. Address: Links Park, Montrose (Tel. 573). Colours: Royal blue shirts and shorts, white stockings. Record victory: 8—0 v. Solway Star, Scottish Cup, 1st Round, Jan. 18, 1930. Record defeat: 9—4 v. Stenhousemuir, Division II, 1934-5.

## MOORE, Robert Frederick O.B.E. (1941- )
Born Barking, Essex, Bobby Moore joined West Ham United straight from school and developed quickly, not only as a commanding wing-half but also as a brilliant captain. From skippering England's Youth team he became England's youngest ever captain at the age of 22 in May 1963, against Czechoslovakia. That was in his 12th international. In his 47th game, three years later, he achieved his greatest honour by captaining England's World Cup-winning team.

Tall and well built, Moore makes great use of the long ball and his strong tackling and sterling work generally has been an inspiration to his team mates.

West Ham United 1958-73. 523(1) apprcs. (20 goals). England Internationals 107. Under-23 games 8. Inter-League games 11. F.A. Cup winners 1964. European Cup Winners' Cup winners 1965. Football League Cup runners-up 1966. World Cup winners 1966.

## MORTON F.C.
Founded 1896. Among original members of Scottish League, Division II, 1893. Honours: Champions, Division II, 1949-50, 1963-4, 1966-7. Runners-up, 1899-1900, 1928-9, 1936-7. Scottish Cup: Winners, 1922, Finalists, 1948. Scottish League Cup: Finalists, 1964. Record attendance: 23,500 v. Celtic, 1921 and v. Rangers, Scottish Cup, 3rd Round, Feb. 21, 1953. Address. Cappielow Park, Greenock (Tel. 0475 23571). Colours: Blue and White hooped shirts, white shorts. Record League goal-scorer: A. McGraw, 51 goals, Division II, 1963-4. Record victory: 11—1 v. Blairgowrie, Scottish Cup, 1st Round, Feb. 1, 1936. Record defeat: 8—2 v. Rangers, Division I, Mar. 15, 1927.

## MORTON, Alan L. (1896-1971)
The Scots claim this player as the greatest outside-left that ever lived and there is plenty of support for this claim beyond the borders of the country in which Morton remained throughout his playing career,

except, of course, for the occasional inter-national or soccer tour. Morton began with Queen's Park and finished with Rangers, and when he finally hung up his boots in 1933 he had created an everlasting picture of a perfectly balanced football genius, leaving the opposition standing as he darted down the wing. Morton possessed magical ball control and a brilliant football brain.

Only 5ft. 4in. tall he was the original "Wee Blue Devil." A name he received after bamboozling the England defence on so many occasions. After giving up playing he was co-opted to the Rangers Board.

Queen's Park 1913-20. Over 200 apprcs. (over 30 goals). Rangers 1920-33, 379 apprcs. (81 goals). Scottish Internationals 31. Inter-League games 15 (plus 2 unofficial 'Victory' games). Scottish League champions 1920-21, 22-23, 23-24, 24-25, 26-27, 27-28, 28-29, 29-30, 30-31. Scottish Cup winners 1928, 1930, runners-up 1921, 1922, 1929.

## MOTHERWELL F.C.

Founded 1885. Among original members of Scottish League, Division II, 1893. Honours: Champions, Division I, 1931-2. Runners-up, 1926-7, 1929-30, 1932-3, 1933-4. Champions, Division II, 1953-4. Runners-up, 1894-5, 1902-3. Scottish Cup: Winners, 1952. Finalists, 1931, 1933, 1939, 1951. Scottish Leagues Cup: Winners, 1951. Finalists, 1955. Record attendance: 36,750 v. Rangers, Scottish Cup, 4th Round (replay), Mar. 12, 1952. Address: Fir Park, Motherwell (Tel. 60 63229). Colours: Amber shirts with claret trim, amber shorts. Record goalscorer in Division I, William McFadyen, 52 goals, 1931-2 (Scottish League Division I record). Record victory: 12—1 v. Dundee United, Division B, Jan. 23, 1954. Record defeat: 10—0 v. St. Mirren, Scottish Southern League, Division A, 1945-6.

**NEEDHAM, Ernest (1873-1936)**
They used to say that this player never had a bad game, and while that may be an exaggeration there is no doubt that the 'Nudger' was one of the most industrious wing half-backs ever seen in the Football League. Only 5ft. 5in. in height he was the king-pin of Sheffield United's 1897-8 Championship-winning team which included the smallest half-back line ever to carry off the League's Blue riband—Rabbi Howell, Tommy Morren and Ernest Needham, all under 5ft. 6 ins.

A strong-tackling, attacking style half-back, Needham was a Sheffield United player for 22 years. He was sometimes criticised for trying to do other men's work as well as his own, but he always contrived to be in the right place at the right time. Born Whittington Moor, near Chesterfield.

Sheffield United 1891-1913, 461 apprcs. England internationals 16. Inter-League games 10. League Champions 1897-8. F.A. Cup winners 1899, 1902, runners-up 1901.

**NETHERLANDS**
The Netherlands F.A. was founded in 1889 and is the oldest outside of Great Britain. There was a soccer club in Haarlem as long ago as 1879, but due to the reluctance of the governing body to accept professionalism the game in that country made only limited progress in the 50-odd years before World War II.

With the football boom in other European countries after World War II and Holland's continued refusal to adopt professionalism several of their best players departed for France, Italy and Germany. The matter was then brought to a head when several of the leading clubs broke away from the F.A. and formed an independent League.

So, in Nov. 1954, professionalism was officially recognised, a professional League inaugurated, and Dutch football embarked on a new era of expansion and improvement. A number of their leading players were encouraged to return home, other professionals joined Dutch clubs, and in recent years they have produced two of the finest club sides in Europe—Feyenoord Rotterdam, winners of the European Cup in 1970, and Ajax Amsterdam who had been finalists in 1969 and who carried off that trophy in 1971, 1972 and 1973, as well as becoming World champions in 1972.

Address of governing body: Koninklijke Nederlandsche Voetbalbond, Verlengde Tolweg 6, 's-Gravenhage. Colours: Orange shirts, white shorts, orange stockings.

Results of internationals:

| | | |
|---|---|---|
| June 4, 1929 | Netherlands 0, Scotland 2; Amsterdam |
| May 8, 1932 | Netherlands 0, Eire 2; Amsterdam |
| April 8, 1934 | Netherlands 5, Eire 2; Amsterdam |
| May 18, 1935 | Netherlands 0, England 1; Amsterdam |
| Dec. 8, 1935 | Eire 3, Netherlands 5; Dublin |
| May 21, 1938 | Netherlands 1, Scotland 3; Amsterdam |
| Nov. 27, 1946 | England 8, Netherlands 2; Huddersfield |
| May 1, 1955 | Eire 1, Netherlands 0; Dublin |
| May 10, 1956 | Netherlands 1, Eire 4; Rotterdam |
| May 27, 1959 | Netherlands 1, Scotland 2; Amsterdam |
| May 9, 1962 | Netherlands 4, Ireland 0; Rotterdam |
| Dec. 9, 1964 | Netherlands 1, England 1; Amsterdam |
| Mar. 17, 1965* | Ireland 2, Netherlands 1; Belfast |
| April 7, 1965* | Netherlands 0, Ireland 0; Rotterdam |
| May 11, 1966 | Scotland 0, Netherlands 3; Hampden Park |
| May 30, 1968 | Netherlands 0, Scotland 0; Amsterdam |
| Nov. 5, 1969 | Netherlands 0, England 1; Amsterdam |
| Jan. 14, 1970 | England 0, Netherlands 0; Wembley |
| Dec. 1, 1971 | Netherlands 2, Scotland 1; Rotterdam |

* World Cup

## NEWCASTLE UNITED F.C.
Founded 1882 as Newcastle East End. Changed to Newcastle United 1892. Elected to the Football League, Division II, 1893. Honours: Champions, Division I, 1904-5, 1906-7, 1908-9, 1926-7. Champions, Division II, 1964-5. Runners-up, Division II, 1897-8, 1947-8. F.A. Cup: Winners, 1910, 1924, 1932, 1951, 1952, 1955. Finalists: 1905, 1906, 1908, 1911. Fairs Cup: Winners, 1969. Record attendance: 68,586 v. Chelsea, Division I, Sept. 3, 1930. Address: St. James's Park, Newcastle upon Tyne NE1 4ST (Tel. 0632-28361). Nickname: Magpies, Colours Black and white striped shirts, black shorts, black stockings with white tops. Record League goal-scorer: H. Gallacher, 36 goals, Division I, 1926-7. Record victory: 13—0 v. Newport County, Dvision II, Oct. 5, 1946. Record defeat: 9—0 v. Burton Wanderers. Division II, April 15, 1895.

## NEWPORT COUNTY F.C.
Founded 1911 by employees of local ironworks. One of the original members of the Football League, Division III, 1920. Honours: Champions, Division III(S), 1938-9. Record attendance: 24,268 v. Cardiff City, Division III(S), Oct. 16, 1937. Address: Somerton Park, Newport, Mon. (Tel. 71543). Nickname: Ironsides. Colours: Tangerine shirts and stockings, black shorts. Record League goal-scorer: T. Martin, 34 goals, Division III(S), 1929-30. Record victory: 10—0 v. Merthyr Town, Division III(S), April 10, 1930. Record defeat: 13—0 v. Newcastle United, Division II, Oct. 5, 1946.

## NEW ZEALAND
Soccer has made tremendous progress in New Zealand since about 1954 when their F.A. did some re-organising and established a coaching scheme for schoolboys.

The New Zealand F.A. was formed as long ago as 1891 but for the greater part of its history interest in the dribbling code in these islands has taken a very poor second place to the Kiwis' favourite sport—rugby.

Now, however, with so much, progress being made in the schools the future seems much brighter as the youngsters take to soccer in ever increasing numbers.

All the major associations (Auckland, Wellington, Canterbury and Otago) together with the majority of minor associations (altogether there are 21 associations in New Zealand) are going all out to coach as many schoolboys as possible. The game has also established itself in the universities.

New Zealand has not yet played any full internationals with teams from the British Isles but there have been a number of "Tests" with F.A. touring teams of 1937, 1961, and 1969, and against an F.A. XI when the New Zealanders visited England in 1964.

The supreme trophy among the associations is the "English Trophy" which was presented to the N.Z.F.A. by the English F.A.

All clubs in New Zealand may enter for the Chatham Cup, the equivalent of the English F.A. Cup. The competition is played off on a regional basis with the North Island finalists meeting the South Island finalists in Wellington, usually during the month of August.

A National League was established in 1970 with eight members, since increased to 10.

Address of the governing body: New Zealand F.A. (Inc.), 21 Palmer Street, P.O. Box 1771, Wellington. Colours: White shirts with black trim, black shorts, white stockings with black rings.

Results of Test matches:
June  5, 1937  New Zealand 0, England (F.A.) 12, Dunedin
June 19, 1937  New Zealand 0, England (F.A.) 6; Auckland
June 26, 1937  New Zealand 1, England (F.A.) 12; Wellington
June  5, 1961  New Zealand 0, England (F.A.) 8; Wellington
June 10, 1961  New Zealand 1, England (F.A.) 6, Auckland
April 13, 1964  F.A. XI 4, New Zealand 0; Northampton
June 11, 1969  New Zealand 0, England (F.A.) 5; Newmarket
July 10, 1971  New Zealand 0, Wales (F.A.) 1; Auckland

## NICKNAMES
Club nicknames appear under the respective club titles.

## NORDAHL, Gunnar (1921-    )
One of the famous trio of brothers who helped Sweden win the Olympic tournament in 1948, Gunnar was an orthodox centre-forward, tall and well built with a powerful shot and good in the air. He turned professional with A.C. Milan early in 1949 and scored over 200 goals for that club, topping the Italian League scoring list in five of six consecutive seasons 1949-55. His total of 35 goals in 1949-50 is still a post-war Italian League record.

I.F.K. Norrkoping 1938-49. A.C. Milan 1949-56. A.S. Roma 1956-58. Karlstad 1959. 33 Swedish internationals. Rest of Europe v. Great Britain 1947. Rest of Europe v. England 1953. Swedish League champions 1943, 1945, 1946, 1947, 1948. Italian League champions 1951, 1955.

## NORTHAMPTON TOWN F.C.
Founded 1897, largely through the enterprise of teachers connected with the local Elementary Schools' Athletic Association. One of the original members of the Football League, Division III, 1920. Honours: Runners-up, Division II, 1964-5. Champions, Division III, 1962-3. Runners-up, Division III(S), 1927-8, 1949-50. Record attendance: 24,523 v. Fulham, Division I, April 23, 1966. Address: County Ground, Northampton NN1 4PS (Tel. 31553). Nickname: Cobblers. Colours: Claret shirts with white sleeves, claret shorts with white trim, white stockings. Record League goalscorer: C. Holton, 36 goals, Division III, 1961-2. Record victory: 10—0 v. Walsall, Division III(S), Nov. 5, 1927. In the old Southern League, 11—1 v. Southend United, Dec. 30, 1909. Record defeat: 10—0 v. Bournemouth & Boscombe, Division III(S), Sept. 2, 1939. In Southern League they were beaten 11—0 by Southampton, Dec. 28, 1901.

## NORTHERN IRELAND
See IRELAND, IRISH FOOTBALL ASSOCIATION and INTERNATIONALS (IRELAND).

## NORWAY
Norway has never adopted professionalism and their most brilliant players have had to go elsewhere to make the most of their talent and gain suitable financial reward.

It is largely because of this that Norway has rarely been able to make much of an impression in international soccer although they have not been entirely without success.

In the Olympic Games of 1920 Norway defeated Great Britain 3—1, and in the 1936 Olympics they gained their most glorious victory by defeating the German "amateurs" 2—0 and went on to gain third place in the Games.

Norway has qualified once for the World Cup Tournament and on that occasion, in 1938, they gave another fine display only losing 2—1 to Italy in extra time. Italy were the holders of the trophy at that time and went on to retain it.

The Norwegian F.A. was formed in 1902 and it is an organisation that must be commended for the way in which it has encouraged the game's development even in the country's northernmost parts where competitions are difficult to organise owing to the distances involved and consequent travelling expenses.

Today there are about 1,200 clubs registered with the Association.

Address of the governing body: Norges Fotballforbund, Ullevaal Stadion, Sognsveien 75, Post Box 42, Oslo 8. Colours: Red shirts, white shorts, blue stockings.

Results of international matches:

| | | |
|---|---|---|
| May 28, 1929 | Norway 3, Scotland 7; Oslo |
| May 14, 1937 | Norway 0, England 6; Oslo |
| Oct. 10, 1937* | Norway 3, Eire 2; Oslo |
| Nov. 7, 1937* | Eire 3, Norway 3; Dublin |
| Nov. 9, 1938 | England 4, Norway 0; Newcastle |
| May 18, 1949 | Norway 1, England 4; Oslo |
| Nov. 26, 1950 | Eire 2, Norway 2; Dublin |
| May 30, 1951 | Norway 2, Eire 3; Oslo |
| May 5, 1954 | Scotland 1, Norway 0; Glasgow |
| May 19, 1954 | Norway 1, Scotland 1; Oslo |
| Nov. 8, 1954 | Eire 2, Norway 1; Dublin |
| May 25, 1955 | Norway 1, Eire 3; Oslo |
| Nov. 6, 1960 | Eire 3, Norway 1; Dublin |
| June 4, 1963 | Norway 4, Scotland 3; Bergen |
| Nov. 7, 1963 | Scotland 6, Norway 1; Glasgow |
| May 13, 1964 | Norway 1, Eire 4; Oslo |
| June 29, 1966 | Norway 1, England 6; Oslo |

* World Cup.

## NORWICH CITY F.C.
Founded 1905 and joined the Southern League. One of the original members of the Football League, Division III, 1920. Honours: Champions, Division II, 1971-2. Champions, Division III(S), 1933-4. Runners-up, Division III, 1959-60. Football League Cup Winners, 1962, Finalists 1973. Record attendance: 43,984 v. Leicester City, F.A. Cup 6th Round, Mar. 30, 1963.

Address: Carrow Road, Norwich NOR 22T (Tel. 21514). Nickname: Canaries. Colours: Yellow shirts with green collars and cuffs, green shorts with yellow stripe down seam, yellow stockings. Record League goal-scorer: R. Hunt, 31 goals, Division III(S), 1955-6. Record victory: 10—2 v. Coventry City, Division III(S) Mar. 15, 1930. Record defeat: 7—0 v. Walsall, Division III(S), Sept. 13, 1930.

## NOTTINGHAM FOREST F.C.
Founded 1865. Elected to Football League, Division I, 1892. Honours: Runners-up, Division I, 1966-7. Champions, Division II, 1906-7, 1921-2. Runners-up, 1956-7. Champions: Division III(S), 1950-51. F.A. Cup: Winners, 1898, 1959. Record attendance: 49,946 v. Manchester United, Division I, Oct. 28, 1967. Address: City Ground, Nottingham NG2 5FJ (Tel. 868236). Nickname: Reds. Colours: Red shirts, white shorts, red stockings with white tops. Record League goal-scorer: W. Ardron, 36 goals, Division III(S), 1950-51. Record victory: 14—0 v. Clapton (A), F.A. Cup, 1st Round, Jan. 17, 1891. Record defeat: 9—1 v. Blackburn Rovers, Division II, April 10, 1937.

## NOTTS COUNTY F.C.
The oldest Football League club, formed 1862. Notts County were one of the original members of the Football League in 1888. Honours: Champions, Division II, 1896-7, 1913-14 1922-3. Runners-up, 1894-5. Champions, Division III(S), 1930-31, 1949-50. Runners-up, 1936-7. Best in Division I, 3rd, 1890-91, 1900-1901. Runners-up, Division III, 1972-3. Champions, Division IV, 1970-71. Runners-up, Division IV, 1959-60. F.A. Cup: Winners, 1894. Runners-up, 1891. Record attendance: 47,301 v. York City, F.A. Cup, 6th Round, Mar. 12, 1955. Address: Meadow Lane, Nottingham NG2 3HJ (Tel. 864152). Nickname: Magpies. Colours: Black and white striped shirts, black shorts, white stockings. Record League goal-scorer: T. Keetley, 39 goals, Division III(S), 1930-31. Record victory: 15—0 v. Thornhill United, F.A. Cup. 1st Round, Oct. 24, 1885. Record defeat: 9—1 v. Blackburn Rovers, Division I, Nov. 16, 1889; v. Aston Villa, Division I, Sept. 29, 1888; v. Portsmouth, Division II, April 9, 1927.

## NUMBERING PLAYERS
Players were first numbered in the F.A. Cup Final in 1933. Then the numbers ran from 1 to 22.

In the same year a proposal was made by Tottenham Hotspur that players should be numbered in Football League games, but it was defeated at the A.G.M.

The proposal was not adopted by the League until 1939 when it was passed by 24 votes to 20.

Despite the delay, however, players had been numbered in Football League games much earlier than this. In the opening games of season 1928-9 Arsenal wore numbers v. Sheffield Wednesday, at Hillsborough, and Chelsea did so for their home game with Swansea Town.

Everton also wore numbers when they appeared at Wolverhampton in another First Division game, May 6, 1933.

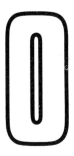

**OCWIRK, Ernst (1926-    )**
Earned a place in soccer history as the last
of the truly great attacking centre half-
backs, a style favoured by the Austrians
long after it had been abandoned elsewhere.
First capped in 1947 he was the dominant
character in the Austrian side which
enjoyed so much success around 1950. He
eventually moved to wing-half, being noted
especially for the accuracy of his cross-field
passes. Later in Italy he figured at inside-
forward. Born Vienna. Captained Rest of
Europe v. Great Britain in 1955.
Stalau, F.A.C. Vienna, F.K. Austria.
Sampdoria 1956-61. F.K. Austria (2nd
time) 1961-62. 62 Austrian internationals.
Rest of Europe v. England 1953, and v.
Great Britain 1955. Austrian League champions 1949, 1950, 1953, 1962.

**OFFSIDE**
The offside rule is the most discussed in the
laws of the game. It is also the most misun-
derstood. The law referring to "offside" is
Law 11 and it can be seen in full under
LAWS OF THE GAME.
It must always be understood that a
player cannot move into an offside position
*after* the ball was last played, nor can he be
offside if the ball was last played by an
opponent, or if he receives the ball direct
from a goal-kick, a corner kick, a throw-in,
or when dropped by the Referee.
The degree to which the offside law
affects tactics can be appreciated from a
consideration of the game both before and
after the law was changed in 1925.
In that year, following a proposal of the
Scottish F.A., the law was altered so that a
player could not be offside if two (instead of
three) opponents were nearer their own
goal-line when the ball was last played.
Under the old rule, which had been in
force since 1867, the full-backs could afford
to play much further up the field providing
they kept in a diagonal line. As soon as a
forward got behind the advanced full-back
he could be in an offside position. And
should he run through after a long ball be-

tween the backs, he still had the other full-
back to beat.
In the early 1920s, full-backs had moved
up almost to the halfway line, one operating
slightly behind the other. They had the offside trap worked to a fine art, and stoppages for offside became monotonous.
When the law was changed stoppages for
offside decreased considerably and for a
while many more goals were scored. In
1924-5 a total of 4,700 goals were scored in
the Football League. In the first season of
the new offside law the total rose by almost
a third to 6,373. Defensive re-organisation
was inevitable.
If the full-backs continued to play well up
and on a slant, an attacker could lie behind
one of them *at all times* and only have the
other to beat. Obviously after 1925 full-
backs were forced to play squarer and
nearer their own goal. But if they lay too
near their own goal they gave the attackers
the chance to shoot without first beating
them with the ball.
Playing square but up field meant that a
long ball down the middle might beat them
both. And if they moved into the centre to
cover this possibility the wingers were given
too much freedom.
The obvious move was to close the gap in
the middle. So a new defensive position
—the third back—was created and was
filled by the centre-half. As a result, there
was one less player concentrating on attack.
Great centre-halves who were always
among the goal-scorers or giving the passes
that provided their colleagues with goal-
scoring chances, men like T. Boyle of
Burnley and J. Cowan of Aston Villa, were
no longer to be seen in football. The
"stopper" or "policeman" centre-half, considered to have been introduced by
Arsenal's famous manager, the late Herbert
Chapman, had arrived.
The change in the offside law not only
brought about an enforced change in the
positioning of the defence, but it has had a
tremendous effect on play throughout the
team. No one can say definitely how much
the change in the law has changed the style
of the game, but it certainly encouraged a
negative type of defensive play which has
been developed to an even greater degree in
recent years.

**OLDHAM ATHLETIC F.C.**
Founded in 1899 in succession to Pine Villa,
a club which had been in existence since
1894. Elected to the Football League, Division II, 1907. Honours: Runners-up, Division I, 1914-15. Runners-up, Division II,
1909-10. Champions, Division III(N), 1952-
3. Runners-up, Division IV, 1962-3. Record

attendance: 47,671 v. Sheffield Wednesday, F.A. Cup, 4th Round, Jan. 25, 1930. Address: Boundary Park, Oldham (Tel. 061-6244972). Nickname: Latics. Colours: Blue shirts and shorts, white stockings. Record League goal-scorer: T. Davis, 33 goals, Division III(N), 1936-7. Record victory: 11—0 v. Southport, Division IV, Dec. 26, 1962. Record defeat: 13—4 v. Tranmere Rovers, Division III(N), Dec. 26, 1935.

## OLYMPIC GAMES

Association Football was first introduced into the Olympic Games in 1900 in Paris, but this was only an exhibition match between the Upton Park Club and a French side which the Londoners won 4—0.

The 1904 Olympics in St. Louis included a soccer tournament with five teams which was won by Galt F.C., representing Canada, and soccer was also included in the intermediate Olympics of 1906 in Athens where Denmark emerged the winners. But the first Olympic soccer tournament to come under the auspices of F.I.F.A. was that in London in 1908.

Today the Olympic soccer tournament is open to all National Associations who are affiliated to F.I.F.A., and the players must, of course, be amateur.

Here are the results of the Finals:

1908 London, Great Britain 2, Denmark 0.
1912 Stockholm, Great Britain 4, Denmark 2.
1920 Antwerp, Belgium 2, Czechoslovakia 0.
1924 Paris, Uruguay 3, Switzerland 0.
1928 Amsterdam, Uruguay 2, Argentine 1 (after draw 1—1).
1932 Los Angeles, No Football Competition.
1936 Berlin, Italy 2, Austria 1.
1948 London, Sweden 3, Yugoslavia 1.
1952 Helsinki, Hungary 2, Yugoslavia 0.
1956 Melbourne, Russia 1, Yugoslavia 0.
1960 Rome, Yugoslavia 3, Denmark 1.
1964 Tokyo, Hungary 2, Czechoslovakia 1.
1968 Mexico City, Hungary 4, Bulgaria 1.
1972 Munich, Poland 2, Hungary 1.

In 1920 the Final was awarded to Belgium, leading 2—0 when the Czechs left the field before half-time after one of their number had been sent off by the referee for kicking an opponent.

The United Kingdom did not enter in 1924 or 1928 because of the split between the Football Association and F.I.F.A. over the question of broken time payments to amateurs.

The United Kingdom were knocked out in the first round by Norway, 3—1, in the 1920 tournament.

1936: U.K. 2, China, 0, Round 1. U.K. 4, Poland 5, Round 2.
1948: U.K. 4, Holland 3, Round 1 (after extra time).
U.K. 1, France 0, Round 2.
U.K. 1, Yugoslavia 3, Semi-finals.
1952: U.K. 3, Luxembourg 5, Preliminary Round (after extra time).
1956: Bulgaria 2, Great Britain 0, Great Britain 3, Bulgaria 3, Preliminary Round.

Despite this defeat the F.A. accepted an invitation to compete at Melbourne to fill a vacancy.

Results in Melbourne:
Great Britain 9, Thailand 0.
Great Britain 1, Bulgaria 6.

In 1960 the 16 teams in the final competition were divided into four groups with the winners of each group going into the semi-finals.

Great Britain 3, Brazil 4.
Great Britain 2, Italy 2.
Great Britain 3, Taiwan 2.

Great Britain was eliminated, Italy winning the group and going forward to the semi-finals.

1964: Preliminary Round.
Iceland 0, G.B.6.
G.B. 4, Iceland 0.
G.B. 2, Greece 1.
Greece 4, G.B. 1.
1968: Preliminary Round.
Spain 1, G.B. 0.
G.B. 0, Spain 0.
1972: Preliminary Round.
G.B. 1, Bulgaria 0.
Bulgaria 5, G.B. 0.

Great Britain's two successful teams were;

1908—H. P. Bailey (Leicester Fosse); W. S. Corbett (Birmingham), H. Smith (Oxford City); K. R. G. Hunt (Wolverhampton Wanderers), F. W. Chapman (South Nottingham), R. M. Hawkes (Luton); A. Berry (Oxford University), V. J. Woodward (Tottenham Hotspur), H. Stapley (Glossop), C. C. Purnell (Clapton), H. P. Hardman (Northern Nomads).

1912—R. G. Brebner (Northern Nomads); T. C. Burn (London Caledonians), A. E. Knight (Portsmouth); D. McWhirter (Bromley), H. C. Littlewort (Glossop), J. Dines (Ilford); A. Berry (Oxford City), V. J. Woodward (Chelsea), H. A. Walden (Bradford City), G. R. Hoare (Glossop), I. G. A. Sharpe (Derby County).

## ORIENT, F.C., THE

Founded 1881. Reconstituted and adopted professionalism, 1901. The club was known as Clapton Orient until 1946 when they became Leyton Orient. Dropped Leyton from the title 1967. Elected to Football League, Div. II, 1905. Honours: Runners-up, Division II, 1961-2. Champions, Division III, 1969-70. Champions, Division III(S), 1955-6. Runners-up, 1954-5. Record attendance: 34,345 v. West Ham United F.A. Cup, 4th Round, Jan. 25, 1964. Address: Brisbane Road, Leyton, London E.10. (Tel. 01-539 1368). Nickname: The "Os". Colours: All red. Record League goal-scorer: T. Johnston, 35 goals, Division II, 1957-8. Record victory: 9—2 v. Aldershot, Division III(S), Feb. 10, 1934 and v. Chester, League Cup, 3rd Round, Oct. 17, 1962. Record defeat: 8—0 v. Aston Villa, F.A. Cup, 4th Round, Jan. 30, 1929.

## ORDERED OFF

See also REFEREES.

In the England v. Argentine World Cup game at Wembley, July 23, 1966, play was held up for seven minutes before the Argentine captain A. Rattin would leave the field after being ordered off by Referee R. Kreitlin (W. Germany).

The first England player to be sent off in a full international—A. Mullery v. Yugoslavia, Nations Cup game, Florence, June 5, 1968.

## ORIGIN OF THE GAME

Considering that soccer and rugby are branches of the same tree then anyone trying to trace the origin of one of these games as distinct from the other is bound to run into a hopeless muddle if any attempt is made to go far beyond the middle of the 19th century.

Football historians are able to refer to the Shrovetide games played in many places including Derbyshire, Chester, Corfe Castle in Dorset, and Scone in the county of Perthshire, but with all due respect to the rugby game those boisterous medieval encounters bear more resemblance (be it only slight) to the handling code than to the game of soccer.

The same historians often claim some connections with various ball games played by the Greeks and Romans, but here again it must be pointed out that the Greek episkyros and the Roman harpastum was more rugby than soccer if only because carrying the ball was a feature of their play.

No indeed, soccer, the game not the name, cannot safely be traced beyond the 1830s when it had its origins in the public schools, but if one really insists on something earlier then we could go to the extreme and mention a form of football that was played with a leather ball in China

at least as early as 200 B.C. and probably much earlier.

Professor H. A. Giles, classical and antiquarian writer who was Professor of Chinese at Cambridge University, proved by his research into the subject that in this game real emphasis was placed upon the ability of the players to dribble the ball, and his findings on this aspect of this ancient Chinese pastime are interesting because it would seem that it bore a much closer resemblance to soccer than any of the Greek and Roman games or the medieval games of mob football.

As has already been mentioned, the modern game of soccer has its origins in the public schools where various forms of football were revived after it had been almost entirely abandoned as a pastime of the working classes.

The rules differed so much from one school to another that although they all played football, some would be more appropriately mentioned in a history of rugby than of soccer, but as far as we are concerned here we can be more specific in mentioning Eton, Westminster, and Charterhouse, as the schools which laid the foundations of the game of Association Football.

From the public schools the obvious course of events was a spread to the universities and it was at Cambridge that one of the earliest attempts was made to adopt a uniform code of rules.

A number of Old Boys got together and formed the first football club, at Sheffield in 1856, and it was the Old Boys and university men who played a leading part in the formation of the Football Association (q.v.) in 1863, and this body originally decided to accept the Cambridge University Rules as a basis upon which to draw up their own rules.

It is well known that the withdrawal of the Blackheath Club two months after the inaugural F.A. meeting in 1863, marks the establishment of the separate games of soccer and rugby. The break, however, did not come, as may be supposed, on the question of handling, but on a disagreement over the F.A.'s ban on running with the ball and 'hacking' (the practice of using the toe either to kick an opponent's shins, or else to trip him up). Strange to relate it was the Blackheath Club which subsequently led a movement to ban 'hacking' from their own game, culminating in the formation of the Rugby Union in 1871.

## OVERSEAS TOUR

See TOURS.

**OWN GOALS**
See GOAL-SCORING (INDIVIDUALS) and (TEAMS), Own Goals.

**OXFORD UNITED F.C.**
Founded 1896 as Headington United. Adopted professionalism 1949 and changed name to Oxford United 1960. Elected to Football League, Division IV, 1962. Honours: Champions, Division III, 1967-8.

Record attendance: 22,730 v. Preston North End, F.A. Cup, 6th Round, Feb. 29, 1964. Address: Manor Ground, Beech Road, Headington, Oxford OX3 7RS (Tel. 0865-61503). Nickname: The U's. Colours: Gold shirts, black shorts, gold stockings. Record League goal-scorer: C. Booth, 23 goals Division IV, 1964-5. Record victory: 7—0 v. Barrow, Division IV, Dec. 19, 1964. Record defeat: 5—0 v. Cardiff City, Division II, Feb. 8, 1969.

## PARAGUAY

Paraguay reached their peak in the 1950s when they not only won the South American Championships (1953) but qualified for the World Cup Tournament both in 1950 and 1958.

They had also competed back in 1930 but then they were eliminated with defeats by the United States and Belgium. In 1950 they gained a 2—2 draw with Sweden and were only beaten 2—0 by Italy. In 1958 they defeated Scotland 3—2 and drew with Yugoslavia 3—3, but in that year it was their 7—3 defeat by France which lost them a place in the semi-finals.

These successes, however, attracted the attention of the wealthier footballing fraternity and Paraguay very soon lost their finest internationals, tempted away by high wages and bonuses.

With a population of only about 1,700,000 and less than 700 clubs affiliated to their F.A., Paraguay's past performances are remarkable indeed, and there seems no doubt that more outstanding performances may be seen in the international field by a country that has a penchant for soccer.

The address of the governing body formed in 1906: Liga Paraquaya de Fútbol, Estadio de Sajonia, Calles Mayor Martinez y Alejo Garcia, Asunción. Colours: Red and white shirts, blue shorts, blue stockings.

Result of international match:
June 11, 1958*   Scotland 2, Paraguay 3; Sweden

* World Cup.

## PARTICK THISTLE F.C.

Founded 1876. Among original members of Scottish League, Division II, 1893. Honours: Champions, Division II, 1896-7, 1899-1900. 1970-71, Runners-up, 1901-2. Best in Division I, 3rd, 1947-8, 1953-4. Scottish Cup: Winners, 1921, Finalists, 1930. Scottish League Cup: Winners, 1972. Finalists, 1957, 1959. Record attendance: 54,723, Scotland v. Ireland, Feb. 25, 1928. Address: Firhill Park, Glasgow, N.W. (Tel. 041-946). Nickname: Jags. Colours: Yellow shirts with red trim, red shorts. Record goalscorer in Division I, A. Hair, 41 goals, 1926-7. Record victory: 16—0 v. Royal Albert, Scottish Cup, 1st Round, Jan. 17, 1931. Record defeat: 10—1 v. Dunfermline Athletic, Division I, 1958-9.

## PELÉ (Edson Arantes Nascimento) (1940- )

A World Cup star at 17 Pelé has become one of the richest and best known sportsmen in the world, and arguably the finest inside-forward of all time, possessing speed, superb ball control and the ability to shoot or head powerfully and accurately. Always difficult to dispossess, no man ever showed more skill in shielding a ball. Capped when only 16 he has figured in four World Cup Final tournaments, helping Brazil win two Finals, but missing the final games of the 1962 tournament which they won while he was absent through injury. Pelé has scored over 1,000 goals in first-class football, his best season being 1959 when he netted 126. Born Tres Coracoes, one of a poor negro family.

Bauru 1955-56. Santos 1956-72. 110 Brazilian internationals. World Cup winners 1958, 1970. World Club Cup champions 1962, 1963. São Paulo League champions 1955, 1956, 1958, 1959, 1960, 1961, 1962, 1964, 1965, 1967, 1968, 1969. Brazil Cup winners 1962, 1963, 1964, 1968.

## PENALTIES

The penalty kick was introduced by the Irish F.A. in season 1890-91. The F.A. (England) accepted it in September 1891.

The first player to score from a penalty kick in a Football League game—J. Heath, Wolverhampton Wanderers v. Accrington, Sept. 14, 1891.

### Cup Final

All four penalty kicks taken in Wembley Cup Finals have been successful.

In the 1937-8 Final, G. Mutch of Preston North End scored the winning goal from the penalty spot in the last minute of extra time. Result: Preston North End 1, Huddersfield Town 0.

In the 1947-8 Final, E. Shimwell scored for Blackpool in the 14th minute. But Blackpool were beaten 4—2 by Manchester United.

In the 1953-4 Final, R. Allen scored a

penalty for West Bromwich Albion against Preston North End 19 min. after the interval. West Bromwich Albion won 3—2.

In the 1961-2 Final, D. Blanchflower scored for Tottenham Hotspur from a penalty awarded against Burnley for "hands" 9 min. from the end. Tottenham Hotspur won 3—1.

## Goalkeepers

A. Birch scored five penalties for Chesterfield in season 1923-4, a record for a goalkeeper in the Football League.

The record number of penalties saved in a Football League game is three. W. Scott saved three for Grimsby Town against Burnley, Feb. 13, 1909. But despite his valiant efforts, Burnley won 2—0.

## Headed

Five players have headed a goal from a penalty kick. On Jan. 5, 1935, in the match Arsenal v. Liverpool, the Arsenal full-back, E. Hapgood, took a penalty kick which Liverpool's goalkeeper, Riley, fisted back, Hapgood headed home the rebound. Arsenal won 2—0. W.R. Dean (Everton) also performed the same feat against West Bromwich Albion (goalkeeper H. F. Pearson), Nov. 7, 1936. Everton won 4—2.

W. Hopper (Workington) headed a similar goal against Aldershot (goalkeeper D. Jones), Division IV, Feb. 14, 1964; also by S. Harland (Bradford City) v. Tranmere Rovers (goalkeeper J. Heath) Division IV, April 11, 1962; D. Simmons (Bournemouth) v. Tranmere Rovers (goalkeeper J. Cumbes) Division III, Jan. 4, 1969.

## Missed

The greatest number of penalties missed by one side in a Football League, Division I, match is three. On Jan. 27, 1912, Fletcher (2) and Thornley missed penalties for Manchester City against Newcastle United. The game resulted in a draw 1—1.

Burnley missed three out of four v. Grimsby Town, Division II, Feb. 13, 1909.

In the last match of the 1923-4 season, L. Davies missed a penalty for Cardiff City v. Birmingham. The result was a goalless draw. If Cardiff City had won they would have been Football League Champions. As it was, they were runners-up on goal average and have never yet won the Championship.

## Relegated

Manchester City missed a penalty against Newcastle United in the last match of the season 1925-6 and were relegated from the First Division. The result was a 3—2 defeat for Manchester City. A draw would have saved them from relegation.

## Season's Aggregates

The highest number of penalties converted in one season of League football by single players are:

13—F. Lee, Manchester City's inside-forward, 1971-2.

11—J. Ball, Sheffield Wednesday's centre-forward, 1932-3. W. Evans, Tottenham Hotspur's outside-left, 1932-3.

10—T. Callendar, Gateshead's centre half-back, 1949-50. J. Evans, Southend United's left-back, 1921-2. P. Morris, Mansfield Town's right-half, 1966-7.

## Single Games

Three players have scored three penalties in a single Division I match:

W. Walker for Aston Villa v. Bradford City, Nov. 21, 1921; C. Mitten for Manchester United v. Aston Villa, Mar. 8, 1950, and K. Barnes for Manchester City v. Everton, Dec. 7, 1957.

During the Division III(N) match between Crewe Alexandra and Bradford on Mar. 8, 1924, there were four penalty kicks in five minutes—a league record.

There were five penalty kicks in the Argentine v. Mexico World Cup game at Montevideo in 1930. Argentine won 6—3.

W. Cook scored from the penalty spot in three consecutive Football League, Division I, games for Everton at Christmas, 1938 v. Blackpool (H), Dec. 24; v. Derby County (H), Dec. 26; and v. Derby County (A), Dec. 27.

## Tie-breakers

The first use of the penalty kick as a tie-breaker in a first-class match in England was in the Watney Cup semi-final between Hull City and Manchester United, Aug. 5, 1970. It was 1—1 after extra time but United eventually won 4—3 on penalties.

## PERU

Peru is another of the smaller countries that have suffered through the loss of their star players to richer clubs of other lands.

Since the war Peru reached their peak in the international field around 1958-9, years in which they not only defeated England 4—1 but twice held mighty Brazil to a draw, 1—1 in the World Cup and 2—2 in the South American Championships.

Following a period in which the exodus of their best players to other countries marred the progress of the game at home, Peru recovered to qualify for the 1970 World Cup in which they reached the quarter-finals.

The address of the governing body which was founded in 1922: Federación Peruana de Fútbol, Estadio Nacional, Calle José Diaz, Puerta 4, Lima. Colours: White shirts with red diagonal stripe, white shorts, white stockings with red tops.

Results of international matches:
May 17, 1959    Peru 4, England 1; Lima
May 20, 1962    Peru 0, England 4; Lima
April 26, 1972    Scotland 2, Peru 0; Glasgow

## PETERBOROUGH UNITED F.C.
Formed 1923. Elected to Division IV 1960. Honours: Champions, Division IV, 1960-61. Record attendance: 30,096 v. Swansea Town, F.A. Cup, 5th Round, Feb. 20, 1965. Address: London Road, Peterborough PE2 8AL (Tel. 3623). Nickname: Posh. Colours: Royal blue shirts, white shorts and stockings. Record League goal-scorer: T. Bly, 52 goals, Division IV, 1960-61. Record victory 8—1 v. Oldham Athletic, Division IV, Nov. 26, 1969. Record defeat: 8—1 v. Northampton Town, F.A. Cup, 2nd Round (2nd replay), 1946-7.

## PLAYERS
The least number of players to appear for a Football League club in one season's competition is 14. Liverpool called on this number when winning the Championship in 1965-6.

In the Scottish League, Division I, the record is 15—Dundee, 1961-2.

At the other end of the scale Coventry City in 1919-20, Sheffield Wednesday in 1919-20, and Hull City in 1946-7, each used as many as 42 players in the season. In the Scottish League, Falkirk and Raith Rovers in 1919-20, each used 38 players.

In the Scottish League, Dumbarton called on 44 players during season 1918-19.

Chelsea finished a Division I game at Blackpool on Oct. 29, 1932 with only six players. The others had left the field because of exhaustion through severe weather conditions. Blackpool won 4—0.

See also under TEAM CHANGES.

## PLAYERS' UNION, THE
See under PROFESSIONAL FOOTBALLERS' ASSOCIATION, THE.

## PLYMOUTH ARGYLE F.C.
Founded 1886. Reconstituted as a professional club 1903. One of the original clubs forming the Football League, Division III, in 1920. Honours: Champions, Division III(S), 1929-30, 1951-2. Runners-up, 1921-2, 1922-3, 1923-4, 1924-5, 1925-6, 1926-7. Champions, Division III, 1958-9. Best in Division II, 4th, 1931-2 1952-3. Record attendance: 43,596 v. Aston Villa, Division III, Oct. 10, 1936. Address: Home Park,

Plymouth (Tel. 52561). Nickname: Pilgrims. Colours: Green shirts with white collars and sleeves, white shorts with green and black stripe down side, green stockings. Record League goal-scorer: J. Cock, 32 goals, Division III(S), 1925-6. Record victory: 8—1 v. Millwall, Division II, Jan. 16, 1932. Record defeat: 9—0 v. Stoke City, Division II, Dec. 17, 1960.

## POINTS
The record number of points gained by clubs in the Football League are:
Division I—1968-9, Leeds United 67.
Division II—1919-20, Tottenham Hotspur 70.
Division III—1971-72, Aston Villa 70.
Division III(S)—1950-51, Nottingham Forest 70. 1954-5, Bristol City 70.
Division III(N)—1946-7, Doncaster Rovers 72.
Division IV—1970-71, Notts County 69.

*Scottish League:*
Division I—1920-21, Rangers 76.
Division II—1966-67, Morton 69.

Five times only in the history of the Football League have the champions of any division finished the season with more points than goals: Nottingham Forest (Division II), 1921-2, 56 points, 51 goals. Notts County (Division II), 1922-3, 53 points, 46 goals. Birmingham City (Division II), 1947-8, 59 points, 55 goals. Gillingham (Division IV), 1963-4, 60 points, 59 goals. Leeds United (Division I), 1968-9, 67 points, 66 goals.

In three successive seasons, 1928-9, 1929-30, and 1930-31, Millwall finished in the same position and with the same number of points. They were 14th with 39 points.

The highest number of points secured by a club relegated from either Division I or II of the Football League is 38 in 1927-8 when Tottenham Hotspur were relegated from the First Division.

### Points deducted
Stockport County had two points deducted from their record for playing J. Smith without permission on Mar. 26, 1927. Sunderland also had two points deducted for playing J. E. Doig on Sept. 20, 1890, before

he was eligible.

Albion Rovers had two points deducted, Scottish League, Division II, 1903-4, for fielding an unregistered player.

In the Italian League, 1959-60, Genoa had 28 points deducted for alleged attempted bribery. They only collected 18 points so they began the following season with a deficit of 10 points.

St. Johnstone had two points deducted in 1922-3 for fielding a player signed after Mar. 16. It cost them the championship of Division II.

Port Glasgow Athletic had seven points deducted for a similar offence in 1893-4.

**Fewest Points**

The lowest number of points obtained in any one season in the Football League is eight by Loughborough Town in Division II, 1899-1900 (won 1, drawn 6, lost 27), and by Doncaster Rovers, Division II, 1904-5 (won 3, drawn 2, lost 29).

In the Scottish League Division A, 1954-5 Stirling Albion gained only 6 points—2 wins and 2 draws in 30 games. A record low.

The fewest number of points to separate the top and bottom teams in any division of the Football League at the end of a season is 16. This happened three times in Division I: in 1901-2, 1927-8 and 1937-8.

The fewest points gained by a Championship winning Football League club in a 42-match season is 52. Sheffield Wednesday in Division I, 1928-9, Arsenal in Division I, 1937-8 and Chelsea in Division I, 1954-5, all won the Championship with only 52 points.

**POLAND**

Before the outbreak of World War II Poland was swiftly developing into one of the leading powers in the football world and although they have not been able to break into the upper crust of football's *élite* during the post-war years they have some notable victories to their credit.

In the 1936 Olympics Poland defeated the United Kingdom 5—4 and finished up in fourth place. In 1938 they defeated Ireland 6—0, and, when that year they appeared in the World Cup Finals for the first time, they surprised the critics by making one of the favourites, Brazil, fight all the way for a 6—5 victory. It was only after extra time that the Poles were beaten.

The Polish amateurs enjoyed their greatest success when they won the 1972 Olympic Tournament. Throughout the competition they suffered only one defeat (3—2 to Bulgaria) and beat Hungary 2—1 in the Final.

Soccer was played in Poland long before the country was declared independent in 1918. For many years before that most of the area now known as Poland was Russian territory and although the formation of football clubs was frowned upon by the Czar some British enthusiasts working in Lodz started a team and interest in the game spread rapidly.

Apparently, however, those British were not quite the first footballers in Poland for the oldest club was formed at Cracow in 1906 when that city was just over the border inside what was then part of Austrian Galicia. There, in 1911, a touring side from Aberdeen created great enthusiasm by playing two games winning them both, 11—1 and 8—1.

The Polish F.A. was formed in 1919. A National League was established in 1927.

Address of the governing body: Polska Sekcja Piłki Nożnej, Ujazdowskie 22, Warsaw. Colours: White shirts, red shorts, red and white stockings.

Results of international matches:

| | | |
|---|---|---|
| May 22, 1938 | Poland 6, Eire 0; Warsaw |
| Nov. 13, 1938 | Eire 3, Poland 2; Dublin |
| May 11, 1958 | Poland 2, Eire 2; Katowice |
| June 1, 1958 | Poland 1, Scotland 2; Warsaw |
| Oct. 5, 1958 | Eire 2, Poland 2; Dublin |
| May 4, 1960 | Scotland 2, Poland 3; Hampden Park |
| Oct. 10, 1962† | Poland 0, Ireland 2; Katowice |
| Nov. 28, 1962† | Ireland 2, Poland 0; Belfast |
| May 10, 1964 | Poland 3, Eire 1; Glasgow |
| Oct. 25, 1964 | Eire 3, Poland 2; Dublin |
| May 23, 1965* | Poland 1, Scotland 1; Chorzow |
| Oct. 13, 1965* | Scotland 1, Poland 2; Hampden Park |
| Jan. 5, 1966 | England 1, Poland 1; Goodison Park |
| July 5, 1966 | Poland 0, England 1; Chorzow |
| May 15, 1968 | Eire 2, Poland 2; Dublin |
| Oct. 30, 1968 | Poland 1, Eire 0; Katowice |
| May 6, 1970 | Poland 2, Eire 1; Poznan |

| Sept. 23, 1970 | Eire 0, Poland 2; Dublin |
| Mar. 28, 1973* | Wales 2, Poland 0; Cardiff |
| May 16, 1973 | Poland 2, Eire 0; Warsaw |
| June 6, 1973* | Poland 2, England 0; Katowice |

* World Cup  † Nations Cup

## PORTSMOUTH F.C.

Founded 1898. Joined Southern League 1899. Joined Football League, Division III, 1920. Honours: Champions, Division I, 1948-9, 1949-50. Runners-up, Division II, 1926-7. Champions, Division III(S), 1923-4. Champions, Division III, 1961-2. F.A. Cup: Winners, 1939. Finalists, 1929, 1934. Record attendance: 51,385 v. Derby County, F.A. Cup, 6th Round, Feb. 26, 1949. Address: Fratton Park, Portsmouth (Tel. 31204). Nickname: Pompey. Colours: Royal Blue shirts with red, white and blue trim, white shirts with red and blue trim, royal blue stockings with red, white and blue tops. Record League goal-scorer: W. Haines, 40 goals, Division II, 1926-7. Record victory: 9—1 v. Notts County, Division II, April 9, 1927. Record defeat: 10—0 v. Leicester City, Division I, Oct. 20, 1928.

## PORTUGAL

Football was introduced into Portugal by English residents of Lisbon in the 1870s and the Lisbon Club was formed in 1875. The game was established on a national basis in 1893 and with a vast increase about that time among the number of boys from Portugal receiving their education in England, the game's popularity developed rapidly. The Portuguese F.A. was formed in 1912.

Portugal reached their peak in 1966 when they proved to be one of the best footballing sides in the World Cup and won third place.

The country's two leading clubs Sporting Lisbon and Benfica have practically monopolised the League Championship in recent years and the latter was the first to break Real Madrid's hold on the European Cup.

The address of the governing body: Federaçao Portuguesa de Futebol, Praça da Alegria 25, Lisbon. Colours: Red shirts, white shorts, green stockings.

Results of international matches:

| June 16, 1946 | Portugal 3, Eire 1; Lisbon |
| May 4, 1947 | Eire 0, Portugal 2; Dublin |
| May 25, 1947 | Portugal 0, England 10; Lisbon |
| May 23, 1948 | Portugal 2, Eire 0; Lisbon |
| May 15, 1949 | Portugal 3, Wales 2; Lisbon |
| May 22, 1949 | Eire 1, Portugal 0; Dublin |
| May 14, 1950 | Portugal 3, England 5; Lisbon |
| May 21, 1950 | Portugal 2, Scotland 2; Lisbon |
| May 12, 1951 | Wales 2, Portugal 1; Cardiff |
| May 19, 1951 | England 5, Portugal 2; Everton |
| May 4, 1955 | Scotland 3, Portugal 0; Hampden Park |
| May 22, 1955 | Portugal 3, England 1; Oporto |
| Jan. 16, 1957* | Portugal 1, Ireland 1; Lisbon |
| May 1, 1957* | Ireland 3, Portugal 0; Belfast |
| May 7, 1958 | England 2, Portugal 1; Wembley |
| June 3, 1959 | Portugal 1, Scotland 0; Lisbon |
| May 21, 1961* | Portugal 1, England 1; Lisbon |
| Oct. 25, 1961* | England 2, Portugal 0; Wembley |
| May 17, 1964 | Portugal 3, England 4; Lisbon |
| June 4, 1964 | Portugal 1, England 1; Sao Paulo, Brazil |
| June 18, 1966 | Scotland 0, Portugal 1; Hampden Park |
| July 26, 1966* | England 2, Portugal 1; Wembley |
| Dec. 10, 1969 | England 1, Portugal 0; Wembley |
| April 21, 1971† | Portugal 2, Scotland 0; Lisbon |
| Oct. 13, 1971† | Scotland 2, Portugal 1; Hampden Park |
| June 6, 1972 | Portugal 2, Eire 1; Brazil |
| Mar. 28, 1973* | Ireland 1, Portugal 1; Coventry |

* World Cup
† European Championship

## PORT VALE F.C.
Founded 1876 as Burslem Port Vale. One of the original members of the Football League, Division II, 1892. Failed to gain re-election, 1896. Returned to Division II two years later but resigned in 1907. Next appeared in Division II when they took over the fixtures of Leeds City in Oct. 1919. Honours: Champions, Division III(N), 1929-30, 1953-4. Runners-up, 1952-3. Champions, Division IV, 1958-9. F.A. Cup: Semi-finalists, 1954 (only the second Division III club to reach this stage of the competition). Record attendance: 50,000 v. Aston Villa, F.A. Cup, 5th Round, Feb. 20, 1960. Address: Vale Park, Burslem, Stoke-on-Trent ST6 1AW (Tel. Stoke-on-Trent 87626). Nickname: Valiants. Colours: White shirts with black edging, white shorts, white stockings with twin black trim. Record League goal-scorer: W. Kirkham, 38 goals, Division II, 1926-7. Record victory: 9—1 v. Chesterfield, Division II, Sept. 24, 1932. Record defeat: 10—0 v. Sheffield United (H), Division II, Dec. 10, 1892; v. Notts County, Division II, Feb. 26, 1895.

## POSTPONED MATCHES
Football League regulations do not permit members to play postponed or replayed F.A. Cup ties on a Saturday.

Where a Football League game is postponed because of an F.A. Cup tie then the two clubs are entitled to claim a sum based on the home club's average gross gate receipts. This money is paid out of the F.A. Cup Pool.

However, such compensation is not paid where games are re-arranged for a Saturday date.

See also WEATHER.

## PRESTON NORTH END F.C.
Founded in 1880 by members of the North End Cricket Club, which had been in existence since 1867. Immediately prior to 1880 they had preferred rugby as their winter game. Became one of the original members of the Football League in 1888 and the first Champions. Honours: Champions, Division I, 1888-89, 1889-90. Runners-up, 1890-91, 1891-2, 1892-3, 1905-6, 1952-3, 1957-8. Champions, Division II, 1903-4, 1912-13, 1950-51. Runners-up, 1914-15, 1933-4. Champions, Division III, 1970-71. F.A. Cup: Winners, 1889, 1938. Finalists, 1888, 1922, 1937, 1954, 1964. Record attendance: 42,684 v. Arsenal, Division I, April 23, 1938. Address: Deepdale, Preston PR1 6RU (Tel. 53818). Nickname: Lily whites. Colours: White shirts, dark blue shorts, white stockings. Record League goal-scorer: E. Harper, 37 goals, Division II, 1932-3. Preston North End is one of the only four clubs ever to achieve "the double"—the League Championship and the F.A. Cup in the same season. They did so in 1888-9. Record victory: 26—0 v. Hyde, F.A. Cup, 1st Round, 1st Series, Oct. 15, 1887. Record defeat: 7—0 v. Blackpool (H), Division I, May 1, 1948.

## PROFESSIONAL FOOTBALLERS ASSOCIATION, THE
See also WAGES.

The first attempt to form a Players' Union was made in Oct. 1893, by W. C. Rose, a goalkeeper with Wolverhampton Wanderers. He sent letters to all the captains of clubs in Division I, proposing the formation of a Union "to protect professional interests".

A Union known as the National Union of Association Players was subsequently formed in 1899 but it soon became defunct.

The present, more powerful and fully recognised body was formed at a meeting held on Dec. 2, 1907, and registered as a trade union on Mar. 10, 1908. It was then known as the Football Players' and Trainers' Union.

In 1908 the F.A. gave official recognition to this Union but when the new body became affiliated with the Federation of Trade Unions trouble started with the F.A. and the Football League. These two organisations feared that football might be suspended through *any* subsequent union strike.

The F.A. withdrew recognition of the Union in 1909, and gave the officials an ultimatum to resign or be forever banned from football. Several Union committee-men chose to obey the F.A.'s instructions, but not all did so, and the Chairman and Secretary were suspended by the F.A.

At the time of the ban, a strike of players was threatened. Several did in fact stand out without pay for 14 weeks before a conference was called at Birmingham in Aug. 1909. The outcome of the meeting was that the players got their wages, and the F.A. and the Union recognised each other.

Since then the Union has done much to improve the lot of the professional footballer. For many years their main bone of contention was the form of contract and the maximum wage rule, and on at least two occasions after World War II the Union threatened to strike to back up their demands.

Fortunately, strikes have been averted and while the Union or the Professional Footballers' Association (they adopted this title in 1958) has never gained all its demands concerning the form of contract they obtained their biggest break through in 1961 when they at last got their way with the abolition of the maximum wage rule.

## Scotland

Scottish players have their own Union. It was formed in 1946, 33 years after the original Scottish Players' Union was dissolved when only two years old.

## PROFESSIONALISM

Today there are about 6,000 professional footballers in Britain, but the identity of the first man to receive payment for playing football will never be definitely established. In its earliest days professionalism was an "under the counter" affair. It was frowned on by the Football Association and, indeed, banned by a rule made in 1882 which permitted only payment for actual wages lost in addition to normal expenses.

However the player who is generally considered to have been the first professional footballer was a Scot, J. J. Lang. North of the Border he had played for Clydesdale and for Glasgow Eastern, but in 1876 he joined Sheffield Wednesday. It is difficult now to prove that he was paid by the Yorkshire club but in later years when he was a steward at Ibrox Park he always claimed that he had been the first Scot to go South solely for the purpose of playing football.

Professionalism was the inevitable outcome of the spread of the game from the schools and universities to the industrial centres in the North and Midlands. It was among the clubs of the industrial North that the practice of paying players first began. As soon as it was seen that so many people were interested in watching football, someone decided to collect "gate money". The money collected was most acceptable for it meant that the clubs could buy better kit and improve their grounds so helping towards attracting bigger crowds.

There was growing enthusiasm for the F.A. Cup. None of the bigger clubs could afford to be out of the competition, but entry meant high travelling expenses so that there was a considerable need to increase revenue.

It is obvious that only winning teams can attract bigger crowds. So that when a club found that it could not form a winning combination from local talent, it looked further afield. Players who were induced to give up their jobs in other towns and move into the neighbourhood of their new clubs naturally needed some incentive other than their love of the game.

About the time that the competition among the Northern clubs for new and more attractive players was becoming so intense (about 1880) Scotland took the lead in the production of talented footballers. The Scots had developed a style of close passing which, as was proved by international results, was far more effective than the old English individual play.

The first clubs to import Scotsmen in any number were Blackburn Rovers and Darwen, between 1879 and 1882. They were soon followed by Preston North End and Bolton Wanderers.

The advent of so many imported players obviously meant professionalism, but the traditionally amateur Football Association seemed peculiarly reluctant to take any definite action against the offending clubs. They introduced a rule in 1882 which stated that any player who received remuneration or consideration of any sort above his actual expenses and any wages lost would be debarred from the Cup or any Association or international matches, and the employing club would be excluded from the Association; but the governing body did not take much action to back up the rule.

The first definite step to bar professionalism was taken by the Lancashire and Birmingham Associations. Their investigations shook the Football Association into action, and early in 1883 a sub-committee was appointed to investigate alleged professionalism. The outcome was disappointing to the opponents of professionalism, for the committee were unable to find proof of payment to players.

There was an ever-growing wave of resentment against professionalism among the amateur clubs. They expressed reluctance in competing for the F.A. Cup while professional players were also engaged in the competition. On the other hand, however, many individuals who had earlier expressed themselves against the growth of professionalism were now beginning to wonder whether professionalism was not, after all, doing the game good.

It seemed that professionalism was encouraging new players from a wider sphere of life; bringing men into the game who would normally have been unable to afford to take part. This meant an increase in the number of expert exponents of the game among men who were not only fighting to keep their places in the team purely for the game's sake, but also because it was their bread and butter. What greater inducement to play well?

The first real move made by the Football Association against professionalism came late in 1883 when it suspended Accrington for paying one of their players. As a result, there was a great deal of bad feeling directed towards the F.A. especially from the Northern clubs. The credit for clearing the air and bringing professionalism into the open belongs to the Preston North End club, and in particular to its President, Major W. Sudell. After Preston North End had drawn with Upton Park in the 4th Round of the F.A. Cup, Jan. 1884, the London club protested to the F.A. insisting that Preston had included professionals in their team.

A special meeting of the F.A. Committee was called, and to everyone's amazement, when Major Sudell came before them, instead of attempting to hide the facts, the Preston chief quite openly admitted professionalism. More than that, he announced that he could provide proof to show that most of the clubs in his part of the country were also paying their players.

Preston North End were disqualified from the competition. But Major Sudell's frankness precipitated the legalisation of professionalism.

However, the lifting of the ban on professionalism was not made immediately. Certain members of the F.A. were not prepared to give up the fight easily. A proposal by Mr. C. W. Alcock (Hon. Sec. of the F.A.) that professionalism should be legalised was countered by a proposal that it was an evil. The latter proposal was carried.

One of the leading opponents of the adoption of professionalism at this time was Mr. J. C. Clegg then the representative of the Sheffield Association, and later to become Sir Charles Clegg, President of the F.A. He considered that the legalisation of professionalism would "place more power in the hands of betting-men and encourage gambling".

In June 1884, the Association passed new rules in their last effort to stem the tide. Under these, payment for wages lost was not allowed for more than one day in any week, and receipts were to be produced by the clubs. But a more drastic rule was that which prevented any but Englishmen from taking part in F.A. Cup ties.

Few, if any, of the clubs who were already paying their players, appeared to take heed of these new rules. Indeed, many preferred to retire from the competition rather than lay themselves open to investigation. A major split was threatened when there was a movement to form a British Football Association in which professionalism would be permitted.

The F.A. now began to realise the futility of their efforts to repress the payment of players. A sub-committee was formed to consider the question afresh. Innumerable meetings took place, proposals and counter-proposals were made, questionnaires circularised to the clubs, until eventually, at a Special General Meeting on July 20, 1885, professionalism was at last recognised. But it was to be strictly controlled. In all Cup matches only professionals who were qualified by birth or residence during the past two years within six miles of the headquarters of their respective clubs, were permitted to take part. This rule was not expunged until four years later.

The other home countries, Scotland in particular, continued to wage war against "this evil" of professionalism, but all in turn, had to submit to the inevitable. Scotland lifted her ban in May 1893.

At first there were no professional clubs in England south of Birmingham. But gradually southern clubs took the plunge, Luton Town (1890), Woolwich Arsenal (1891), Southampton (1892), Millwall (1893), and Tottenham Hotspur (1894), were among the first.

The London F.A. was the last of the leading authorities in this country to accept professionalism. They held out until Feb. 1906.

The spread of professionalism brought the need for more earnest consideration of club fixtures. Football was now a business: the various professional clubs were not in it just for the love of it. More attractive and keener games had to be organised. The outcome of these considerations was the formation of the Football League in 1888 (q.v.).

For more details of the actual payments made to players, see WAGES.

## PROMOTION

Automatic promotion and relegation for the bottom two and the top two teams of Divisions I and II of the Football League was first introduced in season 1898-9. Before this, promotion and relegation had been decided by a series of Test Matches.

The Test Match system was adopted in 1893, the end of the first season of the new Division II. At first, the bottom three teams in Division I met the top three clubs in Division II. Only three matches were played: one Division I team met one of the Division II teams. The winners either retained Division I status or gained promotion accordingly.

This system was revised in season 1895-6 when the bottom two division I teams played each of the top two Division II teams twice. Promotion and relegation were decided on the points obtained by each club from its four games.

See also GOAL AVERAGE.

**Fees**

Clubs promoted to Division II have to pay £200 League membership fee. This figure represents the difference between the initial membership fee of £100 charged to clubs joining Division IV (or who joined the old Third Division) as Associate Members of the Football League, and the fee of £300 charged to Full Members, i.e. those 44 clubs in the top two Divisions.

**Four up and Down**

A proposal that four teams instead of two from each division should change places at the end of each season was made by Derby County as long ago as 1933, but although that same proposal has been made at nearly every A.G.M. of the Football League ever since it has not yet received the three-quarters majority needed for its adoption.

The main reason usually given by those who are against this proposal is that the increase in the scramble for league points would mean more dog fights and less football. However, considering the fact that it is the Division I clubs who have formed the majority of those against the proposal then it is obvious that their thoughts are mainly centred upon preserving their position in the senior section. Little consideration seems to have been given to the point that acceptance of this proposal would also mean that clubs relegated might find it easier to regain the higher status.

In 1956 the Football League Management Committee issued a five-point plan for reorganisation and it was one of their suggestions that there should be an increase in the number of teams promoted and relegated so as to give the clubs in the lower divisions greater incentive and create new interest.

It was subsequently decided to try four-up and four-down promotion and relegation when the two sections of the Third Division were formed into a Third and Fourth Division, but the increased number up and down was only between these two divisions.

However, a real break-through was made in 1973 when the League accepted a proposal for three up and three down between the First, Second and Third Divisions.

See also FOOTBALL LEAGUE.

**PUSKAS, Ferenc (1926-    )**

Made League debut for Kispest (Budapest) in October 1943 and won his first full cap in August 1945, developing into one of the finest inside-forwards of the post-war era with a lethal left-foot shot. Enjoyed one run of 36 consecutive appearances for Hungary and captained the side that reached the World Cup Final of 1954.

Topped the Hungarian League scoring list four times between 1947 and 1954, although considered to be more of a soccer "general" in his home country. However, when he left Hungary during the Revolution of 1956 and later joined Real Madrid he played as a striker and topped the Spanish League scorers in four out of five seasons 1959-64.

After coaching in Canada he returned to Europe and steered Panathinaikos (Greece) to the European Cup Final of 1971.

Kispest 1943-49. Honved 1949-56. Real Madrid 1958-66. 84 Hungarian and 4 Spanish internationals. Olympic Gold medal 1952. European Cup winners 1960, runners-up 1962. World Club Cup winners 1960. Hungarian League champions 1950, 1952, 1954, 1955. Spanish League Champions 1961, 1962, 1963, 1964, 1965. World Cup runners-up 1954.

## QUEEN OF THE SOUTH F.C.
Formed 1919 by the amalgamation of Arrol-Johnston F.C., Dumfries F.C., and K.O.S.B. Elected to Scottish League, Division III, 1923. Reached Division I, 1933. Honours: Champions, Division B, 1950-51, Runners-up, Division II, 1932-3, 1961-2. Runners-up, Division III, 1924-5. Best in Division I, 4th, 1933-4. Record attendance: 25,000 v. Hearts, Scottish Cup, 3rd Round, Feb. 23, 1952. Address: Palmerston Park, Dumfries (Tel. 0387 4853). Colours: Royal blue shirts, white shorts. Record goal-scorer: J. Gray, 33 goals, Division II, 1927-8. Record victory: 11—1 v. Stranraer, Scottish Cup, 1st Round, Jan. 16, 1932. Record defeat: 10—2 v. Dundee, Division I, Dec. 1, 1962.

## QUEEN'S PARK A.F.C.
Founded 1867. Entered Division I of Scottish League, 1900-1901. Honours: Champions, Division II, 1922-3, 1955-6. Scottish Cup: Winners, 1874, 1875, 1876, 1880, 1881, 1882, 1884, 1886, 1890, 1893. Finalists, 1892, 1900. Record attendance: 149,547, Scotland v. England, April 17, 1937. Address: 55 West Regent Street, Glasgow, C.2 (Tel. 041-632 1275). Colours: Black and white hooped shirts, white shorts. Record League goal-scorer: W. Martin, 30 goals, Division I, 1937-8. Record victory: 16—0 v. St. Peter's, Scottish Cup, 1st Round, 1885-6. Record defeat: 9—0 v. Motherwell, Division I, April 26, 1930.

## QUEEN'S PARK RANGERS F.C.
Founded 1885 as St. Jude's Institute F.C. Changed to present title in 1887. Adopted professionalism 1898. Joined Football League, Division III, 1920. Honours: Champions, Division III, 1966-7. Champions, Division III(S), 1947-8. Runners-up, 1946-7. Runners-up, Division II, 1967-8, 1972-3. League Cup Winners, 1967. Record attendance: 33,572 v. Chelsea, F.A. Cup, 6th Round, Feb. 21, 1970. At White City —42,000 v. Leeds United, F.A. Cup, 3rd Round, Jan. 9, 1932. Address: South Africa Road, Shepherd's Bush, London, W12 7PA (Tel. 01-743 2618). Nickname: The "R's". Colours: Blue and white hooped shirts, white shorts and stockings. Record League goal-scorer: G. Goddard, 37 goals, Division III(S), 1929-30. Record victory: 9—2 v. Tranmere Rovers, Division III, Dec. 3, 1960. Record defeat: 8—1 v. Mansfield Town, Division III, Mar. 15, 1965, and v. Manchester United, Division I, Mar. 19, 1969.

## QUICKEST GOALS
See GOAL-SCORING (Fast scoring).

## RAITH ROVERS F.C.

Founded 1883. Became Limited Liability Company, 1907. Elected to Scottish League Division II, 1902. Honours: Champions, Division II, 1907-8, 1909-10 (shared), 1937-8, 1948-9. Runners-up, 1966-7. Best in Division I, 3rd, 1921-2. Scottish Cup: Finalists, 1913. Scottish League Cup: Finalists, 1949. Record attendance: 32,000 v. Hearts, Scottish Cup, 2nd Round, Feb. 7, 1953. Address: Stark's Park, Kirkcaldy (Tel. 0592 3514). Colours: Royal blue shirts and shorts, white stripe on shorts. Record League goal-scorer: W. Penman, 35 goals, Division II, 1948-9. Record victory: 10—1 v. Coldstream (A), Scottish Cup, 2nd Round, Feb. 13, 1954. Record defeat: 11—2 v. Morton, Division II, 1935-6.

## RAMSEY, Sir Alfred Ernest (1920-    )

Sound positional sense and accurate ball distribution made Alf Ramsey one of the finest full-backs of the post-war era. The war ate into his career but at the age of 29 he began a run of 29 consecutive England appearances. As a right-back he was in a class of his own and after being transferred from Southampton to Tottenham Hotspur in May 1949 for a fee of £21,000 he missed only three games during the two successive seasons in which the Spurs carried off the Division II and Division I championships.

Following his appointment as manager of Ipswich Town in August 1955 he proved himself a shrewd soccer boss, steering that club from the Third Division to the Championship of the Football League. In May 1963 he took over as manager of the England team and his greatest triumph —winning the World Cup—followed three years later. Knighted January 1967. Born Dagenham, Essex.

Southampton 1946-49, 90 apprcs. (8 goals). Tottenham Hotspur 1949-55, 226 apprcs. (24 goals). England Internationals 32. Inter-League games 5. England "B" 1. League Champions 1950-51.

## RANGERS F.C.

Founded 1873. One of the original members of the Scottish League, 1890. Honours: Champions, Division I, 1890-91 (jointly with Dumbarton), 1898-9, 1899-1900, 1900-1901, 1901-2, 1910-11, 1911-12, 1912-13, 1917-18, 1919-20, 1920-21, 1922-3, 1923-4, 1924-5, 1926-7, 1927-8, 1928-9, 1929-30, 1930-31, 1932-3, 1933-4, 1934-5, 1936-7, 1938-9, 1946-7, 1948-9, 1949-50, 1952-3, 1955-6, 1956-7, 1958-9, 1960-61, 1962-3, 1963-4. Runners-up, 1892-3, 1895-6, 1897-8, 1904-5, 1913-14, 1915-16, 1918-19, 1921-2, 1931-2, 1935-6, 1947-8, 1950-1, 1951-2, 1957-8, 1961-2, 1965-6, 1966-7, 1967-8, 1968-9, 1969-70. Scottish Cup: Winners (19 times), 1894, 1897, 1898, 1903, 1928, 1930, 1932, 1934, 1935, 1936, 1948, 1949, 1950, 1953, 1960, 1962, 1963, 1964, 1966. Runners-up, 1877, 1899, 1904, 1905, 1921, 1922, 1929, 1969, 1971. Rangers were also finalists in 1908-9 when, after drawing with Celtic, the Cup was withheld because of a riot. European Cup Winners Cup: Winners, 1972. Runners-up, 1961, 1967. Scottish League Cup: Winners, 1947, 1949, 1961, 1962, 1964, 1965, 1971. Runners-up, 1946, 1952, 1958, 1966, 1967. Record attendance: 118,567 v. Celtic, Division I, Jan. 2, 1939. Address: Ibrox Stadium, Glasgow S.W.1 (Tel. 041-427 0159). Nickname: The Blues. Colours: Royal blue shirts, white shorts. Record League goal-scorer: S. English, 44 goals, Division I, 1931-2. Record victory: 14—2 v. Blairgowrie, Scottish Cup, 1st Round, Jan. 20, 1934. Record defeat: 7—1 v. Celtic, Scottish League Cup, Final, Oct. 19, 1957.

## READING F.C.

Founded 1871 and subsequently strengthened by amalgamation with The Hornets (1877) and Earley (1889). One of the original members of the Southern League in 1894, and of the Football League, Division III, 1920. Honours: Champions, Division III(S), 1925-6. Runners-up, 1931-2, 1934-5, 1948-9, 1951-2. Best in Division II, 14th, 1926-7. Record attendance: 33,042 v. Brentford, F.A. Cup, 5th Round, Feb. 19, 1927. Address: Elm Park, Norfolk Road, Reading RG3 2EF (Tel. 57878). Nickname: Biscuitmen. Colours: Blue and white hooped shirts, white shorts, white stockings with two blue rings. Record League goal-scorer: R. Blackman, 39 goals, Division III(S), 1951-2. Record victory: 10—2 v. Crystal Palace, Division III(S), Sept. 4, 1946. Record defeat: 18—0 v. Preston North End, F.A. Cup, 1st Round, 1893-4.

## RECEIPTS

See GATE RECEIPTS.

## RE-ELECTION

Originally it was decided that the bottom four clubs in the Football League should have to apply for re-election at the end of each season. To be precise the rule agreed upon was that the bottom four *in each class* should retire, but be eligible for re-election.

However, a second class, or second division, did not come into existence until 1892 and at the end of season 1892-3 the original rule was not adhered to and only the bottom four in Division II had to apply for re-election.

This system continued until 1896 when it was reduced to the bottom three clubs. In 1909 it became only the last two who had to retire and make a fresh application for membership.

When the Third Division was formed in 1920 the bottom two had to apply for re-election at the end of the first season, and thereafter, with the addition of a Northern Section, the bottom two in each section.

Since the formation of the Fourth Division in 1958 it is the bottom four clubs of this division that have to apply for re-election.

Going back only to the beginning of the Third Division these are the clubs that have had to apply:

Twelve times: Barrow.

Ten times: Hartlepool.

Nine times: Newport County.

Eight times: Southport.

Seven times: Exeter City, Halifax Town, Walsall.

Six times: Chester, Rochdale.

Five times: Accrington Stanley, Bradford, Crewe Alexandra, Darlington, Gillingham, Lincoln City, New Brighton, York City.

Four times: Norwich City.

Three times: Aldershot, Bradford City, Colchester United, Crystal Palace, Merthyr, Swindon Town, Workington.

Twice: Aberdare, Ashington, Bournemouth, Brentford, Gateshead, Millwall, Durham City, Grimsby Town, Nelson, Northampton Town, Oldham Athletic, Queen's Park Rangers, Rotherham United, Southend United, Stockport County, Tranmere Rovers, Watford.

Once: Brighton, Bristol Rovers, Cardiff City, Carlisle United, Charlton Athletic, Doncaster Rovers, Mansfield Town, Port Vale*, Shrewsbury Town, Torquay United, Wrexham.

Thames finished bottom of Division III(S) in 1931-2 but did not seek re-election.

## REFEREES AND LINESMEN

The first mention of a referee in any of the early rules of football (though not specifically soccer) is that found in those which governed the game as played at Cheltenham College in 1867.

For some time prior to this it had become the practice in most important games to appoint two umpires. This had generally been adopted by most of the public schools and one umpire was usually provided by each side. At Cheltenham, however, it was decided that "In every important match there shall be an umpire for each side (each captain to choose his own), and a referee, to be chosen by these umpires. Any point on which the umpires cannot agree shall be decided by the referee."

It should be pointed out, however, that the game which was played at Cheltenham at that time was certainly not soccer. It had been introduced into the college by young men from Rugby where it had been the practice to "run with the ball" since about 1823, and Cheltenham College then eventually adopted the Rugby Union rules.

The first official reference to a referee in Association Football did not appear until 1871 when Rule 15 of the new F.A. Challenge Cup Competition read as follows:

"The Committee shall appoint two umpires and a referee to act at each of the matches in the Final Ties. Neither the umpires nor the referee shall be members of either of the contending clubs and the decision of the umpires shall be final except in the case of the umpires disagreeing when an appeal shall be made to the referee, whose decision shall be final."

The wording of this rule shows just how much the increased competition was already beginning to change the attitude of the players. The days of the gentlemen players, who were proud of the manner in which rival teams generally conducted themselves, and settled any disputes, were beginning to fade. The time had come not only to specify the appointment of both umpires and referees but to insist upon these men being NEUTRAL.

Umpires were first mentioned in the actual laws of Association Football in 1874, but no mention of referees is made until 1880 when the following appeared:

"By mutual consent of the competing clubs in matches, a referee shall be appointed whose duty shall be to decide in all cases of dispute between umpires. He shall also keep a record of the game and act as time-

---

*Port Vale did not finish in bottom four but had been expelled from the League. See under FINES.

keeper, and in the event of ungentlemanly behaviour on the part of any of the contestants, the offender or offenders shall, in the presence of the umpires, be cautioned, and in the case of violent conduct, the referee shall have power to rule the offending player or players out of play, and order him or them off the ground, transmitting name or names to the committee of the Association under whose rules the game was played, and in whom shall be solely vested the right of accepting an apology."

The umpires were abolished in favour of linesmen in 1891 when the referee was moved from the touchline on to the field of play and empowered to give decisions without waiting for appeals.

The referee was now in complete control and soon after this the demand for their services increased so quickly that in Mar. 1893, a Referees' Association was formed.

At its annual meeting on June 4, 1928, the F.A. Council decided that referees should be classified as follows:

Class I. To consist of referees whose competency is guaranteed by their County Associations. Referees of experience recommended for F.A. Cup ties to be starred.

Class II. Other senior referees.

Class III. Junior referees.

Today this classification by the Football Association remains very much the same (there is a similar form of classification in Scotland), although only referees whose ages do not exceed 50 are eligible for classification by the F.A. under I or II.

The Football League draws up a list of referees every season. It normally includes about 80 names. The age limit for the Football League is 47 except in special cases where an extension is granted by the management committee.

The fee for referees originally fixed by the Football League in 1888 was 10s. 6d. per match. Fess for linesmen were fixed at 5s. in 1896. The more recent increases have been made as follows:

May 30, 1938. A uniform scale of payment for referees was instituted: 3gn. for any League game, linesmen to receive 1½gn.

From 1921 to 1938 the fee for referees was 3gn. for Division I and II matches, and 2gn. for Division III matches, linesmen 1½gn. for Division I and II, 1gn. for Division III.

In 1946 there was an increase to 4gn. per match for referees and 2gn. for linesmen and these fees have since been increased several times. The current rate is £12.50 per match for referees and £6.40 for linesmen.

In addition, these match officials are entitled to first class railway fare or 3p per mile if travelling by private car to and from

the match, and a meal allowance of from £1 to £4 according to travelling time. An official who cannot complete his return journey before midnight on the day of the match can also claim a further £1, or £6 if he has to stay overnight.

The Football League have also introduced Merit Awards paid out twice in a season according to the referee's position in the merit list based on average marks awarded them. The maximum payment is £50 per half season.

The scale of fees for referees and linesmen is £12.50 and £6.40 in all Rounds of the F.A. Cup Competition proper, prior to the Final. But in the Final the referee receives £15.75 and the linesmen £8.00. In addition to these fees, the officials are entitled to travelling expenses, and are also presented with a gold medal each.

Fees for referees and linesmen in international matches are now £18 and £9 each respectively.

## Two Referees

The proposal that all games should be controlled by two referees has been brought up from time to time during the past 30 years. The suggestion was given lengthy consideration for the first time in 1935 when the proposal was put to the Annual Meeting of the Football League. It was rejected by 31 votes to 18.

The prime mover of the proposal was the Everton club, and their chairman, Mr. W. C. Cuff, made strong pleas for its introduction.

The dual control plan was tried out in an international trial game, England v. The Rest, at West Bromwich, Mar. 27, 1935, as well as at the game between a Football League XI and West Bromwich Albion on May 8, 1935.

The proposal came forward again in 1937 when it was put to the A.G.M. of the Football Association.

It was suggested that the system be given a trial in practice matches before the opening of the new season and then in certain League games. The proposal was defeated.

## Whistle

It is generally believed that the first time a whistle was used by a referee was in a game between Nottingham Forest and Sheffield Norfolk at Nottingham in 1878.

## Sent Off

The famous occasion on which the referee was "sent off" by a team captain occurred in the annual Sheffield v. Glasgow Inter-City match, Sept. 22, 1930, at Hampden Park, Glasgow. Sheffield were playing in white shirts and black shorts. The referee,

Mr. J. Thomson of Burnbank, wore a white shirt without a jacket. Captaining Sheffield was inside-right, J. Seed. As soon as he found that he was passing the ball to the referee in error, he asked Mr. Thomson to stop the game and put on a jacket. Mr. Thomson obliged.

### F.A. Cup
The referee of the F.A. Cup Semi-final game between Huddersfield Town and Sheffield Wednesday, Mar. 22, 1930, blew for time as a shot from Sheffield Wednesday's centre-forward, J. Allen, was entering the net. The ball had not crossed the line so no goal was awarded. Huddersfield won 2—1.

The youngest referee ever to control an F.A. Cup Final was H. Bamlett of Gateshead. Born Mar. 1, 1882, he was 32 when he took charge of the Final tie between Burnley and Liverpool at the Crystal Palace, 1914.

### Internationals
At the International Board meeting in June 1950, it was decided that referees for international matches must be from a neutral country, unless otherwise agreed by the countries concerned.

## REGISTRATION OF PLAYERS
See also TRANSFERS.

A player must be seventeen years of age before he can be registered as a professional with any club under the jurisdiction of the Football Association or the Scottish F.A.

However, under F.A. rules, youths between the ages of 16 and 17 may be registered as apprentice professionals, each Football League club being limited to 15, of these. As soon as these apprentice professionals have passed their 17th birthday they may register as full professionals. They have until their 18th birthday to decide whether to make this move or, if they wish, they can decide to revert to amateur status.

In Scotland players under the statutory school leaving age (16) may be registered for a club on what is known as "Provisional Form", but such registration does not become operative until the player has reached the statutory school leaving age.

The minimum age at which Football League clubs are permitted to register schoolboys is 14 on the 1st September in any season.

However, this is for the purpose of training and coaching only, and no boy under the age of 16 on 1st September in any season is permitted to play for the club in the League.

Football League clubs are each limited to a maximum of 30 of these schoolboy registrations at any one time.

For many years the form of contract which entitled a club to retain a player indefinitely, providing they were prepared to pay him a certain minimum as laid down by the Football Association, was the main bone of contention when the players threatened to strike on Jan. 21, 1961. The strike was averted and a number of alterations in players' contracts were agreed during protracted discussions which extended over a period of six months and about 17 meetings between Football League representatives and leaders of the Professional Footballer's Association.

While retaining the same broad principles the F.A. originally accommodated the new agreement between the players and the Football League by inserting in their rules the words "subject to the provisions of the competition in which they compete". However, they have since considerably amended their rules.

The Football League would not agree to abandon their right to retain players after the individual registrations expired but they did make certain concessions.

At the present time the rules are such that if a player refuses to re-sign by 30th June (the date when contracts normally expire) then a dispute is deemed to exist between player and club, and either may appeal to the Management Committee who shall adjudicate by not later than 31st July.

If the player has still not re-signed by 31st August then an Independent Tribunal shall determine the dispute not later than 30th September.

Until such time as the dispute is settled the player remains in the employment of his club on the terms of the existing contract.

Another aspect of players' contracts which was discussed in 1961 concerned the maximum period of time for which a player could sign for a club.

For many years it had been the practice to allow clubs to register professionals for one whole season, or during the season for the remainder of that season. If a player joined a club during the last three months of a particular season then he could be registered for the remainder of the current season and the whole of the next.

In 1961 this was amended so that a player in the Football League could be signed for any period up to two years. But even this rule has since been abolished so that now there is no limit to length of contract.

No player can play for his club until his registration has been received and acknowledged at both the Football League and Football Association headquarters. One often hears of last minute registrations, even of a player signing in the morning and playing for his club the same afternoon. This is no longer possible in the Football League where to be eligible for a match the new player's forms must be posted at least 48 hours before that match is due to end, but the F.A. provide special facilities for speedy registrations.

The forms and a copy of the agreement entered into between the player and the club (no registration is accepted without this agreement), is sent by registered post (or recorded delivery) to the F.A., and, at the same time, a telegram is despatched, stating that these forms have been duly signed and posted. Providing the registration is otherwise acceptable, the club may consider the player eligible to play for them from the time such telegram is received at Paddington District Post Office.

Non-British born players cannot be registered as professionals by the F.A. unless they have resided here for at least two years.

Should a professional player wish to continue to play without remuneration (there is no such thing as reverting to amateur status; in the eyes of the Football Association—once a professional always a professional), he has to make application to the F.A., and this costs him 50p. He may then be granted a Permit.*

The Permit entitles him to play for only one club and he may not move to another club during the same season. If he continues with the same club no further Permit is necessary, but a new Permit must be obtained should he move to another club at the end of the season. In any case no Permit is given after Jan. 31 in any season, and never more than one Permit to a player in a single season. A professional playing as an "amateur" under such conditions is termed as "playing under licence".

In 1960 the Football League decided to permit clubs to place amateurs on their retained list at the end of each season.

### F.A. Cup
In all Rounds before the Third Round of the Qualifying competition only professionals who have been registered with their clubs for at least 48 hours before the Cup Tie are eligible to play. In the remaining Rounds the qualifying period is 14 days.

### Scottish Cup
The qualifying period for professionals in the Scottish Cup is 14 days unless he was last registered for, or a playing member of, a club in membership of an affiliated national association or if his customary position is goalkeeper. In the case of the latter he can, of course, only play in goal for his new club if signed within 14 days of the Cup tie.

### RELEGATION
The keenest relegation struggle in the history of the Football League was in Division I in 1927-8. Of the last nine clubs, seven had 39 points, one had 38, and one 37. Tottenham Hotspur and Middlesbrough were relegated.

The only clubs to be relegated twice in successive seasons are Bradford, Brighton, Doncaster Rovers, Fulham, Lincoln City, Northampton Town and Notts County.

Bradford dropped from Division I to Division III in seasons 1920-21 and 1921-2. They missed promotion the following season when they finished runners-up to Nelson.

Fulham dropped from Division I to Division III in seasons 1967-8 and 1968-9.

Huddersfield Town dropped from Division I to Division III in seasons 1971-2 and 1972-3.

Brighton went down from Division II to Division IV in seasons 1961-2 and 1962-3.

Doncaster Rovers and Notts County dropped from Division II to Division IV together in seasons 1957-8 and 1958-9.

Lincoln City dropped from Division II to IV in seasons 1960-61 and 1961-2, while Northampton went down from Division I to III in seasons 1965-6 and 1966-7.

Port Vale also slipped from Division II to Division IV in two seasons but their case is a little different. They were relegated to Division III(S) in 1957 and when, in the following year, the two sections of the Third Division were re-arranged into a new Third and Fourth Division, Port Vale dropped into the lower Division because they were below the halfway mark in the Southern Section. The lower half of each Third Division section made up the new Fourth Division.

The Football League ordered that Peterborough United be relegated from Division III at the end of 1967-8 as punishment for offering players illegal payments.

See also PROMOTION.

### REPUBLIC OF IRELAND
See EIRE.

### RESIGNED
In 1929 Bathgate and Arthurlie were forced to resign from the Scottish League, Division II, through lack of funds.

Wigan Borough resigned from Division III(N) of the Football League on Oct. 26, 1931. The club's record for the season was

---

*Apprentice professionals up to the age of 18 are exempt from this rule.

cancelled.

Leeds City were wound up for alleged irregular practices in Oct. 1919. The remainder of their season's fixtures was taken on by Port Vale.

Stoke resigned from Division II on June 17, 1908 and were replaced by Tottenham Hotspur. Stoke was reformed almost immediately but failed to regain admission to the Football League until 1919.

Other clubs that have resigned from the Football League are Accrington Stanley 1893 and 1962; Glossop North End 1919; New Brighton 1901; and Stalybridge Celtic 1923.

Please note that the above does not include clubs who dropped out of the Football League when they failed to gain re-election.

Thames finished bottom of the Third Division (S) in 1932 and although they did not actually resign, the fact that they did not apply for re-election amounted to the same thing.

## RIVERA, Gianni (1943-    )

Born Alessandria, Italy, and made debut with his home-town club at the age of 15. Delighted the fans as a talented inside-forward who, though so lightly built, packed a powerful shot. A.C. Milan paid something like £73,000 to obtain his transfer in 1960, and his delicate touch and incredible ball-control has made him one of Italy's most entertaining footballers. European Footballer of the Year 1969.

Alessandria 1958-60. A.C. Milan 1960- Italian internationals 53. Italian League champions 1962, 1968. Italian Cup winners 1967. European Cup winners 1963, 1969, 1973. World Club Cup winners 1969. World Cup runners-up 1970.

## ROBERTS, Charles (1883-1939)

When this player was at his peak it was said that he was the most complete footballer ever to have filled the centre-half berth. One may wonder, therefore, why it was that he made only three appearances for England? The reason is not hard to find for Roberts was chairman of the newly formed Players' Union at a time when their affiliation to the Federation of Trade Unions was causing the F.A. and the Football League much heartache.

Charles Roberts was an outspoken personality who did not see eye to eye with the authorities but his work on the field could not be faulted. He is considered to have been among the first players to add real skill and craft to the position of centre-half. Manchester United paid Grimsby Town £400 for his transfer. Born near Darlington.

Grimsby Town 1903-04, 31 apprcs. (4 goals). Manchester United 1904-13, 271 apprcs. (24 goals). Oldham Athletic 1913-15, 68 apprcs. (4 goals). England Internationals 3. Inter-League games 9. League Champions 1907-08, 1910-11. F.A. Cup winners 1909.

## ROBERTS, Herbert (1905-1944)

This player's contribution to Arsenal's phenomenal success in the 1930s is inclined to be overlooked by some historians, but he was the king-pin of a defence that conceded fewer goals than any other First Division side in four out of five successive seasons.

Originally a right-half he was switched into the middle by Herbert Chapman to act as a "stopper." He did this job perfectly and while he was not the first "Policeman" centre-half he was one of the best, being unbeatable in the air. Born Oswestry.

Arsenal 1926-38, 297 apprcs. (4 goals). 1 England international. League Champions 1930-31, 1932-3, 1933-4, 1934-5, F.A. Cup (runners-up 1932, winners 1936).

## ROCHDALE F.C.

Founded 1900 as Rochdale Town. Became limited company as Rochdale A.F.C. in 1910. One of the original members of Division III(N) in 1921. Honours: Runners-up, Division III(N), 1923-4, 1926-7. League Cup: Runners-up, 1962. Record attendance: 24,231 v. Notts County, F.A. Cup, 2nd Round, Dec. 10, 1949. Address: Willbutts Ground, Spotland, Rochdale OL11 5DS (Tel. 44648). Nickname: The Dale. Colours: Blue shirts, white shorts, white stockings with two blue calf bands. Record League goal-scorer: A. J. Whitehurst, 44 goals, Division III(N), 1926-7. Record victory: 8—1 v. Chesterfield, Division III(N), Dec. 18, 1926. Record defeat: 8—0 v. Wrexham, Division III(N), Dec. 28, 1929.

## ROOSE, Dr. Leigh Richmond

An eccentric character who was one of the best known amateurs in the game before World War I. A great practical joker he was full of surprises. When things were quiet at his end this brilliant goalkeeper generally seated himself at the base of an upright. He always wore the same shirt under his jersey and it was said that he refused to have it washed in case it would change his luck. He was the Welsh goalkeeper when they won the International Championship for the first time in 1906-07. Played for the Druids, Aberystwyth and the London Welsh before making Football League debut with Stoke in 1901. He was, for many years, a medical science lecturer at a London hospital.

171

Stoke 1901-04, 80 apprcs. Everton 1904-05, 18 appcs. Stoke 1905-07, 68 apprcs. Sunderland 1907-11, 92 apprcs. Huddersfield 1911, 5 apprcs. Aston Villa 1911-12, 10 apprcs. Woolwich Arsenal 1912, 13 apprcs. Welsh internationals 24.

## ROSS, Nicholas John (1863-1894)

This Scot played in the first Football League representative side—that which drew 1—1 with the Football Alliance at Sheffield in April 1891. He joined Preston from Hearts in July 1883, playing first in the attack but later changing to full-back, and although he was not a member of Preston's "double" winning side of 1888-89, (he spent that one season with Everton) he helped the Deepdale club carry off the League title the following season. A slater by trade he was in the vanguard of Scottish footballers who decided to try their luck as professionals in England. In "Association Football (1899)" N. L. Jackson described him as 'one of the best footballers of any time.' Ross died of consumption when only 31.

Preston North End 1883-88, 89-94, 95 apprcs. Everton 1888-89, 19 apprcs. League Champions 1889-90. F.A. Cup runners-up 1887-8.

## ROTHERHAM UNITED F.C.

Founded as Thornhill United in 1884. Became Rotherham County, 1905. Amalgamated with Rotherham Town, with the present title of Rotherham United, 1925. Elected to Football League, Division II, 1893. Dropped out, 1896; re-elected to Division II, 1919 Honours: Champions, Division III(N), 1950-51. Runners-up, 1946-7, 1947-8, 1948-9. Best in Division II, 3rd, 1954-5. League Cup: Runners-up, 1961. Record attendance: 25,000 v. Sheffield Wednesday, Division II, Jan. 26, 1952, and v. Sheffield United, Division II, Dec. 13, 1952. Address: Millmoor Ground, Rotherham S60 1HR (Tel. 2434). Nickname: Merry Millers. Colours: Red shirts with white collar and sleeves, white shorts, red stockings. Record League goal-scorer: W. Ardron, 38 goals, Division III(N), 1946-7. Record victory: 8—0 v. Oldham Athletic, Division III(N), May 26, 1947. Record defeat: 15-0 v. Notts County, F.A. Cup, 1st Round, Oct. 24, 1885.

## ROYALTY AND FOOTBALL

It is impossible to trace the history of soccer as opposed to rugby much before the middle of the 19th century for there was then only one game—football. Therefore, most of the following references may be included in the history of both codes.

*Edward II*
April 13, 1314. Issued proclamation banning the playing of football.
*Edward III*
June 12, 1349. Royal proclamation issued deploring the falling off in the popularity of archery, and commanding that all able-bodied men should pass their leisure time with bows and arrows to ensure an adequate supply of archers in the event of war.

So that men would be compelled to adopt this pastime they were prevented, under penalty of imprisonment, from "attending to throwing stones, skittles, quoits, fives, football or hockey, or wrestling, or cock-fighting or other foolish games like these which are of no use."
*Richard III*
Passed a statute in 1389 forbidding "all playing at tennise, football, and other games called corts, dice, casting of the stones, railes, and other such importune games."
*James II of Scotland*
Issued a proclamation in 1457: "footballe and golfe be utterly cryed down and not be used."
*James IV of Scotland*
Proclaimed in 1491 that nowhere in the realm "ther be used futeball, golfe, or other sik unprofitable sports."
*Elizabeth I*
1572 proclamation: "No foteballe play to be used or suffered within the City of London."
*Charles II*
He is considered to have been the first monarch to show favour towards the game of football. He patronised a game between his servants and the servants of the Duke of Albemarle in 1681.
*Edward VII*
While Prince of Wales he became the Patron of the F.A. in 1892. He had first patronised the game in Mar. 1886 when he visited Kennington Oval for a charity Festival which included a soccer match between the Gentlemen and Players.
*George V*
The first reigning monarch to attend a Football League match outside of London. On Mar. 27, 1920, he saw the Manchester City v. Liverpool, Division I, game at Hyde Road.

King George V was also the first reigning monarch to attend an F.A. Cup Final. On April 25, 1914, he watched the Burnley v. Liverpool Final at the Crystal Palace. Queen Mary first attended the Cup Final in 1928.

## RUGBY

The split which established the separate

games of Association and Rugby Football is marked by the breaking away of the Blackheath Club from any agreement with the newly formed Football Association in Dec. 1863.

Blackheath objected to the banning of running with the ball and 'hacking' in the Association rules (hacking is the practice of using the toe either to kick an opponent's shins or to trip him up). They insisted that "hacking was the true football game". Despite the fact that the break was made over this question of 'hacking' the Rugby, Union immediately banned 'hacking' on its formation eight years later.

See also ORIGIN OF THE GAME.

The following have gained international caps both at soccer and rugby:

*England*

R. H. Birkett (Clapham Rovers). Soccer: v. Scotland 1879. Rugby: v. Scotland 1871, 1875 and 1876; v. Ireland 1877.

J. W. Sutcliffe (Heckmondwike and Bolton Wanderers). Soccer: v. Scotland 1895 and 1901; v. Wales 1893 and 1903; v. Ireland 1895. Rugby: v. Maoris 1889.

C. P. Wilson (Hendon and Cambridge University), Soccer: v. Scotland and Wales 1884. Rugby: v. Wales 1881.

*Scotland*

H. W. Renny-Tailyour (Royal Engineers). Soccer: v. England 1873. Rugby: v. England 1872.

*Ireland and Eire*

Dr. K. O'Flanagan (London Irish and Arsenal). Soccer: (Eire) v. England, Portugal and Spain 1947. Also for Ireland (Belfast) v. Scotland and Wales. Victory Internationals 1946. Rugby: (Ireland) v. Australia 1948.

M. O'Flanagan (Bohemians and Lands-downe). Soccer: (Eire) v. England 1947. Rugby: (Ireland) v. Scotland 1948.

E. Hammett (Treharris Newport and Blackheath) played as an amateur international for Wales at Association Football (v. England 1912) and a Rugby Union international for England v. Scotland 1920 and 1921; v. Ireland 1921; v. Wales 1920, 1921 and 1922; v. France 1920 and 1921.

D. Davies of Bolton Wanderers was capped at Association Football for Wales and also got his cap in Rugby League Football.

## RUMANIA

Football was introduced to Rumania by British engineers working at the oilfields and the oldest club in that country was formed at Ploesti in 1905.

A National Championship competition was begun in 1900 but progress was interrupted by the First World War and other political upheavals which followed and the game was not established on a proper footing until the return from exile of King Carol in 1930.

This monarch was a real soccer enthusiast and he backed the newly formed Football Association to the hilt. This Association had only been in existence since Feb. 1930 or about four months before Carol's return to his country.

Rumania appeared in the World Cup Finals in 1930, 1934, 1938 and 1970. Their only victories in any of these finals was in 1930 when they defeated Peru 3—1, and in 1970—2—1 v. Czechoslovakia.

The address of the governing body: Federatia Romina de Fotbal, Vasile Conta 16, Bucharest. Colours: Yellow shirts, blue shorts, red stockings.

Results of international matches:

| | | |
|---|---|---|
| May 24, 1939 | Rumania 0, England 2; | Bucharest |
| Nov. 6, 1968 | Rumania 0, England 0; | Bucharest |
| Jan. 15, 1969 | England 1, Rumania 1; | Wembley |
| June 2, 1970* | England 1, Rumania 0; | Guadalajara |
| Nov. 11, 1970† | Wales 0, Rumania 0; | Cardiff |
| Nov. 24, 1971† | Rumania 2, Wales 0; | Bucharest |

\* World Cup
† Nations Cup

## RUSSIA

The British introduced the Russians to football as long ago as 1887 but nearly 60 years had elapsed before the British at home were awakened to the fact that this huge country had quietly developed into a leading soccer nation.

That rude awakening came in Nov. 1945 with the visit of their League champions, Moscow Dynamo.

Interest in this Russian club had reached fever pitch by the time of their first game, with Chelsea at Stamford Bridge, and although it was played in mid-week well over 80,000 spectators crammed the stadium. The result was a draw, 3—3.

The Russians played three more games before returning home undefeated. They beat Cardiff City 10—1, Arsenal 4—3 (in a fog at Tottenham), and drew 2—2 with

173

Rangers at Ibrox Park.

A Russian referee controlled the Arsenal game. He insisted on the match being played to a finish despite the fog which made it impossible to see more than a few yards across the field long before the final whistle was sounded.

The outstanding feature of the Russians' play in all these games was the precision of their forwards' passing. This allied to their strong shooting made them the most accomplished foreign team seen in England up to that time.

Following the visit of the Moscow Dynamo to Britain in 1945 the Russians again withdrew behind their Iron Curtain for a long spell, but their domestic football developed rapidly and when they re-appeared in the international sphere in 1952 they soon established themselves among the leaders of world soccer, winning the Olympic tournament of 1956 and the European Nations Cup in 1960.

The first football club to be established in Russia was Morozowstky in 1887, a team of workers from a cotton mill run by the Char-nock brothers from England.

A League was formed in Moscow as early as 1903 and representative matches between the Muscovites and the other principal soccer centre, St. Petersburg, began in 1908.

The first British team to visit Russia was the Wanderers; not the famous old 19th century side, but a combined Oxford and Cambridge team. They won their three games with an aggregate score of 31—0. This was in 1911.

The First World War and the Russian Revolution put a stop to any further development for a number of years, and indeed, little was seen of the Russian footballers in the international field between the two World Wars. Their matches with other countries were limited to less than a dozen during the period 1920-45 and there is no record of them ever defeating any foreign opposition in those games.

The address of the governing body: U.S.S.R. Football Federation, 4 Skatertny Pereulok, Moscow 69. Colours: Red shirts, white shorts, red stockings.

Results of international matches:

| May 18, 1958 | Russia 1, England 1; Moscow |
| June 8, 1958* | England 2, Russia 2; Sweden |
| June 17, 1958* | England 0, Russia 1; Sweden |
| Oct. 22, 1958 | England 5, Russia 0; Wembley |
| May 30, 1965* | Russia 2, Wales 1; Moscow |
| Oct. 27, 1965* | Wales 2, Russia 1; Cardiff |
| May 10, 1967 | Scotland 0, Russia 2; Hampden Park |
| Dec. 6, 1967 | England 2, Russia 2; Wembley |
| June 8, 1968† | England 2, Russia 0; Rome |
| Sept. 10, 1969* | Ireland 0, Russia 0; Belfast |
| Oct. 22, 1969* | Russia 2, Ireland 0; Moscow |
| June 14, 1971 | Russia 1, Scotland 0; Moscow |
| Sept. 22, 1971‡ | Russia 1, Ireland 0; Moscow |
| Oct. 13, 1971‡ | Ireland 1, Russia 1; Belfast |
| Oct. 18, 1972* | Eire 1, Russia 2; Dublin |
| May 13, 1973* | Russia, 1, Eire 0; Moscow |
| June 10, 1973 | Russia 1, England 2; Moscow |

* World Cup
† Nations Cup
‡ European Championship

## ST. JOHNSTONE F.C.
Founded 1884. Joined Scottish League, Division II, 1911. Honours: Champions, Division II, 1923-4, 1959-60, 1962-3. Runners-up, 1931-2. Best in Division I, 5th, 1934-5. Scottish League Cup: Finalists, 1970. Record attendance: 29,972 v. Dundee, Scottish Cup, 2nd Round, Feb. 10, 1952. Address: Muirton Park, Perth (Tel. 0738 26961). Colours: Royal blue shirts, white shorts. Record League goal-scorer: J. Benson, 36 goals, Division II, 1931-2. Record victory: 8—1 v. Partick Thistle (A), Scottish League Cup, Aug. 16, 1969. Record defeat: 10—1 v. Third Lanark (H), Scottish Cup, 1st. Round, Jan. 24, 1903.

## ST. MIRREN F.C.
Founded 1876 by members of a rugby club. One of the original members of the Scottish League, 1890. Best in Division I, 3rd, 1892-3. Champions, Division II. 1967-8. Runners-up, 1935-6. Scottish Cup: Winners, 1926, 1959. Runners-up, 1908, 1934, 1962. Scottish League Cup: Finalists, 1956. Record attendance: 47,428 v. Celtic, Scottish Cup, 4th Round, Mar. 7, 1925. Address: St. Mirren Park, Love Street, Paisley (Tel. 041-889 2558). Nickname: Saints. Colours: Black with white stripes, black shorts. Record goal-scorer in Division I: D. Walker, 45 goals, 1921-2. Record victory: 15—0 v. Glasgow United, Scottish Cup, 1st Round, Jan. 30, 1960. Record defeat: 9—2 v. Dundee, Division I, Feb. 29, 1964.

## SANTOS, Djalma (1929—    )
Born São Paulo, this powerful negro enjoyed a remarkably long career, playing well over 1,200 games in first-class football. Recognized as the finest right-back ever produced in South America he helped Brazil win the World Cup in 1958 and 1962.

Portuguesa de Desportes 1947-58. Palmeiras 1958-68. Atletico Paranaense 1968-69. 1 Brazilian internationals. Sao Paulo League Champions 1963, 1966. Brazilian Cup winners 1965, 1967. Rest of World v. England 1963.

## SCOTLAND
While it is true that soccer was first popularised in England it was the Scots who first polished up the game and introduced a really high degree of skill.

The oldest club in Scotland is Queen's Park, formed by members of the Glasgow Y.M.C.A. in July 1867, and it is to this club that Scotland owes most for the speedy development of the game in its earliest days north of the Border.

Queen's Park were first to practise the passing game in the 1870s and 1880s and this quickly proved itself to be much superior to the individual style of dribbling then favoured by the Sassenachs.

Scotland's superior style of play brought them six wins to England's two, with two games drawn, in the first 10 meetings, and this not only caused the England selectors great concern but made the more enterprising English clubs turn to Scotland for players to strengthen their sides. It is quite likely that Scots and not Englishmen were the first professional soccer players in the history of the game. (See PROFESSIONALISM).

It was not until these pioneering Scots had spread the gospel of the passing game among the clubs south of the Border, and it had been taken up by such English soccer dignitaries as N. L. Jackson who formed the Corinthians, that England began to hold their own with Scotland in their international matches. Scotland won more than half of their first 20 meetings (to 1891) but the score in the next 20 (to 1911) was 8—6 to England.

There is no doubt that Scottish football as a whole has suffered through the continuous loss of many of their best players to clubs south of the Border, but they have also been hampered by a shortage of really big clubs in their own country. The great traditions of the Scottish game are wrapped up in such fine clubs as Rangers, Celtic, and Hearts, (Queen's Park's reluctance to turn professional put them out of the running nearly 50 years ago) but aside from these and a handful of others the League competition has been forced to include a large number of tail-enders.

Scotland has appeared in the final rounds of only two of the World Cup competitions, but their record has been a dismal one. The two years were 1954 and 1958 but they failed to win any of their five games, their only point being secured from a 1—1 draw with Yugoslavia in 1958. A sad state of affairs for a country that may justly claim to have laid the foundations of the skilful passing game we know today.

References to Scottish football are made

in various sections throughout this book. Special sections devoted to football in Scotland are: SCOTTISH ASSOCIATION CUP, SCOTTISH FOOTBALL ASSOCIATION, SCOTTISH FOOTBALL (GENERAL), SCOTTISH LEAGUE, INTERNATIONALS (SCOTLAND).

### SCOTT, Elisha (1893-1959)

This quiet mannered Irishman from Belfast served Liverpool for 22 years, and for most of that time was rated one of the best goalkeepers in the world. He had a peculiar jumpy action and was always on his toes in the goalmouth but he was not showy. Top scorer "Dixie" Dean, one of Scott's contemporaries, rated the Irishman the finest goalkeeper he ever played against. Scott was 42 years of age when he made his last international appearance in 1936. He went to Belfast Celtic as player-manager in 1934.

Liverpool 1912-34, 429 apprcs. Irish Internationals 31. Inter-League games (Irish League) 2. League Champions 1921-2, 1922-3.

### SCOTTISH ASSOCIATION CUP

The Scottish Cup competition came into being at the same time as the Scottish Football Association in 1873. The original meeting called by the Queen's Park club was, in fact, called primarily to organise a Cup competition on similar lines to that which had already begun in England. The meeting was held on Mar. 13, 1873, and the seven clubs represented decided not only to have a Cup competition but also to form "The Scottish Football Association". The new Association bought a trophy and 12 medals for the winners at a cost of £56.

Sixteen clubs took part in the first season's competition which was won by Queen's Park. They also won the tournament in its second and third seasons. No club has yet succeeded in winning the trophy more than three times in succession although the treble has been achieved six times. Queen's Park won the cup in 1874, 1875 and 1876, and in 1880, 1881 and 1882.Vale of Leven won it in 1877, 1878, 1879. On the last occasion they were awarded the trophy when Rangers failed to turn up for a Final replay. Rangers are the other club that has completed the treble. They

were winners in 1934, 1935 and 1936; 1948, 1949, 1950; and in 1962, 1963, 1964.

**Appearances**
For men who have won both Scottish Cup and F.A. Cup medals see CUP MEDALS.

Most appearances in a Scottish Cup winning side were made by J. McMenemy: six with Celtic, 1904-14, and one with Partick Thistle, 1921; and R. McPhail, one with Airdrieonians, 1924, and six with Rangers, 1928-36.

Although he only appeared in two Scottish Cup games during seasons 1947-8 and 1948-9, W. Williamson, centre-forward or inside-forward, gained two Cup winners' medals. The two matches were both Cup Finals with Rangers.

**Attendances**
See separate section.

**Final**
In 1879 Vale of Leven were awarded the Cup when Rangers failed to turn up for the Final replay. The first game was drawn 1—1, but Rangers had a goal disallowed for offside. They appealed against the referee's decision, claiming they had won, but the Scottish F.A. decided against them. In protest at this decision, Rangers refused to take part in a replay.

Oddly enough, Vale of Leven were concerned in a similar affair in 1884 when they did not turn up for the Cup Final with Queen's Park who were accordingly awarded the trophy.

**In England**
Several Scottish Cup ties have been played in England on the Berwick Rangers' ground, Northumberland.

**Receipts**
See separate section—GATE RECEIPTS.

**Replays**
In season 1908-9, Broxburn and Beith met five times in a 1st Round tie. The last three games were played on three consecutive days. Beith finally emerged victorious on a Friday by 4 goals to 2. On the following day, Beith met St. Mirren, their fourth game on successive days.

### Results of Finals

| 1874 | Queen's Park | bt. | Clydesdale | 2–0 |
| 1875 | Queen's Park | bt. | Renton | 3–0 |
| 1876 | Queen's Park | bt. | Third Larnark | 2–0 |
| | (after draw 1—1) | | | |
| 1877 | Vale of Leven | bt. | Rangers | 3–2 |
| | (after draws 0–0 and 1–1) | | | |
| 1878 | Vale of Leven | bt. | Third Lanark | 1–0 |

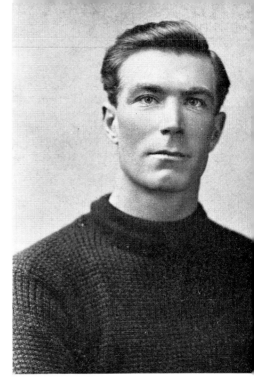

MEREDITH, BILLY. Playing for Manchester United against Queens Park Rangers, 1908. (*Photo*: Radio Times Hulton Picture Library) (*right*) PYM, DICK. This is the famous Bolton Wanderers goalkeeper who won three F.A. Cup medals and never conceded a goal at Wembley. He was Bolton's last line of defence when they won the trophy in 1923, 1926 and 1929.

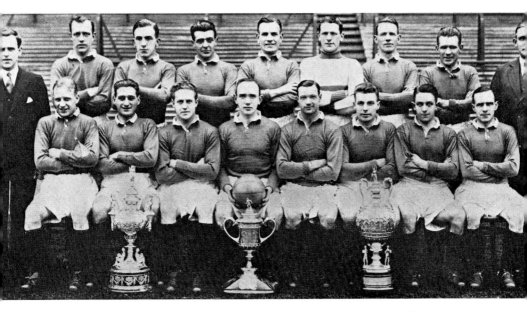

RANGERS F.C. This is the 1929-30 team that swept the board in Scotland by winning the League and Cup as well as the Glasgow Cup and Glasgow Charity Cup. Back row, Kerr (trainer), Meiklejohn, Marshall, Archibald, Fleming, Hamilton, Buchanan, Craig, W. Struth (manager); front row, Brown, Gray, McDonald, Muirhead, McPhail, Hamilton, Nicholson, Morton. (*Photo: The Glasgow Herald*).

SEELER, UWE. The West German goalscoring ace tries a flying header against
Italy in the 1962 World Cup tournament. (*Photo*: Planet News).

THIRD DIVISION. Clubs from this Division win at Wembley. (*opposite bottom*) Queen's Park Rangers shooting the first goal of their League Cup win against West Bromwich Albion in 1967. (*above*) Gould scores for Arsenal in the League Cup Final of 1969, but Swindon Town were the winners. (*Photos*: United Press International and Central Press Photos).

TRANSFERS. These players were transferred for record fees: Pietro Anastasi (*below left*) and David Nish (*below right*). (*Photos*: United Press International and Provincial Press Agency).

WEMBLEY. The first Cup Final at Wembley Stadium, 1923, when Bolton Wanderers defeated West Ham 2-0. The start was delayed for forty minutes when the crowd swarmed on to the pitch (*above*). Meanwhile the players waited (*below*) for police to make play possible. At least 150,000 saw the game. (*Photos*: The Topical Press Agency and Radio Times Hulton Picture Library).

WOLVERHAMPTON WANDERERS F.C. There were plenty of stars in the Wolves League Championship-winning team of 1953-54. Back row, Short, Slater, Flowers, Williams, Swinbourne, Pritchard; front row, Hancocks, Broadbent, Wright, Wilshaw, Mullen. (*Photo:* Provincial Press Agency)

WORLD CUP. After proving themselves to be the outstanding side in the 1954 World Cup the Hungarians were surprisingly beaten by West Germany in the Final, and this is the goal that clinched it. Rahn (20) beats the diving Grosics. (*Photo*: United Press International).

WORLD CUP. England's third goal in their World Cup Final victory over West Germany at Wembley, 1966. (*Photo*: Bippa).

WORLD CUP. The vital Brazilian goal in the match with England, 1970. Scorer Jairzinho watches the ball enter the net. Martin Peters jumps over Gordon Banks, the England goalkeeper. (*Photo:* United Press International)

WORLD CUP. Pele heads the ball past Burnich to score the first goal in Brazil's victory over Italy in the Final at Mexico City, 1970. (*Photo:* Associated Press)

ZAMORA. The great Spanish goalkeeper seen coming under pressure from Dixie Dean during the England v. Spain game at Highbury in 1931. (*Photo:* Radio Times Hulton Picture Library)

| 1879 | Vale of Leven awarded Cup after drawn game 1–1 and Rangers declined to replay. | | | |
|---|---|---|---|---|
| 1880 | Queen's Park | bt. | Thornliebank | 3–0 |
| 1881 | Queen's Park | bt. | Dumbarton | 3–1 |
| | (after protested game 2–1 for Queen's Park) | | | |
| 1882 | Queen's Park | bt. | Dumbarton | 4–1 |
| | (after draw 2–2) | | | |
| 1883 | Dumbarton | bt. | Vale of Leven | 2–1 |
| | (after draw 2–2) | | | |
| 1884 | Queen's Park awarded Cup. Vale of Leven failing to appear. | | | |
| 1885 | Renton | bt. | Vale of Leven | 3–1 |
| | (after draw 0–0) | | | |
| 1886 | Queen's Park | bt. | Renton | 3–1 |
| 1887 | Hibernian | bt. | Dumbarton | 2–1 |
| 1888 | Renton | bt. | Cambuslang | 6–1 |
| 1889 | Third Lanark | bt. | Celtic | 2–1 |
| | (after protested game 3–0 in favour of Third Lanark) | | | |
| 1890 | Queen's Park | bt. | Vale of Leven | 2–1 |
| | (after draw 1–1) | | | |
| 1891 | Heart of Midlothian | bt. | Dumbarton | 1–0 |
| 1892 | Celtic | bt. | Queen's Park | 5–1 |
| | (after protested game 1–0 for Celtic) | | | |
| 1893 | Queen's Park | bt. | Celtic | 2–1 |
| 1894 | Rangers | bt. | Celtic | 3–1 |
| 1895 | St. Bernards | bt. | Renton | 2–1 |
| 1896 | Heart of Midlothian | bt. | Hibernian | 3–1 |
| 1897 | Rangers | bt. | Dumbarton | 5–1 |
| 1898 | Rangers | bt. | Kilmarnock | 2–0 |
| 1899 | Celtic | bt. | Rangers | 2–0 |
| 1900 | Celtic | bt. | Queen's Park | 4–3 |
| 1901 | Heart of Midlothian | bt. | Celtic | 4–3 |
| 1902 | Hibernian | bt. | Celtic | 1–0 |
| 1903 | Rangers | bt. | Heart of Midlothian | 2–0 |
| | (after draws 1–1 and 0–0) | | | |
| 1904 | Celtic | bt. | Rangers | 3–2 |
| 1905 | Third Lanark | bt. | Rangers | 3–1 |
| | (after draw 0–0) | | | |
| 1906 | Heart of Midlothian | bt. | Third Lanark | 1–0 |
| 1907 | Celtic | bt. | Heart of Midlothian | 3–0 |
| 1908 | Celtic | bt. | St. Mirren | 5–1 |
| 1909 | Cup withheld following riot at replay which ended in a draw Rangers 1, Celtic 1. The teams had previously drawn 2–2 | | | |
| 1910 | Dundee | bt. | Clyde | 2–1 |
| | (after draws 2–2 and 0–0) | | | |
| 1911 | Celtic | bt. | Hamilton Academicals | 2–0 |
| | (after draw 0–0) | | | |
| 1912 | Celtic | bt. | Clyde | 2–0 |
| 1913 | Falkirk | bt. | Raith Rovers | 2–0 |
| 1914 | Celtic | bt. | Hibernian | 4–1 |
| | (after draw 0–0) | | | |
| 1920 | Kilmarnock | bt. | Albion Rovers | 3–2 |
| 1921 | Partick Thistle | bt. | Rangers | 1–0 |
| 1922 | Morton | bt. | Rangers | 1–0 |
| 1923 | Celtic | bt. | Hibernian | 1–0 |
| 1924 | Airdrieonians | bt. | Hibernian | 2–0 |
| 1925 | Celtic | bt. | Dundee | 2–1 |
| 1926 | St. Mirren | bt. | Celtic | 2–0 |
| 1927 | Celtic | bt. | East Fife | 3–1 |
| 1928 | Rangers | bt. | Celtic | 4–0 |
| 1929 | Kilmarnock | bt. | Rangers | 2–0 |
| 1930 | Rangers | bt. | Partick Thistle | 2–1 |
| | (after draw 0–0) | | | |

| 1931 | Celtic | bt. | Motherwell | 4–2 |
|------|--------|-----|------------|-----|
| | | (after draw 2–2) | | |
| 1932 | Rangers | bt. | Kilmarnock | 3–0 |
| | | (after draw 1–1) | | |
| 1933 | Celtic | bt. | Motherwell | 1–0 |
| 1934 | Rangers | bt. | St. Mirren | 5–0 |
| 1935 | Rangers | bt. | Hamilton Academicals | 2–1 |
| 1936 | Rangers | bt. | Third Lanark | 1–0 |
| 1937 | Celtic | bt. | Aberdeen | 2–1 |
| 1938 | East Fife | bt. | Kilmarnock | 4–2 |
| | | (after draw 1–1) | | |
| 1939 | Clyde | bt. | Motherwell | 4–0 |
| 1947 | Aberdeen | bt. | Hibernian | 2–1 |
| 1948 | Rangers | bt. | Morton | 1–0 |
| | | (after draw 1–1) | | |
| 1949 | Rangers | bt. | Clyde | 4–1 |
| 1950 | Rangers | bt. | East Fife | 3–0 |
| 1951 | Celtic | bt. | Motherwell | 1–0 |
| 1952 | Motherwell | bt. | Dundee | 4–0 |
| 1953 | Rangers | bt. | Aberdeen | 1–0 |
| | | (after draw 1–1) | | |
| 1954 | Celtic | bt. | Aberdeen | 2–1 |
| 1955 | Clyde | bt. | Celtic | 1–0 |
| | | (after draw 1–1) | | |
| 1956 | Heart of Midlothian | bt. | Celtic | 3–1 |
| 1957 | Falkirk | bt. | Kilmarnock | 2–1 |
| | | (after draw 1–1) | | |
| 1958 | Clyde | bt. | Hibernian | 1–0 |
| 1959 | St. Mirren | bt. | Aberdeen | 3–1 |
| 1960 | Rangers | bt. | Kilmarnock | 2–0 |
| 1961 | Dunfermline | bt. | Celtic | 2–0 |
| | | (after draw 0–0) | | |
| 1962 | Rangers | bt. | St. Mirren | 2–0 |
| 1963 | Rangers | bt. | Celtic | 3–0 |
| | | (after draw 1–1) | | |
| 1964 | Rangers | bt. | Dundee | 3–1 |
| 1965 | Celtic | bt. | Dunfermline | 3–2 |
| 1966 | Rangers | bt. | Celtic | 1–0 |
| | | (after draw 0–0) | | |
| 1967 | Celtic | bt. | Aberdeen | 2–0 |
| 1968 | Dunfermline | bt. | Hearts | 3–1 |
| 1969 | Celtic | bt. | Rangers | 4–0 |
| 1970 | Aberdeen | bt. | Celtic | 3–1 |
| 1971 | Celtic | bt. | Rangers | 2–1 |
| | | (after draw 1–1) | | |
| 1972 | Celtic | bt. | Hibernian | 6–1 |
| 1973 | Rangers | bt. | Celtic | 3–2 |

The Final was first played at the present Hampden Park in 1904 and has been played there every season since 1925.

## Second Division
The only Division II club to win the Scottish Cup is East Fife in 1938.

## Withheld
The Cup was withheld in 1909 after the Hampden riot. Rangers and Celtic were the finalists. They drew the first game, 2—2, and at the end of 90 min. in the replay the result was again a draw, 1—1. At the time there was no rule which said that extra time must be played in such circumstances, but a section of the crowd was under the misapprehension that extra time was to be played. When the players were leaving the field and it became apparent that there was to be no more play, the crowd broke loose, tore up the goal-posts, broke down payboxes, and actually started a bonfire at the side of the pitch. Police who tried to intervene were badly manhandled and stoned.

## SCOTTISH FOOTBALL ASSOCIATION

The S.F.A. was formed at a meeting at Dewar's Hotel, Glasgow attended by the representatives of seven clubs on Mar. 13, 1873. The clubs were Clydesdale, Dumbreck, Eastern, Granville, Queen's Park, Third Lanark and Vale of Leven. An eighth club, Kilmarnock, had written to pledge their support.

Mr. Archibald Rae, the secretary of the Queen's Park Club, was the enthusiast who initiated the move to form an Association and he became the first secretary.

In the early 1880s the Scottish F.A. threatened to discontinue international games with England because of differences in the interpretation of the Laws of the Game. The English Association suggested a meeting of the four home Associations to draw up a uniform code of rules but at first Scotland refused. When a split seemed inevitable, there came a change of feeling in the Scottish F.A. It agreed to a meeting at Manchester on Dec. 6, 1882, and a code of rules acceptable to all four Associations was drawn up. This meeting led to the formation of the International Board (q.v.).

Professionalism was adopted by the Scottish F.A. after prolonged resistance in May 1893.

The Council which conducts the Association's affairs usually meets about eight times a year and consists of the president, two vice-presidents (one appointed by the Scottish League), the treasurer, 11 divisional representatives, 18 representatives of affiliated associations, and 11 Scottish League representatives.

Address: 6 Park Gardens, Glasgow, G3 7YF. Colours: Navy blue shirts, white shorts, navy blue stockings with red tops.

## SCOTTISH FOOTBALL
### General

The oldest football club in Scotland is Queen's Park, formed by members of the Glasgow Y.M.C.A. in July 1867.

In season 1929-30 Rangers won the following honours: Scottish Cup, Scottish League Championship, Glasgow Cup, Scottish Second Eleven Cup, and the Glasgow Charity Cup. The Charity Cup was won by the toss of a coin after playing for two hours against Celtic without reaching a definite result (the score was 2—2).

In season 1948-9 and 1963-4 Rangers won the Scottish League Championship, the Scottish Cup and the Scottish League Cup.

Celtic also achieved this treble in 1966-7 and 1968-9.

## SCOTTISH INTERNATIONALS
See INTERNATIONALS (Scotland).

## SCOTTISH LEAGUE

The Scottish League was formed after a series of meetings in Glasgow in 1890. Several clubs felt that their existence was threatened if fixtures could not be arranged with some certainty of them being carried out. One or two of the larger clubs were constantly approached with the offers of fixtures, but the lesser-known clubs were finding it increasingly difficult to satisfy their supporters with attractive games.

It was obvious that some regulating body should be formed among the clubs just as it had been done in England two years earlier. Not without some opposition from the Scottish Football Association and certain clubs who feared that the formation of such a League would favour professionalism, an agreement was made between 11 clubs, Abercorn, Celtic, Cowlairs, Cambuslang, Dumbarton, Hearts, Rangers, St. Mirren, Renton, Third Lanark, and Vale of Leven. The Scottish League was in being.

The move to form a League had been largely initiated by Renton who were unable to take full advantage of their enterprise when they were suspended by the Scottish Football Association after playing only five of their League matches. Renton had disobeyed a ban placed on all affiliated clubs restraining them from playing matches with St. Bernards, a club which had been pronounced guilty of a breach of the laws of amateurism. In fact, Renton played a new club called Edinburgh Saints, but the S.F.A. had already ruled them to be one and the same as the banned St. Bernards club. Renton's record in their first five League matches was consequently cancelled. However, they returned to the League the following season.

Division II of the League was formed in 1893. It was suspended in 1915 and re-formed in 1921 when automatic promotion and relegation was also introduced.

A Third Division was formed in 1923 but did not complete its third season. It was re-formed in 1946 and divided into two sections in 1950, but it was scrapped in 1955 when the Reserve League came into existence.

In the history of the competition only one club has succeeded in winning all its League matches in any one season. Rangers won all 18 games played in season 1898-9.

Rangers hold the record for the highest number of Championship wins. They have achieved this distinction 34 times (including once as joint holders of the title with Dumbarton in 1891). Celtic have won the Championship on 25 occasions.

There was such a rush of games at the end of season 1915-16 that Celtic actually played two League games in one day —April 15, 1916. They beat Raith Rovers 6—0 at Celtic Park and in the evening beat Motherwell 3—1 at Fir Park.

Entrance fee for clubs joining Scottish League is £10.

## Champions

*Scottish League:* 1890-91 Dumbarton and Rangers; 1891-2 Dumbarton; 1892-3 Celtic.

First Division: 1893-4 Celtic; 1894-5 Hearts; 1895-6 Celtic; 1896-7 Hearts; 1897-8 Celtic; 1898-9 Rangers; 1899-1900 Rangers; 1900-1901 Rangers; 1901-2 Rangers; 1902-3 Hibernian; 1903-4 Third Lanark; 1904-5 Celtic*; 1905-6 Celtic; 1906-7 Celtic; 1907-8 Celtic; 1908-9 Celtic; 1909-10 Celtic; 1910-11 Rangers; 1911-12 Rangers; 1912-13 Rangers; 1913-14 Celtic; 1914-15 Celtic; 1915-16 Celtic; 1916-17 Celtic; 1917-18 Rangers; 1918-19 Celtic; 1919-20 Rangers; 1920-21 Rangers; 1921-2 Celtic; 1922-3 Rangers; 1923-4 Rangers; 1924-5 Rangers; 1925-6 Celtic; 1926-7 Rangers; 1927-8 Rangers; 1928-9 Rangers; 1929-30 Rangers; 1930-31 Rangers; 1931-2 Motherwell; 1932-3 Rangers; 1933-4 Rangers; 1934-5 Rangers; 1935-6 Celtic ; 1936-7 Rangers; 1937-8 Celtic; 1938-9 Rangers; 1946-7 Rangers; 1947-8 Hibernian; 1948-9 Rangers; 1949-50 Rangers; 1950-51 Hibernian; 1951-2 Hibernian; 1952-3 Rangers†; 1953-4 Celtic; 1954-5 Aberdeen; 1955-6 Rangers; 1956-7 Rangers; 1957-8 Hearts; 1958-9 Rangers; 1959-60 Hearts; 1960-61 Rangers; 1961-2 Dundee; 1962-3 Rangers; 1963-4; Rangers; 1964-5 Kilmarnock†; 1965-6 Celtic; 1966-7 Celtic; 1967-8 Celtic; 1968-9 Celtic; 1969-70 Celtic; 1970-71 Celtic; 1971-2 Celtic; 1972-3 Celtic.

Second Division: 1893-4 Hibernian; 1894-5 Hibernian; 1895-6 Abercorn; 1896-7 Partick Thistle; 1897-8 Kilmarnock; 1898-9 Kilmarnock; 1899-1900 Partick Thistle; 1900-1901 St. Bernard; 1901-2 Port Glasgow; 1902-3 Airdrieonians; 1903-4 Hamilton Academicals; 1904-5 Clyde; 1905-6 Leith Athletic; 1906-7 St. Bernard; 1907-8 Raith Rovers; 1908-9 Abercorn; 1909-10 Leith Athletic and Raith Rovers (shared); 1910-11 Dumbarton; 1911-12 Ayr United; 1912-13 Ayr United; 1913-14 Cowdenbeath; 1914-15 Cowdenbeath; 1916-21 no competition; 1921-2 Alloa Athletic; 1922-3 Queen's Park; 1923-4 St. Johnstone; 1924-5

Dundee United; 1925-6 Dunfermline Athletic; 1926-7 Bo'ness; 1927-8 Ayr United; 1928-9 Dundee United; 1929-30 Leith Athletic†; 1930-31 Third Lanark; 1931-2 East Stirlingshire†; 1932-3 Hibernian; 1933-4 Albion Rovers; 1934-5 Third Lanark; 1935-6 Falkirk; 1936-7 Ayr United; 1937-8 Raith Rovers; 1938-9 Cowdenbeath; 1940-46 no competition; 1946-7 Dundee; 1947-8 East Fife; 1948-9 Raith Rovers†; 1949-50 Morton; 1950-51 Queen of the South†; 1951-2 Clyde; 1952-3 Stirling Albion; 1953-4 Motherwell; 1954-5 Airdrieonians; 1955-6 Queen's Park; 1956-7 Clyde; 1957-8 Stirling Albion; 1958-9 Ayr United; 1959-60 St. Johnstone; 1960-61 Stirling Albion; 1961-2 Clyde; 1962-3 St. Johnstone; 1963-4 Morton; 1964-5 Stirling Albion; 1965-6 Ayr United; 1966-7 Morton; 1967-8 St. Mirren; 1968-9 Motherwell; 1969-70 Falkirk; 1970-71 Partick Thistle; 1971-2 Dumbarton‡; 1972-3 Clyde.

† Won on goal average.
‡ Won on goal difference.

## SCOTTISH LEAGUE CUP, THE

After World War II the President of the Scottish League presented a trophy to be competed for as the Scottish League Cup, a competition which succeeded the war-time Southern League Cup in 1946.

Arranged on a League basis with the clubs divided into nine groups at the start, the winners of each group subsequently play on a knock-out basis until the Final is reached in December.

Results of Finals— 46-47 Rangers bt Aberdeen 4—0; 47-48 East Fife bt Falkirk 4—1 (after 1—1 draw); 48-49 Rangers bt Raith R. 2—0; 49-50 East Fife bt Dunfermline 3—0; 50-51 Motherwell bt Hibernian 3—0; 51-52 Dundee bt Rangers 3—2; 52-53 Dundee bt Kilmarnock 2—0; 53-54 East Fife bt Partick T. 3—2; 54-55 Hearts bt Motherwell 4—2; 55-56 Aberdeen bt St. Mirren 2—1; 56-57 Celtic bt Partick T. 3—0 (after 0—0 draw); 57-58 Celtic bt Rangers 7—1; 58-59 Hearts bt Partick T. 5—1; 59-60 Hearts bt Third Lanark 2—1; 60-61 Rangers bt Kilmarnock 2—0; 61-62 Rangers bt Hearts 3—1 (after 1—1 draw); 62-63 Hearts bt Kilmarnock 1—0; 63-64 Rangers bt Morton 5—0; 64-65 Rangers bt Celtic 2—1; 65-66 Celtic bt Rangers 2—1; 66-67 Celtic bt Rangers 1—0; 67-68 Celtic bt Dundee 5—3; 68-69 Celtic bt Hibernian 6—2; 69-70 Celtic bt St. Johnstone 1—0; 70-71 Rangers bt Celtic 1—0; 71-72 Partick T. bt Celtic 4—1; 72-73 Hibernian bt Celtic 2—1.

*Celtic won deciding match with Rangers.

## SCOTTISH PLAYERS IN ENGLAND

Early in the 1955-6 season Accrington Stanley set up a Football League record by fielding a side which included all Scottish-born players. Their all Scottish side made several appearances in the Third Division (N) during that season and, indeed, all but four of the 19 players who appeared for this club during 1955-6 were born in Scotland.

In the First Division the record for fielding a side containing the most Scotsmen goes to Newcastle United in whose team on Oct. 6, 1928, when they defeated Leeds United 3-3, only centre-half, E. Wood, was not Scottish born.

For 30 years, West Bromwich Albion never had a Scottish professional on their books until they signed G. Dudley, a centre-forward from Glasgow who had previously played for Albion Rovers, in Nov. 1937.

See also FOOTBALL ASSOCIATION CHALLENGE CUP (Scotland) and F.A. AMATEUR CUP (Scotland).

## SCUNTHORPE UNITED F.C.

Founded 1904. Amalgamated with Lindsey United 1910 as Scunthorpe and Lindsey United. Dropped name "Lindsey" from title 1951. Elected to Football League, Division III(N), 1950. Honours: Champions, Division III(N), 1957-8. Record attendance: 23,935 v. Bolton Wanderers, F.A. Cup, 3rd Round, Jan. 10, 1959. Address: Old Show Ground, Scunthorpe (Tel. 2954). Nickname: Irons. Colours: All red. Record League goal-scorer: B. Thomas, 31 goals, Division II, 1961-2. Record victory: 9—0 v. Boston United, F.A. Cup, 1st Round, Nov. 21, 1953. Record defeat: 8—0 v. Carlisle United, Division III(N), Dec. 25, 1952.

## SEELER, Uwe (1936-    )

A pocket-size human dynamo whose wholehearted efforts on the football field have made him one of West Germany's most popular sportsmen. Capped for his country before his 18th birthday he went on to create a German record with 72 international appearances. Noted for his acrobatic shooting and heading (despite his lack of height he could beat most opponents in the air) he has been an inspiration to both club and country, being a real 90-minute player who never gives up trying. Topped the West German League scoring list five times between 1955 and 1964, his best figure being 36 goals in 1959-60.

Hamburger S.V. 1952-. 72 West German internationals. West German League champions 1960. West German Cup winners 1963. European Cup-winners Cup runners-up 1968. World Cup runners-up 1966.

## SHEFFIELD UNITED F.C.

Founded 1889, by members of the Yorks County Cricket Club and the Sheffield United C.C.C. One of the original members of the Football League, Division II, 1892. Honours: Champions, Division I, 1897-8. Runners-up, 1896-7, 1899-1900. Champions, Division II, 1952-3. Runners-up, 1892-3, 1938-9, 1960-61, 1970-71. F.A. Cup: Winners, 1899, 1902, 1915, 1925. Runners-up, 1901, 1936. Record attendance: 68,287 v. Leeds United F.A. Cup, 5th Round, Feb. 15, 1936. Address: Bramall Lane, Sheffield S2 4SU. (Tel. 0742-25585). Nickname: Blades. Colours: Red and white striped shirts, black shorts, white stockings with two red hoops at top. Record League goal-scorer: J. Dunne 41 goals, Division I, 1930-31. Record victory: 11—2 v. Cardiff City, Division I, Jan. 1, 1926. Record defeat: 13—0 v. Bolton Wanderers, F.A. Cup 2nd Round, Feb. 1, 1890.

## SHEFFIELD WEDNESDAY F.C.

Founded 1867 by the Wednesday Cricket Club, the fifth oldest Football League club. Officially known as The Wednesday until June 1929 when present title adopted. Elected to the Football League, Division I, 1892. Honours: Champions, Division I, 1902-3, 1903-4, 1928-9, 1929-30. Runners-up, 1960-61. Champions, Division II, 1899-1900, 1925-6, 1951-2, 1955-6, 1958-9. Runners-up, 1949-50. F.A. Cup: Winners 1896, 1907, 1935, Runners-up, 1890, 1966. Record attendance: 72,841 v. Manchester City, F.A. Cup, 5th Round, Feb. 17, 1934. Address: Hillsborough, Sheffield S6 1SW (Tel. 0742-343122). Nickname: Owls. Colours: Royal blue and white striped shirts with blue collar, royal blue shorts, white stockings. Record League goal-scorer: D. Dooley, 46 goals, Division II, 1951-2. Record victory: 12—0 v. Halliwell, F.A. Cup, 1st Round, Jan. 17, 1891. Record defeat: 10—0 v. Aston Villa, Division I, Oct. 5, 1912.

## SHINGUARDS

Shinguards were invented by Samuel W, Widdowson, the Nottingham Forest forward who played for England against Scotland in 1880. It is believed they may have been used in 1874 but were not actually mentioned in the rules of the game until 1880.

## SHREWSBURY TOWN F.C.

Founded 1886. Elected to Football League, Division III(N), 1950. Transferred to Division III(S), 1951. Highest in Division III, 3rd, 1959-60. Record attendance: 18,917 v. Walsall, Division III, April 26, 1961.

Address: Gay Meadow, Shrewsbury (Tel. 56068). Nickname: The Salop. Colours: Blue shirts with amber stripe and V-neck insert, blue shorts with amber stripe, blue stockings with amber hoops at top. Record League goal-scorer: A. Rowley, 38 goals, Division IV, 1958-9. Record victory: 7—0 v. Swindon Town, Division III(S), 1954-5. Record defeat: 8—1 v. Norwich City, Division III(S), 1952-3, and v. Coventry City, Division III, Oct. 22, 1963.

## SMITH, Gilbert Oswald (1872-1943)

This amateur centre-forward played a leading role in the development of the passing game, spurning the individual dribbling style which was still favoured by so many Englishmen when this brilliant footballer first made his mark with Oxford University in the early 1890s. G. O. Smith was also a clever dribbler when circumstances required it, but he was noted especially for the manner in which he brought his wingmen into the game with pinpoint passes.

In contrast to so many centre-forwards of his day G. O. Smith was gentle and rather frail looking but for many years after his retirement he was still acknowledged as the greatest centre-forward in the game's history. He led the England attack more often than any other player before World War II. An all-rounder, G. O. Smith got his Oxford "Blue" at both cricket and Association football, and also played the summer game with Surrey.

Oxford University 1891-96. Old Carthusians. Corinthians 1892-1903, scoring 105 goals in 131 games. England internationals 20 (plus one amateur game v. Germany not accorded official status). F.A. Amateur Cup runners-up 1895, winners 1897.

## SOUTH AFRICA

Football has been played in South Africa for more than 80 years but for the greater part of that time it has taken a poor second place to rugby.

The soccer revival which has established the game as number one favourite ahead of the handling code began soon after World War II and received its biggest boost in 1959 when professionalism was adopted and a National League formed by the leading clubs in the Transvaal and Natal. A second division was added in 1960.

However, while great strides have been made on the domestic front South Africa's international football aspirations received a severe set-back in 1964, when they were suspended from F.I.F.A., a suspension which is still in force.

The oldest Association, the Natal Football Association, was formed in 1882, and the first overseas tour of an English club (outside of Europe) followed in 1897 when the Corinthians visited this part of the world. The famous amateur club revisited South Africa in 1903 and 1907.

The South African F.A. was affiliated to the Football Association of England from 1903 until 1962.

South Africa has never met our full international team. They have, however, played what are known as "Test Matches" against F.A. Touring teams. The results of these matches are as follows:

| | | |
|---|---|---|
| June 29, 1910 | South Africa 0, England 3; | Durban |
| July 23, 1910 | South Africa 2, England 6; | Johannesburg |
| July 30, 1910 | South Africa 3, England 6; | Cape Town |
| June 26, 1920 | South Africa 1, England 3; | Johannesburg |
| July 17, 1920 | South Africa 1, England 9; | Cape Town |
| July 19, 1920 | South Africa 1, England 3; | Durban |
| June 15, 1929 | South Africa 2, England 3; | Durban |
| July 13, 1929 | South Africa 1, England 2; | Johannesburg |
| July 17, 1929 | South Africa 1, England 3; | Cape Town |
| June 17, 1939 | South Africa 0, England 3; | Johannesburg |
| June 24, 1939 | South Africa 1, England 2; | Durban |
| July 1, 1939 | South Africa 1, England 2; | Johannesburg |
| June 23, 1956 | South Africa 3, England 4; | Johannesburg |
| July 1, 1956 | South Africa 2, England 4; | Durban |
| July 9, 1956 | South Africa 0, England 0; | Cape Town |
| July 14, 1956 | South Africa 1, England 4; | Salisbury |

The South Africans have made three tours of the United Kingdom. In 1924 they played 26 matches, winning 16 and losing 10. In 1953 they won five and drew four of their 20 matches, and in 1958 they played another 17 games, winning seven, drawing four and losing six.

Many South Africans have appeared in the Football League and they are far too numerous to mention here, but the following have also appeared in full internationals:

G. Hodgson (Liverpool, Aston Villa, Leeds United), England v. Scotland, Ireland, Wales, 1930-31; W. Perry (Blackpool), England v. Ireland, Scotland, and Spain, 1955-6; J. Hewie (Charlton Athletic), Scotland v. England, 1955-6, 1956-7, v. Ireland and Wales, 1956-7, 1959-60, plus eight appearances against foreign countries; P. Kelly (Barnsley), Ireland v. Scotland, 1949-50; F. Osborne (Fulham, Tottenham Hotspur), England v. Ireland and France, 1922-3, v. Belgium, 1924-5, 1925-6. R. Osborne (Leicester City), England v. Wales 1927-8.

The address of the governing body: South African F.A., 500 Volkskas, Market Street, P.O. Box 2694, Johannesburg. Colours: Green shirts, white shorts, green and gold stockings.

## SOUTHAMPTON F.C.
Founded 1885 by the Young Men's Association of St. Mary's Church. Adopted present title, 1897. One of the original members of the Football League, Division III, 1920. Honours: Runners-up, Division II, 1965-6. Champions, Division III(S), 1921-2. Runners-up, 1920-21. Champions, Division III, 1959-60. F.A. Cup: Finalists, 1900, 1902. Record attendance: 31,044 v. Manchester United, Division I, Oct. 8, 1969. Address: The Dell, Southampton SO9 4XX (Tel. 23408). Nickname: Saints. Colours: Red and white striped shirts, black shorts, red stockings with white hoop around ankle. Record League goal-scorer: D. Reeves, 39 goals, Division III, 1959-60. Record victory: 9—3 v. Wolverhampton Wanderers, Division II, Sept. 18, 1965. In a Southern League game they beat Northampton Town, 11—0, Dec. 28, 1901. Record defeat: 8—0 v. Tottenham Hotspur, Division II, Mar. 28, 1936, and v. Everton, Division I, Nov. 20, 1971.

## SOUTHEND UNITED F.C.
Founded 1906 from the older Southend Athletic amateur club. One of the original members of the Football League, Division III, 1920. Honours: Runners-up, Division IV, 1971-2. Record attendance: 28,059 v. Birmingham City, F.A. Cup, 4th Round, Jan. 26, 1957. Address: Roots Hall, Southend-on-Sea SS2 6NQ (Tel. 40707). Nickname: Shrimpers. Colours: Blue shirts, blue shorts with white trim, white stockings. Record League goal-scorer: J. Shankly, 31 goals, Division III(S), 1928-9, and S. McGrory, Division III(S), 1957-8. Record victory: 10—1 v. Golders Green, F.A. Cup, 1st Round, Nov 24, 1934, and 10—1 v. Brentwood, F.A. Cup, 2nd Round, Dec. 7, 1968. Record defeat: 9—1 v. Brighton &

Hove Albion, Division III, Nov. 27, 1965. In a Southern League game they were beaten 11—1 by Northampton Town, Dec. 30, 1909.

## SOUTHERN LEAGUE
This organisation was for many years the principal competition outside the Football and Scottish Leagues. Before the formation of Division III of the Football League in 1920, the Southern League held an important position in the football world.

The formation of this League followed the spread of professionalism to clubs in the London and Home Counties area. Royal Arsenal was first to suggest such a competition. In 1892 Arsenal circularised several clubs with its proposal and a number of meetings were held, but for many there was still the fear of being ostracized by the London F.A. for playing with professionals and support for the idea was very limited. The following year Arsenal secured admission to the newly-formed Division II of the Football League, and abandoned its proposals.

Millwall Athletic was the next club to advocate the formation of such a League, and it was directly due to Millwall's enterprise that a meeting was held at which the Southern League was formed on Jan. 12, 1894. In addition to Millwall, representatives of Ilford, Luton Town, Clapton, 2nd Scots Guards, Reading and Chatham were present at the discussion. Other clubs were circulated and nine clubs—Royal Ordnance and Swindon Town in addition to the seven at the original meeting—formed the First Division of the new League. 2nd Scots Guards dropped out before the first season started and Southampton St. Mary's was elected in their place. There was also a Second Division containing seven clubs.

The first three places in the Southern League were held by the same three clubs in the first two seasons, Millwall Athletic, Luton Town and Southampton St. Mary's. In the next three seasons, Southampton, the outstanding club in the history of the competition, carried off the title.

The most eventful year in the history of the Southern League was 1920 when the First Division members applied en bloc to become members of the Football League. The Football League accepted them in a newly-formed Division III as Associate Members. With all its leading clubs gone, the Southern League lost its status as a major competition. However, it carried on with an English Section of 13 clubs (including 9 who fielded only their reserve teams) and a Welsh section of 11 clubs.

In 1923 the Welsh Division was dropped and the League divided into Eastern and Western sections. In 1933 a Central Section was included. The League continued in three sections until 1936 when a single division of 16 clubs was formed. This became 18 in 1937, and 23 in 1938. There was also a mid-week section for three seasons just before World War II.

When the competition was resumed in 1945, there were only 11 clubs, but later the number increased to 23.

For season 1958-9 it was divided into S.E. and N.W. sections totalling 35 clubs, but in 1959 the number of clubs was increased to 44 and a new formation of a Premier Division and a First Division was established. The First Division was split into North and South sections in 1971.

The record for the highest number of points registered by any club in a single season in the top division is held by Merthyr Tydfil who collected 71 points in season 1949-50.

The Southern League entered into an agreement with the Football League and the Scottish League in 1909, regarding the transfer of players. This was broken in 1919 following a dispute with West Ham United and the Football League when West Ham United made a last-minute decision to join Division II of the Football League.

Following this dispute the Southern League also discontinued competition with the Football, Scottish and Irish Leagues in inter-League games.

## SOUTHPORT F.C.
Founded 1881 as Southport Central. A limited company was formed in 1919 and the club became known as Southport F.C. One of the original members of the Football League, Division III(N), 1921. Honours: Champions, Division IV, 1972-3. Runners-up, 1966-7. Record attendance: 20,010 v. Newcastle United, F.A. Cup, 4th Round (replay), Jan. 26, 1932. Address: Haig Avenue, Southport (Tel. 5353). Nickname: Sandgrounders. Colours: Gold shirts, royal blue shorts with gold stripe, gold stockings. Record League goal-scorer: A. R. Waterson, 31 goals, Division III(N), 1930-31. Record victory: 8—1 v. Nelson, Division III(N), Jan. 1, 1931. Record defeat: 11—0 v. Oldham Athletic, Division IV, Dec. 26, 1962.

## SPAIN
Spain has produced three or four of the greatest club sides in the history of the game. Outstanding among these, of course, has been Real Madrid, six times European Cup Winners and once unofficial World Champions, and yet, during these glorious post-war years the Spanish international side has never been able to establish itself among the leaders of world soccer, although they did succeed in winning the European Nations' Cup in 1964.

This is the enigma of Spanish soccer. They undoubtedly possess many of the world's finest players in their club sides, but although they have included most of these in their national XI, irrespective of the fact that many are not Spanish-born, they have seldom made the same impression as such clubs as Real Madrid, Barcelona and Atletico Madrid have done in international competitions.

The game is believed to have been first introduced into the country by British mining engineers working around Vizcaya and they formed the first club, Atletico Bilbao, in 1898.

The Spanish Football Federation was founded in 1905 and today it controls over 2,400 clubs.

The Spanish League was formed in 1928 and it was in the following year that Spain became the first foreign country to defeat England in a full international—(full details are given under INTERNATIONALS (England).

Spain did not enter for the World Cup in either 1930 or 1938. They qualified for the final tournament in 1934, 1950, 1962 and 1966, but failed to qualify in 1954, 1958 and 1970. Their best performance in this competition was their 1—1 draw with Italy, the eventual winners, in 1934. In the replay Italy won by the only goal scored.

Address of the governing body: Real Federación Española de Fútol, Calle Alberto Bosch, 13, Apartado postal 347, Madrid 14. Colours: Red Shirts, blue shorts, black stockings with red and yellow tops.

| | |
|---|---|
| May 15, 1929 | Spain 4, England 3; Madrid |
| April 26, 1931 | Spain 1, Eire 1; Barcelona |
| Dec. 9, 1931 | England 7, Spain 1; Highbury |
| Dec. 13, 1931 | Eire 0, Spain 5; Dublin |
| June 23, 1946 | Spain 0, Eire 1; Madrid |
| Mar. 2, 1947 | Eire 3, Spain 2; Dublin |
| May 30, 1948 | Spain 2, Eire 1; Barcelona |
| June 12, 1949 | Eire 1, Spain 4; Dublin |

| July 2, 1950* | Spain 1, England 0; Rio de Janeiro |
|---|---|
| June 1, 1952 | Spain 6, Eire 0; Madrid |
| May 18, 1955 | Spain 1, England 1; Madrid |
| Nov. 27, 1955 | Eire 2, Spain 2; Dublin |
| Nov. 30, 1955 | England 4, Spain 1; Wembley |
| May 8, 1957* | Scotland 4, Spain 2; Glasgow |
| May 26, 1957* | Spain 4, Scotland 1; Madrid |
| Oct. 15, 1958 | Spain 6, Ireland 2; Madrid |
| May 15, 1960 | Spain 3, England 0; Madrid |
| Oct. 26, 1960 | England 4, Spain 2; Wembley |
| April 19, 1961* | Wales 1, Spain 2; Cardiff |
| May 18, 1961* | Spain 1, Wales 1; Madrid |
| May 30, 1963† | Spain 1, Ireland 1; Bilbao |
| June 13, 1963 | Spain 2, Scotland 6; Madrid |
| Oct. 30, 1963† | Ireland 0, Spain 1; Belfast |
| Mar. 11, 1964† | Spain 5, Eire 1; Seville |
| April 8, 1964† | Eire 0, Spain 2; Dublin |
| May 5, 1965* | Eire 1, Spain 0; Dublin |
| May 8, 1965 | Scotland 0, Spain 0; Glasgow |
| Oct. 27, 1965* | Spain 4, Eire 1; Seville |
| Nov. 10, 1965* | Eire 0, Spain 1; Paris |
| Dec. 8, 1965 | Spain 0, England 2; Madrid |
| Oct. 23, 1966† | Eire 0, Spain 0; Dublin |
| Dec. 7, 1966† | Spain 2, Eire 0; Valencia |
| May 24, 1967 | England 2, Spain 0; Wembley |
| Apr. 3, 1968† | England 1, Spain 0; Wembley |
| May 8, 1968† | Spain 1, England 2; Madrid |
| Nov. 11, 1970‡ | Spain 3, Ireland 0; Seville |
| Feb. 16, 1972‡ | Ireland 1, Spain 1; Hull |

\* World Cup
† Nations Cup
‡ European Championship

## SPECTACLES (GLASSES)

J. F. Mitchell, an English amateur international and Olympic Games goalkeeper, who played for Manchester University, Manchester City and Preston North End, is believed to be the only player to take part in an F.A. Cup Final wearing glasses when he kept goal for Preston North End against Huddersfield Town in 1922.

Apart from goalkeepers it is believed that there have been only two other bespectacled players to appear regularly in first-class football: H. S. Bourne, West Ham United full-back, 1908-11, and A. Raisbeck, Liverpool and Scotland centre-half of the early 1900s.

Josef Jurion, capped 67 times by Belgium as an inside forward 1955-1967, played in spectacles.

At the present time there are a number of first-class players who wear contact lenses.

## STEPHENSON, Clement (1891-1961)

Although this player made only one England appearance there is no doubt that he was among the finest inside-forwards in the period between the two World Wars,
indeed, the fact that he schemed Huddersfield Town through three consecutive Championship-winning campaigns in itself marks him down as one of the all-time greats. The perfect link-man, Stephenson was a master tactician. Huddersfield signed him from Aston Villa in 1921 when some thought he was past his best, but he continued to play until 1929. Born Seaton Delaval he joined Villa from West Stanley in 1910.

Aston Villa 1910-21, 190 apprcs. (85 goals). Huddersfield Town 1921-29, 248 apprcs. (42 goals). 1 England international. Inter-League games 2. Football League Champions 1923-4, 1924-5, 1925-6. F.A. Cup winners 1913, 1920, 1922, runners-up 1928.

## STENHOUSEMUIR F.C.

Founded: 1884. Elected to Scottish League, Division II, 1921. Honours: nil. Record attendance: 12,500 v. East Fife, Scottish Cup, 4th Round, Mar. 11, 1950. Address: Ochilview Park, Stenhousemuir (Tel. 032-45 2992). Colours: Maroon shirts with white trim, white shorts. Record League

185

goal-scorer: E. Morrison, 29 goals, Division II, 1928-9 and R. Murray, 29 goals, Division II, 1936-7. Record victory: 9—2 v. Dundee United, Division II, 1936-7. Record defeat: 11—2 v. Dunfermline Athletic, Division II, 1930-31.

## STIRLING ALBION F.C.
Founded 1945. Elected to Scottish League, Division C, 1946. Honours: Champions, Division C, 1946-7. Champions, Division B, 1952-3. Runners-up, 1948-9, 1950-51. Champions, Division II, 1957-8, 1960-61, 1964-5. Record attendance: 26,400 v. Celtic, Scottish Cup, 4th Round, Mar. 14, 1959. Address: Annfield Park, Stirling (Tel. 0786 3584). Colours: All red. Record League goal-scorer: R. Gilmour, 22 goals, Division I, 1958-9. Record victory: 7—0 v. Albion Rovers, 1947-8; Montrose, 1957-8; St. Mirren, 1959-60 and Arbroath, 1960-61, all in the Scottish League. Record defeat: 9—0 v. Dundee United, Division I, Dec. 30, 1967.

## STOCKPORT COUNTY F.C.
Founded 1883. Adopted present title 1891 (previously known as Heaton Norris Rovers). Elected to Football League, Division II, 1900. Failed to gain re-election, 1904. Returned when Division II was increased from 18 to 20 clubs, 1905. Honours: Champions, Division III(N), 1921-2, 1936-7. Runners-up, 1928-9 1929-30. Champions, Division IV, 1966-7. Best in Division II, 10th, 1905-6. Record attendance: 27,833 v. Liverpool, F.A. Cup, 5th Round, Feb. 11, 1950. Address: Edgeley Park, Stockport SK3 9DD (Tel. 061 480-8888). Nickname: Hatters. Colours: White, shirts with blue collar and cuffs, white shorts with blue stripe, white stockings with blue tops. Record League goal-scorer: A. Lythgoe, 46 goals, Division III(N), 1933-4. Record victory: 13—0. v. Halifax Town, Division III(N), Jan. 6, 1934. Record defeat: 8—1 v. Chesterfield, Division II, April 19, 1902.

## STOKE CITY F.C.
The second oldest club in the Football League. Founded 1863 by employees of the North Staffordshire Railway. One of the original members of the Football League, 1888. Not re-elected, 1890. Returned after 12 months' absence, 1891. Resigned 1908, returned 1919. Honours: Champions, Division II, 1932-3, 1962-3. Runners-up, 1921-2. Champions, Division III(N), 1926-7. Best in Division I, 4th, 1935-6, 1946-7. F.L. Cup: Winners, 1972, Finalists, 1964. Record attendance: 51,380 v. Arsenal, Division I,

Mar. 29, 1937. Address: Victoria Ground, Stoke-on-Trent ST4 4EG (Tel. 44660). Nickname: Potters. Colours: Red and white striped shirts, white shorts, white stockings with red hoops. Record League goal-scorer: F. Steele, 33 goals, Division I, 1936-7. Record victory: 10—3 v. West Bromwich Albion, Division I, Feb. 4, 1937. Record defeat: 10—0 v. Preston North End, Division I, Sept. 14, 1889.

## STRANRAER F.C.
Founded: 1870. Elected to Scottish League, Division II, 1955. Honours: nil. Record attendance: 6,500 v. Rangers, Scottish Cup, 1st Round, Jan. 24, 1948. Address: Stair Park, Stranraer (Tel. 0776 3271). Colours: Royal blue shirts, white shorts. Record League goal-scorer: J. Hanlon, 23 goals, Division II, 1962-3. Record victory: 7—0 v. Brechin City, Division II, 1964-5. Record defeat: 11-1 v. Queen of the South, Scottish Cup, 1st Round, Jan. 16, 1932.

## SUBSTITUTES
The evolution of the substitute:

1932—International Board decide to allow them in internationals with foreign countries if previously agreed.

1950—J. Mullen (Wolverhampton W.) became first substitute to score for England —v. Belgium, Brussels, May 18th.

1958—Board recommended that in non-competition matches substitute goalkeepers may be brought on at any time and a substitute for any other player before end of first half.

1965—Football League allow one substitute per team in case of injuries. First substitute called on was K. Peacock of Charlton Athletic, at Bolton, Aug. 21, 1965.

1966-67 season—F.A. Cup and Football League Cup allow the one substitute. Scottish F.A. and League follow suit. Substitute goalkeepers allowed in Home Internationals.

June 1967—International Board decides to allow two substitutes per team and not only for injuries, but F.A. and Football League agreed to continue with one substitute.

1968—D. Clarke (W.B.A.) became first substitute called on in an F.A. Cup Final —v. Everton, May 18th.

1968-69—Two substitutes (one to be goalkeeper) allowed in European Champions and Cup Winners Cups.

1972—International Board alter Laws of Game so as to allow for up to five substitutes in matches outside the rules of any competition provided both teams agree.

Although substitute goalkeepers were not

officially permitted in the Home International Championship before 1966 it should be noted that at Wrexham in 1908, L. R. Roose was injured playing for Wales against England and the F.A. consented to D. Davies of Bolton Wanderers appearing in goal for Wales in the second half.

## SUNDAY FOOTBALL

The popularity of Sunday football has spread so rapidly that there are more people playing on this day than on any other day of the week. The largest proportion of these are in the London, Birmingham and Liverpool areas, but there are also well established organisations for Sunday football in Manchester and Hampshire as well as other thickly populated areas.

Until 1955 the F.A. did not permit clubs or players under their jurisdiction to take part in Sunday football. In that year, however, it lifted the ban, but also made it clear that they did not intend to organise or control Sunday football. Five years later when the question was considered once again the F.A. at last decided to allow Sunday Football Leagues to become affiliated, and in 1964 they went a step further, actually inaugurating their own Sunday Cup Competition for amateurs.

However, the F.A. has retained its rule which states that no club, player, official, referee or linesman shall be compelled to take part in football on Sundays, Good Friday or Christmas Day.

The F.A. rules also state that Professional Players' Registration forms signed on a Sunday are not valid. Indeed, it is an offence for a club to induce a player to sign on a Sunday.

The first professional competition match played on Sunday in England—Wisbech v. Dunstable Town, Southern League, Mar. 19, 1967.

## SUNDERLAND F.C.

Founded 1879, as Sunderland and District Teachers' A.F.C. Adopted present title 1881. Elected to Football League, Division I, 1890. Honours: Champions, Division I, 1891-2, 1892-3, 1894-5, 1901-2, 1912-13, 1935-6. Runners-up, 1893-4, 1897-8, 1900-1901, 1922-3, 1934-5. Runners-up, Division II, 1963-4. F.A. Cup: Winners, 1937, 1973. Finalists, 1913. Record attendance: 75,118 v. Derby County, F.A. Cup, 6th Round (replay), Mar. 8, 1933. Address: Roker Park, Sunderland SR6 9SW (Tel. 72077). Nickname: Rokerites. Colours: Red and white striped shirts, white shorts, red stockings with white tops. Record League goal-scorer: D. Halliday, 43 goals, Division I, 1928-9. Record victory: 11—1, v. Fairfield, F.A. Cup, 1st Round, Feb. 2, 1895. Record defeat: 8—0 v. West Ham United, Division I, Oct. 19, 1968.

## SUPPORTERS' CLUBS

### National Federation of Football

"To Help—not Hinder" is the motto of the National Federation of Football Supporters' Clubs. Their members have a proud record of valuable help to their parent clubs over the past three decades.

During this time thousands of pounds have been collected by the sale of programmes, ball tickets, other draw tickets, dances, socials, etc. Many football clubs big and small owe their existence to the hard work and generosity of its Supporters' Club.

The Federation was formed early in 1927. Brentford, Bournemouth, Brighton, Charlton, Northampton and Plymouth were the original members. Today there are over 360 clubs affiliated, associated with both professional and amateur teams. The first amateur club whose supporters' organisation became a member of the Federation was Barking.

## SUSPENSION

See also BETTING and FINES.

### Clubs

Crook Town A.F.C. officials and players, were permanently suspended by Durham F.A., Jan. 7, 1928, for alleged breaches of the amateur rules. The club was also suspended from the F.A. Amateur Cup competition, and Bishop Auckland, whom they had defeated, were allowed into the next Round.

Following further investigation into Durham football by the F.A. on June 30, 1928, 342 players and 61 club officials were suspended and fines amounting to nearly £400 were imposed. All the suspended players were declared professionals.

The Council of Durham F.A. also passed a resolution suspending themselves for a year.

### Grounds

If a ground is suspended by the F.A., then the club concerned cannot play on any ground within a radius of 12 miles until the suspension is lifted.

Clubs whose grounds have been closed by order, thus forcing them to play a number of "home" games away include: Arsenal 1895; Clapton Orient 1930*; Cry-

*Note that this was because ground was declared unsuitable rather than for crowd misbehaviour as in most other cases listed here.

stal Palace 1920; Crewe Alexandra 1896; Gillingham 1961; Hull City 1934; Leeds United 1971; Manchester United 1971; Millwall 1920, 1934, 1947, 1950; Plymouth Argyle 1961; Q.P.R. 1930; Stockport County 1921; Stoke 1911; Sunderland 1903; Wolverhampton W. 1919.

## Players

In 1915 the F.A. permanently suspended eight of the players who had taken part in a Division I game between Manchester United and Liverpool on April 2. This was the outcome of an investigation during which it was alleged that the match had been "fixed" for betting. In 1919 a number of these suspensions were lifted as a mark of appreciation for war service.

A number of players, including internationals, were suspended for life in 1964-5 following sensational disclosures in the "People" newspaper concerning bribery and match fixing.

In 1971 the F.A. decided to allow players suspended for life the right of appeal after a period of seven years.

## SWANSEA CITY F.C.

Founded 1912 as Swansea Town. Became Swansea City February 1970. One of the original members of the Football League, Division III, 1920. Honours: Champions, Division III(S), 1924-5, 1948-9. Best in Division II, 5th, 1925-6. Record attendance: 32,796 v. Arsenal, F.A. Cup, 4th Round, Feb. 19,1968. Address: Vetch Field, Swansea SA1 3SU (Tel. 42855). Nickname: Swans. Colours: White shirts with black V-neck insert and black cuffs, white shorts, white stockings with two black hoops at top. Record League goal-scorer: C. Pearce, 35 goals, Division II, 1931-2. Record victory: 8—1; v. Bristol Rovers, Division III(S), April 15, 1922, and v. Bradford City, Division II, Feb. 22, 1936. Record defeat: 8—1 v. Fulham, Division II, Jan. 22, 1938.

## SWEDEN

Retaining what is largely an amateur system Sweden has suffered through the departure of their best players to other countries, notably to Belgium, where they can earn high wages for playing football, but the country has not been without its successes in the international sphere.

At a time when their players were more strictly amateur than they are today Sweden won the Olympic Soccer title in London in 1948. This was the success that first opened the eyes of the world to the high standard of football achieved by many Swedish players and began the exodus of those stars to other countries.

With a number of these professionals recalled for international duty Sweden won third place in the World Cup finals in Brazil in 1950, while their amateurs gained another third place in the Olympics at Helsinki in 1952.

This was a remarkable run of success and although it was broken when they failed to qualify for the World Cup tournament of 1954 in Switzerland and the 1956 Melbourne Olympics, they gave a good account of themselves when the 1958 World Cup finals were played in their own country.

Indeed, 1958 was the high spot of Swedish soccer history, for they won through to the Final before losing 5—2 to the brilliant Brazilians.

Since then the Swedes have only qualified for one of the three World Cup final tournaments, that of 1970.

The early history of the game in Sweden is very sketchy and records contain many contradictions. It is obvious, however, that soccer first became popular in the principal cities, Stockholm and Gothenburg being introduced in the 1880s by British Embassy officials in the capital and by Scottish textile workers at Gothenburg. The latter formed a soccer section of the Orgryte club which is recognised as the oldest in the country.

A National Championship was established as early as 1896 but this was on a limited scale until the formation of the National League in 1924.

The Swedish F.A. was officially founded in 1904, although there had been a similar organisation in existence since 1902. The Corinthians visited Stockholm in 1904 and played three games which they won by an aggregate of 29—1.

Address of the governing body which controls over 3,000 clubs: Svenska Fotbollförbundet, Box 1216, S-171 23 Solna. Colours: Yellow shirts, blue shorts, yellow stockings.

Results of internationals:

| | | |
|---|---|---|
| May 21, 1923 | Sweden 2, England 4; | Stockholm |
| May 24, 1923 | Sweden 1, England 3; | Stockholm |
| May 17, 1937 | Sweden 0, England 4; | Stockholm |
| Nov. 19, 1947 | England 4, Sweden 2; | Highbury |
| May 13, 1949 | Sweden 3, England 1; | Stockholm |
| June 2, 1949* | Sweden 3, Eire 1; | Stockholm |

Nov. 13, 1949*  Eire 1, Sweden 3; Dublin
May 30, 1952   Sweden 3, Scotland 1; Stockholm
May  6, 1953   Scotland 1, Sweden 2; Hampden Park
May 16, 1956   Sweden 0, England 0; Stockholm
June 15, 1958*  Sweden 0, Wales 0; Stockholm
Oct. 28, 1959  England 2, Sweden 3; Wembley
Nov.  1, 1959  Eire 3, Sweden 2; Dublin
May 18, 1960   Sweden 4, Eire 1; Malmo
May 16, 1965   Sweden 1, England 2; Gothenberg
May 22, 1968   England 3, Sweden 1; Wembley
Oct. 14, 1970†  Eire 1, Sweden 1; Dublin
Oct. 28, 1970†  Sweden 1, Eire 0; Malmo

* World Cup
† Nations Cup

## SWIFT, Frank Victor (1914-1958)
When Manchester City's two senior goal-keepers were unable to play through injury during 1933 they introduced a youngster signed the previous season from a Black-pool junior club. This was Frank Swift and so capable did he prove to be that once in the side he did not miss a game for the next five years—192 consecutive League appear-ances.

A spectacular goalkeeper Frank Swift was always entertaining. He was also a great humourist and became one of the most popular players in the game. With his huge hands he would hold a football in the same way most people would handle a tennis ball. No goalkeeper ever made a closer study of his most regular opponents and he perfected the art of throwing the ball to a team mate rather than booting it upfield.

"Big Swifty" (he was 6ft 2½in) was born at Blackpool and he died in the Munich air disaster which involved the Manchester United team in 1958.

Manchester City 1933-50, 341 apprcs. England international 15 (plus 4 Victory and 10 war-time games). League Cham-pions 1936-7. F.A. Cup winners 1934.

## SWINDON TOWN F.C.
Founded 1881. Adopted professionalism and joined newly formed Southern League, 1894. Third Division, 1920. Honours: Run-ners-up, Division III, 1962-3, 1968-9. League Cup: Winners, 1969. Record atten-dance: 32,000 v. Arsenal F.A. Cup, 3rd Round, Jan. 15, 1972. Address: County Ground, Swindon (Tel. 22118). Nickname: Railwaymen. Colours: Red shirts with white edgings, black shorts with three white vertical stripes, black stockings with red and white hoop. Record league goal-scorer:

H. Morris, 47 goals, Division III(S), 1926-7. Record victory: 10—1 v. Farnham United Breweries (A), F.A. Cup, 1st Round, Nov. 28, 1925. In the Southern League, Dec. 30, 1909, they beat Northampton Town 11—1. Record defeat: 10—1 v. Manchester City, F.A. Cup, 4th Round (replay), Jan. 25, 1930.

## SWITZERLAND
Switzerland has post-war victories over all the home countries and they certainly shocked England when holding them to a 1—1 draw at Wembley in November 1971, but on the whole their international form has suffered from a lack of consistency.

At their best, when coached by Karl Rappan, they reached the World Cup final tournaments of 1938 and 1950. As hosts they automatically qualified in 1954 and again surprised a lot of people by twice beating Italy to reach the quarter-finals before going under to Austria. With Rappan in retirement they failed to qua-lify in 1958 but he returned to coach them into the 1962 finals, although on this occasion they failed to get a point. They had a similar experience in 1966, while two defeats by Rumania put them out of the qualifying competition in 1970.

The Swiss F.A. was founded in 1895 and a League inaugurated two years later. Today the F.A. controls just over 1,000 clubs, the best known among these being the Grasshoppers, F.C. Basle and F.C. Zurich.

Address of the governing body: Association Suisse de Football, Laubegg-strasse 70, B.P.24, 3000 Berne 32. Colours: Red shirts, white shorts and red or white stockings.

Results of international matches:

| | | |
|---|---|---|
| May 24, 1931 | Switzerland 2, Scotland 3; Geneva |
| May 20, 1933 | Switzerland 0, England 4; Berne |
| May 5, 1935 | Switzerland 1, Eire 0; Basle |
| Mar. 17, 1936 | Eire 1, Switzerland 0; Dublin |
| May 17, 1937 | Switzerland 0, Eire 1; Berne |
| May 21, 1938 | Switzerland 2, England 1; Zurich |
| Sept. 18, 1938 | Eire 4, Switzerland 0; Dublin |
| May 11, 1946* | England 4, Switzerland 1; Chelsea |
| May 15, 1946* | Scotland 3, Switzerland 1; Hampden Park |
| May 18, 1947 | Switzerland 1, England 0; Zurich |
| May 17, 1948 | Switzerland 2, Scotland 1; Berne |
| Dec. 2, 1948 | England 6, Switzerland 0; Highbury |
| Dec. 5, 1948 | Eire 0, Switzerland 1; Dublin |
| May 26, 1949 | Switzerland 4, Wales 0; Berne |
| April 26, 1950 | Scotland 3, Switzerland 1; Hampden Park |
| May 16, 1951 | Wales 3, Switzerland 2; Wrexham |
| May 28, 1952 | Switzerland 0, England 3; Zurich |
| June 20, 1954† | Switzerland 0, England 2; Berne |
| May 19, 1957† | Switzerland 1, Scotland 2; Basle |
| Nov. 6, 1957 | Scotland 3, Switzerland 2; Hampden Park |
| May 9, 1962 | England 3, Switzerland 1; Wembley |
| June 5, 1963 | Switzerland 1, England 8; Basle |
| Oct. 14, 1964† | Ireland 1, Switzerland 0; Belfast |
| Nov. 14, 1964† | Switzerland 2, Ireland 1; Lausanne |
| Oct. 13, 1971‡ | Switzerland 2, England 3; Basle |
| Nov. 10, 1971‡ | England 1, Switzerland 1; Wembley |
| June 22, 1973 | Switzerland 1, Scotland 0; Berne |

* Victory internationals
† World Cup
‡ European Championship

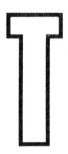

## TACTICS AND TEAM EVOLUTION
See also OFFSIDE.

In its early days football was played between sides of unlimited numbers and without any particular formation. But by 1850 it had become the practice for opposing teams to field between 15 and 20 men each.

These numbers were favoured by several clubs until late in the 1860s, although the famous Queen's Park Club of Glasgow fielded 15 or more players in a team for several years after it had become normal to play with only 11 or 12 men.

Teams of nine forwards and two defenders came into fashion around, 1860 and this formation quickly developed into a combination of goalkeeper, one back, two half-backs and seven or eight forwards. The Sheffield Association club seem to have preferred the 12-player team.

An all-round rule of 11 players a side was not adopted until about 1870 when the formation was usually a goalkeeper, one full-back, two half-backs, and seven forwards. The forward line being made up of two right wings, three centres and two left wings.

When England met Scotland for the first official international in 1872, the Scots played with a goalkeeper, two backs, two half-backs and six forwards, while England kept to a goalkeeper, one back (then known as a three-quarter back), one half-back and eight forwards.

As one may gather from the disposition of the players in those days, the emphasis was definitely on attack. Most sides played with virtually nine or ten forwards, for the half-backs were really attackers who paid little attention to defence.

In those early days there was practically no teamwork as we know it today although there was a system of backing-up players of your own side who were in possession of the ball so as to be able to take it on if one's colleague should over-run it or lose possession. Sides were composed of individual artists who when they got the ball, did their best to beat the opposing side on their own. So

were the great dribblers developed. Whatever we may now think of such tactics there must have been real pleasure in watching these football artists weaving their way through the opposition, taking the ball almost from one end of the field to the other before shooting at goal.

Towards the middle of the 1870s it became the practice to line-up with a goalkeeper, two backs, two half-backs and six forwards, the combination first favoured by the Scots. Also about this time the Scots were fast developing stronger teams with the introduction of more unselfish methods. It was in Scotland that it first became the fashion to pass the ball before being tackled.

It was hard to break the English of their individualistic type of football. They still preferred to try and dribble through the opposition on their own, and so remarkable was their ability in this respect that they were not entirely without success.

However, when, after 10 games against Scotland, England had only won two, it became obvious that the passing game must bring greater dividends in the long run. This success of Scotland in international matches not only prompted the adoption of the passing game, but it also encouraged the importation of many Scottish players into England in the 1880s.

In 1882 it also inspired N. L. Jackson, then honorary assistant-secretary of the Football Association, to form the Corinthians, a club which subsequently became noted for the excellent brand of their combined football.

However, even before the advent of the Corinthians the success of the forward combinations who adopted this new style of play made it obvious that some tightening up was necessary in defence. Several teams began to experiment with three half-backs instead of two, but still retained only the one full-back. The Cambridge University team was probably the first to adopt a line-up similar to that of the present day with a goalkeeper, two full-backs, three half-backs and five forwards. This was in 1877. Wrexham also adopted this formation for the first time when they beat the Druids 1—0 in the Welsh Cup final of 1878. However, most teams continued with six forwards for some time after this.

England first played three half-backs against Scotland in 1884, but the Scots did not adopt this system until 1887 when it became the general practice with all clubs to field three half-backs. Among the first clubs to play regularly with three half-backs was Preston North End. This formation, plus their development of the Scottish passing game, brought them great successes towards the end of the 1880s.

The club which probably did more than any other towards establishing without doubt the real advantages of the passing game was, as already mentioned, the Corinthians. They were the first to show how to draw an opponent and then pass into an open space.

While there may not be as many great individualists in football today, the power of the team as a team is more effective. Indeed, the strength of the modern defensive system is greater than it has ever been. This has developed out of the "third back" game which followed the change in the offside law in 1925 (see under OFFSIDE), but even without considering the defensive strength of the modern team it can be seen that the regimentation and the adherence to a planned system as well as super fitness makes the team today a different force than it was even 20 years ago.

Unfortunately, too many sides nowadays seem to have a positive mania for defensive tactics, but because such tactics often breed success, they are difficult to criticise. The partisan spectator cares little about tactics providing his side is winning. The truth is, however, that defensive football cannot possibly be such an attractive spectacle as the better brand of fast, combined, attacking play.

Perhaps the great dribblers of the past were better attackers. But with a few exceptions this type of play meets with disapproval nowadays. The cry is "get rid of it", and the game has been marred because so many players have taken heed of this cry, booting the ball away before they have found a worthwhile place to put it. This fault may also be part of the modern craze for speed. Unfortunately, too many players cannot think as quickly as this modern game demands.

The claim that the game has declined in recent years is difficult to substantiate. It is true that the modern emphasis on systems such as 4-2-4, 4-3-3 or what have you, has almost completely destroyed individualism and enterprise on the part of the players who are now so strictly tied to the system. But despite what the old-timers would have us believe one still doubts whether the Corinthians would prove a match for the so well drilled modern team.

Where the decline has undoubtedly occurred is not in efficiency but in the quality of entertainment provided. Footballers have become too stereotyped and the lack of enterprise shown by some teams, especially when playing away from home, is strongly deplored.

One of the most successful combinations of the post-war era was the Hungarian side of the 1950s. They were an all-out attacking combination in which each man was a brilliant ball-player like the dribblers of old, but each man also knew just where he should be when not in possession of the ball.

The Hungarian defence was perhaps not as good as that of many Football League clubs, but it was difficult to criticise the rearguard as a separate part of the eleven, when in that Hungarian scheme they were an integral part of an all-out attacking team. And is not attack the best form of defence?

What has been said of the Hungarians can also be said of the Brazilians. No one who saw the Brazilians in the World Cup of 1970 would dare to say that football tactics are inferior to those of 60 years ago. They provided an astonishing contrast to the modern concept of the game. To begin with each player was a master of the basic techniques of dribbling, passing, shooting and heading, and they played with flair, imagination and great genius, all the time concentrating on attack.

It was hoped that the lesson of Brazil's victory would have had a greater effect on the style of play favoured in other countries. But, unfortunately, the adoption of the enterprising attacking style has been resisted. The system of two-leg home and away ties in major Cup competitions has done nothing to help influence coaches in the way many had hoped after watching the Brazilians. But starting at the bottom it is obvious that at home we must pay more attention to developing those basic techniques so that we may never again see either one-footed attackers or poor headers in a world class tournament.

## TEAM CHANGES
See under PLAYERS for the greatest number and least number to appear for a club in a single season.

The Huddersfield Town defence of W. J. Wheeler; R. Staniforth, L. Kelly; W. H. McGarry, D. W. McEvoy and W. L. Quested, remained unchanged throughout season 1952-3 when they won promotion to Division I.

Norwich City fielded an unchanged team in their first 21 Division III(S) games of 1950-51.

When Oldham Athletic visited Barrow in Division III(N), Sept. 14, 1957, only outside-left, R. Fawley, retained his position from the previous game.

Derby County also made 10 changes in their League side on one occasion. That was on April 2, 1960, when only centre-half, R. Young, retained his position in the side which defeated Huddersfield Town.

## TELEVISION

Whereas the Football Association has agreed to the televising of certain matches played under their immediate jurisdiction, the spread of this medium since the war has not been met with open arms by the Football League. For some time the League banned live television from their matches, although the ban was reviewed every season.

In 1960, the Football League made a £150,000 agreement with I.T.A. for the screening of a number of matches, but this scheme fell through when some of the leading clubs refused to take part.

In Aug. 1964 the Football League agreed to allow B.B.C. 2 to screen an edited 55-minute version of one League game per week, to be shown two hours after the game. This was subsequently reduced to 45 minutes following protest by the F.A.

The most recent agreement between the Football League and the Television authorities restricts filming of matches to 45 minutes with no prior announcement of the match to be shown.

The first F.A. Cup Final at which any part of the game was televised was the 1937 Final between Sunderland and Preston North End.

When the B.B.C. resumed television after the war the first game seen on television was Barnet v. Tooting and Mitchum, Oct. 19, 1946, at Barnet.

The first post-war F.A. Cup Final to be televised from start to finish was Charlton Athletic v. Burnley, April 26, 1947.

The first F.A. Cup tie to be televised —other than the Final—was Charlton Athletic v. Blackburn Rovers, 5th Round Feb. 8, 1947.

The first Football League game to be televised was Blackpool v. Bolton Wanderers, on I.T.V., Sept. 10, 1960.

Closed circuit television of an away game was first seen on the Coventry City ground on Wednesday, October 7, 1965. Four large screens were used to show Coventry's game with Cardiff City as it was played at Ninian Park.

The record attendance for an F.A. Cup tie other than the Final was created on March 11, 1967, when 105,000 saw Everton and Liverpool in their 5th Round tie.

A crowd of 64,851 were present at Goodison Park, but another 40,149 were also watching the game on closed circuit television at Anfield.

The first match to be screened in colour —Liverpool v. West Ham United, Nov. 15, 1969.

## TEST MATCHES
See Promotion.

## TEXACO CUP

One of the sponsored competitions introduced into first-class football recently, this is for those First Division clubs who have failed to gain a place in any of the major European Cup competitions. It includes six from the Football League, six from the Scottish League and two each from the League of Ireland and the Irish League.

Winners: 1970-71—Wolverhampton Wanderers bt. Heart of Midlothian 3—1, 0—1. 1971-72—Derby County bt. Aidrieonians 0—0, 2—1. 1972-73—Ipswich Town bt. Norwich City 2—1, 2—1.

## THROW-IN

The "throw-in" was established by the newly-formed Football Association, 1863.

It had been previously mentioned in the Sheffield Laws of the Game as early as 1858, but in the majority of games before 1863 the ball was kicked back into play after it had crossed the touch-lines. Even in the Cambridge rules published only a couple of months before those of the F.A., the ball was to be kicked into play.

According to the earliest F.A. rules, it was the first player to reach the ball after it had passed out of play who was given the advantage of throwing it in. There was nothing in the rules to prevent a player taking a run-up to the line and throwing it one-handed or two-handed in any fashion he thought best.

The two-handed throw-in was first introduced in 1882, and it was not until 1895 that the rules stated that a player must stand on the touch-line when taking the throw-in.

Of course, players have never been permitted to score direct from a throw-in, but until 1920 they could be given offside when a throw was being taken.

In 1925 the F.A. further improved on the rule that a player must stand on the touch-line when taking a throw-in, by compelling him to have both feet on the line. For many years it was the practice to award a free kick against a player making a foul throw. It was not until 1931 that it became law for the throw-in to revert to the opposing side.

The record distance for a throw-in is claimed by R. Woodruff of Wolverhampton Wanderers. In practice on the Molineux ground in October 1965 he threw the ball 40 yards 2 feet 1 inch, thus beating the previous record of 37 yards 2 feet 6 inches by R. Lunnis (Portsmouth) set up at Fratton Park.

**Goal-scoring**
There is only one instance on record of a player scoring with a throw-in. It occurred in a 4th Round F.A. Cup tie at Oakwell between Barnsley and Manchester United on Jan. 22, 1938. F. Bokas took a throw-in near a corner flag and threw the ball right into the goalmouth where T. Breen, the Manchester United goalkeeper, deflected it into his own net.

## TICKETS
In all F.A. Cup ties before the Semi-final Round the visiting clubs are entitled to claim 25 % of all seating accommodation providing they request their share within three days of the draw (in the Scottish Cup 20% of all tickets sold in advance may be claimed).

In the F.A. Cup Semi-final the two competing clubs can each claim 40% of the tickets and the club on whose ground the match is being played can claim 20%.

**F.A. Cup Final Tickets**
The F.A. Cup Final has been an all-ticket game since 1923 when Wembley Stadium was stormed by thousands of fans.

The capacity of Wembley in 1923 was around 127,000 but it is estimated that this figure was exceeded by at least 70,000 on the day. Such was the congestion that the F.A. later had to return £2,797 to ticket holders who had been unable to claim their seats.

Some clubs adopted the practice of issuing Cup Final tickets to "lucky programme number" holders. This system has received the blessing of the F.A. with certain conditions. For instance, the programmes must be sold at their usual price and the club must announce in advance the dates of the matches at which draws will take place and mention the number of tickets to be distributed.

## TORQUAY UNITED F.C.
Founded 1898, Elected to Football League, Division III(S), 1927. Honours: Runners-up, Division III(S), 1956-7; 3rd in Div. IV, 1959-60, 1965-6. Record attendance: 21,908 v. Huddersfield, F.A. Cup, 4th Round, Jan. 29, 1955. Address: Plainmoor, Torquay TQ1 3PS (Tel 38666). Nickname: Gulls. Colours: Gold shirts with blue trim, gold shorts with 2 blue stripes, gold stockings with two blue rings at top. Record League goal-scorer: R. Collins, 40 goals, Division

III(S), 1955-6. Record victory: 9—0 v. Swindon Town, Division III(S), Mar. 8, 1952. Record defeat: 10—2 v. Fulham, Division III(S), Sept. 7, 1931; v. Luton Town, Division III(S), Sept. 2, 1933.

## TOTTENHAM HOTSPUR F.C.
Founded 1882. Elected to Football League, Division II, 1908. Honours: Champions, Division I, 1950-51, 1960-61. Runners-up, 1921-2, 1951-2, 1956-7, 1962-3. Champions, Division II, 1919-20, 1949-50. Runners-up, 1908-9, 1932-3. F.A. Cup: Winners, 1901, 1921, 1961, 1962, 1967. Tottenham Hotspur is one of the only four clubs to have completed the "double"—League Championship and F.A. Cup Winners in the same season. They did so in 1960-61. Football League Cup: Winners, 1971, 1973. Winners European Cup-winners' Cup, 1963. U.E.F.A. Cup: Winners, 1972. Record attendance: 75,038 v. Sunderland, F.A. Cup, 6th Round, Mar. 5, 1938. Address: 748 High Road, Tottenham, N17 0AP (Tel. 01-808 1020). Nickname: Spurs. Colours: White shirts, dark blue shorts, white stockings. Record League goal-scorer: J. Greaves, 37 goals, Division I, 1962-3. Record victory: 13—2 v. Crewe Alexandra, F.A. Cup, 4th Round (replay), Feb. 3, 1960. Record defeat: 7—2 v. Liverpool, Division I, Oct. 31, 1914, v. Newcastle United, Division I, Sept. 1, 1951, and v. Blackburn Rovers, Division I, Sept. 7, 1963, and v. Burnley, Division I, April 22, 1964.

## TOURS
The first overseas tour by an English team was that made by Oxford University when they visited Germany in 1875. The second overseas tour of an English club side did not take place until 1897 when the Corinthians visited South Africa.

The first Scottish club to play abroad was Queen's Park. They played two games in Copenhagen in 1898, winning 7—0 and 3—0.

The first tour, either at home or abroad, was made by the Royal Engineers in Dec. 1873. They played Sheffield, Derby and Nottingham, and won all three games.

Clubs affiliated to the F.A. are obliged to seek permission before playing anywhere abroad.

The Football League makes a stipulation that clubs on tour abroad must not pay their players more than £2 per day for out-of-pocket expenses, further, that the players must not profit from such payments. Clubs are entitled to pay the usual £4 (win) and £2 (draw) bonuses.

The first continental tour to be made by a representative F.A. team took place during the 1899-1900 season when a side which included such famous players as C. W. Alcock, W. Bassett and C. Wreford-Brown, visited Berlin, Prague and Karlsruhe.

## TRAINERS

### Champions
J. Grierson trained six Football League Championship winning teams: Aston Villa in 1894, 1896, 1897, 1899, 1900 and 1910.

### F.A. Cup
J. Lewis trained three F.A. Cup Final teams: Wolverhampton Wanderers 1893, Everton 1897 and Bolton Wanderers 1904.

### Long Service
W. Williams was trainer of Sunderland for 32 years during which time he never missed any of his club's League or Cup matches. He was appointed trainer, Feb. 8, 1897, and retired, April 1929.

### Player
G. Lathom (Cardiff City trainer) played inside-right against Blackburn Rovers at Ewood Park in a First Division game, Jan. 2, 1922.

J. Gallagher (Exeter City trainer) played centre-half against Norwich City at Carrow Road, Division III(S) Jan. 1, 1949, when the team was suffering from food poisoning.

## TRANMERE ROVERS F.C.
Founded 1883. One of the original members of the Football League, Division III(N), 1921. Honours: Champions, Division III(N), 1937-8. Relegated after one season in Division II. Record attendance: 24,424 v. Stoke City. F.A. Cup, 4th Round. Feb. 5, 1972. (Address: Prenton Park, Birkenhead (Tel. 051-608 3677). Colours: White shirts with royal blue edgings, royal blue shorts, white stockings with single blue band. Record League goalscorer: R. Bell, 35 goals, Division III(N), 1933-4. Record victory: 13—4 v. Oldham Athletic, Division III(N), Dec. 26, 1935. Record defeat: 9—1 v. Tottenham Hotspur, F.A. Cup, 3rd Round (replay), Jan. 14, 1953.

## TRANSFERS
See also REGISTRATION OF PLAYERS.

Transfer fees continue to soar, but the suggestion that transfer fees could be limited by the authorities has long since been proved impracticable. As long ago as 1899 the F.A. made a suggestion to the Football League that there should be a limit of £10. A limit actually came into force nine years

later on Jan. 1, 1908 at a much larger figure of £350. But only four months later, at the F.A.'s Annual Meeting, the regulation was expunged.

There were too many easy ways of dodging such a limit. For instance, what was there to stop a club handing over £2,000 for a player, but—to keep within the regulations—signing on a half-dozen other worthless players so as to spread the fee?

Some critics of the present system have gone so far as to label it akin to "white slave trafficking". But is it not the fairest and only practical system? A club wants a certain player from another club . . . so why should they not pay for him? A transfer fee is the only proper compensation for a club's loss. It also enables the club, if it wishes, to obtain a replacement.

Certainly, if there had never been such a system there would not now be so many first-class clubs in existence. Several of these clubs who are able to bring first-class football home to their local supporters have had to transfer to live.

The paying of transfer fees for players became the practice among the leading clubs even before there was any necessity for them to part with money to obtain a player's services. According to the earliest regulations, a player was bound to his club for a single season only, and at the end of that term he was free to join any other club he wished. Transfers during the season could only be arranged with the special permission of the F.A. Council. Yet fees were paid, and the legislators took very little action, beyond calling it "unsportsmanlike".

Today, players are not permitted to move from club to club at will. Once a professional is signed by a club he may remain the club's property for so long as it is prepared to exercise the option which is written into his contract and providing the terms offered are not less favourable than those originally agreed. Whether he continues to play for the club is another matter, but he cannot play for any other club affiliated to the Football Association, or indeed, any other Association belonging to the world-wide Federation, as long as the club which originally obtained his signature keep him on their retained list. The player, however, can appeal to the Management Committee if not released by his club by June 30. He *may* then be placed on the transfer list.

At the end of each season, and in other special circumstances, professionals are either offered terms by their respective clubs, placed on the "open to transfer" list, or given a "free transfer". "Open to transfer" means that a club is willing to receive offers for the player. "Free transfer" means that a club is no longer interested in the player and he is free to go where he pleases.

Clubs are not permitted to make a direct approach to try and obtain the services of players retained by another club or on the "open to transfer" list. In all cases (except, of course, for those given a "Free transfer") any inquiries must be made to the club holding the player's registration. The same applies on the player's side. He must not offer his services to any other club until his existing engagement has ended.

No club can transfer a player without his consent, and players have the right of appeal to the League Management Committee which has the power to overrule clubs in any decision affecting transfers. If, for instance, a player considers that the fee placed on him by his club is so high that it may restrict his chances of obtaining a transfer, he may appeal to have that figure reduced.

The transfer system was upheld in Law in 1912 when the test case of Lawrence J. Kingaby v. Aston Villa was heard in the King's Bench Division on Mar. 26-7. This was really the Players' Union v. the Football League, for the League undertook to indemnify the club against all costs, and the player was backed by the union. Kingaby claimed damages for loss of employment. The defence submitted that the case was simply a question of law and therefore not one for a jury but for a judge's decision alone. This submission was upheld and the case came before Mr. Justice Lawrence.

The player pleaded that another club had offered him employment but that he was unable to take it because of the transfer fee fixed by his present employers—Aston Villa. He further alleged that his employers had maliciously made their fee excessive.

Judgment was given for the defendants with costs. Mr. Justice Lawrence found no evidence of malice and that the action of the defendants (Aston Villa) was justified by the terms of the employment.

A much more recent case, that concerning G. Eastham and Newcastle United in 1963, resulted in a declaration being made to the effect that the system of retaining a player after the expiration of his contract was not binding in law, but this has been overcome by the insertion of an option clause (previously mentioned) in the player's contract.

The transfer of players in the Football League after the second Thursday in March in each season is controlled by the Management Committee of the League. Players transferred after this date are not able to

play for their new club in League matches unless permission is received. This rule, made in 1911 (originally the deadline was March 16) is designed to prevent clubs engaged in promotion or relegation struggles from strengthening their team at so vital a stage of the season.

The last occasion permission was granted for a club so concerned to include a player signed after deadline, was when Blackburn Rovers were fighting to avoid relegation to Division II at the end of the 1935-6 season. There were special circumstances. They had three goalkeepers out of commission with fractured limbs and permission was obtained to play K. J. Hamill, a goalkeeper signed on April 15.

In 1967 the Football League instituted a system of Temporary Transfers wherein each club is permitted two players on loan.

### F.A. Cup

Players transferred cannot play for their new clubs in the F.A. Cup competition if they have already taken part in the competition during the season with another club.

In 1958, because of the Munich disaster, Manchester United was granted special permission to include S. Crowther in their Cup team although he had already appeared for Aston Villa that season.

In season 1945-6 J. Scoular appeared for Gosport in a Preliminary Round of the competition and for Portsmouth in the 3rd Round Proper.

### Four-Figure Fees

The first four-figure transfer fee was £1,000, paid by Middlesbrough to Sunderland for the transfer of A. Common, Feb. 1905. Common proved his worth. On Feb. 25, Middlesbrough, who were in a dangerous position near the bottom of Division I, won their first away League game for nearly two years. They defeated Sheffield United with the only goal of the match, scored from the penalty spot by Common. Middlesbrough's previous away win was also against Sheffield United, 3—1, Mar. 7, 1903.

Common's transfer caused such a sensation that a special commission was set up to investigate. They were unable to report anything unlawful or underhand.

The first four-figure transfer between Irish clubs is said to be £1,000, paid by Distillery to Derry City for wing-half G. Bowler, during the last war.

### Private and Confidential

Transfer fees as stated in the National Press are usually only estimated. In 1922 the Football League decided that all transfer fees should be treated as private and confidential.

## Record Fees

The world record transfer fee is approximately £435,000. This amount is believed to have been paid by the Italian club Juventus to Varese for the transfer of P. Anastasi in 1968.

The record fee in a transfer deal involving only one player with a Football League club is understood to be about £225,000, the amount said to have been paid by Derby County to Leicester City for D. Nish in Aug. 1972.

The record fee between two Scottish clubs—£100,000 by Rangers to Hibernian for C. Stein, Oct. 1968.

## Signing-on Fee

When a player signs for any particular Football League club for the first time (as a professional) then, unless transferred at his own request without good reason he is entitled to a signing-on fee which is 5% of his transfer fee (minimum share £250) or, if given a free transfer then his new club must agree to pay the minimum £250 over the period of the contract.

Before the Football League altered the rules in 1920 so that players were no longer permitted to receive a share of their transfer fee, the record amount received by a player under the old agreement is believed to have been £1,000, paid to centre-forward J. Lane, transferred from Blackpool to Birmingham for £3,300, season 1919-20.

Since the Football League decided to allow players to receive 5% of the fee (that was in 1967) then it is assumed that D. Nish (see Record Fees in this section) has received the British record signing-on fee of £11,250.

In many countries abroad players have been known to receive huge signing-on fees and Italian and Spanish clubs have led the world in this respect.

Information concerning these fees is not always reliable for many reports are grossly exaggerated. However, while the accuracy of the following list cannot be guaranteed it is included here as a fair reflection of the degree of inducements offered to the world's top players to sign for some foreign clubs. These are signing-on fees paid at time of transfer from one club to another. In most foreign countries, especially Italy and Spain, large signing-on fees are offered to players by their clubs each time they sign a new contract.

| | |
|---|---|
| L. Suarez, Barcelona to Internazionale (Milan), 1961 | £59,000 |
| L. Del Sol, Real Madrid to Juventus (Turin), 1962 | £47,500 |
| H. Haller, Bologna to Juventus, 1968 | £38,000 |
| T. S. Amarildo, Botafogo to Milan, 1963 | £32,000 |
| J. Schiaffino, Penarol (Uruguay) to A. C. Milan, 1954 | £23,000 |
| E. O. Sivori, River Plate (Argentine) to Juventus, 1957 | £20,000 |
| A. Simonsson, Gothenburg to Real Madrid, 1960 | £14,000 |
| E. I. Netto (Vava), Atletico Madrid to Corinthians (Brazil), 1960 | £13,000 |
| G. Hitchens, Aston Villa to Internazionale, 1961 | £12,000 |

## Special and Unusual Transfers

When Arsenal signed C. Buchan from Sunderland in 1925 they paid a fee of £2,000, and also agreed to pay Sunderland an extra £100 for each goal Buchan scored during his first season. He scored 21 goals.

When Tottenham Hotspur signed W. G. Hall from Notts County in 1932, they agreed to pay an additional fee of £500 if Hall was "capped" as a Tottenham player. Hall got the first of several caps in Dec. 1933, when he played against France.

A. Pape, Clapton Orient's centre forward, travelled with his side to Manchester to play a Division II match against Manchester United on Feb. 7, 1925, but just before the game he was transferred to Manchester United. The Football League sanctioned the transfer when contacted by telephone and Pape helped to defeat his old club 4—2.

F. Laycock, a Barrow forward, was called off the field during a Division III game with Rotherham County in order to sign forms transferring him to Nelson. It was the last day of the season for transfers, Mar. 16, 1925.

There has been at least one player who has played for both sides in the same League match, J. Oakes, a left-back, who captained Charlton Athletic's promotion-winning side of the 1930s, played for Port Vale in a Division II game against Charlton Athletic at The Valley on Boxing Day, 1932. The game was abandoned before the end owing to bad light. When the re-arranged fixture came up, later in the season, Oakes was left-back for Charlton Athletic, having been transferred to the London club in the interim.

The list that follows is only intended to show the increase in transfer fees among British clubs over the years:

| | | |
|---|---|---|
| 1893 | J. Southworth, Blackburn Rovers to Everton | £400 |
| 1902 | J. McMahon, Preston North End to Manchester City | £450 |
| 1903 | G. Dorsett, West Bromwich Albion to Manchester City | £450 |
| 1904 | A. Common, Sheffield United to Sunderland | £520 |
| 1904 | A. McCombie, Sunderland to Newcastle United | £700 |
| 1905 | A. Common, Sunderland to Middlesbrough | £1,000 |
| 1907 | G. Wilson, Everton to Newcastle United | £1,600† |
| 1908 | A. Brown, Sheffield United to Sunderland | £1,600 |
| | A. Shepherd, Bolton Wanderers to Newcastle United | £1,650 |
| 1911 | J. Simpson, Falkirk to Blackburn Rovers | £1,800 |
| | W. Hibbert, Bury to Newcastle United | £1,950 |
| 1912 | D. Shea, West Ham United to Blackburn Rovers | £2,000 |
| 1913 | T. Logan, Falkirk to Chelsea | £2,500 |
| 1920 | J. Lane, Blackpool to Birmingham | £3,300 |
| | J. Crosbie, Ayr United to Birmingham | £3,500 |
| | S. Fazackerley, Sheffield United to Everton | £4,000 |
| 1921 | T. Hamilton, Kilmarnock to Preston North End | £4,600 |
| 1922 | S. Puddefoot, West Ham United to Falkirk | £5,000 |
| | W. Cresswell, South Shields to Sunderland | £5,500 |
| 1925 | R. Kelly, Burnley to Sunderland | £6,500 |
| 1927 | J. Gibson, Partick Thistle to Aston Villa | £7,500 |
| 1928 | D. Jack, Bolton Wanderers to Arsenal | £10,890 |
| 1934 | J. Allen, Portsmouth to Aston Villa | £11,000 |
| 1938 | B. Jones, Wolverhampton Wanderers to Arsenal | £13,000 |
| 1946 | A. Stubbins, Newcastle United to Liverpool | £13,500 |
| 1947 | W. Steel, Morton to Derby County | £15,000 |
| | T. Lawton, Chelsea to Notts County | £20,000 |
| 1949 | J. Morris, Manchester United to Derby County | £25,000 |
| | E. Quigley, Sheffield Wednesday to Preston North End | £26,000 |
| 1950 | T. Ford, Aston Villa to Sunderland | £30,000 |
| 1951 | J. Sewell, Notts County to Sheffield Wednesday | £34,500 |
| 1958 | C. Jones, Swansea Town to Tottenham Hotspur | £35,000 |
| | A. Quixall, Sheffield Wednesday to Manchester United | £45,000 |
| 1959 | M. Charles, Swansea Town to Arsenal | £40,000§ |
| 1960 | D. Law, Huddersfield Town to Manchester City | £55,000 |
| 1962 | J. Byrne, Crystal Palace to West Ham United | £58,000‡ |
| 1962 | A. H. Kay, Sheffield Wednesday to Everton | £60,000 |
| 1964 | F. Pickering, Blackburn Rovers to Everton | £80,000 |
| 1965 | J. Baxter, Rangers to Sunderland | £85,000 |
| 1966 | M. England, Blackburn Rovers to Tottenham Hotspur | £95,000 |
| 1966 | T. Hateley, Aston Villa to Chelsea | £100,000 |
| 1966 | A. Ball, Blackpool to Everton | £110,000 |
| 1968 | W. Morgan, Burnley to Manchester United | £118,000 |
| 1968 | M. Chivers, Southampton to Tottenham Hotspur | £125,000‡ |
| 1968 | A. Clarke, Fulham to Leicester City | £150,000‡ |
| 1969 | A. Clarke, Leicester City to Leeds United | £165,000 |
| 1970 | M. Peters, West Ham United to Tottenham Hotspur | £180,000‡ |
| 1971 | A. Ball, Everton to Arsenal | £220,000 |
| 1972 | D. Nish, Leicester City to Derby County | £225,000 |

‡ These deals involved a second player in part exchange.

† Newcastle United was reported to have paid £1,000 to Everton and the remaining £600 to Belfast Distillery.

§ Arsenal also let Swansea Town have two players.

Transfer fees are supposed to be confidential and while it is difficult to establish the precise amounts involved in deals between British clubs it is almost impossible to obtain the precise figure of fees involving foreign clubs. However, here, for what they are worth, are the estimated amounts of some of the more important transfer deals where one or more foreign clubs have been involved:

| 1968 | P. Anastasi, Verese to Juventus | £435,000 |
| 1972 | J. Mulder, Anderlecht to Ajax | £300,000 |
| 1972 | D. Zoff, Naples to Juventus | £280,000 |
| 1968 | M. Bertini, Fiorentina to Internazionale | £267,000 |
| 1968 | H. Haller, Bologna to Juventus | £267,000 |
| 1963 | A. Sormani, Mantua to A.S. Roma | £243,000 |
| 1968 | R. Benetti, Palermo to Juventus | £233,000 |
| 1969 | S. Clerici, Atlanta Bergamo to Verona Hellas | £233,000 |
| 1966 | R. Rosato, Torino to AC Milan | £231,000 |
| 1962 | L. Del Sol, Real Madrid to Juventus | £200,000 |
| 1966 | V. De Paoli, Brescia to Juventus | £197,000 |
| 1962 | J. Peiro, Atletico (Madrid) to Torino (Turin) | £170,000 |
| 1961 | L. Suarez, Barcelona to Internazionale (Milan)* | £150,000 |
| 1963 | T. S. Amarildo, Botafogo to Milan‡ | £142,850 |
| 1966 | Anquilletti, Atalanta to AC Milan | £132,000 |
| 1962 | D. Law, Torino (Turin) to Manchester United | £115,000 |
| 1957 | B. Julinho, Florence to Palmeiras (Brazil) | £111,000 |
| 1966 | L. Pizabella, Atalanta to A.S. Roma | £109,000 |
| 1961 | B. Di Giacomo, Napoli to Torino (Turin) | £105,000 |
| 1961 | D. Law, Manchester City to Torino (Turin) | £100,000 |
| 1957 | E. Sivori, River Plate (Argentine) to Juventus | £100,000 |
| 1961 | J. Greaves, Milan to Tottenham Hotspur | £99,999 |
| 1962 | V. Angelillo, Internazionale (Milan) to A.S. Roma | £90,000 |
| 1961 | J. Umberto, Academica (Portugal) to Internazionale (Milan) | £90,000 |
| 1961 | J. Greaves, Chelsea to Milan | £85,000 |
| 1958 | E. Firmani, Sampdoria (Genoa) to Internazionale | £81,000 |
| 1961 | G. Hitchens, Aston Villa to Internazionale | £80,000 |
| 1954 | J. Schiaffino, Penarol (Uruguay) to Milan | £72,000 |
| 1961 | J. Baker, Hibernian to Torino (Turin) | £70,000 |
| 1962 | U. Maschio, Atalanta (Genoa) to Internazionale† | £68,000 |
| 1957 | W. J. Charles, Leeds United to Juventus (Turin)§ | £65,000 |
| 1962 | J. Baker, Torino (Turin) to Arsenal | £65,000 |

* The player received £59,000 of this amount.
† Plus two other players.
§ The player received £10,000 of this amount.
‡ The player received £32,000 of this amount.

**TRAVELLING**
On Good Friday, April 10, 1936, Swansea Town defeated Plymouth Argyle 2—1 in a Division II match at Home Park, Plymouth. The following day Swansea Town met Newcastle United at St. James' Park, Newcastle. Swansea Town lost 2—0.

Between the two games they travelled about 400 miles, a record distance for a League club between matches on successive days.

**TROPHIES**
Players who have received F.A. Cup medals, League Championship medals and full international honours in the same season are: F. Dewhurst and J. Goodall of Preston North End, 1888-9, C. Athersmith of Aston Villa, 1896-7, D. Blanchflower, D. Mackay, C. Jones, R. Smith and J. White of Tottenham Hotspur, 1960-61, and F. McLintock, P. Rice and P. Storey of Arsenal, 1970-71.

D. Mackay (Tottenham Hotspur) has a unique distinction. He is the only player to have appeared in both F.A. Cup and Scottish F.A. Cup winning teams (Heart of Midlothian 1956, Tottenham Hotspur 1961, 1962 and 1967); Scottish League and Football League Champions (Heart of Midlothian 1957-8, Tottenham Hotspur 1960-61); Scottish League Cup winners (Heart of Midlothian 1955, 1959); Scottish League v. Football League, Mar. 1957, Oct. 1958; Football League v. Scottish League, Mar. 1960; in addition to Scottish International appearances.

**TURKEY**
Soccer has been played in Istanbul for more than 70 years and the leading club in Turkey, Fenerbahce, can trace its history back to 1907, or two years after Galatasaray, their first club was formed.

Turkey first appeared in an international match in 1923 when they drew 2—2 with

199

Rumania in Istanbul and they entered the Olympic tournament in Paris in the following year, but their pre-war matches were very few and far between, and it is in the last decade or so that this country has really begun to make a name in internationals.

In 1954 they qualified for the World Cup tournament, but unfortunately found themselves grouped with the two eventual finalists Germany and Hungary.

In Feb. 1956, they halted the Hungarians' run of successes with a shock 3—1 victory over the Mighty Magyars in Istanbul.

Professionalism was officially adopted by the Turks in 1952 and the Turkish Football Federation which was founded in 1923 now controls nearly 2,000 clubs.

Address of the governing body: Turkiye Futbol Federasyonu, Ulus Is Hani A Blok Kat: 4, Ankara. Colours: White shirts, white shorts, red and white stockings.

Results of international matches:

| | | |
|---|---|---|
| June 8, 1960 | Turkey 4, Scotland 2, Ankara |
| Nov. 16, 1966† | Eire 2, Turkey 1; Dublin |
| Feb. 22, 1967† | Turkey 2, Eire 1; Ankara |
| Oct. 23, 1968* | Ireland 4, Turkey 1; Belfast |
| Dec. 11, 1968* | Turkey 0, Ireland 3; Istanbul |

* World Cup
† Nations Cup

## TWINS
See FAMILIES (Brothers).

## UEFA CUP

The full title of this competition is the Union of European Football Associations Cup and it came into being in 1971 when this organisation took over what was previously known as the European Fairs Cup. A match between the first and last winners of the old trophy, Barcelona and Leeds United respectively, played to decide the permanent holders, was won 2-1 by the Spanish side.

Although a new trophy has been presented the story of this competition may be said to have begun in 1955 as the International Industries Fairs Inter-Cities Cup and was originally intended for representative sides from cities who annually hold Industries Fairs. That title was changed in 1969 to European Fairs Cup, and in 1971 to UEFA Cup.

The first competition was played over a period of three years with teams from 12 cities. London and Barcelona emerged as finalists in 1958.

The idea of entering representative sides from each city soon gave way to the entry of club teams, and in the second competition which began in 1958, Chelsea represented London and Birmingham was represented by the club of that name.

Results of Finals with the number of entries in brackets:

*Fairs Cup*:

1955–58 (12) Barcelona bt. London, 6–0, 2–2
1958–60 (16) Barcelona bt. Birmingham City, 0–0, 4–1
1960–61 (16) AS Roma bt. Birmingham City, 2–0, 2–2
1961–62 (28) Valencia bt. Barcelona, 6–2, 1–1
1962–63 (32) Valencia bt. Dynamo Zagreb, 2–0, 2–1
1963–64 (32) Real Zaragoza bt. Valencia, 2–1
1964–65 (46) Ferencvaros bt. Juventus, 1–0
1965–66 (45) CF Barcelona bt. Zaragoza, 0–1, 4–2*
1966–67 (48) Dynamo Zagreb bt. Leeds Utd. 2–0, 0–0
1967–68 (44) Leeds Utd. bt. Ferencvaros, 1–0, 0–0
1968–69 (62) Newcastle Utd. bt. Ujpest Dosza, 3–0, 3–2
1969–70 (64) Arsenal bt. Anderlecht, 1–3, 3–0
1970–71 (64) Leeds Utd. bt. Juventus, 2–2, 1–1†

*UEFA Cup:*

1971–72 (64) Tottenham Hotspur bt. Wolverhampton W., 2–1, 1–1
1972–73 (63) Liverpool bt. Borussia Mönchengladbach, 3–0, 0–2

*After extra time    †Won on away goals rule

## UNDEFEATED

See DEFENSIVE RECORDS (Undefeated).

## UNION OF EUROPEAN FOOTBALL ASSOCIATIONS

In 1952 the suggestion was made that the Football Associations of the various European countries should form themselves into a group to consider all matters relating to football in this continent and to promote the development of friendly sporting relations between the member countries.

A referendum was conducted among the European countries and upon general agreement the Union came into being in June 1954 with Mr. Ebbe Schwartz of Denmark elected the first Chairman.

The Union is not a separate body to F.I.F.A. but is one of six Continental Confederations operating under the auspices of the world-wide Federation.

There are now 33 members of U.E.F.A. and the address of the headquarters is: Case Postale 16, 3,000 Berne 32, Switzerland.

Competitions under their immediate control include: European Champion Clubs' Cup, European Cup-winners' Cup, European Championship (Nations), and UEFA Cup.

## UNITED STATES OF AMERICA

Since World War II soccer has made a big increase in popularity in the United States. This has been due not only to the influx of immigrants from Europe but to the return of American servicemen from countries where they had the opportunity to watch and play football, and catch the enthusiasm for the game from the British, French, Germans, etc.

Soccer, however, is still a poor fourth to the Americans' most popular games of baseball, American football and basketball, and although the introduction in 1960 of the U.S. International Soccer League in New York and the inauguration in 1967 of coast to coast professional Leagues added a terrific impetus to the game in the States it still has a long way to go before the average home-born American mentions it in the same breath as any of the major sports just named.

Football of sorts was played in New England in the middle of the 19th century but this was little more than rough and tumble similar to the old Shrove Tuesday game played on this side of the Atlantic.

However, although early American football subsequently developed into a game resembling rugger rather than soccer, there were many points about the early game as played at some of the colleges in the 1870s that linked it with the latter sport.

Harvard University played a form of soccer as early as 1860 but they subsequently led the field in the development of American football.

The first inter-collegiate match was played between Rutgers and Princetown, at New Brunswick, in Nov. 1869.

Football has been played at Yale since about 1840 but it was not until the 1870s that they began to meet other colleges in regular games. It is interesting to note that at about this time running with the ball was not permitted at Yale although it could be handled and knocked from hand to hand. Goals were scored under and not over the bar and dribbling was also practised.

Twenty-a-side was the normal practice but in 1873 a team of Englishmen, captained by an Old Etonian, met Yale at New Haven and in this game the teams were each composed of 11 men. In fact, 1873 was the first year in which any widely accepted code of rules was adopted in America.

As already indicated the change of direction in development of the American game towards rugger rather than soccer was led by Harvard, in 1875, and they subsequently persuaded Yale to follow suit.

It was not until April 1884 that a meeting was held in New York at which the American Football Association was formed. This subsequently became defunct, but was re-formed in 1913.

The United States first met Canada at Association Football in 1886, clubs sprang up in many parts of the country in the 1890s, and the Californian F.A. (one of the strongholds of soccer in the States) was established in 1902.

An Inter-University Association Football League was formed in 1905, the same year in which the Pilgrims F.C. went out from England to play 23 games in America, winning 21 of them. They toured the United States again in 1909, while the famous Corinthians went out in 1906 and 1911.

A National Challenge Cup competition was established in 1913 and a National Amateur Cup in 1922.

The United States has suffered several big defeats in the Olympic Games soccer tournament. Their best performance in this competition was probably that in Berlin in 1936 when a side which included several Scots was only beaten 1—0 by Italy.

In 1930 the U.S. reached the semi-finals of the World Cup before being eliminated 6—1 by the Argentine. A 7—1 defeat by Italy put them out in the first round in Italy in 1934, and the only year since then in which they have appeared in the World Cup Finals was 1950. In that year, however, they gained their most shattering victory, beating England 1—0 in Brazil. The teams on that occasion were:

England: Williams; Ramsey, Aston; Wright, Hughes, Dickinson; Finney, Mannion, Bentley, Mortensen, Mullen.

United States: Borghi; Keough, Macca; McIlvenny, Colombo, Bahr; Wallace, Pariani, Gaetjens, J. Sousa, E. Sousa.

Gaetjens scored the only goal of the match.

In 1960 the inaugural tournament of the United States International Soccer League included 12 clubs, each from a different country. The final was won by Bangu (Brazil) who beat Kilmarnock, 2—0. This competition was repeated during the summer months in each succeeding year to 1966.

The first major step to introduce professional soccer into the United States on a national scale was taken during 1966 with the formation of two Leagues, both with considerable financial backing—The National Professional Soccer League and the North American Soccer League (later changing its title to The United Soccer Association).

These two competitions amalgamated in December 1967 and formed a 17-team League which became known as the North American Soccer League, but a considerable amount of money was lost in all-out efforts to indoctrinate a largely disinterested American public, and at the end of only one season the majority of clubs withdrew.

However, despite the comparative failure of the American enthusiasts to promote professional soccer as bigtime entertainment for the masses, a great deal of progress has been made since 1966 in introducing the game to the schools, a development which augurs well for the future.

Although still small, attendances at North American League matches during 1972 showed an increase of over 50%.

The address of the governing body which has been affiliated to F.I.F.A. since 1913 and now controls something like 3,000 clubs is the United States Soccer Football Association, Inc., Empire State Building, Room 4010, New York, N.Y. 10001. Colours: White shirts, blue shorts, red stockings.

Results of international matches:

| | | |
|---|---|---|
| June 16, 1924 | Eire 3, United States 1; Dublin |
| June 29, 1950* | England 0, United States 1; Belo Horizonte, Brazil |
| April 30, 1952 | Scotland 6, United States 0; Hampden Park |
| June 8, 1953† | United States 3, England 6; New York City |
| May 28, 1959 | United States 1, England 8; Los Angeles |
| May 27, 1964 | United States 0; England 10; New York City |

  * World Cup
  †Under floodlights

## UNIVERSITY FOOTBALL

Although the universities of Oxford and Cambridge have not been able to maintain the strong position they once held in the football world, forced into the background by the keener competitive elements of the professional game, they played a leading role in the game's early development and readers who refer to the index will be able to trace several references to these universities throughout this volume.

Cambridge University men drew up the first code of rules of the game in the middle of the 19th century and Oxford University produced one of the most powerful combinations to enter the F.A. Cup during the earliest years of this competition. Oxford were semi-finalists 1875, 1876, finalists 1873, 1877 and 1880, and winners 1874. Cambridge were semi-finalists in 1877. They dropped out in 1880-81.

The first Oxford v. Cambridge match was played at Kennington Oval in 1874 and was won 1—0 by Oxford. A return match played later in the same year was won 2—0 by Cambridge. This game has been played in every season since with the exception of five seasons 1914-19 and six seasons 1939-45.

During the period before the introduction of professionalism and until the amateurs were no longer able to hold their own with the professional, many university men appeared in full internationals. Indeed, 78 were chosen for England, Ireland and Wales, the last man to receive this honour being C. T. Ashton of Cambridge who actually captained England against Ireland in Oct. 1925.

University Blues who subsequently played as professionals for Football League clubs: G. T. L. Ansell (Oxford University 1928, 1929, 1930) turned professional with Brighton and Hove Albion, 1932. M. King (Oxford University, 1956), Colchester United 1956. A. Smith (Oxford University 1946), Aston Villa 1951, M. Pinner (Cambridge University, 1953), Leyton Orient, 1963, K. Sanderson (Cambridge University), Plymouth Argyle, 1964, P. Phillips (Cambridge University 1966, 67, 68), Luton Town, 1969.

## URUGUAY

The footballers of Uruguay have proved themselves to be among the finest in the world and only the loss of so many of their star players to Italy and the Argentine has prevented them from becoming established permanently among the half dozen leading soccer nations.

Uruguay won the football tournament of the 1924 Olympic Games by defeating Switzerland 3—0 in Paris. They retained their Olympic title at Amsterdam four years later when they defeated the Argentine 2—1 after a drawn game. In 1930 they carried off the World Cup on their home ground by beating Argentine, 4—2, and when they next entered this competition, in Brazil in 1950, they again carried off the trophy, this time by beating the host nation, 2—1 In all, a remarkable record in international football.

Since then Uruguay has lost many of their best players. They were beaten in the semi-finals of the World Cup in 1954; failed to qualify in 1958; were eliminated through defeats by Russia and Yugoslavia in the final tournament of 1962, but did better again in 1966 when they won through to the quarter-finals before being eliminated by West Germany. In 1970 they reached the

semi-finals, with a hard uncompromising style of defensive football, before losing 3—1 to Brazil.

An English professor at Montevideo University formed the first club in 1882, and Britishers engaged in building the railways established another club in 1891 which subsequently became the famous Penarol club of today.

The leading Uruguayan clubs have been professional since 1932 and the F.A. which was founded in 1900 now controls about 600 clubs including over 1,000 professional players.

The address of the governing body: Asociación Uruguaya de Football, 18 de Julio 1520-28, Montevideo. Colours: Sky blue shirts with white collars and cuff, black shorts, blacks stockings with sky blue tops.

Results of international matches:

| | |
|---|---|
| May 31, 1953 | Uruguay 2, England 1; Montevideo |
| June 19, 1954* | Uruguay 7, Scotland 0; Basle |
| June 26, 1954* | Uruguay 4, England 2; Basle |
| May 2, 1962 | Scotland 2, Uruguay 3; Hampden Park |
| April 29, 1964 | Ireland 3, Uruguay 0; Belfast |
| May 6, 1964 | England 2, Uruguay 1; Wembley |
| July 11, 1966* | England 0, Uruguay 0; Wembley |
| June 8, 1969 | Uruguay 1, England 2; Montevideo |

* World Cup

**U.S.S.R.**
See Russia.

**WADSWORTH, Samuel John (1896-1961)**
When Nelson needed some cash to help pay for a new stand they sold this full-back to Huddersfield Town in 1920 and he developed into one of the most constructive defenders in the League, assisting Huddersfield to win the F.A. Cup and then their triple championship success. He subsequently captained England before his transfer to Burnley in September 1929. Roy Goodall and Sam Wadsworth in the Huddersfield defence (they played together in well over 200 games) must be one of the finest pairs of club full-backs in the game's history.

Huddersfield Town 1920-29, 281 apprcs. (3 goals). Burnley 1929-31, 7 apprcs. England internationals 9. Inter-League games 6. League Champions 1923-4, 1924-5, 1925-6. F.A. Cup winners 1922.

## WAGES
The early history of players' wages is dealt with in general terms under PROFESSIONA-LISM. It will be seen there that wages were paid to players before official sanction was given for such payments. In the eyes of the Football Association all Footballers were amateurs. When the first rumours of payments being made to players began to spread, the F.A. made a rule in 1882 that any member of a club would be debarred from football if it was found that he received "remuneration or consideration of any sort above his actual expenses and any wages actually lost".

Several evasions were adopted to make the payment of wages possible. Duplicate sets of books were often kept: one under the counter and one to be made available for perusal by the F.A. should the occasion arise. In other instances, players were given bogus jobs for which they received payment, the money being refunded to the "employers" by the clubs. Another scheme was to pay players out of the gate money before the total was entered in the books as gross gate receipts.

Preston North End and Blackburn Rovers were among the first clubs to pay wages to players. Another club, Stoke, paid their first professionals 2s. 6d (12½p) a week, until one day it leaked out that one of the men was receiving the stupendous sum of 5s. (25p). The bulk of the players immediately went on strike until the club eventually agreed to an all-round increase to 5s.

Around 1883, Bolton Wanderers were paying their players 2s. 6d. bonus for winning games and deducting that amount for defeats.

Following the legalisation of professionalism in 1885, there was still no stipulation as to either minimum or maximum wages. One of the greatest players of all times, S. Bloomer, became a professional with Derby County in the 1890s at a wage of 7s. 6d. (37½p) a week. About the same time Sunderland were paying their players as much as 30s. (£1.50) a week. Birmingham's players agreed to receive a share of the gate as their wages when the club turned professional in 1885. Professionals at Fulham were paid 10s. (50p) a week and given an "outside job".

The first move to regulate payment to players concerned the signing-on fee. In 1891 the Football League ruled that this should not exceed £10. (It was not increased until 1958.)

The wages problem came to a head in 1893 when the Football League proposed that players should be limited to £140 per year including a maximum of £1 per week in the close season. But this proposal did not receive the necessary majority and the idea of limiting wages was shelved.

The first maximum wage rule came into force in 1901 when the limit was fixed at £4 per week. Nearly nine years later this figure was raised to £5, providing that the increase was given in two rises of 10s. (50p) after two and four years of service.

The Football Association took no further part in the control of weekly wages to players after 1910. This is now left to the respective Leagues and competitions. Until 1966 they retained some interest in the actual amounts paid by stipulating the minimum which a club must offer any player they wished to retain for a further period of service, but even this has since been erased by the new form of contract.

During World War I there were reductions in wages. But in Mar. 1920, following a request by the Players' Union, proposals for an increased maximum came before a Special General Meeting of the Football League. The result was an increase to £9 per week throughout the year (during both the playing season and the close season).

The new wage was not for all players. From a £5 minimum for new players, the rise was to be given in annual increments of £1. It was also decided that players entitled to receive only the £5 maximum (and players receiving less) could sign an agreement with their clubs whereby they would receive £1 extra for each first team appearance. A year later this £1 extra was allowed to all players making first team appearances on a wage of £8 or less.

The Players' Union soon demanded further alterations in the rate of increments and a maximum wage of £10. But 12 months after its demands, the League Management Committee proposed a reduction in the maximum wage. Its proposals were passed by the League on April 12, 1922, and took effect immediately—maximum £8 per week during playing season of 37 weeks, and a maximum £6 per week during the remaining 15 weeks.

Despite the efforts of the Players' Union to secure further alterations in the wage scale, there was no other change until 1945 when the maximum close season wage was increased to £7 per week.

During the war-time seasons special wage rates were in force. From 1939 to 1943 players were paid 30s. (£1.50) per match plus travelling expenses but no bonus. For season 1943-4 this was increased to £2, while players in Championship teams received a bonus of £5, runners-up £3. The rate in 1945-6 was £4 per match.

A most significant wage agreement was made in 1947, thanks largely to the efforts of the Players' Union. For the first time a *minimum* wage level was fixed for all full-time Football League professionals. A National Arbitration Tribunal under the chairmanship of Lord Terrington, was responsible for making the award which stipulated a minimum of £7 in the season and £5 in the summer for all players over 20 years of age.

The tribunal also decided that the maximum wage should be raised to £12 in the playing season and £10 in the close season, based on length of service, the maximum wage being reached after five years' service with any club in the Football League, Scottish League, Irish League or Eire League.

Further increases were as follows:

June 1951: Maximum raised to £14.

July 1953: Maximum raised to £15 in the playing seasons and £12 in the close season. Minimum raised to £3 10s. (£3. 50) for a 17-year-old and £7 10s. (£7. 50) for a 20-year-old in the playing season and £5 10s. (£5. 50) in the close season.

June 1957: Maximum raised to £17 and £14, minimum to £4 10s. (£4.50) at 17, £8 10s. (£8.50) and £6 10s. (£6.50) at 20.

June 1958: Maximum raised to £20 and £17. Minimum to £5 at 17, £8 at 20.

The players made further wage demands in 1960 and when these were backed by a threat to strike on Jan. 21, 1961, the Football League agreed to a number of alterations. The most important of these which concerned wages was the abolition of the maximum.

At the same time it was also decided to raise the minimum wage and graduate from £624 to £780 per annum according to the division of the League in which the player's club is engaged. All these rates are for full-time professionals at age 20 and over in the Football League.

Part-time players of any age must be paid at least £5 per week.

Apprentice professionals must be paid at least £5 per week or up to a maximum of £8 at 16, or £10 at 17 years of age.

**Bonus**

In addition to their regular wage, players may receive certain other payments such as match bonuses.

 In the Football League the rate of bonus is £4 for a win and £2 for a draw.

The bonus for the various Rounds of the F.A. Cup competition is as follows:

For a win in Rounds 1, 2, 3, 4, 5, 6 respectively, £4, £4, £5, £6, £8, £10.

For a win in the Semi-final £20.

For a win in the Final £25.

In the case of drawn games the teams receive half the above amounts.

Where matches are televised live each player may receive a payment of up to £10.50 out of the fee paid by the television company, but this payment shall not be made when only short extracts of matches are filmed for transmission.

It should be noted that there is no limit to bonuses paid by clubs who win European Competitions. For instance the Manchester United players each collected £2,000 for winning the European Cup in 1968.

**Fees for Internationals**

| | | |
|---|---|---|
| 1886—10s. per match | | |
| 1887—£1 | ,, | ,, |
| 1908—£4 | ,, | ,,* |
| 1920—£6 | ,, | ,, |
| 1937—£8 | ,, | ,, |

---

*England players were getting as much as £10 per game before there was a general agreement with the other home countries in 1908 to pay £4.

1939—£10 ,,        ,,
1946—£20 ,,        ,,
1952—£30 ,,        ,,
1953—£50 ,,        ,,
1961—£60 ,,        ,,
1972—£100,,        ,,
Players in Under-23 games receive £20.

See also REFEREES AND LINESMEN, TOURS, and TRANSFERS (Signing-on fee).

## WALES
See under INTERNATIONALS (WALES); WALES, FOOTBALL ASSOCIATION; WELSH CUP; WELSH LEAGUE.

## WALES, THE FOOTBALL ASSOCIATION OF.
In Jan. 1876, a number of Welsh football enthusiasts gathered at the Wynnstay Arms Hotel, Wrexham, to discuss the possibility of arranging an international match with Scotland. They also decided to form the Football Association of Wales. A Committee was elected and final details were agreed at a second meeting on Feb. 2, 1876.

The international match with Scotland took place at Glasgow in Mar., Wales losing 0—4, but the game served to increase Welsh interest despite protests from certain individuals in South Wales that the side could not be truly representative of the country unless it included players from the South. The F.A. of Wales (nearly all men from North Wales) asserted that the Southerners had been given every opportunity to submit the names of candidates. As a matter of fact it was several years before South Wales took an active part in the affairs of the F.A. of Wales.

Mr. L. Ll. Kenrick, of Wynne Hall, Ruabon, North Wales, a member of the Shropshire Wanderers F.C. who played in the first international match v. Scotland, was the prime mover. He became Chairman and Hon. Secretary.

The earliest club formed in Wales was The Druids who played at Plasmadoc Park, Ruabon, and they were soon followed by clubs at Wrexham, Oswestry and Chirk. It was not until 1890 that the game became sufficiently popular in South Wales to warrant the organisation of an Association League.

This was followed in 1893 by the establishment of the South Wales and Monmouthshire F.A. But it was not until the early part of the present century that the dribbling code was adopted on a first-class basis. Soccer's growth in Wales was due largely to the efforts of Mr. E. Robbins, who was secretary of the Welsh F.A. from 1910 until his death in 1946.

Address: F.A. of Wales, 3 Fairy Road, Wrexham LL13 7PS. Colours: All red.

## WALKER, William Henry (1897-1964)
Born Wednesbury, Staffordshire, Billy Walker enjoyed a distinguished career of more than 40 years as player and manager. He made his first team debut in an F.A. Cup tie with Aston Villa in January 1920 and remained with that club throughout his playing career until joining Sheffield Wednesday as manager in November 1933. He later had a spell as manager of Chelmsford before taking charge of Nottingham Forest in March 1939, finally retiring from this post in 1960.

Originally a centre-forward Billy Walker later master-minded the Villa attack at inside-left and his deceptive body-swerve often had defenders stumbling.

Aston Villa 1919-33, 480 apprcs (213 goals). England internationals 18. Inter-League games 6. F.A. Cup winners 1920, runners-up 1924.

## WALSALL F.C.
Founded 1888 by amalgamation of Walsall Swifts (1877) and Walsall Town (1879). Elected to the Football League Division II, 1892. Failed to gain re-election 1895. Returned 12 months later. In 1901 they dropped out again. Were not seen in the Football League until the formation of Division III(N) in 1921. Best in Division II, 6th, 1898-9. Honours: Champions, Division IV, 1959-60. Runners-up, Division III, 1960-61. Record attendance: 25,453 v. Newcastle United, Division II, Aug. 29, 1961. Address: Fellows Park, Walsall WS2 9DB (Tel. 22791). Nickname: Saddlers. Colours: White with red trim, red shorts, white stockings. Record League goal-scorer: G. Alsop, 39 goals, Division III(N), 1933-4 and 1934-5. Record victory: 10—0 v. Darwen, Division II, Mar. 4, 1899. Record defeat: 12—0 v. Small Heath, Division II, Dec. 17, 1892; v. Darwen, Division II, Dec. 26, 1896.

## WAR-TIME FOOTBALL
During both World Wars the Football League competition was abandoned. One season was played at the beginning of World War I (season 1914-15), but at the beginning of World War II the competition was immediately abandoned with most clubs having played three games of the new season.

In World War I the Football League carried on with two groups, Lancashire and Midlands, with the exception of five clubs in the South who, with the Southern League clubs, played in a London Combination.

The Football League's regional competition was also divided between a Principal Tournament and a Subsidiary Tournament. The latter was run towards the end of the season when the Principal Tournament had been completed.

The London Combination was also divided between a Principal Tournament and what was known as a Supplementary Tournament.

As the champions of these competitions are not normally included in most record books, here they are:

### League Competition

*Principal Tournament*
Lancashire Section
    1915-16   Manchester City
    1916-17   Liverpool
    1917-18   Stoke
    1918-19   Everton

Midland Section
    1915-16   Nottingham Forest
    1916-17   Leeds City
    1917-18   Leeds City
    1918-19   Nottingham Forest

In seasons 1917-18 and 1918-19 the champions of each section met each other at home and away, the winner on the aggregate score being declared League Champions.

    1917-18   Leeds City 2, Stoke 0;
        Stoke 1, Leeds City 0;
Leeds City declared Champions.
    1918-19   Nottingham Forest 0,
                    Everton 0;
        Everton 0, Nottingham
                  Forest 1;
Nottingham Forest declared Champions.

*Principal Tournament*

London Combination
    1915-16   Chelsea
    1916-17   West Ham United
    1917-18   Chelsea
    1918-19   Brentford

In Scotland during World War I, Division I carried on as usual, but the Scottish F.A. Cup was abandoned.

During World War I the F.A. made a rule that no payment or consideration be made to a club or player for the player's services.

In World War II, however, the Football League sanctioned a payment of 30s. per match but no bonus for either wins or draws. This fee was the rule for seasons 1939-40, 1940-41, 1941-2 and 1942-3. Fees were increased to £2 per match in 1943-4,

and £4 per match in 1945-6.

A system of Regional League football was adopted during World War II. The F.A. Cup was abandoned until 1945, when it resumed on a home and away basis.

The Scottish League, too, played on a regional basis.

Here are the Champions of the principal war-time competitions:

### 1939-40

Regional League:
South "A" Division—Arsenal.
South "B" Division—Queen's Park Rangers.
South "C"—Division—Tottenham Hotspur.
South "D" Division—Crystal Palace.
Western Division—Stoke City.
South-Western Division—Plymouth Argyle.
Midland Division—Wolverhampton Wanderers.
East Midland Division—Chesterfield.
North-West Division—Bury.
North-East Division—Huddersfield Town.
Scottish West and South—Rangers.
Scottish East and North—Falkirk.

### 1940-41

North Regional—Preston North End.
South Regional—Crystal Palace.
Scottish Southern League—Rangers.

### 1941-2

North Regional—Blackpool.
South Regional—Leicester City.
Scottish Southern League—Rangers.

### 1942-3

North Regional—Blackpool.
South Regional—Arsenal.
Scottish Southern League—Rangers.

### 1943-4

North Regional—Blackpool.
South Regional—Tottenham Hotspur.
Scottish Southern League—Rangers.

### 1944-5

North Regional—Huddersfield Town.
South Regional—Tottenham Hotspur.
Scottish Southern League—Rangers.

### 1945-6

North Regional—Sheffield United.
South Regional—Birmingham City.

*League War Cup Winners:*
    1939-40—West Ham United.
    1940-41—Preston North End.
    1941-42—Wolverhampton Wanderers.
    1942-43—Blackpool (North).

Arsenal (South).
1943-44—Aston Villa (North)
Charlton Athletic (South)
1944-45—Bolton Wanderers (North)
Chelsea (South).

## War-time goal-scorers

The aggregate goal-scoring records for World War II are difficult to establish with real accuracy, because of the number of competitions into which the Football League clubs were divided and because many players appeared for so many clubs as "guests".

However, there can be little doubt that the following three players were top of the aggregate scoring list in war-time Football League Regional matches 1939-46, inclusive. The figures are as accurate as possible:

A. Stubbins (Newcastle United) 226; E. Dodds (Blackpool) 221; T. Lawton (Everton, Tranmere Rovers, Aldershot and Chelsea) 212.

The leading Scottish goal-scorers, 1939-46 include: T. Walker (Hearts), D. Wallace (Clyde), G. Smith (Rangers), R. Flavell (Airdrieonians), J. Calder (Morton and Albion Rovers), D. Wilson (Hamilton Academicals), and K. Dawson (Falkirk).

During World War I, principal goal-scorers included such men as S. Puddefoot (West Ham United), H. Barnes (Manchester City), J. McColl (Celtic), W. Davis (Millwall), E. Simms (Luton Town), H. G. Yarnall (Airdrieonians), and R. Thomson (Chelsea).

In the London Combination in season 1916-17, E. Simms scored 40 goals in 29 matches.

In season 1917-18, S. Puddefoot scored 40 of West Ham United's total of 103 goals in the London Combination.

R. Thomson scored 39 goals in 31 London Combination matches for Chelsea, season 1915-16.

## War-time Internationals

War-time and Victory internationals did not count as full internationals and no caps were awarded. The following players made the most appearances in War-time and Victory internationals:

*England*
S. Matthews (Stoke City), 29; J. Mercer (Everton), 27; T. Lawton (Everton), 23; H. Carter (Sunderland), J. Hagan (Sheffield United), and G. Hardwick (Middlesbrough), 17; L. Scott (Arsenal), 16; F. Swift (Manchester City), 14; L. Smith (Brentford and Aston Villa), 13.

*Scotland*
T. Walker (Hearts), 11; W. Waddell (Rangers), J. Carabine (Third Lanark), J. Caskie (Everton) and J. Dawson (Rangers), 9.

*Ireland*
(Victory internationals only)
T. Breen (Linfield), W. McMillan (Belfast Celtic), and J. Vernon (Belfast Celtic), 3 each.

*Wales*
D. Dearson (Birmingham) 15; W. Hughes (Birmingham), 14; C. Sidlow (Liverpool), 11; R. Burgess (Tottenham Hotspur), H. Cumner (Arsenal) and T. G. Jones (Everton), 10.

## WATFORD F.C.

Founded 1891 when West Herts and Watford St. Mary's amalgamated. Joined Football League, Division III, 1920. Honours: Champions, Division III, 1968-9. Record attendance: 34,099 v. Manchester United, F.A. Cup, 4th Round (replay), Feb. 3, 1969. Address: Vicarage Road, Watford WD1 8ER (Tel. 21759). Nickname: Brewers or Hornets. Colours: Gold shirts, black shorts with gold stripe, gold stockings. Record League goal-scorer: C. Holton, 42 goals, Division IV, 1959-60. Record victory: 10—1 v. Lowestoft Town, F.A. Cup, 1st Round, Nov. 27, 1926. Record defeat: 10—0 v. Wolverhampton Wanderers, F.A. Cup, 1st Round (replay), Jan. 13, 1912.

## WATNEY CUP

Watney Mann Ltd., the brewery firm, are among the official patrons of the Football League and were one of the first companies to offer big money when football sponsorship was accepted by the Football League in 1969.

The Watney Cup is a pre-season competition open to the top two scoring sides in each division of the Football League, with the exception of those promoted and those entering European competitions.

Winners: 1970-71—Derby County bt. Manchester United 4-1; 1971-2—West Bromwich Albion bt. Colchester United 4—3 on penalties after drawing 4—4; 1972-73—Bristol Rovers bt. Sheffield United 7—6 on penalties after drawing 0—0.

## WEATHER

All previous records regarding postponements and abandonments due to the weather were broken in the winter of 1962-3.

The severe spell of cold which lasted for about six weeks began to trouble the football clubs just before Christmas and before the thaw had set in over 400 League and

Cup games had been postponed or abandoned in England, Scotland and Wales.

The F.A. Cup programme most affected by the weather was on Jan. 5, 1963. Of the 32 3rd Round ties due to be played 29 were postponed. The entire F.A. Cup programme was postponed, Feb. 8, 1969, but that day only eight 5th Round ties were due to be played.

In League Football in England and Scotland the worst day for a full peace-time programme was Saturday, Feb. 9, 1963. Then there were 57 games postponed because of snow and ice. In all only seven Football League games were completed while the Scottish League programme was completely wiped out.

The Football League programme actually suffered worse on Jan. 12, 1963, and again on Feb. 2, 1963, when only four out of 44 and four out of 43 games respectively were completed. But on that first date Scotland managed to get through eight of their League and Cup games (only seven being postponed), while on the other day the total games postponed amounted to 52, including 13 in Scotland, where four games were played.

During World War II, on Feb. 3, 1940, only one Regional League game was played out of a total of 56 in the whole of England and Scotland. That was between Plymouth Argyle and Bristol City.

Other bad days in the history of the game arranged here according to the total number postponed or abandoned in Football League, F.A. Cup, Scottish League and Scottish Cup:

Jan. 19, 1963—54 games either postponed or abandoned; Feb. 16, 1963—51; Dec. 30, 1961—43; Dec. 29, 1962—42; Jan. 1, 1968—42; Jan. 15, 1955—41; Jan. 26, 1963—41; Feb. 8, 1969—40; Feb. 15, 1958—39; Jan. 17, 1959—39.

The worst season for postponed and abandoned matches in the Football League prior to season 1962-3 was 1946-7 when the total was 146. But the worst day in that season did not produce such alarming figures as those mentioned above. It was Mar. 8, 1947 when only 18 of the 44 Football League games were played.

The hottest day on which a full League programme was carried out is believed to have been Saturday, Sept. 1, 1906, when the temperature in most parts of the country was just under 90deg. Fahrenheit.

## WEDLOCK, William John (1881-1965)
This Bristolian who stood only 5ft 4½in tall was England centre-half against Scotland in six consecutive seasons, a record for an England pivot in full peace-time internationals. Despite his lack of height he could beat most of his taller opponents in the air and was known as the "India rubber man." When Bristol City won promotion in the First Division in 1905-06 Wedlock played in every game. Appeared in three first team games for Bristol City before being allowed to join Aberdare in 1900, and won two Welsh Cup finalists' medals before returning to Bristol City 1905.

Bristol City 1905-21, 363 apprs. (16 goals). England internationals 26. Inter-League games 3. F.A. Cup, runners-up, 1909.

## WEIGHT
The lightest player ever to appear in the Football League is believed to have been W. Hepworth, a Barnsley inside-right of the 1890s, who weighed around 7st. 5lb.

Next to Hepworth comes outside-right F. Le May who weighed about 7st. 10lb. during his League career with Thames (1930-31), Watford (1931-2), and Clapton Orient (1932-3).

The heaviest Football League player was probably W. Foulke, the Sheffield United, Bradford City and England goalkeeper of the 1890s and early 1900s. With Sheffield United he gradually increased weight from 15st. to over 20st., and later, while playing for Bradford City, he was said to weigh 25st.

## WELSH CUP
The Welsh Cup competition was established in 1877 but it was not until more than a year later that the Cup was actually obtained and more than two years before the Welsh F.A. had sufficient funds to complete payment for this handsome trophy said to have cost about £150.

Wrexham were the first winners when they defeated Druids, 1—0, at Acton Park, Wrexham. They have since won the competition 18 times, more times than any other club.

## WELSH INTERNATIONALS
See INTERNATIONALS (WALES).

## WELSH LEAGUE
The Welsh Football League was founded in 1902. Today it has a membership of 48 clubs who are divided into three Divisions.

Cardiff City hold the record for the highest number of points in a single season in the Welsh League. They gained 72 in season 1922-3.

Lovells Athletic have a remarkable record in the competition. They won the championship five times in succession in seasons 1937-8, 1938-9, 1945-6, 1946-7, 1947-8.

## WEMBLEY, THE EMPIRE STADIUM

The venue of the F.A. Cup Finals since 1923 and the principal home of the England national team, Wembley Stadium is neither a stadium reserved solely for football, nor the property of the Football Association, nor the home of any particular football club.

It is the property of a limited company and is merely hired to the Football Association on certain occasions.

It was in Jan. 1922, that the Duke of York, later to become King George VI, cut the first turf to mark the beginning of the building of this great sports arena. It was completed in under a year at a cost of £750,000. Some 250,000 tons of clay had to be dug out to form the bowl of the stadium and the stands and terraces were built with 25,000 tons of concrete, reinforced with 600 tons of steel rods. The stands were erected with 1,500 tons of steel girders held together with something like 500,000 rivets.

The F.A. Cup Final between Bolton Wanderers and West Ham United was the first event to take place in the new stadium in April 28, 1923. 126,047 people were officially admitted and the total receipts were £27,776. However, a conservative estimate of the number of people who entered the stadium, including those who broke in, puts the number at 150,000. It may have been nearer 200,000.

The first Wembley international match was between England and Scotland, April 12, 1924.

In 1962-3 £500,000 was spent on transforming Wembley Stadium into a more up-to-date sports arena. Major operation was the erection of a new roof all the way around so as to afford complete protection to all 100,000 spectators (45,000 seated and 55,000 standing). The inner apron of this roof is covered in fibre glass sheeting to allow maximum daylight to the playing pitch.

### League Games

Clapton Orient met Brentford and Southend United in Third Division games at Wembley Stadium in season 1930-31. Their ground at Lea Bridge was banned because it did not fulfil official requirements.

See also AMATEURS (FOOTBALL LEAGUE) The Argonauts A.F.C.

## "WEMBLEY WIZARDS"

This title was given to the Scottish international XI which gave such a remarkable display of football in defeating England 5—1, at Wembley, Mar. 31, 1928.

It was England's third defeat of the season in the International Championship, the first time they had ever lost all three games.

The Scottish side which so out-classed England on this occasion included eight Anglo-Scots.

The complete line-up was:

*England:*

Hufton (West Ham United); Goodall (capt.) (Huddersfield Town), Jones (Blackburn Rovers); Edwards (Leeds United), Wilson, T. (Huddersfield Town), Healless (Blackburn Rovers); Hulme (Arsenal), Kelly (Huddersfield Town), Dean (Everton), Bradford (Birmingham), Smith, W. H. (Huddersfield Town).

*Scotland:*

J. D. Harkness (Queen's Park); Nelson (Cardiff City), Law (Chelsea); Gibson (Aston Villa), Bradshaw (Bury), McMullan (capt.) (Manchester City); Jackson (Huddersfield Town), Dunn (Hibernian), Gallacher (Newcastle United), James (Preston North End), Morton (Rangers).

Scorers: England—Kelly. Scotland —Jackson (3) and James (2).

Half-time score: 2—0.

Referee: Mr. W. Bell (Scotland).

## WEST BROMWICH ALBION F.C.

Founded 1879. Known as West Bromwich Strollers until title changed to West Bromwich Albion in 1880. One of the original members of the Football League, 1888. Honours: Champions, Division I, 1919-20. Runners-up, 1924-5, 1953-4. Champions, Division II, 1901-2, 1910-11. Runners-up, 1930-31, 1948-9. F.A. Cup: Winners, 1888, 1892, 1931, 1954, 1968. Finalists, 1886, 1887, 1895, 1912, 1935. League Cup: Winners, 1966. Runners-up, 1967, 1970. Record attendance: 64,815 v. Arsenal, F.A. Cup, 6th Round, Mar. 6, 1937. Address: The Hawthorns, West Bromwich (Tel. 021-553 0095). Nickname: Throstles. Colours Navy Blue and white striped shirts, white shorts, navy blue stockings with one white ring at top. Record League goal-scorer: W. "G." Richardson, 39 goals, Division I, 1935-6. Record victory: 12—0 v. Darwen, Division I, April 4, 1892. Record defeat: 10—3 v. Stoke City, Division I, Feb. 4, 1937.

## WEST GERMANY

See GERMANY.

## WEST HAM UNITED F.C.

Founded 1900 following the disbandment of the five-year-old Thames Ironworks

Club. Elected to Division II, 1919. Honours: Champions, Division II, 1957-8. Runners-up, 1922-3. Best in Division I, 6th, 1926-7, 1958-9. F.A. Cup: Winners, 1964. Finalists, 1923. Winners, European Cup Winners Cup, 1965. Football League Cup: Finalists, 1966. Record attendance: 42,322 v. Tottenham Hotspur, Division I, Oct. 17, 1970. Address: Boleyn Ground, Green Street Upton Park, London, E.13 (Tel. 01-472 0704). Nickname: Hammers. Colours: Claret shirts with blue sleeves, claret and blue trim, white shorts and stockings. Record League goal-scorer: V. Watson, 41 goals, Division I, 1929-30. Record victory: 8—0 v. Rotherham United, Division II, Mar. 8, 1958 and v. Sunderland, Division I, Oct. 19, 1968. Record defeat: 8—2 v. Blackburn Rovers, Division I, Dec. 26, 1963.

## WINNING RUNS
See also AWAY WINS, HOME WINS, DEFENSIVE RECORDS.

In season 1905-06 Bristol City won 14 consecutive League matches and set up a Football League record which was not equalled until 1950-51 when Preston North End recorded the same number. Both clubs were in Division II.

From the start of season 1963-4 Morton gained 23 consecutive victories in Scottish League, Division II. They did not drop a single point until losing 3—1 at East Fife.

In season 1898-99 Rangers (Glasgow) won all 18 of their Scottish League, Division I games. They won the first four games of the following season but then their run of victories was halted with a 1—1 draw against Heart of Midlothian at Tynecastle.

Celtic had a run of 23 victories (including League, League Cup and European Cup games) to Nov. 5, 1966 when they were held to a 1—1 draw by St. Mirren.

Tottenham Hotspur began season 1960-61 with 11 consecutive victories in Division I. This is a Football League record for the beginning of a season.

## WINS, MOST IN A SEASON

| Football League | | Wins | Games | |
|---|---|---|---|---|
| Division I | Tottenham Hotspur | 31 | 42 | 1960–61 |
| Division II | Tottenham Hotspur | 32 | 42 | 1919–20 |
| Division III(S) | Millwall | 30 | 42 | 1927–28 |
| | Plymouth Argyle | 30 | 42 | 1929–30 |
| | Cardiff City | 30 | 42 | 1946–47 |
| | Nottingham Forest | 30 | 46 | 1950–51 |
| | Bristol City | 30 | 46 | 1954–55 |
| Division III(N) | Doncaster Rovers | 33 | 42 | 1946–47 |
| Division III | Aston Villa | 32 | 46 | 1971–72 |
| Division IV | Notts County | 30 | 46 | 1970–71 |
| Scottish League | | | | |
| Division I | Rangers | 35 | 42 | 1920–21 |
| Division II | Morton | 33 | 38 | 1966–67 |

## WITHOUT A WIN
The longest run without a win in the Football League was made by Crewe Alexandra during 1956-7. After beating Scunthorpe United, 2—1, Sept. 19, 1956, they did not win again until April 13, 1957, when they defeated Bradford City 1—0—a run of 30 games in Division III(N) without a victory.

Merthyr Town created a Football League record with a run of 61 away games without a win in Division III(S), September 1922 to September 1925.

The highest number of consecutive ties without a victory (by a Football League club) is 16 by Leeds United, from 1952 to 1963.

See also DEFEATS.

## WOLVERHAMPTON WANDERERS F.C.
Founded 1877. One of the original members of the Football League, 1888. Honours: Champions, Division I, 1953-4, 1957-8, 1958-9. Runners-up, 1937-8, 1938-9, 1949-50, 1954-5, 1959-60. Champions, Division II, 1931-2. Runners-up, 1966-7. Champions, Division III(N), 1923-4. F.A. Cup: Winners, 1893, 1908, 1949, 1960. Finalists, 1889, 1896, 1921, 1939. UEFA Cup: Finalists, 1972. Record attendance: 61,315 v. Liverpool, F.A. Cup, 5th Round, Feb. 11, 1939. Address: Molineux Grounds, Wolverhampton WV1 4QR (Tel. 24053). Nickname: Wolves. Colours: Gold shirts, black shorts, gold stockings. Record League

scorer: D. Westcott, 37 goals, Division I, 1946-7. Record victory: 14—0 v. Crosswell's Brewery, F.A. Cup, 2nd Round, 1886-7. Record defeat: 10—1 v. Newton Heath, Division I, Oct. 15, 1892.

## WOMEN'S FOOTBALL

Anyone who believes that women's football is a modern innovation would be sadly mistaken as there were a number of women's clubs in the 1890s and one in North London was reported to have attracted a 10,000 gate to a game on the Crouch End ground.

Preston was the stronghold of women's football in the early days, the famous Dick Kerr's XI being formed there in 1894 and earning a lot of money for charity. The present Preston lady's club was formed in 1917 and toured the U.S.A. as long ago as 1922.

The F.A. (England) refused to recognise women's football when it was increasing in popularity after World War I, indeed, in 1921 they decided that club's must not allow ladies matches on their grounds.

Women's football has spread rapidly throughout Europe and other parts of the world in recent years, and a number of unofficial international tournaments have been held at which gates of over 100,000 have been achieved. The Danes have generally been to the fore in these competitions.

The big break-through at home came in December 1969 when the F.A. decided to recognise women's football and allow ladies clubs to affiliate to County Associations. This was followed within a couple of weeks by the formation of the Women's Football Association which became officially recognised by the F.A. in November 1971.

Today the Women's F.A. (England) has a membership of nearly 300 clubs and over 20 Leagues. The Northern Irish and Scottish Women's Football Associations are Honorary members.

The first official international in Britain was played at Greenock, November 18, 1972, when England beat Scotland 3—2.

## WOODWARD, Vivian John (1879-1954)

The last of the truly amateurs to make his presence felt among the professionals in League and International football, this centre or inside-forward from Kennington was one of the most prolific goalscorers ever to wear an England jersey.

An architect by profession, Woodward first came into prominence with Tottenham Hotspur, helping them win promotion to the First Division in 1908-09, and subsequently he figured in the Chelsea side that regained First Division status in 1911-12.

In contrast to the majority of centre-forwards of his time Woodward was rather frail looking but he used his brains and subtle skills to such advantage that he scored over 70 goals in all his International appearances.

Tottenham Hotspur 1901-09, 27 apprcs. (19 goals). Chelsea 1909-15, 106 apprcs. (31 goals). England internationals 23. England Amateur internationals 38. Great Britain (Olympic) appearances 6.

## WORKINGTON F.C.

Founded 1884. Re-formed 1921. Elected to Football League, Division III(N), 1951. Record attendance: 21,000 v. Manchester United, F.A. Cup, 3rd Round, Jan. 4, 1958. Address: Borough Park, Workington CA14 2DT (Tel. 2871). Nickname: The Reds. Colours: Red shirts, white shorts red and white stockings. Record League goalscorer: J. Dailey, 26 goals, Division III(N), 1956-7. Record victory: 9—1 v. Barrow, League Cup, 1st Round, Sept. 2, 1964. Record defeat: 8—0 v. Wrexham, Division III(N), Oct. 24, 1953.

## WORLD CHAMPION CLUB

The championship of the world is contested each year between the winners of the European Cup (League Champion Clubs' Competition) and the South American Clubs' Cup. It is decided on a two leg home and away basis. Originally points decided the winner, but since 1968 it has been decided on goal aggregate.

1960 Real Madrid Champions:
Penarol (Uruguay) 0, Real Madrid (Spain) 0; Montevideo
Real Madrid 5, Penarol 1; Madrid
1961 Penarol Champions:
Benfica (Portugal) 1, Penarol (Uruguay) 0; Lisbon
Penarol 5, Benfica 0; Montevideo
Decider:
Penarol 2, Benfica 1; Montevideo
1962 Santos Champions:
Santos (Brazil) 3, Benfica (Portugal) 2; Rio de Janeiro
Benfica 2, Santos 5; Lisbon

1963 Santos Champions:
Milan 4, Santos 2; Milan
Santos 4, Milan 2; Rio de Janeiro
Santos 1, Milan 0; Rio de Janeiro
1964 Internazionale Champions:
Independiente (Argentine) 1, Internazionale (Italy) 0; Buenos Aires
Internazionale 2, Independiente 0; Milan
Internazionale 1, Independiente 0 (after extra time); Madrid
1965 Internazionale Champions:
Internazionale 3, Independiente 0; Milan
Independiente 0, Internazionale 0; Buenos Aires
1966 Penarol Champions:
Penarol 2, Real Madrid 0; Montevideo
Real Madrid 0, Penarol 2; Madrid
1967 Racing Club Champions:
Glasgow Celtic 1, Racing Club (Argentine) 0; Hampden Park
Racing Club 2, Glasgow Celtic 1; Buenos Aires
Racing Club 1, Glasgow Celtic 0; Montevideo
1968 Estudiantes Champions:
Estudiantes (Argentine) 1, Manchester United 0; Buenos Aires
Manchester United 1, Estudiantes 1; Old Trafford
1969 A. C. Milan Champions:
A. C. Milan 3, Estudiantes 0; Milan
Estudiantes 2, A. C. Milan 1; Buenos Aires
1970 Feyenoord Champions:
Estudiantes 2, Feyenoord (Holland) 2; Buenos Aires
Feyenoord 1, Estudiantes 0; Rotterdam
1971 Nacional Champions:
Panathinaikos (Greece)* 1, Nacional 1; Athens
Nacional (Uruguay) 2, Panathianaikos 1; Montevideo
1972 Ajax Champions:
Independiente 1, Ajax 1; Buenos Aires
Ajax 3, Independiente 0; Amsterdam

* Took place of Ajax who refused to play

## WORLD CUP

Since World War II the World Cup has developed into one of the most important international sporting competitions and the interest created in almost every part of the globe has had far reaching effects which are felt well outside the limited sphere of football.

The trophy originally presented to the World Cup winners was a gold cup known as the Jules Rimet Cup after the late Monsieur Jules Rimet, who was Honorary President of F.I.F.A. from 1921 to 1954. This trophy was won outright by Brazil with their victories in 1958, 1962 and 1970.

The new trophy is of solid gold 36cm high and known offically as "F.I.F.A. World Cup". The sculptor is an Italian and his design was selected from 53 submitted.

F.I.F.A. inaugurated the World Congress of 1928 when it was decided to hold a World Championship every fourth year.

Uruguay requested the opportunity of organising the first of these competitions in 1930, but when it took place it was only a pale imitation of a World Cup series, and certainly nothing like as universal as the more recent tournaments. Only 13 countries entered and the competition was won by the hosts.

Italy were hosts of the next World Cup in 1934 and again the host nation emerged as winners. 29 countries took part.

In 1938 the tournament was held in France and from an entry of 25, Italy retained the title.

Because of the war the next competition did not take place until 1950. This was the first time that the home Associations were included among the entries. England, Scotland, Ireland and Wales were not members of F.I.F.A. from 1928 to 1946. (See FEDERATION INTERNATIONALE DE FOOTBALL ASSOCIATION.)

In 1950 the home International Championship was made part of the qualifying competition for the World Cup tournament, the finals of which took place in Brazil. The two top countries in the International Championship qualified for the finals, but while England (winners) went to Brazil, Scotland (runners-up) declined the invitation.

It is now a matter of football history that this was the most disastrous year ever for English football prestige abroad.

On June 25, 1950, at the giant new Rio Stadium, England won her first game against Chile, 2—0. Four days later, however, came the shock: England lost 0—1 at Belo Horizonte, beaten by the rank outsiders—United States of America.

England's final elimination from the competition with a defeat by Spain (0—1) was not so much a surprise, but it proved conclusively that England was no longer at the top of the soccer ladder.

In the Final of this 1950 World Cup the record crowd for a football match, 199,850, assembled at the Rio Stadium to see Uruguay win the trophy for the second time, beating Brazil, 2—1.

In 1954, 35 countries entered. The final tournament took place in Switzerland, and this time, Scotland, as well as England, were among the 14 nations who emerged from the qualifying competition. Added to these were Uruguay and Switzerland, exempted from the qualifying rounds as Champions and hosts respectively.

England's elimination from the competition this year was not as sudden as it had been in 1950. She won through the first round with a 2—0 victory over Switzerland and a 4—4 draw with Belgium. But in the quarter finals, against the Cup holders, Uruguay, England went down 2—4 fighting all the way.

Scotland's display was probably as disastrous a debut for them as the 1950 tournament had been for England. The Scots could not score a goal in their two games and were eliminated in the first round with a 0—1 defeat by Austria and a 0—7 defeat by the Cup holders, Uruguay. Like England, Scotland had fallen from the high pedestal of the soccer masters.

The 1954 tournament will always be notorious because it not only produced one of the finest games ever seen, but also one of the toughest and roughest of international matches. The rough game was the quarter-final between Hungary and Brazil. Hungary won, 4—2, but not before English referee, A. Ellis, of Halifax, had sent off two Brazilian players and one Hungarian, as well as awarding a penalty to either side. Scenes at the end of the game, both on and off the field, were unforgettable as well as unforgivable. Several players, officials and policemen were injured.

Some critics suggested that after this exhibition the World Cup should be abandoned, but all relented when soon afterwards it was seen what good football this

tournament could produce. No one can expect to see a finer exhibition off football than the semi-final match between Hungary and Uruguay played at Lausanne on June 30, 1954, and refereed by B. M. Griffiths of Newport (Mon.), Hungary won 4—2.

There is little doubt that the great Hungarian team was still feeling the strain of that game when they met Germany in the Final, four days later. They were well below form and lost 3—2 after being two goals up. The Germans had an outstanding forward line and were deserving winners on the day's play, for they were faster on the rain-soaked pitch. This final was refereed by W. Ling (Cambridgeshire).

The entry for the 1958 World Cup increased to 51 countries. Four of these withdrew without playing a game.

England, N. Ireland and Scotland qualified for the final tournament, while Wales, though eliminated with a defeat by Czechoslovakia, subsequently got through after being appointed to meet Israel when Egypt and Sudan had withdrawn. Wales then beat Israel to qualify.

In the final tournament which took place in Sweden, England and Scotland were eliminated in the first round, but both Wales and Ireland got through to the quarter-finals by dint of some surprisingly good performance. For instance, Wales shook the soccer world by holding Hungary to a draw and later by defeating that same country when they met again in a play-off. Ireland had two victories over Czechoslovakia. The second being a particularly gallant effort achieved despite injuries and in a strenuous game which went into extra time.

It was no surprise when Ireland's valiant effort was brought to a close with a 4—0 defeat by France, while Wales, resorting largely to negative football, were beaten 1—0 by Brazil.

Brazil, who had not made a very convincing show in getting to the Final, then produced their real form in that match to beat Sweden 5—2.

England was the only representative of the British Isles to reach the final tournament of 1962 in Chile. 56 countries had entered for this competition and England went as far as the quarter-finals before losing 3—1 to Brazil who carried off the trophy by beating Czechoslovakia 3—1 in the final played in Santiago.

53 countries competed for the 1966 World Cup in which England as the host country was automatically seeded to the final tournament and then went on to win the coveted trophy with some determined

football and a particularly well organised defence.

England finished top of her group and then beat Argentine in a dramatic quarter-final, Portugal in a so entertaining semi-final, and West Germany in a final which proved to be a real test of endurance, the game going into extra time before England emerged the winners by 4 goals to 2.

England's team in the Final tie: Banks; Cohen, Wilson; Stiles, Charlton, (J.), Moore; Ball, Hurst, Hunt, Charlton (R.), Peters.

Automatically seeded to the Finals of 1970 which were played in Mexico, England were eliminated by West Germany in the quarter-finals, the Germans fighting back from 2—0 to win 3—2 in extra time.

Although highly organised and particularly strong in defence this series served to highlight the weakness of England's attackers in the art of shooting and heading as compared with the Brazilians who deservedly won the trophy with delightful, scintillating and exciting football. The Brazilian's style was like a breath of fresh air being such a contrast to the stifling defensive game favoured by so many less talented teams and they beat the Italians 4—1 in the Final.

The record individual scoring feat for a single game in the World Cup Final tournament is four goals. Eight players have scored this number as follows:

G. Wetterstroem, Sweden v. Cuba, 1938; Leonidas da Silva, Brazil v. Poland, 1938; E. Willimowski, Poland v. Brazil, 1938; Ademir, Brazil v. Sweden, 1950; S. Kocsis, Hungary v. W. Germany, 1954; J. Schiaffino, Uruguay v. Bolivia, 1950; J. Fontaine, France v. West Germany, 1958; Eusebio, Portugal v. N. Korea, 1966.

Best individual aggregates for Final tournaments (six or more goals)—13, Fontaine (France), 1958; 11, Kocsis (Hungary), 1954; 10, Mueller (W. Germany), 1970; 9, Eusebio (Portugal), 1966; 8, Stabile (Argentine), 193, Leonidas (Brazil), 1938; 7, Szengeller (Hungary), 1938, Ademir (Brazil), 1950, Jairsinho (Brazil), 1970; 6, Morlock (W. Germany), 1954, Pelé (Brazil), and Rahn (W. Germany), 1958.

Record individual score in the Cup Final is 3 by G. Hurst (England) v. West Germany, 1966.

The leading goal-scorer in each tournament can be seen in the above list except the 1934 finals when top place was shared by Schiavio (Italy), Nejedly (Czechoslovakia), and Conen (Germany), each with four goals, and the 1962 finals when top scorer was Jerkovic (Yugoslavia) with five.

Brazil created a record by playing through 13 games undefeated (P. 13, W. 11, D. 2) in the Final Tournaments of 1958, and 1962, and until beaten 3—1 by Hungary in their second game in England in 1966.

Results of World Cup Finals (the name of the "host" and the number of National Associations who actually took part in each competition are given in parentheses):

1930   Uruguay 4, Argentine 2 (Uruguay) (13). 90,000
1934   Italy 2, Czechoslovakia 1† (Italy) (29). 50,000
1938   Italy 4, Hungary 2. (France) (25). 45,000
1950   Uruguay 2, Brazil 1. (Brazil) (29). 199,850
1954   West Germany 3, Hungary 2 (Switzerland) (35). 60,000
1958   Brazil 5, Sweden 2 (Sweden) (47). 49,737
1962   Brazil 3, Czechoslovakia 1 (Chile) (53). 68,679
1966   England 4, West Germany 2† (England) (53). 93,802
1970   Brazil 4, Italy 1 (Mexico) (69). 107,412

† After extra time

## WRIGHT, William Ambrose, C.B.E. (1924- )

Began with Wolverhampton Wanderers as a boy on the ground staff and remained with the club throughout his playing career, eventually proving to be an inspiring captain both for club and country. Originally selected to play for England at inside-left but actually appeared right-half when another player was forced to drop out. That was against Belgium in 1946, and, thereafter he missed only three of England's next 107 games, including a run of 46 consecutive games at centre-half. Such remarkable figures speak for themselves. His 105 appearances in full internationals was made up of 51 games at right-half, 46 at centre-half, and 8 at left-half. He captained England in 90 games. Born Ironbridge, Shropshire.

Wolverhampton Wanderers 1941-59, 490 apprcs. England internationals 105 (plus 4 Victory games). England "B" games 2. Inter-League games 21. League Champions 1953-4, 1957-8, 1958-9. F.A. Cup winners 1949.

## WREXHAM F.C.

The oldest Association Football club in Wales, founded 1873. One of the original members of Division III(N), 1921. Honours: Runners-up, Division III(N), 1932-3. Runners-up, Division IV, 1969-70. Record attendance: 34,445 v. Manchester United, F.A. Cup, 4th Round, Jan. 26, 1957. Address: Racecourse Ground, Mold Road, Wrexham LL11 2AH (Tel. 2414). Nickname: Robins. Colours: Red shirts with white trim, white shorts with red stripe, red stockings. Record League goal-scorer: T. Bamford, 44 goals, Division III(N), 1933-4. Record victory: 10—1 v. Hartlepools United, Division IV, Mar. 3, 1962. Record defeat: 9—0 v. Brentford, Division III, Oct. 15, 1963.

## YASHIN, Lev (1929-    )

Real name Ivanovitch and Russia's most famous footballer, keeping goal for his country in 78 internationals from 1954. A tremendous personality, his astonishing acrobatics between the posts delighted his Moscow Dynamo supporters in over 600 games. First attracted world-wide attention when he won a gold medal in the 1956 Olympics in Melbourne.

Moscow Dynamo 1949-71. 78 Russian internationals. Rest of Europe v. Scandinavia and v. Yugoslavia in 1964. Rest of World v. England 1963. European Nations Cup winners 1960, runners-up 1964. Russian League champions 1954, 1955, 1957, 1959, 1963. Russian Cup winners 1953, 1967.

## YORK CITY F.C.

Founded 1922. Elected to Football League, Division III(N), 1929. Record attendance: 28,123 v. Huddersfield Town, F.A. Cup, 5th Round, Mar. 5, 1938. Address: Bootham Crescent, York YO3 7AQ (Tel. 24447). Colours: Maroon shirts with white collar and cuffs, white shorts, maroon stockings. Record League goal-scorer: W. Fenton, Division III(N), 1951-2, and A. Bottom, Division III(N), 1955-6, 31 goals. Record victory: 9—1 v. Southport, Division III(N), Feb. 2, 1957. Record defeat: 12—0 v. Chester, Division III(N), Feb. 1, 1936.

## YOUTH FOOTBALL

Since World War II a number of national and international competitions catering for players under the age of 18 (usually they are between 16 and 18) have been created.

The principal competitions in what is known as "Youth Football" are as follows:

*International Youth Championship:* Representative teams of each of the four British Associations, namely, the F.A., the Scottish F.A., the F.A. of Wales and the Irish F.A. meet each other once during each season, the championship being decided on a points basis. Only players who are under 18 years of age on the 1st Sept. of the current season and are members of an "Amateur" club under the jurisdiction of one of the four National Associations are eligible to take part.

This competition was inaugurated in season 1947-8.

*International Youth Tournament:* This is another amateur competition for youths of the same age as the above but this under the auspices of UEFA, includes most of the European countries. The tournament is played over a period of eight or nine days, usually at Whitsun, at a different centre each year.

The inaugural tournament took place in England in season 1947-8 and included teams from eight different countries.

*Internationals:* Youth internationals other than the above competitions are also played each season between the home Associations and foreign Associations, but these games include professionals. All players are under the age of 18 at the start of the then current season.

*F.A. County Youth Challenge Cup Competition:* A knock-out cup competition for amateurs under the age of 18 (on Sept. 1). Each team being representative of one of the County F.A.s in England affiliated to the Football Association.

This competition was inaugurated in 1944-5 when it was won by Staffordshire F.A.

*F.A. Youth Challenge Cup:* This competition is also played on a knockout basis but it differs from the above in that it is played between club sides and professionals may be included. All players must be under the age of 18 on *1st Sept. of the current season.* Professionals must have been registered with their clubs as professionals for at least 14 days before the match, unless already qualified as amateurs, and the latter must have been a recognised playing member of his club for the same minimum period.

This competition was inaugurated in season 1953-4 with the trophy being donated by the Football League, which was appropriate enough as most of the Football League clubs enter their youth sides.

## YUGOSLAVIA

Yugoslavia was the first Continental side to escape defeat in England in a full international. That was in November 1950 when they forced a 2—2 draw at Highbury. They have since gained two further draws in three visits to England and could certainly be described as England's "bogey" team.

Yugoslavia's record in international matches since the war places her well to the fore among the leading football powers in the world, although the country has in recent years suffered from the exodus of so many of their star players to clubs abroad where the financial returns are much greater.

World Cup: 1930—Semi-finalists. 1934—Failed to qualify. 1938—Failed to qualify. 1950—Eliminated in first round of final tournament. 1954—Quarter-finalists. 1958—Quarter-finalists. 1962—Semi-finalists. 1966 and 1970—failed to qualify.

Opympic Games: 1920—1st round. 1924—1st round. 1928—1st round. 1936—Did not enter. 1948—Runners-up. 1952—Runners-up. 1956—Runners-up. 1960—Winners. 1964—Quarter-finalists. 1968—Did not enter. 1972—2nd round.

European Championship: Runners-up 1968.

Yugoslavia, as a country whose boundaries resemble those in existence today, did not come into being until 1918, and their Football Association was founded in the following year, but it is known that football was played in Belgrade at least 20 years earlier. The oldest of the senior League clubs is Hajduk (Split) formed in 1911.

After four or five years of part-time or severely restricted semi-professionalism the Government lifted their ban and full-time professionalism was adopted in 1966.

Address of the governing body: Futbalski Savez Jugoslavije, P.O. Box 263, 35, Terazije, Belgrade. Colours: Blue shirts, white shorts, red stockings.

Results of international matches:

| | |
|---|---|
| May 18, 1939 | Yugoslavia 2, England 1; Belgrade |
| Nov. 22, 1950 | England 2, Yugoslavia 2; Highbury |
| May 21, 1953 | Yugoslavia 5, Wales 2; Belgrade |
| May 16, 1954 | Yugoslavia 1, England 0; Belgrade |
| Sept. 22, 1954 | Wales 1, Yugoslavia 3; Cardiff |
| May 15, 1955 | Yugoslavia 2, Scotland 2; Belgrade |
| Sept. 19, 1955 | Eire 1, Yugoslavia 4; Dublin |
| Nov. 21, 1956 | Scotland 2, Yugoslavia 0; Glasgow |
| Nov. 28, 1956 | England 3, Yugoslavia 2; Wembley |
| May 11, 1958 | Yugoslavia 5, England 0; Belgrade |
| June 8, 1958* | Scotland 1, Yugoslavia 1; Sweden |
| May 11, 1960 | England 3, Yugoslavia 3; Wembley |
| May 9, 1965 | Yugoslavia 1, England 1; Belgrade |
| May 4, 1966 | England 2, Yugoslavia 0; Wembley |
| June 5, 1968† | England 0, Yugoslavia 1; Florence |
| June 29, 1972 | Scotland 2, Yugoslavia 2; Belo Horizonte |
| Oct. 11, 1972 | England 1, Yugoslavia 1; Wembley |

\* World Cup
† Nations Cup

**ZAMORA, Ricardo (1901-     )**

When Real Madrid signed this legendary player from Espanol in 1930 the fee was about £6,000 and a world record for a goalkeeper, a fact which surprises many who believe that Continental football only came into the big-money bracket after World War II. Unfortunately, Zamora's reputation in English eyes was destroyed by one disastrous display for Spain at Highbury in 1931 when he was beaten seven times, but he was really a talented though typically flashy continental style goalkeeper. His international career spread over 14 years.

Espanol 1916-19. C.F.Barcelona 1919-22. Espanol 1922-30. Real Madrid 1930-36. 47 Spanish Internationals. Spanish League champions 1932, 1933. Spanish Cup winners 1920, 1922, 1929, 1934, 1936.

# Index